Guide to
Strategic Infrastructure Security: Becoming a Security Network Professional

by Randy Weaver and Dawn Weaver

COURSE TECHNOLOGY
CENGAGE Learning

Australia • Brazil • Japan • Korea • Mexico • Singapore • Spain • United Kingdom • United States

**Guide to Strategic Infrastructure Security:
Becoming a Security Network
Professional**
Randy Weaver and Dawn Weaver

Vice President, Career and Professional
Editorial: Dave Garza

Director of Learning Solutions: Matt Kane

Executive Editor: Stephen Helba

Managing Editor: Marah Bellegarde

Product Manager: Robin M. Romer

Developmental Editor: Lisa M. Lord

Contributing Authors: Michael Palmer,
Sydney Shewchuk

Technical Editor: Sydney Shewchuk

Quality Assurance Coordinator: Christian
Kunciw, MQA

Editorial Assistants: Dawn Daugherty,
Claire Jeffers

Vice President, Career and Professional
Marketing: Jennifer McAvey

Marketing Director: Debbie Yarnell

Marketing Manager: Erin Coffin

Marketing Coordinator: Shanna Gibbs

Production Director: Patty Stephan

Content Project Manager: Heather Furrow

Art Director: Kun-Tee Chang

Cover Designer: Abby Scholz

Manufacturing Coordinator: Julio Esperas

Proofreader: Karen Annett

Compositor: GEX Publishing Services

For product information and technology assistance, contact us at
Cengage Learning Customer & Sales Support, 1-800-354-9706

For permission to use material from this text or product,submit all
requests online at **cengage.com/permissions**
Further permission questions can be emailed to
permissionrequest@cengage.com

Some of the product names and company names used in this book have
been used for identification purposes only and may be trademarks or registered trademarks of their respective manufacturers and sellers.

Any fictional data related to persons or companies or URLs used throughout this book is intended for instructional purposes only. At the time this
book was printed, any such data was fictional and not belonging to any real
persons or companies.

ISBN-13: 978-1-4188-3661-0
ISBN-10: 1-4188-3661-3

Course Technology
25 Thomson Place
Boston, MA 02210
USA

Cengage Learning is a leading provider of customized learning solutions
with office locations around the globe, including Singapore, the United
Kingdom, Australia, Mexico, Brazil, and Japan. Locate your local office at:
international.cengage.com/region

Cengage Learning products are represented in Canada by Nelson
Education, Ltd.

For your lifelong learning solutions, visit **course.cengage.com**
Purchase any of our products at your local college store or at our preferred
online store **www.ichapters.com**

Printed in Canada
1 2 3 4 5 6 7 12 11 10 09 08

BRIEF Contents

TABLE OF
Contents

Introduction

Perimeter defense takes an outside-in approach to securing a network's entry points, but infrastructure security focuses more on internal systems, interaction between them, and the pathways that lead them outside the security perimeter. Infrastructure security includes security policies, risk analysis, penetration testing, patching and upgrading systems, capturing and analyzing packets, cryptography, hardening of operating systems, and more. This book examines the technologies involved in securing the critical network infrastructure.

This book was written with two goals. The first goal is to give students a solid foundation in advanced infrastructure security fundamentals. Essential security practices, such as penetration testing, systems hardening, packet analysis, and securing Internet and Web resources are explained. The critical role a comprehensive security policy plays is demonstrated, and the processes of performing a risk analysis and developing a security policy are explained. The second goal is to prepare students to take the Strategic Infrastructure Security exam (SC0-471) for the Security Certified Network Professional (SCNP) certification.

Intended Audience

Guide to Strategic Infrastructure Security: Becoming a Security Network Professional is intended for students and professionals who need hands-on experience with intermediate security management techniques, such as developing security policies, hardening and testing servers, and implementing cryptographic systems. This book assumes that you're familiar with the Internet; advanced networking concepts such as TCP/IP, gateways, routers, and Ethernet networks; and intermediate OS security concepts such as installing and upgrading OSs, navigating Windows file systems, and working with client OSs. It also assumes that you have prerequisite knowledge and experience that's equivalent to CompTIA's Security+ certification. In addition, the Course Technology *Guide to Tactical Perimeter Defense* is a highly recommended prerequisite, but you can complete the projects in this book without it.

HOW TO USE THIS BOOK

This book should be studied in sequence. The first two chapters offer a thorough background on risk analysis and security policies and establish the basis for the running case project (discussed later in "The Running Case Project"). Each chapter builds on the previous one and expands on knowledge from prerequisite courses.

The Running Case Project

This book's running case project is designed to give you practical experience in applying skills and concepts and attempts to mirror a real-life setting as closely as possible. Throughout the book, you work on a full-scale network security project for a fictitious company, Green Globe R&D, Inc., an environmental research and "green" design company. Green Globe works with architects, construction companies, and others in designing environmentally sound structures and conducts independent environmental impact studies for government agencies, corporations, and educational institutions. Some field work is outsourced, with one or more project managers and several engineering staff overseeing short-term projects in more than 100 countries. Long-term studies often use doctoral students from American universities in addition to a small group of Green Globe staff. The company's employees are highly diversified.

Green Globe has recently closed a deal to provide design oversight and research services to a large international construction corporation. It has also been negotiating with the EPA to provide impact studies on a wide range of projects. As a result, the company needs to expand its base of operations to support expected growth of more than 300% over the next 18 months and 150% per year for the next five years.

Because of the sensitive nature of the company's work and the competition it faces, it requires high security. Additionally, it has received threats from unknown sources. Federal law enforcement agencies are investigating these threats, but the company is concerned about being a target for cyberterrorists, especially when working in socially and politically volatile regions.

Green Globe has one location capable of supporting expansion in terms of space and needs secure mobile services for staff in the field around the globe as well as at its main offices. It has no plans to move or open satellite offices at this time but is considering adding on to its current building, a large warehouse in an airpark. It has allocated a generous budget to purchase equipment.

Your firm has been hired to design a secure network for Green Globe. Your supervisor has dispatched you to its location to evaluate its needs, assess the location, and complete a preliminary design. The facility layout is shown in a diagram your instructor will provide.

Your design should meet these major requirements:

- One fully networked location, 100% company owned, in Phoenix, AZ. This location will be the permanent base of operations.

- Capable of supporting up to 200 full-time users in these departments: Account Management; Project Management; Research and Development; Engineering; Sales and Marketing; Legal; Administration (includes office staff and management); Reports and Publications; Client Services; and Facilities and Technology Support.

- High security required. Extremely sensitive data must remain secure.

- Temporary access to specific resources must be available for external entities, which includes some limited mobile access.

- The company must adhere to applicable state and federal laws on information security and privacy.

Chapter Descriptions

Here is a summary of the topics covered in each chapter of this book:

Chapter 1, "Performing Risk Analysis," reviews risk analysis factors and methods and outlines the process of conducting a risk analysis. In addition, this chapter explains important techniques for minimizing risks.

Chapter 2, "Creating Security Policies," covers best practices in creating a security policy for your organization, outlines the seven main steps of policy developments, and gives you an overview of handling security incidents. You also learn the basics of security policy life cycle management, such as conducting periodic reviews and incorporating updates.

Chapter 3, "Penetration Testing Techniques," introduces the main methods of network reconnaissance that attackers use. You examine network attack techniques and malicious code attacks and learn guidelines for reducing the risk of these attacks.

Chapter 4, "Analyzing Packet Structures," explains the components of a packet capture and how to analyze normal and abnormal network traffic signatures. You explore some tools and techniques for capturing packets and see how to identify suspicious events that warrant further investigation.

Chapter 5, "Cryptography," gives you a brief background on historical cryptographic techniques and outlines the components of cryptographic protocols, such as encryption and hashing algorithms, digital signatures, and cryptographic primitives. You also examine cryptography standards and modern cryptanalysis methods.

Chapter 6, "Internet and Web Security," discusses the underlying structure of the Internet, including weak points that are vulnerable to attack. You examine attacks against Web sites and Internet users and learn techniques and tools for hardening Internet and Web resources, such as securing DNS transfers.

Chapter 7, "Hardening Linux Systems," starts with an overview of the Linux file system and navigation. You also examine methods of secure system management, ways to manage user and file system security, and techniques for securing your network configuration.

Chapter 8, "Windows Server 2003 Security Fundamentals," covers the security-related components of a Windows Server 2003 network, such as planning an Active Directory deployment and using group policies. You also examine Windows Server 2003 authentication, auditing, and logging.

Chapter 9, "Configuring Windows Server 2003 Security," explains ways to secure your Windows Server 2003 network. You begin with a quick review of Windows file systems and learn how to secure resources such as files, folders, printers, and the Registry. You learn to use security configuration tools, including security templates, and examine methods of configuring network security, such as Routing and Remote Access Services and Virtual Private Network services.

Appendix A, "SC0-471 Objectives," maps the objectives in the Security Certified Network Professional (SCNP) SC0-471 Strategic Infrastructure Security exam to this book's corresponding chapter and section. If you need to brush up on a specific topic to prepare for the exam, you can use this appendix as a handy reference.

Appendix B, "Additional Resources," lists several security-related organizations, groups, and other information sources you can turn to for up-to-the-minute news about trends and emerging threats.

Features

To help you fully understand networking security concepts, this book includes many features designed to enhance your learning experience:

- **Chapter Objectives.** Each chapter begins with a list of the concepts to be mastered in that chapter. This list gives you a quick reference to the chapter's contents and serves as a useful study aid.

- **Figures and Tables.** Numerous diagrams of physical and virtual configurations help you visualize concepts. In addition, tables provide details and comparisons in an organized, easy-to-grasp manner. Because most labs use Microsoft operating systems, Microsoft products are used for most of the screenshots and Hands-On Projects in this book, except in Chapter 7, which covers Linux.

- **In-Chapter Activities.** Each chapter has activities integrated into the main text. Their purpose is to provide immediate reinforcement of a newly learned skill or concept and give you an opportunity to apply knowledge and skills as a way to maintain interest and motivation.

- **Chapter Summaries.** Each chapter's material is followed by a summary of the concepts introduced in that chapter. These summaries are a helpful way to review the ideas covered in each chapter.

- **Key Terms.** Following the Chapter Summary, the Key Terms list gathers all the terms introduced in that chapter with boldfaced text and provides full definitions for each term. This list encourages a more thorough understanding of the chapter's key concepts and is a useful reference.

- **Review Questions.** The end-of-chapter assessment begins with a set of review questions that reinforce the main concepts in each chapter. These questions help you evaluate and apply the material you have learned.

- **Hands-On Projects**. Although understanding the theory behind networking technology is important, practice in real-world applications of this theory is essential. Each chapter includes projects aimed at giving you experience in planning and development tasks or hands-on configuration tasks.

- **Case Projects.** Each chapter closes with the corresponding segment of this book's running case project (described previously in "The Running Case Project"), which gives you a chance to draw on your common sense as well as skills and knowledge you have learned.

Lab Setup

The lab setup for this book is straightforward, requiring Internet access for projects and research and access to a computer capable of supporting Windows XP Professional with Service Pack 2, Windows Server 2003, and Linux in a triple-boot configuration. The hard drive should be at least 30 GB and partitioned to give each OS at least 10 GB. Your partitioning and boot scheme might vary, depending on the Linux distribution you use: SUSE Linux, Red Hat Linux, Fedora Linux, and so forth.

Text and Graphic Conventions

Where appropriate, additional information and exercises have been added to this book to help you better understand the topic at hand. Icons throughout the text alert you to additional materials. The following icons are used in this book:

The Note icon draws your attention to additional helpful material related to the subject being covered.

Tips based on the author's experience offer extra information about how to attack a problem or what to do in real-world situations.

The Caution icon warns you about potential mistakes or problems and explains how to avoid them.

Each in-chapter activity is preceded by the Activity icon and a description.

Each end-of-chapter project in this book is preceded by the Hands-On icon and a description of the exercise that follows.

These icons mark Case Projects, which are scenario-based assignments. In these case examples, you're asked to apply independently what you have learned.

INSTRUCTOR'S RESOURCES

The following supplemental materials are available when this book is used in a classroom setting. All supplements available with this book are provided to instructors on a single CD. You can also retrieve these supplemental materials from the Course Technology Web site, *www.course.com*, by going to the page for this book, under "Download Instructor Files & Teaching Tools."

Electronic Instructor's Manual. The Instructor's Manual that accompanies this book includes additional instructional material to assist in class preparation, including suggestions for classroom activities, discussion topics, and additional case projects.

Solutions. Solutions to all end-of-chapter material are included, with answers to Review Questions and, when applicable, Activities, Hands-On Projects, and Case Projects.

ExamView. This book is accompanied by ExamView, a powerful testing software package that instructors can use to create and administer printed, computer (LAN-based), and Internet exams. ExamView includes hundreds of questions that correspond to the topics covered in this book, enabling students to generate detailed study guides that include page references for further review. The computer-based and Internet testing components allow students to take exams at their computers and have them graded automatically to save instructors time.

PowerPoint presentations. This book comes with Microsoft PowerPoint slides for each chapter. These slides are meant to be used as a teaching aid for classroom presentation, to be made available to students on the network for chapter review, or to be printed for classroom distribution. Instructors can also add their own slides for other topics introduced to the class.

Figure files. All figures in the book are reproduced on the Instructor's Resources CD. Similar to the PowerPoint presentations, they are included as a teaching aid for classroom presentation, to make available to students for review, or to be printed for classroom distribution.

COPING WITH CHANGE ON THE WEB

Sooner or later, the Web-based resources mentioned in this book will become out of date or be replaced by newer information. In some cases, the URLs listed lead you to their replacements; in other cases, the URLs lead nowhere, leaving you with the dreaded "Not found" error message.

When that happens, don't give up! There's always a way to find what you want on the Web, if you're willing to invest some time and energy. Most Web sites offer a search engine, and if you can get to the main site, you can use this tool to help you find what you need. You can also use general search tools, such as *www.google.com* or *www.livesearch.com*, to find related information. In addition, although standards organizations offer the most specific information on their standards, many third-party sources of information, training, and assistance are available. The bottom line is that if you can't find something where the book says it's located, start looking around, which is an excellent way to improve your research skills.

Visit the Book's Web Site

Additional materials designed especially for you might be available for your course. Go to *www.course.com* periodically and search for this book title for more details.

ACKNOWLEDGMENTS

We would like to thank Course Technology for the opportunity to write this book on a topic of such value and importance. Thanks also go to the editorial and production staff, including Robin Romer, Product Manager, and Heather Furrow, Content Project Manager. Thanks also to Lisa Lord, Developmental Editor, for her guidance, her words of encouragement, and her periodic reminders that kept us on track. Sydney Shewchuk, Technical Editor and Contributing Author, went above and beyond the call of duty to provide suggestions based on his experience and knowledge. Thank you to Benedict H. Eu for his contributions.

Special thanks go to Michael Palmer, a consummate professional and well-known Course Technology author, who graciously applied his expertise to writing Chapter 7. He also agreed to write Chapter 9 when a family illness and tragedy threw us off track. The entire team was so supportive in our time of sorrow. They are all the finest professionals we have ever had the privilege of working with.

We would like to express our thanks for the patience and cooperation of our family throughout this time-consuming and sometimes frustrating process. Jennifer, thanks for keeping the music down and understanding when Mom needed peace and quiet with no interruptions.

We would also like to thank the following reviewers, who guided us with helpful feedback on each chapter:

Michael Anderson, ECPI College of Technology, Newport News

Julia Bell, Walters State Community College

Dr. Philip Craiger, University of Central Florida

Keith Elijah, Digital Network Analysis and Joint Network Attack School, Department of Defense

Mark Krawcyzk, Greenville Technical College

David Pope, Ozarks Technical Community College

DEDICATION

For Dad: *I wish you could have danced just one more dance. Save me a good fishing spot up there. Love, Dawn*

1

PERFORMING RISK ANALYSIS

> **After reading this chapter and completing the exercises, you will be able to:**
> ♦ Explain the fundamental concepts of risk analysis
> ♦ Describe different approaches to risk analysis
> ♦ Explain the process of risk analysis
> ♦ Describe techniques to minimize risk

Computer crime is becoming more sophisticated. As one vulnerability is patched to counter a threat, another threat crops up to take its place. Those charged with securing systems and the data stored on them must be vigilant. They must also have the support of management and develop a plan to deal with security for their organization. This plan is called a security policy.

One of the first steps toward achieving an effective security policy is risk analysis. This chapter, along with Chapter 2, explains the processes in creating and implementing a security policy. First, you learn the fundamentals of risk analysis, and then you explore different methods of conducting risk analysis. Next, you need to decide how to deal with or manage those identified risks. Risk analysis is not a one-time process that, when it's complete, can be trusted to remain accurate. Threats change constantly, so risk analysis must be conducted regularly to reassess the environment and determine whether changes to policies and procedures are needed.

RISK ANALYSIS CONCEPTS

The consensus among security professionals is that there's no zero-risk situation—in other words, there's no situation in which security is perfect. Your first task, when developing a security policy, is to assess the risk to your employees, your network, and your databases of customer, job, and personnel information. Your ultimate goal is not to reduce risks to zero, but to devise ways to manage risks in a reasonable fashion. This process, called **risk analysis**, determines the threats an organization faces, what resources are at risk, and what priority should be given to each resource. It's the first step in formulating a **security policy**, a statement that specifies what defenses should be configured to block unauthorized access, how the organization will respond to attacks, and how employees should safely handle the organization's resources to prevent loss of data or damage to files.

Because threats change constantly along with technology, determining risks and developing a security policy to manage those risks are ongoing processes, as shown in Figure 1-1, rather than a one-time operation.

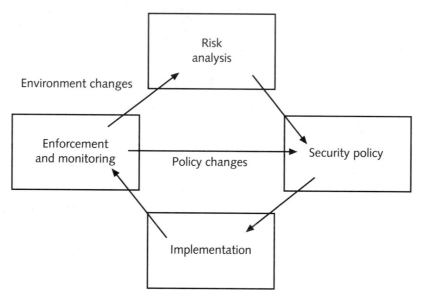

Figure 1-1   The process of risk analysis

Many companies overlook security policies and risk assessments in the process of developing network defenses and countermeasures. When you ask whether a security policy is in place, don't be surprised to hear remarks such as "*What* security policy?" or "We started working on one three years ago, but it never got anywhere." In the rush to cope with everyday business processes and amid normal employee turnover, security policies can easily be overlooked. One of your first tasks might be selling managers and employees on the need to develop a risk analysis and security policy cycle for your organization.

The following sections lay the groundwork for understanding risk analysis, the first step in developing a network security policy. You learn the fundamental concepts underlying risk analysis, different approaches to conducting risk analysis, principles for making risk analysis an ongoing process rather than an isolated occurrence, and ways to analyze the economic effect of threats.

 TIP If you're looking for statistics to back up your risk analysis and security policy drafts, visit the CERT Coordination Center (*www.cert.org*), which maintains current information on new threats and statistics of virus attacks and other security incidents.

Risk Analysis Factors

Risk is defined as the possibility of damage or loss, so risk analysis is the study of the likelihood of damage or loss in a particular situation or environment. In terms of a network connected to the Internet, risk analysis should encompass computer hardware and software plus data warehouses—storehouses of valuable customer, job, and personnel information that a company needs to safeguard.

The following sections describe these six factors that go into creating a risk analysis:

- Assets
- Threats
- Probabilities
- Vulnerabilities
- Consequences
- Safeguards

Assets

Assets in an organization play a central role in risk analysis—after all, they are the hardware, software, and informational resources you need to protect by developing and implementing a comprehensive security policy. You're likely to encounter four types of assets:

- *Physical assets*—Equipment and buildings in the organization
- *Data assets*—Databases, personnel records, customer or client information, and other data the organization stores and transmits electronically
- *Software assets*—Server programs, security programs, and other applications used to communicate and carry out the organization's typical activities
- *Personnel assets*—People who work in the organization as well as customers, business partners, contractors, and freelance employees

Some assets are tangible objects, such as computers. Other assets are intangible, such as a company's reputation and the level of trust it inspires in its customers. You might consider other assets to be essential business concepts, such as confidentiality, integrity of information, and availability of resources. The most valuable information, such as a database with contents that need to be confidential and accurate, is what you should focus on first. Data, even though it isn't tangible, might be the most important asset to continuing business operations. It's also the most difficult to evaluate. In fact, listing every single asset you have can be difficult. You might be able to analyze only the most important ones in detail.

Threats

Threats are events and conditions that haven't occurred but could potentially occur, and their presence increases risk. Some dangers are universal, such as weather-related disasters. Others are more specific to your system, such as a server storing a customer database, with the obvious danger being the threat of an attacker gaining access to the system. Other examples of circumstance-specific threats include the following:

- *Power supply*—The power supply in your area might be unreliable, making your company subject to brownouts, blackouts, and sudden surges called voltage spikes.

- *Crime rate*—If you work in a high-crime area or other offices in your area have been broken into, your risk increases.

- *Facility-related*—If your building has old wiring prone to fluctuations or has insufficient fire suppression, the risk of fire damage increases.

- *Industry*—If your organization operates in a highly competitive industry or in one requiring high security, a security breach could result in litigation or major loss of revenue or even force the business to close.

The seriousness of a threat depends on the probability that it will occur, as explained in the following section.

Probabilities

Geographic or physical location, habitual factors, and other factors affect the **probability** that a threat will occur. A geographic factor might include earthquakes being common in a region. Physical location might influence threat probability because of an electrical problem in the building housing your systems. Habitual factors could be poor security practices, such as employees keeping passwords written down near their computers, that increase the probability of a security breach. These factors are a large part of what risk assessment seeks to uncover. Risk analysis evaluates each factor and rates its potential impact or exposure.

Your **exposure** to risk increases if you have one or more factors that increase threat probabilities. For example, if you live in a part of the country with frequent severe storms or floods, the threat of weather-related damage increases. If you have a group of disgruntled employees who worked with sensitive information and have just been fired, the probability of losing that information increases unless you take steps to protect it before they leave. If your office has an alarm system wired to a security service, the probability of burglary is reduced.

Make a list of the major threats to your computer network, and rank them in order of probability. The Australian Standard AS 4360 Risk Management, developed by Standards Australia (*www.riskmanagement.com.au*), uses seven steps to describe probability: Negligible, Very Low, Low, Medium, High, Very High, and Extreme. Ranking threats by using the form in Table 1–1 can be helpful.

Table 1-1   Sample threat probabilities

Threat	Probability
Earthquake	Medium
Fire	Low
Flood	High
Attack from the Internet	Very High
Virus infection	Very High
Employees giving out information	Low

The Australian Standard is a general guide for risk management that can be applied to any industry or sector and customized to fit different business needs. It offers a framework for organization-wide risk assessment, analysis, and management. The disadvantage of the Australian Standard is that you must purchase it from Standards Australia, and it isn't inexpensive. If an organization can afford it, the standard is worth the price; however, plenty of free resources for risk analysis are available.

NOTE   For risk management guidelines specific to computer networking and IT, the Risk Management Guide for Information Technology Systems (Special Publication 800-30) from the National Institute of Standards and Technology (NIST) of the U.S. Department of Commerce outlines the risk assessment and management process step by step. NIST is a great resource for information, and best of all, the guide is free. You can find NIST's Risk Management Guide at *http://csrc.nist.gov/publications/nistpubs/800-30/sp800-30.pdf*.

Vulnerabilities

Vulnerabilities are situations or conditions that increase the probability of a threat, which, in turn, increases risk. Examples include connecting computers to the Internet, putting computers out in the open where anyone can use them, installing Web servers outside the corporate network in the vulnerable demilitarized zone (DMZ), and so on.

You can easily come up with examples of vulnerable situations that affect networked hardware and software. Some common flaws involve OS software (particularly several versions of Windows, although Linux needs to be secured as well and has fallen victim to attacks such as the Lion worm). Others involve application software (most notoriously, Internet Information

Services, Internet Explorer, and Outlook Express). Even the freeware Web server Apache has fallen victim to security compromises as a result of software flaws. Although some systems have more security flaws than others, remember that every system can and will have flaws. Opening a network to remote users whose desktop computers are unprotected by antivirus or firewall software can expose it to intrusions and virus infections. Poorly configured firewalls or packet filters, unprotected passwords, log files that aren't reviewed closely or regularly, new intrusion threats affecting wireless networks, and the complexity of modern computer networks mean that any number of components can give attackers an opening. If you remember that your system always has at least one more vulnerability than what you have found, you'll be a successful information security professional.

Security professionals have many resources for finding information on current vulnerabilities or possible network attacks. One important resource that should be bookmarked in any security professional's Web browser is the Common Vulnerabilities and Exploits (CVE) list, discussed in more detail in Chapter 4.

 Helpful Web sites and security resources are listed in Appendix B.

TIP

Consequences

Substantial adverse consequences can result from a virus that forces you to take your Web site offline for a week or a fire that destroys all your computer equipment. You can extend the earlier identification of threats to include ratings that evaluate consequences of those threats, as shown in Table 1-2.

Table 1-2   Probability and consequences of threats

Threat	Probability	Consequences
Earthquake	Medium	Significant
Fire	Low	Significant
Flood	High	Minor
Attack from the Internet	Very High	Serious
Virus infection	Very High	Serious
Employees giving out information	Low	Significant

In Table 1-2, the probability of threats has been extended to a rating of their impact. Ranking these items can be difficult because the severity often depends on the specific virus or your particular physical location. A flood doesn't have as much impact on computers stationed on the 50th floor of an office tower as it does on those on the ground floor, for instance.

Besides the consequences of getting a system back online after an attack, there are cost impacts and other effects more difficult to anticipate, including insurance claims, police reports, shipping or delivery charges, and the time and effort to obtain and reinstall software or hardware. A return on investment (ROI) calculator, such as Cisco Security Agent, can help you calculate these losses, which can amount to far more than just the price of hardware (see Figure 1-2). As you can see in this figure, an investment in Cisco Security Agent software of $26,230 would be recovered in 15.7 months, based on the calculated dollar savings of avoiding attacks, downtime, and recovery time.

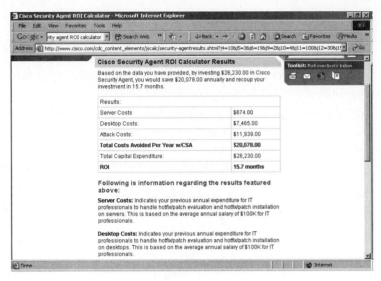

Figure 1-2   Cisco Security Agent ROI calculator

Activity 1-1: Calculating ROI

Time Required: 15 minutes

Objective: Learn how to find and use online resources, such as an ROI calculator, to evaluate products and help justify equipment investments.

Description: Part of risk analysis is estimating the value of lost data and computers that store your data as well as the indirect costs of lost productivity and recovery. Cisco Security Agent (CSA) is a powerful enterprise security tool that uses behavior-based assessment to detect suspicious traffic and prevent malicious behavior. CSA can perform firewall and intrusion detection system (IDS) functions as well as OS assurance and audit log consolidation. The ROI calculator is intended to help you justify the purchase of CSA. In this activity, you determine the time needed to recoup the purchase cost of CSA. You can enter random values or values your instructor specifies.

1. Start your Web browser and go to **www.cisco.com/en/US/products/sw/ secursw/ps5057/prod_brochure09186a00801e1249.html**.

2. When the calculator is displayed, enter values to answer each question or use values your instructor supplies. (*Tip*: For Question 19, enter the number of agents you need to secure all your servers and desktops. Based on the preceding values, enter or select appropriate values from the drop-down lists.)

3. After you've finished entering values, click **Submit** at the bottom of the page.

4. How long would it take you to recover the investment cost of CSA? Did you expect the total costs avoided per year (cost of attacks, downtime, disasters, and so on) to be higher or lower than the value shown?

_____

_____

_____

5. If time permits, go back and enter different values to better understand how each cost affects your results. After reading the results, exit your browser.

The actual cost of an incident is usually much higher than the cost of replacing equipment and restoring data (if it can be restored). When you go to management to justify investing in security, estimating the cost of the investment and benefit to the company (commonly called a **cost-benefit analysis**) is vital. The most critical numbers you want management to understand are the actual costs per year the company is paying because of security incidents. The benefit is the amount per year saved by preventing incidents.

Safeguards

Safeguards are measures you can take to reduce threats, such as installing firewalls and IDSs, locking doors, and using passwords and encryption. These measures interact with one another to help manage risk. When deciding how to manage risk, you must identify and classify risks first. Next, you determine priorities of threatened assets. The next step is to determine whether to accept, transfer, or mitigate the risk.

An asset has an associated amount of risk. Threats and vulnerabilities increase the risk; countermeasures work to reduce risk. **Residual risk** is what's left over after countermeasures and defenses are implemented; risk never actually equals zero. Figure 1-3 illustrates this process.

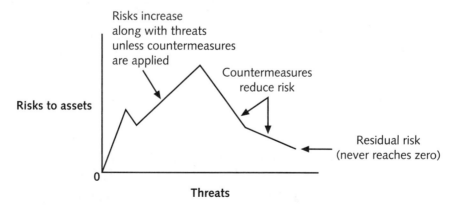

Figure 1-3   Countermeasures reduce but never completely eliminate risk

ACTIVITY

Activity 1-2: Conducting Asset Identification, Threat Analysis, and Safeguards in Your Environment

1

Time Required: 45 minutes

Objective: Learn to apply risk assessment concepts.

Description: A first step in risk analysis is identifying the assets to be protected. In this activity, you perform asset identification and a threat analysis of your environment. Your instructor will set the boundaries of the environment. Your task is to conduct a thorough, objective assessment of assets in your classroom, and then prioritize assets and propose ideas for safeguards. This activity can be done individually or in groups.

1. First, make a chart with four columns, and label the columns **Asset**, **Threats**, **Probabilities**, and **Safeguards**. Be sure to leave enough room for your notes.

2. Starting at the classroom door, begin writing down assets. Write a short description of each asset in the Asset column, such as "student computer."

3. After you have listed all assets in your classroom, assess the threats. Starting with the first asset listed, write down threats that could damage or destroy it. Examples of threats are a leaky roof, exposed wires, food or drink that could spill, and so forth. Be sure to look in all directions, including the ceiling. (*Hint*: Be sure to note drop ceilings or false floors because they are a potential point of access for intruders.)

4. Now that you have assessed the threats, examine the probabilities of a threat occurring. Use the information in Table 1-2 as a guide. For example, if you listed a leaky roof as a threat and live in an area with frequent rainfall, the probability of that threat occurring and causing damage is high. If you live in an arid desert climate, that probability is not as high.

5. Next, determine safeguards to reduce threats. Beginning with your first asset, look for ways to manage risks to it, and write down your safeguards. For a leaky roof above an expensive computer, the cost of repairing the roof might be warranted, but simply moving the computer reduces the risk and is more cost effective. On the other hand, if the power supply to the server room is prone to fluctuations that could damage delicate electronics, investing in uninterruptible power supplies (UPSs) or a generator could be less expensive than replacing damaged equipment. Remember that the priority level determines the investment in security.

6. If time permits, share your findings with the class. Discuss the results and justify your assessments and recommendations. Were the results similar? Discuss similarities and differences in findings.

RISK ANALYSIS METHODS

After listing assets you need to protect, threats to those assets, the probability that they will occur, consequences if they occur, and safeguards you can take to protect them, you have the building blocks you need to prepare a risk analysis. You can use different methods of risk analysis to create a security policy and then evaluate how well the policy is performing so that you can update and improve it. The following sections describe the two methods you're most likely to use.

Survivable Network Analysis

Survivable Network Analysis (SNA) is a security process developed by the CERT Coordination Center (*www.cert.org*). SNA starts with the assumption that a computer system or network will be attacked. It leads you through a four-step process designed to ensure the **survivability** (the capability to continue functioning during attacks, system faults, accidents, or disasters) of a network if an attack occurs.

Survivability focuses on a network's essential services and assets and critical capabilities and depends on four key properties of a network:

- *Resistance*—The capability of a system to repel attacks
- *Recognition*—The capability to detect attacks when they occur and to evaluate the extent of damage and compromise
- *Recovery*—The capability to maintain essential services during an attack and restore all services following an attack
- *Adaptation and evolution*—The capability to improve system survivability based on knowledge gained from attacks

The study of a network's survivability builds on other concepts related to risk analysis, including **fault tolerance** (the capability of an object or a system to continue operations despite a failure, such as a system shutdown), safety procedures, security systems, and ongoing testing. Most software products aren't designed with survivability in mind. That's why survivability studies can be valuable. Instead, software is often designed to work for a certain number of users or a certain amount of information, until it's replaced by new and improved versions.

The steps in SNA are as follows:

- *System definition*—First, you create an overview of the system's organizational requirements. You analyze system architecture while taking into account its hardware components, software installations, databases, servers, and other computers that store your information.
- *Essential capability definition*—You identify a system's essential services and assets that are critical to fulfilling your organization's missions and goals.
- *Compromisable capability definition*—You design situations in which intrusions to the system occur, and then trace the intrusion through your system architecture to identify what can be accessed and what sorts of damage can occur.
- *Survivability analysis*—You identify potential points of fault in the system—integral components that can be compromised. You then make recommendations for

correcting the points of fault and suggest specific ways to improve the system's resistance to intrusions and capability to recover from attacks, accidents, and other disasters.

The emphasis is on an ongoing process rather than a series of steps ending in a report of a configuration regarded as secure and permanent. You might start with better password management, then upgrade the system to encrypt critical data, and then install software that filters out potentially harmful e-mail so that the system's capability to survive improves continually.

Threat and Risk Assessment

Threat and Risk Assessment (TRA) approaches risk analysis from the standpoint of threats and risks to an organization's assets and the consequences of those threats and risks if they occur. Like SNA, TRA has four steps:

- *Asset definition*—You identify software, hardware, and information you need to defend.

- *Threat assessment*—You identify the kinds of threats that place the asset at risk, including vandalism, fire, natural disasters, and attacks from the Internet. Threat assessment also includes an evaluation of the probability and consequences of each threat.

- *Risk assessment*—You evaluate each asset for any existing safeguards, the severity of threats and risks to assets, and the consequences of the threat or risk taking place. The combination of these factors creates an assessment of the actual risk to each asset.

- *Recommendations*—Based on the risks and current safeguards, you make recommendations to reduce the risk. These recommendations should then be made part of a security policy.

TRA is carried out in different ways by security agencies all over the world. One of the clearest and most systematic statements of how to perform TRA is by the Information Security Group of the Australian Government's Defense Signals Directorate. The document "Australian Communications - Electronic Security Instruction 33 (ACSI 33)" describes a variety of ratings systems. Instead of assigning numeric values to risks and threat levels, these systems use terms such as "high," "low," and "medium." Often, these systems are enough to assess risk and are easier to use than statistical tools. Table 1-3 shows ratings you can assign to describe the probability of threats occurring.

Table 1-3   Threat ratings system

Rating	What it means
Negligible	Unlikely to occur
Very Low	Likely to occur only two or three times every five years
Low	Likely to occur within a year or less
Medium	Likely to occur every six months or less
High	Likely to occur after a month or less

Table 1-3   Threat ratings system (continued)

Rating	What it means
Very High	Likely to occur multiple times per month or less
Extreme	Likely to occur multiple times each day

TIP   ACSI 33 is available online at *www.dsd.gov.au/_lib/pdf_doc/acsi33/acsi33_u_0904.pdf*. If you want to research other governments' approaches to TRA, you can find links to TRA guidelines in Canada and other countries at *www.infosyssec.net/infosyssec/threat1.htm*.

After rating the severity of a threat or risk, you evaluate the consequences if it actually occurs. ACSI 33 lists a set of standard descriptors, shown in Table 1-4.

Table 1-4   Describing consequences

Description	Consequences
Catastrophic	Threatens the continuation of the program and causes major problems for customers
Major	Threatens the continuation of basic functions of the program and requires senior-level management intervention
Moderate	Does not threaten the program; however, the program could be subject to major review and modification of operating procedures
Minor	Could threaten the program's efficiency or effectiveness but can be dealt with internally
Insignificant	Can be dealt with by normal operations

After evaluating the threats to assets and describing the consequences, you can combine the two ratings (level of threat and consequences of the threat occurring) to come up with an analysis of the risk to each asset, as described in the following section.

RISK ANALYSIS PROCESS

Risk analysis is not a one-time activity used to create a security policy. Rather, risk analysis evolves to take into account an organization's changing size and activities, the progression to larger and more complex computer systems, and new threats from inside and outside the corporate network.

The initial risk analysis is used to formulate a security policy; the security policy is then enforced and security is monitored. New threats and intrusion attempts create the need for reassessing the risk an organization faces.

General Activities to Follow

Whatever method you use, risk analysis is a group of related activities that typically follow this sequence:

- *Holding initial team sessions*—First, hold meetings to get groups of workers together in one place; hold interviews or hand out questionnaires to collect pertinent information. It's especially important to talk to all managers to set the objectives and scope for the risk analysis, schedule how long the project should take, and identify the important people you need to interview.

- *Conducting asset valuation*—After you determine the scope of the risk analysis, you need to identify assets to protect and determine their value. This activity can be subjective or speculative. If it's subjective, you're assessing the impact of losing assets that might not be tangible, and you should use your best judgment or solicit opinions from other qualified employees. If it's speculative, you're estimating whether information might fall into the hands of unauthorized people and what the company's cost would be to recover the information. Personal interviews with managers can help you determine a realistic assessment.

- *Evaluating vulnerability*—You investigate the levels of threat and vulnerability in relation to the value of the organization's assets. Ask IT staff to evaluate the threat of virus attacks or other intrusions on a scale of one to five, for instance.

- *Calculating risk*—After you have the asset value and an idea of vulnerabilities threatening those assets, you can calculate risk. Usually, a numeric value is assigned. For instance, 1 is given to a low-level baseline security need and 7 to a very high security priority.

NOTE

Remember that the first step in risk management and designing and implementing a security policy is gaining the backing of upper management (board of directors, CEO, CIO, and so on). This support makes your efforts much easier. The cooperation you get from colleagues, other departments, and employees will be more forthcoming if they know you're acting with full support from the highest levels of management. "Selling" a security policy to managers isn't difficult if you know what they care about: the bottom line, profits. If you consider how security affects profitability, selling the point isn't hard. Just remember you must be able to back up the numbers you give them, and don't exaggerate potential costs of a security incident.

Analyzing Economic Impacts

An important part of conducting a risk analysis is preparing estimates of the financial impact of losses. If you're familiar with statistics, you can use a number of different models for estimating impacts. You can also use a software program to help you prepare reports that substantiate your estimates and produce charts and graphs to support your figures. Project Risk Analysis by Katmar Software, for example, gives you a structure for listing hardware and software assets in your organization (see Figure 1-4). You work with this program in Activity 1-3.

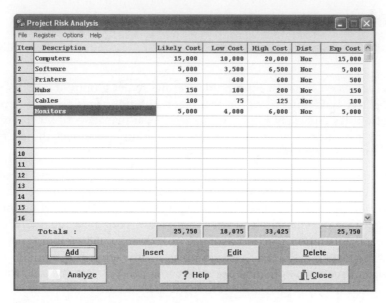

Figure 1-4   Project Risk Analysis offers a structure for making cost estimates

With this program, you can make cost estimates by using a variety of statistical models. For those who are unfamiliar with statistics, the simplest model uses the following:

- *Likely cost*—The most realistic estimate of the money you need to spend to replace the item

- *Low cost*—The lowest dollar amount for replacing the item

- *High cost*—The highest dollar amount for replacing the item

When you create a record of an asset in Project Risk Analysis and estimate its replacement cost, you enter these values using the Normal distribution setting, as shown in Figure 1-5.

One advantage of a risk analysis program is being able to analyze cost estimates and present them in a report format (see Figure 1-6). In addition, these programs can quickly calculate the mean cost of replacing hardware, software, or other items.

Project Risk Analysis performs calculations by using a statistical formula called a **Monte Carlo simulation**—an analytical method that simulates a real-life system by randomly generating values for variables. The charts and reports these programs create are valuable documentation for preparing a risk analysis; these visuals have a lot of impact when presented to managers.

For more information on Monte Carlo simulations, see *www.decisioneering.com/monte-carlo-simulation.html*.

TIP

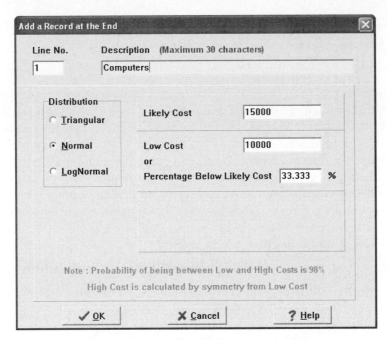

Figure 1-5 Entering values for likely cost and low cost to estimate replacement cost

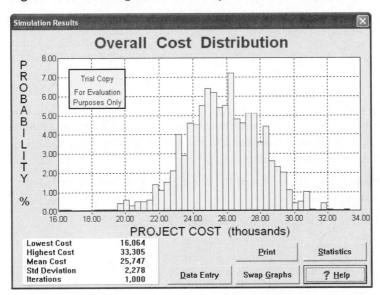

Figure 1-6 Graphical reports in risk analysis software

ACTIVITY

Activity 1-3: Calculating Replacement Costs

Time Required: 15 minutes

Objective: Use a risk analysis tool to calculate replacement costs for equipment.

Description: A software tool can bring some consistency and objectivity to the process of risk analysis. In this activity, you download a trial version of a risk analysis tool for Windows called Project Risk Analysis (PRA) by Katmar Software. You then enter the characteristics of network resources in your school's lab and calculate the contingency funds needed to replace lab equipment if a disaster strikes. You need a computer running Windows XP and a file-archiving utility, such as WinZip. Enter values for computer equipment in your lab and an estimate of data on them. If you aren't in your computer lab or don't know about all the equipment in it, assume you're in a lab with 10 PCs, two printers, one network hub, and one removable disk drive. Each PC has a replacement value of $1500, is equipped with $1000 worth of software, and stores data valued at $500.

1. Start your Web browser and go to **www.katmarsoftware.com/pra.htm**.

2. Read the description of the program, and then click the **Download Now!** link.

3. When you're prompted to open or save the Projrisk.zip file, click **Save** and save it to a folder on your file system.

4. When the file download is finished, click **Close** in the Download Complete dialog box. Exit your Web browser, and then double-click the file to open it with WinZip. Extract the files to the folder where you placed the .zip file you downloaded.

5. Double-click the **ProjRisk_Setup.exe** file and follow the steps in the setup program to install it on your computer.

6. Click **Start**, point to **All Programs**, point to **Risk Analysis**, and click **ProjRisk** to start the program. The first time you run the program, you see a Thank You for Installing PRA window, which states the terms under which the program can be run. (It runs 30 times as an evaluation.) Click **OK**, and then click **OK** again when you see a second shareware reminder.

7. Click **Add** to open the Add a Record at the End dialog box. In the Description text box, type **Computers**.

8. In the Distribution section, click the **Normal** option button.

9. In the Likely Cost text box, type **15000**. (*Note:* Don't use commas in number entries.)

10. In the Low Cost text box, type **10000**.

11. Click **OK** to return to the main Project Risk Analysis window, where your estimate is entered in the first row.

12. Repeat Steps 7 through 11 for **Software** (likely cost 5000, low cost 3500), **Printers** (likely cost 500, low cost 400), **Hubs** (likely cost 150, low cost 100), **Cables** (likely cost 100, low cost 75), and **Monitors** (likely cost 5000, low cost 4000). (*Note:* Remember to click **Normal** for Step 8 each time.)

1

13. In the main Project Risk Analysis window, click the **Analyze** button to see the Overall Cost Distribution graph. What are the Lowest Cost, Highest Cost, and Mean Cost figures displayed in this window?

   _____

   _____

   _____

14. Click the **Statistics** button. What is the mean cost listed in the Simulation Statistics Report dialog box?

   _____

   _____

15. Close the Simulation Statistics Report dialog box, and exit Project Risk Analysis. If necessary, click **Yes** in the message box warning you that the data has not been saved. Leave your system running for the next activity.

TECHNIQUES FOR MINIMIZING RISK

After analyzing the level of risk to hardware and software assets in your network, you can recommend safeguards for minimizing the risk. **Risk management**, in fact, is the term for the process of identifying, choosing, and setting up countermeasures for the risks you identify. The countermeasures you describe are the statements that go into your security policy. In the following sections, you learn about important points to consider when deciding how to secure hardware, how to secure information databases in your network, how to conduct routine analysis, and how to respond to security incidents.

Securing Hardware

Your company's physical computing assets—the hardware devices that keep data flowing throughout the network—are the most obvious objects that need to be identified. You have to decide how you're going to protect your hardware. First, think about obvious kinds of physical protection, such as environmental controls to keep machines cool in hot temperatures and fire protection systems. Then consider whether you're going to lock up all hardware in your organization or use theft protection only for servers. (Placing your servers in a locked room with an alarm system so that unauthorized employees can't access them is critical; this equipment should never be left out in the open.)

Be sure to pay special attention to laptop computers in your organization. These machines can be lost or stolen easily, and any proprietary information on them could be compromised. These incidents happen regularly and often with serious consequences. To alleviate the problem of data on lost or stolen laptops being compromised, be sure to install startup passwords as well as screen saver passwords; experienced thieves can circumvent them, of course, but at least they make it more difficult to access files. In addition, you can encrypt files on your laptop with a program such as Pretty Good Privacy (PGP), which is available at *www.pgp.com*. For Windows computers, you should consider enabling Encrypting File System (EFS) on all company laptops.

Conducting a Hardware Inventory

Make a list of servers, routers, cables, computers, printers, and other hardware the company owns. Be sure to include your company's **network assets**—the routers, cables, servers, and firewall hardware and software that enable employees to communicate with one another and other computers on the Internet. Make a topology map that shows how the devices are connected and includes an IP allocation register, such as the one in Figure 1-7.

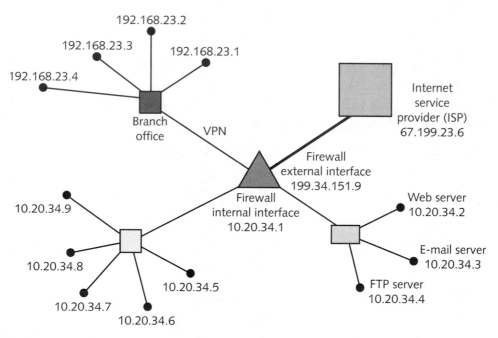

Figure 1-7   A topology map can supplement a hardware inventory

Ranking Resources To Be Protected

In listing physical, electronic, network, and system assets, assigning a value to each object is helpful. The value can be an arbitrary number; what's important is to rank resources in order of importance so that you can focus your security efforts on the most critical resources first. The team that helps you prepare your security policy will probably determine that data is more important than the devices on which it's stored.

TIP   The numbers you come up with might seem somewhat arbitrary; however, deriving rankings with the cooperation of your organization's higher management is helpful. Developing a lengthy list of resources and rankings on your own without input from managers is likely to result in extensive revisions. You'll get better results if you submit a list of resources to management and ask them to develop their own rankings. Also, ask them to consider the cost to replace software and computers you have listed. Suggest that they rank assets on a scale of 1 to 10.

Using Encryption

One of the best and least costly methods of securing data is to apply encryption to lock it down. Encryption doesn't prevent accessing or viewing encrypted data or even prevent its theft, for that matter. However, it can prevent data from being exploited. The following sections describe several areas in which using encryption could be helpful in minimizing the risk of sensitive data being compromised.

Mobile Computers

Thieves and attackers are targeting mobile computers (laptops, notebooks, PDAs, and so forth) more often as sources of sensitive data, so they should be considered high-security devices. Many instances of mobile computer theft have occurred recently that resulted in large-scale unauthorized access to sensitive corporate and personal data. The resulting damage could have been prevented easily through physical security, password protection, and data encryption on these devices.

Removable Media

When you're considering data vulnerability, removable media, such as disks, tapes, CDs, flash drives, and so on, are much like mobile computers. Removable media are easy to transport and conceal and capable of containing large quantities of data. As with mobile computers, removable media containing millions of sensitive, cleartext records have been lost or stolen to the detriment of corporations and private individuals. Again, physical security, password protection, and, most of all, data encryption could have prevented sensitive data from being compromised.

Data Transfers

Moving data over wired and wireless media is common. Often devices sharing data use encrypted authentication methods to establish their communication link. However, just as often, after communication paths have been established, data is transferred in cleartext, thus making it vulnerable to theft and exploitation. Data encryption before communication doesn't prevent data theft, but it does minimize the risk of data being exploited.

Securing Information

After you have decided on safeguards for your hardware, you need to determine how best to protect your company's **electronic assets**—word processing, spreadsheet, Web page, and other documents on your network computers. Logical assets include e-mail, any records of instant messaging conversations, and log files compiled by firewalls and IDSs. Data assets include personnel, customer, and financial information that your company needs to protect.

Maintaining Customer and Employee Privacy

Many companies now conduct all or part of their business operations on the Internet. If your organization conducts e-commerce, you need to strike a balance between making it easy to find goods for sale and complete electronic transactions and keeping customer and business information confidential.

One way to protect the information your customers send via the Internet is to isolate the information from the Internet so that attackers can't access it. In many high-profile attacks that have plagued Web sites recently, attackers manage to break into a site and access credit card numbers and other data. In your security policy, you might want to state that to minimize the risk of attackers stealing critical customer data, your company needs to move information to a computer that's physically isolated from the Internet. You can configure backup software to save critical files in isolated locations automatically on a nightly or weekly basis. You can also use the following measures to protect information:

- *Encryption*—By encrypting data, you can protect it as it passes from one network to another so that it can't be read if it's intercepted or captured.

- *Message filtering*—This measure keeps potentially harmful messages from entering the network from the outside.

- *Data encapsulation*—The data in packets can be encrypted in such a way that the packets are encapsulated (or "wrapped") for extra protection.

- *Redundancy*—By providing redundancy through backup systems, you ensure that databases and other stores of information remain accessible if primary systems go offline.

- *Backups*—Systematic and periodic backups of information on the network are one of the most basic and important ways to protect that information.

TIP You can separate customer databases from Web servers by using hardware/ software products, such as Forefront by Microsoft, to keep data flowing securely between the external Web server and internal database servers.

Protecting Corporate Information

Do employees at your organization handle confidential, proprietary, or private information? If so, this information needs to be covered in the security policy. Safeguards are needed to inform these employees of their information protection duties and to tell them what they can and can't do with sensitive information. To minimize risks, you could specify the following measures in a security policy:

- Never leave company-owned laptops or handheld devices unattended.

- Always password-protect information on corporate devices.

- Encrypt any confidential information.

- Password-protect all job records and customer information.

- Restrict all personnel information to human resources staff and upper management.

You need to make sure all employees read and understand the policy. You might consider distributing the policy in the form of a manual issued to all new employees and published on the company Web site for current employees to review. Having employees sign a statement that they have read and understand their responsibilities is also a good idea.

Conducting Routine Risk Analysis

Risk analysis is an ongoing operation. A company changes constantly in terms of the information it handles, number of customers, number of employees, and number of computers on the network. Risk analysis should be done routinely despite common obstacles, such as indifference of IT staff and employees, heavy workload in critical areas, and lack of available personnel to do the evaluation.

Deciding how your organization performs routine risk analysis starts with the following questions:

- How often will risk analysis be performed? Every year at budget time is a logical, consistent level of frequency. However, conducting risk analysis more often, such as every six months, enables you to keep up with new threats better.

- Who will conduct risk analysis? The same professionals who manage security for the organization are the ones who should participate, along with accounting or bookkeeping staff.

- Do all hardware and software resources need to be reviewed every time? You might not need to conduct a new risk analysis for every asset you have; you might decide that only assets that have increased or changed substantially should be reexamined.

The calculations and evaluations in risk analysis require subjective evaluations of how much an asset is "worth" and how "valuable" it is. Human emotions can influence evaluations, so many companies don't allow employees to perform these calculations manually. Because of the often complex calculations, using risk analysis software can be easier as well as more objective.

One of the best-known software tools for risk analysis, CRAMM, is available from Insight Solutions (*www.insight.co.uk/products/cramm.htm*).

CHAPTER SUMMARY

❑ Risk analysis plays a central role in formulating a security policy. Risks need to be calculated and security policies amended on an ongoing basis as a network configuration changes and new threats emerge.

❑ Risk analysis covers a company's computer hardware, software, and informational assets and should be done before *and* after a security policy is created. The goal is not to reduce risks to zero (which isn't possible) but to manage risk at reasonable levels on an ongoing basis.

❑ Your first task is to identify the assets you need to protect. Then, you assess threats to your network, such as attacks, power outages, and environmental disasters.

❑ Next, you determine the probability that those threats might happen. You then use the data you have assembled to perform a risk analysis, using an approach such as Survivable Network Analysis (SNA) or Threat and Risk Assessment (TRA). A risk analysis describes the level of risk to each asset in the organization as well as the economic impact if it's lost or damaged.

❑ After assessing the level of risk to assets, you need to determine countermeasures and safeguards for minimizing risk. You decide how to secure computing assets, logical assets (IM records, e-mail, and log file records), data stored in your databases, application software, and personal assets of employees. You then come up with a plan for conducting risk analysis routinely and a plan for handling security incidents.

KEY TERMS

assets — The hardware, software, and informational resources you need to protect by developing and implementing a comprehensive security policy.

cost–benefit analysis — A technique for comparing the costs of an investment with the benefits it proposes to return.

electronic assets — The word processing, spreadsheet, Web page, and other documents on your network computers.

exposure — Vulnerability to loss resulting from the occurrence of a threat, such as accidental or intentional disclosure or destruction or modification of information resources. Exposure increases with the presence of multiple threat factors.

fault tolerance — The capability of an object or a system to continue operations despite a failure.

Monte Carlo simulation — An analytical method meant to simulate a real-life system by randomly generating values for variables.

network assets — The routers, cables, bastion hosts, servers, and firewall hardware and software that enable employees to communicate with one another and other computers on the Internet.

probability — The possibility that a threat will actually occur, influenced by geographic, physical, habitual, or other factors that increase or decrease the likelihood of occurrence.

residual risk — The risk remaining after countermeasures and defenses are implemented.

risk — The possibility of incurring damage or loss.

risk analysis — A process of analyzing the threats an organization faces, determining precisely what resources are at risk, and deciding the priority to give each asset.

risk management — The process of identifying, choosing, and setting up countermeasures justified by the risks you identify.

safeguards — Measures you can take to reduce threats, such as installing firewalls and intrusion detection systems, locking doors, and using passwords and encryption.

security policy — A statement that spells out exactly what defenses will be configured to block unauthorized access, what constitutes acceptable use of network resources, how the organization will respond to attacks, and how employees should handle the organization's resources safely to discourage loss of data or damage to files.

survivability — The capability to continue functioning in the presence of attacks or disasters.

Survivable Network Analysis (SNA) — A security process that starts with the assumption that a computer system will be attacked and follows a set of steps to build a system that can survive such an attack.

Threat and Risk Assessment (TRA) — An approach to risk analysis that starts from the standpoint of threats and accounts for risks to an organization's assets and the consequences of those threats and risks if they occur.

threats — Events and conditions that haven't occurred but could potentially occur; the presence of these events or conditions increases risk.

vulnerabilities — Situations or conditions that increase threat, which, in turn, increases risk.

REVIEW QUESTIONS

1. Which of the following should be done before formulating a security policy?

   a. intrusion handling plan

   b. risk analysis

   c. security review

   d. list of assets

2. Personnel records fit into which category of assets?

   a. personnel assets

   b. software assets

   c. data assets

   d. physical assets

3. Survivable Network Analysis begins with what assumption?

   a. that you have laid the groundwork for a risk analysis

   b. that your network will be attacked

   c. that the probability of threats is increasing constantly

   d. that an effective security policy can reduce risk to zero

4. Survivable Network Analysis looks for which of the following in a network?

   a. failure points

   b. bottlenecks

   c. collisions of data

   d. software incompatibilities

5. Name three factors that can increase the cost (beyond the actual sticker price) of replacing hardware that has been damaged or stolen.

6. List and describe the four steps of a Survivable Network Analysis in the order in which they should occur.

7. The hardware and software you need to protect can be valued most easily by following what approach?

   a. getting the most recent prices online

   b. keeping records of purchase costs

   c. using your experience and expertise

   d. interviewing support personnel

8. If an organization doesn't have a full-fledged security staff on duty, what should it do? (Choose all that apply.)

   a. Hire a group such as CERT.

   b. Designate IT staff to hold concurrent security positions.

   c. Designate managers to fulfill security functions.

   d. A standalone security staff is not needed.

9. When should an organization conduct a new round of risk analysis?

   a. every month

   b. every three months

   c. as frequently as possible

   d. when equipment or staff change significantly

10. A risk analysis report should call attention to _____ .
    a. all identified risks
    b. the most urgent risks
    c. the newest risks
    d. the risks that are easiest to manage

11. Which of the following is the process of identifying, choosing, and setting up countermeasures for the risks you identify?
    a. risk assessment
    b. risk identification
    c. threat management
    d. risk management

12. The ultimate goal of formulating a security policy is which of the following?
    a. reduce the risks to zero
    b. get the policy done right the first time so that it doesn't have to be rewritten constantly
    c. convince management you deserve a raise
    d. none of the above

13. What are the hardware, software, and informational resources you need to protect called?
    a. threats
    b. tangibles
    c. assets
    d. business holdings

14. Equipment and buildings in the organization are called _____ assets.
    a. facility
    b. tangible
    c. physical
    d. hard

15. Which of the following risk factors are events and conditions that haven't occurred but could happen?
    a. dangers
    b. disasters
    c. threats
    d. vulnerabilities

16. Documents on network computers, e-mail messages, log files compiled by firewalls and IDSs, and confidential information on personnel, customers, and finances are considered what type of asset?

    a. physical

    b. tangible

    c. electronic

    d. data

17. Ensuring that databases and other stores of information remain accessible if primary systems go offline is known as _____ .

    a. fault tolerance

    b. failover

    c. redundancy

    d. resiliency

18. The presence of one or more factors that increase threat probabilities increases your _____ .

    a. risk

    b. threats

    c. exposure

    d. consequences

19. The routers, cables, servers, and firewall hardware and software that enable employees to communicate with one another and other computers on the Internet are considered _____ assets.

    a. desktop

    b. server

    c. communications

    d. network

20. Which of the following technologies helps protect sensitive data even after it has been stolen from a secured medium?

    a. virus protection

    b. authentication

    c. encryption

    d. Spybot

HANDS-ON PROJECTS

1

Hands-On Project 1-1: Collecting Hardware and Software Inventory Information

Time Required: 15 minutes

Objective: Create a hardware and software inventory of your network and save it to a file.

Description: Making a complete hardware or software inventory of your network can be a daunting task. Luckily, several methods, from simple VBScripts to high-end software programs, can automate this chore. In this project, you use Network Asset Tracker from MIS Utilities to gather hardware and software data about your computer and save it to a file.

At the time of this writing, the latest version of Network Asset Tracker was 2.8. If you download a more recent version, your screens might look slightly different from the figures shown in these steps.

NOTE

1. Start your Web browser and go to **www.misutilities.com/download.html**.

2. Scroll down and click the download link for **Network Asset Tracker**.

3. When you're prompted to open or save the Natracker.exe file, click **Save** and save it to a directory on your file system.

4. When the file download is finished, click **Close** in the Download Complete dialog box, and then close your Web browser.

5. Go to the directory where you downloaded the program, and double-click the **Natracker.exe** file. If necessary, when the Security Warning dialog box opens, click **Run**.

6. Click **Next** to accept the default setting of English (United States) in the Language Selection dialog box, as shown in Figure 1-8.

7. Click **Next** in the Welcome to the Installation Wizard window. Scroll through and read the Readme Information window, and then click **Next**.

8. Click to select the **Yes, I agree with all the terms of this license agreement** check box, and then click **Next**.

9. Click **Next** to accept the default installation directory, and then click **Next** in the Select Components window. Click **Next** two more times to start the installation, and then click **Finish**.

10. Click **Start**, point to **All Programs**, point to **Network Asset Tracker**, and click **Network Asset Tracker** to start the program. Click **Close** in the Tip of the Day message box.

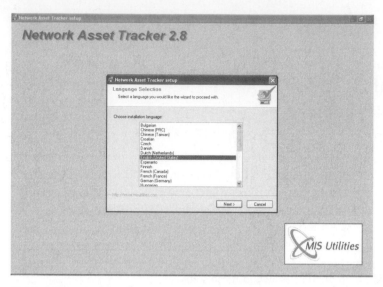

Figure 1-8   Network Asset Tracker setup

11. Right-click the **LOCALHOST** computer icon, and click **Get/Update Info**. A window similar to the one in Figure 1-9 is displayed with details about your system.

12. Click **Report**, **System Info** from the menu. Under Type of report, click to select the **List** option button, and then click **OK**.

13. Click **Export** and save the System Info file to a directory on your C drive. Click **OK** in the Report exported successfully message box, and then click **Close**.

14. Navigate to the directory where you saved the System Info file, and double-click the **System Info.html** file. Read through the file to examine the information that was gathered. When you're finished, close the file.

15. Repeat Steps 12 through 14, substituting **Software Info** for **System Info**.

16. Click **File, Exit** from the menu to close the program.

1

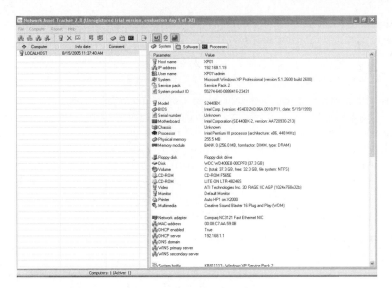

Figure 1-9 The Get/Update Info window

Case Projects

Case Project 1-1: Conducting Risk Assessment and Analysis

Risk assessment can be as simple as noting an unlocked door or a password written on a note, or it can be a complex process requiring several team members and months to complete. A large enterprise environment probably has multiple locations, diverse activities, and a wide array of resources to evaluate. You don't need such a complex network, however, for your running case project; the main idea is to learn how to apply your knowledge methodically to produce useful and accurate data. Approaching risk assessment without a strategy means repeating steps, wasting resources, and missing critical information.

Your instructor will provide a floor plan for Green Globe R&D, Inc., and if you haven't already done so, create a network diagram and complete the hardware and software inventory for this network. Your instructor will also provide documentation templates for risk assessment. Make additional copies as needed. In a real risk analysis, one of the first steps is meeting with all department managers, upper management, employee representatives, workers in the production environment, human resources staff, and other employees to get their input. Without input from the people actually doing the work, you might not think of essential factors, so direct any questions you have to your instructor, or do independent research to find your answers.

NOTE

Remember that threats can affect multiple assets and vice versa, so the same asset might be listed more than once.

1. First, identify the business processes that must continue for the organization to keep functioning—for example, collecting money from customers, receiving and processing contracts, developing new products, and so on. Document major business processes that drive Green Globe, using the Business Process column of the Business Process Identification Worksheet. (You need your imagination and some common sense for this step.) Assign a priority level to each process (using the priority rankings in the following list). Write down the department that performs the process, and leave the Assets Used column blank for now.

   - *Critical*—Absolutely necessary for business operations to continue. Loss of a critical process halts business activities.

   - *Necessary*—Contributes to smooth, efficient operations. Loss of a necessary process doesn't halt business operations but degrades working conditions, slows production, or contributes to errors.

   - *Desirable*—Contributes to enhanced performance and productivity and helps create a more comfortable working environment, but loss of a desirable process doesn't halt or negatively affect operations.

2. Next, identify the organization's assets. Using the Asset Identification Worksheet your instructor provides, list each asset, its location, and approximate value, if known. (For multiple identical assets, describe the asset and list the quantity instead of listing each asset.) In organization-wide risk assessments, you list all assets, including office furniture, industrial equipment, personnel, and other assets. For this project, stick to IT assets, such as computers, servers, and networking equipment, based on your network diagram. All the equipment needed to build your network should be listed here as well as any cabling in the facility. (Assume the facility is already wired for a computer network with network drops available for each computer.) *Hint*: Remember to list items such as electricity and Internet connections.

3. Determine which assets support each business process. On your Business Process Identification Worksheet, list the assets needed for each business process in the Assets Used column.

4. Each process should be documented and have a priority assigned to it. Next, transfer the priority rankings to your Asset Identification Worksheet. Now you know which assets are the most critical to restore and warrant the most expense and effort to secure. You also have the documentation to back up your security actions for each item.

5. The final step is assessing existing threats. Table 1-5 shows examples of ways to evaluate some types of threats and suggests ways to quantify them. On the Threat Identification and Assessment Worksheet, list each possible threat. Be sure to consider threats from geographic and physical factors, personnel, malicious attack or sabotage, and accidents. Also,

examine the facility diagram for flaws in the facility layout or structure that could pose a threat, such as air-conditioning failure or loss of electrical service. Assess the probability of occurrence (POC) on a 1 to 10 scale, with 1 being the lowest and 10 being the highest, and assign those ratings in the POC column for each threat.

Table 1-5 Threat evaluation and quantification methods

Type of threat	How to quantify
Severe rainstorm, tornado, hurricane, earthquake, wilderness fire, or flood	Collect data on frequency, severity, and proximity to facilities. Evaluate the past quality and speed of local and regional emergency response systems to determine whether they helped minimize loss.
Train derailment, auto/truck accident, toxic air pollution caused by accident, or plane crash	Collect data on the proximity of railroads, highways, and airports to facilities. Evaluate the construction quality of transportation systems and the rate of serious accidents on each system.
Building explosion or fire	Collect data on the frequency and severity of past incidents. Evaluate local emergency response to determine its effectiveness.
Militant group attacking facilities, riot, or civil unrest	Collect data on the political stability of the region where facilities are located. Compile and evaluate a list of groups that might have specific political or social issues with the organization.
Computer hack (external) or computer fraud (internal)	Examine data on the frequency and severity of past incidents. Evaluate the effectiveness of existing computer security measures.

6. Using the Asset Identification Worksheet, determine which assets would be affected by each threat. List those assets in the Assets Affected column of the Threat Identification and Assessment Worksheet. For an electrical outage, for example, list all assets requiring electricity to operate; for a hardware failure, list all assets a hardware failure would disrupt, damage, or destroy.

7. In the Consequence column, enter the consequences of the threat occurring, using the following designations:

   - *Catastrophic (C)*—Total loss of business processes or functions for one week or more. Potential complete failure of business.

   - *Severe (S)*—Business would be unable to continue functioning for 24 to 48 hours. Loss of revenue, damage to reputation or confidence, reduction of productivity, complete loss of critical data or systems.

   - *Moderate (M)*—Business could continue after an interruption of no more than 4 hours. Some loss of productivity and damage or destruction of important information or systems.

   - *Insignificant (I)*—Business could continue functioning without interruption. Some cost incurred for repairs or recovery. Minor equipment or facility damage. Minor productivity loss and little or no loss of important data.

8. Then rate the severity of each threat in the Severity column, using the same designations as in the preceding list for consequences (C, S, M, or I). You derive these ratings by combining the probability of occurrence, the asset's priority ranking, and the potential consequences of a threat occurring. For example, if an asset has a Critical (C) priority ranking and a Catastrophic (C) consequence rating, it has a Catastrophic (C) severity rating. If you have mixed or contradictory ratings, you need to reevaluate the asset and use common sense. A terrorist attack that destroys the facility and kills half the staff might have a probability of occurrence (POC) of only 1 (depending on your location), but if it happened, the consequences would definitely be catastrophic. Even so, because of the low POC, you wouldn't necessarily rank its severity as catastrophic.

9. Finally, on the Threat Mitigation Worksheet, list assets that are ranked as the most critical and threatened with the highest severity. In the Mitigation Techniques column, list recommendations for mitigating threats to those assets. For example, to mitigate the threat of an electrical outage damaging a critical server, you might suggest a high-end uninterruptible power supply (UPS).

10. Review your work, and submit it to your instructor.

2

CREATING SECURITY POLICIES

> ## After reading this chapter and completing the exercises, you will be able to:
>
> ♦ Explain important concepts in security policies
> ♦ Identify security policy categories
> ♦ Define incident-handling procedures

Computer crime is a continuing problem for businesses. The 2006 Annual CSI/FBI Computer Crime and Security Survey (*www.gocsi.com/forms/fbi/csi_fbi_survey.jhtml*) indicated that computer crimes and financial losses resulting from security incidents are on the decrease, which is good news for security professionals. Many organizations now integrate security as part of everyday business practices, although it means a higher investment in security. Additionally, several areas of industry, notably health care and financial services, are subject to new legislation that makes lack of security a major liability. That trend is likely to continue, and businesses must consider security and its costs as part of daily operations. Information security is being addressed more often with a logical and structured methodology, with positive results.

Progress has been made, but computer-related losses still happen and will continue to be a problem requiring ongoing management. Faced with these challenges, information security professionals and management need to evaluate the risks their organizations face and plan the deployment of standard methodologies to defend their systems. Armed with a detailed and accurate risk assessment, the next step is to develop a security policy—a statement that spells out exactly what defenses are configured to block unauthorized access, how the organization responds to attacks, and how employees should handle the organization's resources safely to prevent loss of data or damage to files.

WHAT MAKES A GOOD SECURITY POLICY?

In organizations, hearing the question "Do we really need a security policy?" is common. You should remind skeptical fellow employees that a security policy is indeed necessary, particularly if the organization falls into one of the following categories:

- Employees work with confidential or proprietary information.

- Damage, theft, or corruption of systems or data would result in severe financial losses that could endanger business continuity.

- The organization has trade secrets that are important to its goods or services.

- Employees regularly access the Internet and use e-mail or other means of electronic communication at risk of attack or infection.

- The company is in an industry regulated by state and federal legislation on information security and privacy.

- The company uses Internet connections with partner businesses or application service providers (ASPs)—companies that provide Web-based services for a fee.

To help your case, you can also relate examples of public relations and human relations dilemmas that can occur if a clearly defined security policy isn't in place. Here are some to consider:

- A copyeditor spent a lot of time on the job surfing the Internet for personal pursuits as well as work-related research. Management was unable to discipline this employee because no policy was in effect stating what constituted excessive personal use. The employee's supervisor later discovered that the copyeditor had downloaded pornography; for this reason, the employee was fired. However, the employee subsequently appealed the dismissal with the Civil Service Board, claiming that he couldn't be fired because he had never been told he couldn't download pornography. After a hearing, the board ordered him to be reinstated with back pay.

- A clerk laid off because of downsizing at an insurance company was hired by a competing company. The insurance company discovered that many of its customer files had been accessed and copied, and a number of its clients had switched to the competitor after they were offered lower insurance rates. The original company didn't have a policy for protecting its passwords or switching passwords after employees left the company. The laid-off clerk was able to access her former employer's network and steal files so that her new employer could market itself aggressively to potential customers.

The benefits of a security policy are wide ranging. In general, however, a security policy provides a foundation for an organization's overall security stance. A security policy not only gives employees guidelines on how to handle sensitive information and IT staff instructions on what defensive systems to configure, but also reduces the risk of legal liability for the company and its employees. Employees who are fired or laid off often sue their previous employers or file a grievance, and in these cases, a well-defined security policy can make the difference between the company having to pay damages and not being liable at all.

To protect overall security, it's important to formulate a clear policy that states what rights employees have and how they should handle company resources responsibly. All employees should sign the policy when they are first hired. In some instances, asking an employee who works with sensitive or proprietary information to sign a nondisclosure or confidentiality agreement is a wise precaution.

A good security policy is comprehensive and flexible; often, it's not a single document but a group of documents, each with a specific emphasis. The next section discusses general best practices for security policies. Then you examine major factors that result in an effective set of rules and procedures: the consideration of cyber risk insurance coverage; the need to base a policy on a thorough risk assessment; the need to teach employees about acceptable use of network resources; the need to specify what an employee's expected privacy rights are when on company property and using company equipment; the need to enable management to set priorities; the need to help administrators do their jobs; and the need to see a security policy as making subsequent risk analyses possible.

General Security Policy Best Practices

A security policy for a large corporation might rival a metropolitan phone book in length and encompass every possible aspect of business, or it can be a simple document describing a few fundamental rules for a small company with only two computers and nine employees. Whatever your organization's size, environment, and needs, you need to understand a few basic concepts about building an effective security policy:

- If it's too complex, no one will follow it. In fact, users might circumvent it.

- If it affects productivity negatively, it will fail.

- It should state clearly what can and can't be done on company property and with company equipment. Avoid jargon or complex descriptions, but be as thorough as possible.

- Include a generalized clause in statements, such as "Employees are not permitted to download games, screen savers, wallpaper, images, video clips, art, *or any other form of multimedia applications or files.*" The corporate attorney might need to fine-tune the wording, but the italicized clause covers anything not specifically mentioned. Another phrase that's frequently used is "including but not necessarily limited to."

- People need to know why a policy is important. They are more likely to accept it as necessary if they understand it.

- Involve representatives of all departments, including rank-and-file employees. The benefits are twofold:
  - You'll design a more accurate and appropriate policy if you tailor it to fit the needs of people using the systems. You find out what those needs are by having input from the people who do the work.
  - By involving every level of the company, you have given employees a personal stake in the process. This encourages taking ownership, which leads to a more involved attitude and better morale—and that equates to a more effective and enforceable security policy.
- The policy should contain a clause stating specific consequences an employee could face for violating the policy.
- It must have support from the highest level of the company, and that support must flow down through the ranks. If management doesn't endorse or obey the policy, why should employees?
- Have every employee sign a document acknowledging his or her understanding of the policy and agreement to abide by it. Some might think this practice conveys a lack of trust, but it's simply a sensible precaution and serves as an audit trail.
- Keep your security policy updated with current technologies. For example, include mobile device guidelines and regulate the use of portable storage devices. The point isn't to cover specific devices; it's to cover technology categories. For example, instead of listing "cell phones" or "USB drives," mention "wireless devices" or "portable storage devices." In addition, remove outdated material that no longer applies or has been integrated into another area. For example, the policy might have contained a clause about laptop or portable computers. When the policy is updated, laptops and portable computing devices are addressed in the section on mobile devices (cell phones, PDAs, wireless devices, and so on). To avoid conflicts, remove any other statements about laptops or portable computers.
- Make certain your policy directives are consistent with applicable laws. Retaining legal counsel to review your policy draft might be prudent to make sure all bases are covered and the policy doesn't violate civil rights or other laws. For example, in the United States, it's illegal to forbid employees from publicly protesting a company's actions, unless they all agree to that provision. Even then, this clause could be challenged based on the First Amendment of the U.S. Constitution. Also, make sure the security policy doesn't conflict with other corporate policies.

This task might seem overwhelming, but it isn't as bad as it sounds. Templates and other free resources with guidance on handling specific situations are available, and you can customize them to fit your situation.

ACTIVITY

Activity 2-1: Using Online Resources for Security Policy Development

Time Required: 20 minutes

Objective: Use a security policy template to guide the policy development process.

Description: For network administrators, security administrators, and IT staff, being understaffed and overworked with a less-than-adequate budget is more the rule than the exception. Although you realize a security policy is crucial, finding the time to develop one is difficult. One resource you can use is templates available on the Internet. In this activity, you sign up for a free membership to TechRepublic, which has thousands of free research documents, templates, checklists, and white papers, and locate a security policy template.

1. Start your Web browser and go to **http://techrepublic.com/**.

2. At the upper-right corner, click the **Get a free membership** link. Enter the required information, and click **Continue**.

3. On the Free E-newsletters page, select the ones you want to receive (if any), and then click **Complete my membership**.

4. TechRepublic will send a confirmation e-mail to the address you entered in Step 2. Respond to the e-mail as instructed to complete your registration.

5. After your registration is completed, log on to TechRepublic. Enter the search term **security policy** in the Search box at the top, and click **Search**.

6. The results are categorized by resource types. On the right side in the Content Types area, click **Download resources**.

7. In the Downloads section, scroll down until you see the entry **Information security policy**. (You might have to click the **Next** link to find it on another page.) Click the item title to go to the Download page, and click the **Download** button. When the Download dialog box opens, click the **Download Now** button.

8. When the File Download dialog box opens, click **Save**. Using the default filename, save the file to your desktop.

9. After the download is finished, double-click the **information_security_policy.zip** icon on your desktop. (The file is zipped, but Windows XP has a built-in utility that opens the file.)

10. Open the Microsoft Word document **information_security_policy.doc**. Take a few moments to read through the policy template.

11. Leaving the policy template open, exit your Web browser.

Keep this example in mind as you progress through the next sections, and refer back to the policy template to see how the following information relates to it.

Considering Cyber Risk Insurance

The dynamics of technology change business needs in some unexpected ways and can affect seemingly unrelated industries. Until a few years ago, **cyber risk insurance** wasn't available, but the insurance industry is beginning to find methods of evaluating coverage requirements and costs. Cyber risk insurance is simply an insurance policy, like your homeowner's or auto policy, that protects against losses to information assets. Policies are available that cover losses from cybercrime (such as break-ins that cause damage to, destruction of, or theft of sensitive data), malicious code damage (viruses, worms, and so on), and natural disasters. Determining value is straightforward for hardware items, such as routers, switches, servers, and computers, but it gets tricky when insurance underwriters try to evaluate electronic assets, such as data, accurately.

Cyber risk insurance is now being evaluated much like any other insurance. For your homeowner's policy, the insurance company wants to know certain things about your home, such as where it is, how much it cost, what security measures are used (such as a smoke alarm, carbon dioxide detector, and burglar alarm), and where the nearest police and fire services are located. They are beginning to apply the same criteria to cyber risk insurance. They want to know what losses are likely for your organization and what steps the organization is taking to prevent losses.

This approach should give you a good idea of how insurance and a security policy are related. Many answers to insurance application questions come from the security policy, and this policy could even earn your company a break on rates, much like a good driver discount. Because many businesses view information security as part of daily operations, concerns such as cyber risk insurance policies are also becoming part of day-to-day business and should be addressed in your security policy.

Most of the steps for developing a sound security policy play a prominent role in securing cyber risk insurance. Even the most thorough security mechanisms can't eliminate the risks an organization faces, so it makes sense that businesses would turn to insurance for protection against financial losses resulting from security incidents. That is noteworthy because auditing insurance coverage for IT systems is a task that naturally fits into the security policy development cycle.

NOTE

For more information on cyber risk insurance, visit the SANS reading room at *www.sans.org/rr/whitepapers/legal/1412.php*. In particular, read the seven-page questionnaire toward the end. By the end of this chapter, you'll be able to identify how many of these questions are part of your security policy or included in the process you used to develop it.

Activity 2-2: Investigating Cyber Risk Insurance

Time Required: 15 minutes

Objective: Learn how a company security policy can help in applying for cyber risk insurance coverage.

Description: In this activity, you search the Internet for companies offering cyber risk insurance.

1. Start your Web browser, and perform a search on the keywords **cyber risk insurance**.

2. In the list of results, click the first promising link you see. (*Note:* At the time of this writing, using the Google search engine, one of the first results was *www.insuretrust. com*. Results will vary over time and depend on the search engine used.)

3. On your selected insurance site, locate an application document or form. On the InsureTrust site, you would click **Policies and Applications** and then click the **Complete an application form** link. (*Hint:* If your site doesn't offer an online application link, return to the search results and select another insurer's site.)

4. As shown in Figure 2-1, InsureTrust asks many questions related to computer security. What information does the company request on its application form that would also be found in a security policy? Discuss this topic as a class or as specified by your instructor.

Developing Security Policies from Risk Assessment

If you're asked "Where do we start with a security policy?" you should be able to come up with an answer based on your review of risk analysis in Chapter 1 and what you learned in Activity 2-1. You start by identifying what needs to be protected. You then define threats the network faces, the probability that those threats will occur, and the consequences each threat poses. Finally, you propose safeguards and define how to respond to incidents.

The information you gather during the risk analysis phase should go into the security policy along with a statement of the policy's overall goals and the importance of employees reading and following its guidelines. In the document template you reviewed, the penalties for violating the policy are stated near the top. This is no accident; in litigation, the company attorney can argue that the employee couldn't have missed this section and so had to be aware that violating the policy could result in disciplinary action. Most policies state termination as a possible penalty, mainly to protect the company from wrongful termination lawsuits or similar grievances. One main function of a security policy (for most companies) is to reduce legal liability. Defining security measures and specifying procedures are other important functions, but to upper management, reduced liability is a major consideration in approving security policy development, implementation, and enforcement.

After the security policy is implemented, its effectiveness must be monitored. There's a difference between theory and practice, so it's reasonable to assume that some ideas might not work as planned. Like any large system with interdependencies among its parts, an

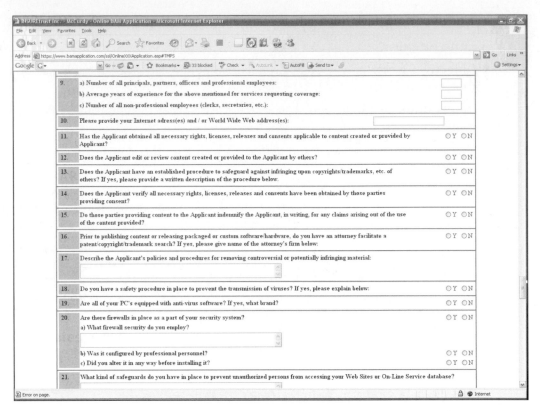

Figure 2-1   InsureTrust's online cyber risk insurance application

organization-wide security policy requires periodic revision. Sometimes an immediate change is required in response to a problem, but other revisions can be made on a regular cycle. Remember that a security policy is a fluid document that must adapt to new circumstances to remain effective. Based on any problems, intrusions, or incidents that occur, you can update the policy as needed; the sequence of policy design, implementation, monitoring, and reassessment is an ongoing cycle.

Teaching Employees About Acceptable Use

The issue of trust is an integral part of a security policy. The policy needs to define who to trust and what level of trust should be placed in those people. It's easy to say that members of the organization should not be trusted at all, but you should clarify in writing how they should use system resources correctly so that acceptable use is no longer a matter of trust.

In reality, organizations have to achieve a balance between trust and issuing orders. You need to allow employees to use their computers to communicate and be productive. By placing too little trust in people and prescribing everything they should do in an excessively rigid fashion, you not only hamper their work, but also hurt morale and make attempts to circumvent safeguards more likely. (Employee awareness is discussed in "Developing a Security Policy" later in the chapter.)

Outlining Penalties for Violations

The cornerstone of many security policies is the acceptable use policy, which spells out how employees should make use of the organization's resources, including the Internet, e-mail, and software programs they use every day. More important, the policy should spell out what constitutes unacceptable use, such as downloading or viewing objectionable or offensive content, using company equipment for personal business, removing company property (including any digitized information) without specific permission, and other major use problems. That doesn't mean employees should be fired for checking personal e-mail accounts two or three times a day, any more than they should be fired for calling home to check on their children.

Policy declarations exist to guide management and employees on the proper use of corporate resources. Penalty clauses exist mainly so that companies can discipline someone whose computer activities interfere with productivity. The policy should also contain guidelines for the penalty process so that employees who have read and agreed to the policy can't claim they didn't know they were violating it or didn't understand possible penalties. For example, the first offense can be a warning, the second offense could be a write-up or probation period, and the third offense results in terminating the employee. Of course, if management views a violation as severe enough, the penalty could be immediate termination. In extenuating circumstances, an employee could be given another chance. The idea is to establish flexible methods of punishment that can be applied at management's discretion but protect the company from litigation. Wrongful termination lawsuits are common and can result in high costs for a company. Penalty clauses, if worded correctly, can protect companies from this type of lawsuit. Having legal counsel review any major corporate policies is usually a good idea, and a security policy is no exception.

Criminal Computer Offenses

What happens if the security policy violation is a criminal offense, such as possessing child pornography? Law enforcement must be notified, and the investigation is turned over to them.

In this situation, you need to be aware of some pitfalls. After an investigation is turned over to the police, the U.S. Constitution's **Fourth Amendment** protections for search and seizure apply. Your responsibilities as administrator of company systems possibly containing evidence change when the public sector (police and government) is involved. There's a tremendous burden of liability on you if you assist the police without being served with a **subpoena** or **search warrant**. A subpoena is an order issued by a court demanding that a person appear in court or produce some form of evidence (documents, papers, or other tangible items). A subpoena specifies what evidence is required, whether it's personal testimony, paper documents, or data files from the suspect's computer. A search warrant is similar to a subpoena, in that it's issued by the court and compels you to cooperate with law enforcement officers conducting an investigation. However, it also describes the place to be searched and specifies what evidence officers are allowed to search for.

The reasons for search warrants and subpoenas can be found in the Fourth Amendment, which grants the right to **due process** and protects U.S. residents against illegal search and seizure. Due process is the constitutional guarantee of a fair and impartial trial. A defendant can sue you for violating his or her constitutional rights to due process if you provide evidence without being served with a warrant or subpoena. Providing assistance without being served is known as becoming a "de facto agent of law enforcement." This doesn't mean you are being paid by, or are employed by, law enforcement; it means you're acting under their direction and aiding them in an investigation, so you're bound by the same procedures and laws that bind public-sector investigators. When turning the case over to police officers, you can give them all the evidence you have gathered to that point, but you can't continue to investigate after that point unless you're ordered to do so. If you have been served with a subpoena or officers arrive to carry out a search warrant, you have no choice but to comply, thus removing any potential liability. Even if you want to help law enforcement, in a criminal case, you must not cooperate or turn over evidence unless you're ordered to do so.

Finally, there's the issue of an employee's expected right to privacy. The lines between Fourth Amendment protection and privacy expectations versus company-owned property can get blurry, unless you spell out what privacy an employee can expect while using company equipment at work. Your security policy must address this issue, stating clearly that company equipment and all digital information on it or accessed through it belong exclusively to the company, and the company reserves the right to search and inspect its property at any time. An employee has no expectation of privacy while using company resources. Unless this expectation is stated specifically, the company and anyone involved in an investigation could be liable if evidence is revealed that incriminates an employee. For example, if an employee is terminated for statements made in an e-mail, he could argue successfully that he didn't realize the company would be reading what he considered private e-mail, and he shouldn't be held accountable for what he said. Some companies might want to have employees sign a separate acknowledgement of this clause.

NOTE

For more information on the Fourth Amendment and Constitutional protections, visit *http://straylight.law.cornell.edu/constitution/* for the text of the Bill of Rights and links to the full text of the Constitution. For more information on interpreting the Fourth Amendment, visit *http://caselaw.lp.findlaw.com/data/constitution/ amendment04/*.

Activity 2-3: Discovering the Rules of Criminal Search and Seizure of Electronic Evidence

Time Required: 30 minutes

Objective: Learn about federal rules for searching and seizing digital evidence in the workplace.

Description: In this activity, you read selected excerpts from the U.S. Department of Justice manual, *Searching and Seizing Computers and Obtaining Electronic Evidence in Criminal Investigations*.

1. Start your Web browser and go to **www.cybercrime.gov/s&smanual2002.htm**.

2. Take a moment to review the Table of Contents, and then click **D. Special Case: Workplace Searches**.

3. Read this section thoroughly, and answer the following questions:

   ▪ How can an officer of law enforcement search a workplace without a warrant?

   _____

   _____

   ▪ What is the difference between private-sector and public-sector searches?

   _____

   _____

   ▪ What does the manual say about employer searches in private-sector workplaces? What segment of this statement relates to your involvement as an administrator cooperating with law enforcement?

   _____

   _____

4. Return to the Table of Contents. Scroll down and click **Appendix A** on network banner language. How do network banners affect a private-sector (nongovernmental) employee's reasonable expectations of privacy?

   _____

   _____

   _____

   _____

5. How should this information be incorporated into a security policy?

   _____

   _____

Enabling Management to Set Priorities

Security policies give employees guidelines they can follow during everyday work activities, but they are also helpful to management. They protect management in case disputes with employees happen or employees complain about security measures the organization uses.

Security policies do more than assist with dispute resolution, however. They give management a way to identify security priorities for the company. A security policy lists the network resources that managers find most valuable in the organization and are most in need of protection. It spells out whether the organization's priority is to allow personnel to access the Internet or restrict access to the Internet and internal corporate network. In addition, it describes measures the company takes if resources are misused or information is compromised by people outside or inside the company.

When you prepare a project proposal for developing full-fledged security policies or spending extensively on security-related hardware and software, management will probably ask what kind of return on investment (ROI) the company will realize. As discussed in Chapter 1, ROI indicates how long before the savings from preventing security incidents pay back the investment. Advise management to think about the issue not only in terms of ROI, but also in terms of the cost of doing nothing. Large organizations with employees who connect remotely are far more vulnerable to security breaches than other businesses. They need to consider three factors:

- How much information systems and the data on them are worth
- Possible threats they've already encountered and will encounter
- The chances that those security threats will result in losses of time and money

These days, security threats can originate from many sources and have a wide variety of signatures, and no single solution can block them all. A comprehensive security plan is not just intended to provide an ROI, but also a way of protecting systems and customers' personal information. Ask management to quantify the future revenue lost when attackers steal customers' credit card numbers and post them on the Internet, which destroys the company's credibility and exposes it to possible criminal and civil litigation. In addition, ask management to estimate the cost to the business if information is unavailable for weeks or months. You should present these situations diplomatically, and you must have statistics to back up your points. Nothing can make a proposal go down in flames as fast as unsubstantiated scare tactics, even if they're true.

Avoid making quantitative statements that can't be verified with precision because equipment depreciates and an office's environment changes. Businesses are usually dynamic, so new employees, products, and technologies are constantly added, and employees leave, old technologies are removed from service, and so on. Instead of trying to assign hard numbers to these items, have management consider the following business factors that can be affected adversely by intrusions:

- Costs related to financial loss and disruption (includes cost of downtime and lost productivity, among others)
- Personnel safety

- Personal information
- Legal and regulatory obligations
- Commercial and economic interests
- Intangibles such as consumer trust and company image or reputation

Dealing with the Approval Process

Developing a security policy can take several weeks to several months, depending on the organization. When you have cooperation from all relevant employees, preparing a security policy in two or three weeks is possible. Don't rush the process, however. Take the time to do it right and cover all bases. The only thing worse than no security policy is a bad security policy, which could result in management not backing the project.

One aspect of development to address is the need for upper management, executives, and other stakeholders to review and approve the security policy, and this process can take several weeks to several months. Don't be dismayed if the process of scheduling meetings, holding discussions, and getting approval takes longer than you expect. For a security policy to work, employees must accept it. You might encounter resistance, which is natural with any policy that affects an entire organization. A security user awareness program, in which employees are instructed formally about the organization's security strategy, can help.

Feeding Security Information to the Security Policy Team

Any changes made to the organization's security configuration should be conveyed to the security policy team. This team can suggest changes to the policy; the policy then dictates whether new security tools need to be purchased or new security measures need to be taken.

Management's participation and backing can help in amending the security policy. Encourage managers to inform employees that protecting company assets is everyone's responsibility. Provide training to users to make them aware of security issues, and explain why data collection and management should be conducted securely. Educate users so that they have the knowledge to carry out their jobs in a secure manner. Listen to employees' concerns. Develop sensible security solutions that allow daily business to be conducted yet provide an acceptable level of protection against risks.

Helping Network Administrators Do Their Jobs

Network administrators responsible for instructing employees on how to access shared resources, change passwords, sort through e-mail, and other functions can get considerable assistance from security policies. A security policy can spell out simple but important information that an administrator would otherwise have to convey personally, such as:

- Users aren't allowed to share accounts with other employees or with visitors or family members.
- Users are allowed to install only software programs in the Downloadables directory on the Shared Project server. Any other software is subject to approval.
- Users aren't allowed to make copies of office-owned software.

- Users are required to use password-protected screen savers during the day and shut down their computers each night.

- Only members of the IT staff are allowed to add hard drives or install networking devices on office computers.

- The network administrator needs to assign a username and password to anyone who connects to the office network from a remote location. In addition, any remote PCs used to connect to the network must be protected with firewall and antivirus software.

Administrators can be covered by a specific part of a security policy called a **privileged access policy**. This policy covers the access administrators can have to network resources and specifies whether they're allowed to run network-scanning tools, run password-checking software, and have root or domain administrator access.

To see an excellent example of a privileged access policy, visit *http://socrates. berkeley.edu:7015/proceds/access.html.*

Using Security Policies to Conduct Risk Analysis

After a security policy has been drafted, the work doesn't end there. After employees and managers have been educated about the policy's requirements and provisions, the safeguards are put in place. In addition to information gathered by preexisting security systems, such as log files, network traffic signatures, and peak traffic loads, further network monitoring after firewalls and other intrusion detection systems (IDSs) are installed can be helpful. You can use this information to determine how the network is performing in terms of speed and loads and use the data in further rounds of risk analysis.

It's up to you to decide how often to do another round of risk analysis. The first time you analyze the level of risk might be after a fairly short period, such as a month or six weeks. After you make any needed adjustments to the security configuration as a result of threats that have occurred, you might decide to conduct ongoing risk analysis every three months or six months; there's no hard-and-fast rule. Conducting risk analysis after a major change is important, such as when new equipment is installed or there's a lot of staff turnover. The risk analysis that occurs after implementing the security policy involves the same steps as the first round of risk analysis. The difference is that you have real-world data on which to base your evaluations of risk and its consequences instead of being limited to "what-if" situations.

Developing a Security Policy

In the preceding sections, you learned that formulating a security policy begins with analyzing the level of risk to the organization's assets. A security policy usually contains many component documents. After you know what assets are at risk and have developed suggestions for safeguards, you can put these component documents together to form a security policy.

Additionally, you can assess the legal risks your company faces and the potential need for cyber risk insurance. These issues might seem unrelated to a security policy but are becoming important. Companies are always trying to find ways to protect themselves from the risks of doing business. A security policy can help do just that.

The following sections outline the steps in creating a security policy and offer tips and examples of types of policies you can create. When these different types of policies are put together, they form a complete security policy.

Seven Steps to Creating a Security Policy

As you learned in Chapter 1, after conducting a risk analysis, you should summarize your findings in the form of a report that points out the most urgent risks the company needs to address. You might summarize these risks in an introductory paragraph or section, and then present a grid listing the most important assets in the company and the level of risk you have determined. Table 2-1 shows an example of this grid.

Table 2-1 Risk analysis example

Asset	Threat	Probability	Consequences	Risk assessment
Physical assets	Low	Low	Significant	Medium
Data	Medium	Medium	Damaging	High
Software	Negligible	Minor	Minor	Low
Personal assets	Low	Low	Significant	Medium
Hardware	High	Medium	Damaging	High

Remember to include definitions of types of assets and describe your assessment method. Explain the risk assessment you assigned to each category of assets, too. For example, in Table 2-1, the hardware risk might be high because servers are left in openly accessible work areas that aren't protected by locks or any special environmental controls, so they can be stolen or damaged easily.

The risk analysis report you completed for Case Project 1-1 should be distributed to management. After you have approval from top-level managers, the CIO, or whoever is responsible for approving the project, you follow these steps to create the security policy:

1. Form a group that meets to develop the security policy. Because of the political nature of security policies and their effect on employees, be sure to include a senior administrator, a member of the legal department, some IT staff, and a representative of rank-and-file employees.

2. Determine whether the organization's overall approach to security should be restrictive or permissive. A restrictive approach limits activity on the network to only a few authorized activities. A permissive approach allows traffic to flow freely and restricts only vulnerable ports, services, or computers.

3. Identify the assets you need to protect. You should have already done the groundwork for this step in your risk analysis.

4. Determine what needs to be logged and which network communications need to be audited. Then decide how often the results should be reviewed. **Auditing** is the process of reviewing records of network computers' activities; these records include who's connecting to a computer, what resources are being requested, and whether access was granted or blocked. This information is typically recorded in a log file.

5. List the security risks that need to be addressed.

6. Define acceptable use of the Internet, office computers, passwords, and other network resources.

7. Create the policy. The risks specified in the policy can be presented as separate sections of one security policy document or as separate policies that together make up the organization's overall security policy.

Identifying Security Policy Categories

After the security policy group has determined what should go into the security policy, the contents need to be written. Specific members of the group can be assigned the task of preparing different parts of the policy. A team approach ensures that all relevant points are covered. Many different kinds of policies can make up a policy; the following sections briefly describe common categories you're likely to need.

In policy examples in the following sections, Company is used as a generic company name.

NOTE

Acceptable Use

An **acceptable use policy** establishes what is acceptable use of company resources and usually offers specifics on what's considered unacceptable use. An acceptable use policy might state the following:

The following acceptable use policy covers the use of Company's computers, network components, software applications, and other hardware. The term "other hardware" includes, but is not limited to, personal computers, laptops, PDAs, floppy disks, CD-ROM drives and disks, servers, cables, routers, and tape backup systems. The term "user" is defined as a person who has an account to use Company's network resources. All users of Company's network are expected to conduct themselves in a responsible, legal, nonthreatening manner at all times, specifically:

- *Users aren't allowed to make unauthorized copies of copyrighted software except with the permission of the copyright holder.*

- *Users are responsible for storing personal data on their computers. If they need assistance with storing data, they should consult the network administrator.*

- *Users aren't permitted to engage in any activity, online or offline, that harasses, threatens, or abuses other users.*

- *E-mail accounts are for business use only; personal e-mail messages and messages that might be judged obscene, harassing, or offensive, shall not be sent from or stored on Company's systems.*

Users who violate these policies will be reported to security staff. Offenses might result in loss of network privileges or termination of employment. If the offense warrants, the company may press civil or criminal charges against the user.

I have read and understand Company's acceptable use policy and agree to abide by it.

The user's signature follows; some companies include the signature of a witness and the date the policy was signed. These provisions are a few examples of what can be included in an acceptable use policy. Your own policy can go into more detail on the use of network resources.

TIP The Virginia Department of Education offers some helpful tips and examples of creating acceptable use policies. You can find them at *www.pen.k12.va.us/go/ VDOE/Technology/AUP/home.shtml*.

The acceptable use policy is usually stated at the beginning of a security policy because it affects most employees in an organization, and it can generate the most controversy. Because everyday work routines might be changed to comply with the new policy, gaining cooperation from all employees can be difficult. The transition is easier if upper management and direct supervisors begin an awareness campaign early. Also, having a representative from rank-and-file employees on the policy development group is wise for a few reasons. First, employees' interests are represented. Second, their input on decisions can help avoid making changes that affect production negatively. Finally, with an employee representative on the committee, managers and supervisors are more likely to talk to employees about the policy, why it is important, and why employees should support it. These discussions are usually called a **security user awareness program** and should be part of the implementation plan. Efforts should start as early as possible to get employees involved and excited about the policy.

The first step in an awareness effort could be posting informational memos on bulletin boards. Then supervisors might call departmental meetings to talk to employees about the new policy and answer questions. A company can also post information about the policy on its internal Web site or devise games, such as brief quizzes on the security policy or giving employees hypothetical situations to handle. Departments are awarded points for correct answers, and at the end of the game, the department with the most points wins a party or bonuses.

The point is to make sure a policy isn't sprung on employees with a mandate to obey it. That approach would practically ensure failure because the policy depends on employees following it. An awareness program also needs to explain how the policy benefits employees, such as increased revenue resulting in better pay or improved working conditions from using new technologies. However this task is approached, it must be consistently carried out before, during, and after security policy implementation.

NOTE

Many companies require employees to read and sign an acceptable use policy before they are given a user account or when they are first hired.

Extranets and Third-Party Access

Allowing third-party access to the company network is often a requirement when outsourcing jobs or working with contractors. An **extranet** is a private network a company sets up as an extension of its corporate intranet for the purpose of allowing outside entities (contractors, suppliers, partners, and so on) access to only a limited portion of the network infrastructure. Parties who have access to the extranet should be included in the security policy. This third-party access policy should include, at a minimum, the following points:

- Access should be permitted only for business being conducted with your company.
- Third parties should be subject to a security screening process.
- Precise methods of permitted and nonpermitted connectivity should be defined.
- The duration of permitted access and how termination of access will be carried out should be stated.
- Penalties and consequences for violating access terms should be spelled out because they will be different from those being applied to employees.

TIP

You can find examples of extranet or third-party access policies at *www.sans.org/resources/policies/Extranet_Policy.pdf* and *https://extranet. brownrudnick.com/ua.htm*.

Violations and Penalties

As mentioned earlier, many companies include a section in their policies on what constitutes a violation and how violations are dealt with. These clauses vary in wording, but the

2

meaning is usually the same. In large companies, legal counsel reviews and sometimes writes the corporate security policy to make sure it's legal and binding and helps ensure that important points are clear, such as violations and penalty clauses.

Defining these points can help a company avoid legal problems. New employees are often required to sign a statement acknowledging their understanding of company policies, including any penalties resulting from violations of company policies.

NOTE Now would be a good time to refer to the policy template from Activity 2-1 and note the passage on violations. In this policy template, the violations clause refers to the company policy. Because it's an information security policy, it's specific to computing resources.

User Accounts, Password Protection, and Logical Access Controls

By creating a policy that guides how user accounts are to be used, you gain flexibility in developing and enforcing the security policy because you don't limit yourself to employees who work onsite. User accounts include employees and contractors who work at home and suppliers who connect to your network from their own facilities. Your security policy might specify user account policies, such as the following:

- Users aren't permitted to gain access to an unauthorized resource.
- Users can't block an authorized user from gaining access to an authorized resource.
- Users can't give their account usernames and passwords to others for any reason. If a password is lost or a user account is disabled, contact the administrator or help desk for assistance.
- Users must protect their usernames and passwords in a secure location that's not visible on their desktops.
- Users must abide by the password policy of the company, specifically:
  - Passwords must meet complexity requirements: Strong passwords use a random combination of letters, numbers, and symbols and use both uppercase and lowercase characters.
  - Passwords must be at least eight characters.
  - Passwords must not be words from the dictionary, names, dates, or other information that can be associated with the user or company.
  - Passwords must be changed every 90 days. Users may not reuse old passwords for a period of one year.

Passwords represent a first line of defense for many organizations. They allow users to access e-mail and control access to the network from outside, access to shared directories on servers, and more. Often companies require users to protect their computers or Web browsers by means of passwords so that other staff or visitors can't use them after hours. Your company can use these guidelines or might have others suiting its needs and security goals.

Whatever the case, a password policy should be established in the security policy and enforced by software means whenever possible.

One of the information access problems companies face is ensuring that employees have ready access to the information needed to perform their jobs but making sure inappropriate access to confidential information is limited. For example, granting read access but not change or delete access to an employee for specific information is often necessary. Unlimited access to this information might be granted to only one or a few employees. Logical access controls are used as a protection mechanism for limiting access. They are software components that narrow the scope of users' access to information, restricting system and information access to only those areas they are permitted to use.

Logical access controls might be part of the network operating system or logic built into existing network utilities and applications. Some logical access controls are supplied by third-party software vendors as OS security add-ins or are included as software components of sophisticated network devices, such as routers and switches. Your security policy should include a section specifying that users should not breach or attempt to override logical access control mechanisms.

Remote Access and Wireless Connections

Organizations often use freelancers and consultants who work with them via broadband connections, e-mail, virtual private networks (VPNs), and wireless connections. Even now, however, a surprising number of workers still use dial-up connections. In addition, mobile workers often need to connect to the home office while on the road or at home, and business partners want to update their orders or view account information by connecting to the company network.

These types of workers represent an opportunity for increased productivity but also increase security vulnerabilities. If a user who connects to the corporate network is working at a computer that's infected with a virus or has been compromised by an attacker, that attacker or virus could access the corporate network while the user is connected to it. Mobile devices can be stolen, and thieves can then attempt to gain access to your network.

A **remote access and wireless connection policy** specifies the use of **role-based authentication**, which gives users limited access based on the role they are assigned in the company and what resources the role is allowed to use. The sensitivity of those applications determines the type of authentication to be used, which can also be specified in the policy. For example, access to applications or data sources that aren't considered confidential can be granted with a simple password; access to confidential resources can be secured with a smart card or token, a piece of hardware used with a password to provide **two-factor authentication**. This type of authentication combines something the owner *is* (fingerprints, signature, retina scan), *has* (a card or token), or *knows* (a password or PIN). Any two of these factors combined qualifies as two-factor authentication. The idea is to provide an extra layer of protection to authentication, so adding a second requirement doubles the security. For example, if you simply have to insert your bank card to make purchases, all a thief would need is your card. Because you also have to enter a PIN or sign the receipt, a thief has a harder time using your card to buy airline tickets. Using public or private keys for authentication would also work.

Other options for network access that have become popular because of their effective and inexpensive nature are VPNs and wireless connectivity. VPNs create a tunnel to transport information through public communications media, such as regular phone lines. The data is kept safe by the use of **tunneling protocols** and encryption. Wireless connections offer the same range of tools available on wired connections but without the burden of cabling. However, wireless connectivity has security problems, too. Your security policy must specify who can use wireless connectivity and how and where it can be used.

You can find an example of a remote access policy at *www.sans.org/resources/policies/Remote_Access_Policy.pdf* and a wireless communications policy example at *www.sans.org/resources/policies/Wireless_Communication_Policy.pdf*.

TIP

Secure Use of the Internet and E-mail

An **Internet use policy** can be integrated with an acceptable use policy or the overall security policy. However, because Internet use is becoming so integral to day-to-day work functions, it's worth creating a separate security policy section that covers how employees can access and use the Internet.

A clear policy governing the use of e-mail is essential. Without this type of policy, the following incident is an example of what might occur: An employee receives a virus hoax sent by e-mail. The message indicates that if other users receive a message with the heading "You're a Winner!" they shouldn't read it because it will erase all files on the user's hard disk. As a result, the employee broadcasts the e-mail to all other employees. Many of those people send the same e-mail to other parts of the organization, thinking they are doing others a favor. Because no policy defined how they should handle these warnings, the company's mail servers are flooded with e-mail, and IT employees are called to diagnose the trouble, which wastes staff time and resources. E-mail hoaxes are more than nuisances. They can cause real problems on the network.

Visit *http://hoaxbusters.ciac.org* or *www.snopes.com* to investigate e-mail hoaxes.

TIP

An Internet use policy prohibits broadcasting any e-mail messages. Instead, users should contact the network administrator about suspicious e-mail. The policy should also specify whether users are allowed to download software or streaming media from the Internet, and if so, state limits on the size of file downloads. The policy could prohibit users from opening executable e-mail attachments that might contain viruses. It could also specify whether the company has blocked any objectionable Web sites and inform users how the company will protect their privacy with regard to e-mail.

Network Security

A **network security policy** should clearly define and establish responsibility for the network and for protecting information that's processed, stored, and transmitted on the network. The primary responsibility can be assigned to the data owner—the manager of the organization that creates and processes the data. Secondary responsibility is then assigned to users who have access to the information. Primary responsibility means ensuring that policies and procedures to protect data are followed.

Network management should clearly define the role of the people responsible for maintaining the network's availability. This policy should describe the following:

- *Applicability*—What constitutes the network environment and what parts, if any, are exempt from the policy
- *Evaluations*—The value of information stored on the network
- *Responsibilities*—Who's responsible for protecting information on the network
- *Commitment*—The organization's commitment to protecting information and the network

The sample network security policy that follows defines responsibilities for these employees:

- *Functional managers*—Employees who have primary responsibility
- *Local administrators*—Employees who are responsible for ensuring that end users have access to network resources on their servers
- *End users*—Any employees who have access to the organization's network (those responsible for using the network in accordance with the network security policy)

All users of data are responsible for complying with the security policy established by those with primary responsibility for security of data and for reporting any suspected security breach to management.

NOTE The material in this section reflects the Federal Information Processing Standard (FIPS) 191, Guideline for the Analysis of LAN Security. Reading the full text of FIPS 191, available at *www.itl.nist.gov/fipspubs/fip191.htm*, is highly recommended.

The following is an excerpt of a sample network security policy developed by NIST in FIPS 191:

> *A computer security incident is any adverse event whereby some aspect of computer security could be threatened: loss of data confidentiality, loss of data or system integrity, or disruption or denial of availability. In a LAN environment, the concept of a computer security incident can be extended to all areas of the LAN (hardware, software, data, transmissions, etc.), including the LAN itself.*

2

Contingency plans in a LAN environment should be developed so that any LAN security incident can be handled in a timely manner, with minimal impact on the ability of the organization to process and transmit data. A contingency plan should consider: (1) incident response, (2) backup operations, and (3) recovery.

The purpose of incident response is to mitigate the potentially serious effects of a severe LAN security problem. It requires not only the capability to react to incidents, but the resources to alert and inform the users, if necessary. It requires the cooperation of all users to ensure that incidents are reported and resolved and that future incidents are prevented. NIST Special Publication 800-61, Computer Security Incident Handling Guide, is recommended as guidance in developing an incident response capability. A copy of this document can be downloaded from *http://csrc.nist.gov/publications/nistpubs/800-61/sp800-61.pdf.*

Backup operation plans are prepared to ensure that essential tasks (as identified by a risk analysis) can be completed after the LAN environment is disrupted and continue until the LAN is sufficiently restored.

Recovery plans are made to permit smooth, rapid restoration of the LAN environment following interruption of LAN usage. Supporting documents should be developed and maintained that minimize the time required for recovery. Priority should be given to applications, services, and so forth that are deemed critical to the organization's functioning. Backup operation procedures should ensure that critical services and applications are available to users.

Server Security

A **server security policy** doesn't usually target the general employee population. Its purpose is to regulate IT staff who have privileged access to company servers. This policy should cover all servers, including Web and database servers, and should encompass, at a minimum, the following areas:

- Names and positions of IT staff responsible for operating and maintaining servers
- Specific identification details for all servers, including serial numbers and part numbers
- Username and password security requirements
- Configuration details, including hardware and software versions
- Monitoring requirements and schedules and logging requirements
- Data and system backup requirements, storage, schedules, and responsibilities
- System audit requirements and schedules
- Policy compliance and enforcement

To see an example of a server security policy, visit *www.sans.org/resources/ policies/Server_Security_Policy.pdf*.

Physical and Facility Security

Physical and facility security encompasses a broad range of issues related to locking down hardware components of a corporate network. Computer facility security has to be integrated into the overall security policy for the entire corporate facility. Common sense plays a major role in designing adequate physical security and formulating a sound physical security policy:

- A separate enclosed space should be set aside to house servers and other essential computer network components.

- The facility should be located on the building's ground floor or higher in an area prone to flooding or other forms of environmental hazards.

- The facility should have no windows and a limited number of doors—preferably one door, if the fire code permits. If possible, it should be located away from exterior building walls.

- All access points, including ventilation shafts, should have unbreakable coverings and be double locked. Access codes should be held by as few people as possible. Not all staff working in the facility require access codes.

- Access should be limited to those who work in the enclosed facility. If cleaning or maintenance workers have access to the facility, they should be supervised at all times by a facility staff member.

- Fire suppression and intrusion alarm systems should be in place.

- A 24-hour video surveillance system should be maintained and viewed regularly.

- Secure off-site storage should be arranged for backup data.

Examples of physical security topics and policies can be found at *www.infosyssec.com/infosyssec/security/physfac1.htm*.

HANDLING SECURITY INCIDENTS

While formulating a security policy, you should describe in detail who responds to security incidents, what needs to be done, and why these procedures need to happen. This part of a security policy is called the incident response section. You should begin by describing the need for careful and expeditious handling of an intrusion if it occurs. You might also describe types of incidents that need to be addressed, such as the following:

- Alarms sent by intrusion detection systems
- Repeated unsuccessful logon attempts

- New user accounts that suddenly appear without explanation
- New files with unfamiliar filenames that appear on system servers
- Unexplained changes to data or deletion of records
- System crashes
- Poor system performance

The incident-handling process should then be outlined in the security policy. Tell employees to identify whether an intrusion has actually occurred. They can do this by auditing the system to see whether new files have been added. If so, they need to determine what resources have been compromised. The affected resources should then be contained, viruses or other files introduced into the system should be eradicated, and resources should be recovered.

You might want to fill out a form designed to record what happens during a break-in. You don't have to prepare this form from scratch; you can use one of the forms published on the Federal Agency Security Practices Web site of NIST. A sample form is shown in Figure 2-2.

Assembling a Response Team

If an incident occurs, the security policy should spell out exactly which security staff should be notified. Include e-mail addresses and phone numbers. Also, specify a location where team members should assemble in case they are unable to access the facility or communicate. Teamwork is essential in responding to network security incidents successfully, and it's common for an organization to designate a **security incident response team (SIRT)**—a group of employees designated to take countermeasures when an incident is reported.

NOTE You might also see a SIRT referred to as a computer emergency response team (CERT), which can respond to any type of system failure, not just a security-related intrusion.

A SIRT is primarily intended to respond to security-related breaches and usually includes functions such as the following in its mission statement:

- Reacting to security breaches that originate from outside as well as inside the organization
- Isolating, reviewing, and interpreting information about security incidents
- Assessing the extent of damage caused by a security incident
- Determining the causes of intrusions and other incidents and recommending countermeasures to prevent them from reoccurring
- Monitoring the integrity of the organization's network on an ongoing basis

Sample Generic Policy and High-Level Procedures for Incident Response

Issue Statement

XX Agency must be able to respond to computer security–related incidents in a manner that protects its own information and helps protect the information of others who might be affected by the incident.

A security incident is defined as any adverse event that threatens the security of information resources. Adverse events include compromise of integrity, denial of service, compromise of data (for example, sold or used in an authorized manner), loss of accountability, or damage to any part of the system.

Organization's Position

XX Agency has established a Large Service Application (LSA) Computer Security Incident Response Capability (CSIRC) to address computer security incidents, including theft, misuse of data, intrusions, hostile probes, and malicious software. When an incident occurs, the supervisor must provide a verbal report to the ISSO within one working day after the incident. A written preliminary report must be submitted within two working days. Within five working days of the resolution of an incident, a written final report

Figure 2-2   A sample incident-handling form

Typically, a SIRT contains IT operations and technical support staff, IT application staff, a chief security officer, and other information security specialists. In some large organizations, a special position called Incident Response Manager might be created; this person is responsible for responding to incidents, doing an initial assessment, and summoning the SIRT and other employees as needed. A SIRT can also include members from other areas of the organization, such as department management, public relations, and legal counsel. All staff involved in the SIRT should be identified in the security policy; if the primary contact person can't be found, another person on the list can be summoned.

Specifying Escalation Procedures

An **escalation procedure** is a set of roles, responsibilities, and measures taken in response to a security incident. It describes how an organization increases its state of readiness when a threat or security incident occurs. Incidents are usually divided into three levels of escalation:

- *Level One (minor to moderate)*—These incidents are the least severe and typically must be managed within one working day from when they occur.

2

- *Level Two (major)*—These incidents are of moderate seriousness. They should be managed the same day the event takes place—ideally, within four hours.

- *Level Three (catastrophic)*—These incidents are the most serious; they must be handled immediately.

Escalation procedures also specify the employees who handle each level. A large organization might have a full-fledged department whose members are assigned only to maintaining security. They often have titles such as security analyst, security architect, and chief security officer. Many organizations assign technical staff to these roles, who are responsible for handling escalation in addition to their other responsibilities. In either case, escalation procedures in a security policy must spell out who needs to respond.

In addition, Level Two or Level Three incidents might require the participation of outside security groups, such as Computer Incident Advisory Capability (CIAC) or CERT. These highly regarded organizations keep records of serious security attacks; if your organization is hit by a new virus or an unusually strong distributed denial-of-service (DDoS) attack, you should let others on the Internet know about the attack.

If an intrusion is found to have occurred and damage is more severe than originally thought—or if the intrusion is currently happening and files are being accessed—the security policy should describe stages of response that escalate along with the incident's consequences. To determine how a response might escalate, you can come up with a system for ranking an incident's severity (for instance, using the rankings listed in Table 2-2). Each ranking could then be mapped to an escalation chain—a hierarchy of employees who should be involved in responding to incidents and making decisions. Table 2-2 shows one possible mapping.

Table 2-2   Mapping an escalation chain to incident severity rankings

Incident severity	Escalation chain
Catastrophic (Level Three)	Business owner or manager, chief security officer, senior network administration staff, all department heads, public relations officer
Major (Level Two)	On-duty manager, on-duty network administration staff, security architect
Moderate (Level One)	Immediate supervisor, on-duty security analyst, help desk
Minor or insignificant	Immediate supervisor

Table 2-2 could be extended to list actions to take in response to incidents, based on their severity. Incidents of minor to moderate severity might require a virus scan or log file review; major incidents might call for disconnecting the local network from the Internet or other network segments while the response is ongoing.

Responding to Security Incidents

To determine how incidents should be escalated, the security policy's section on incident handling should clearly define the types of incidents to watch out for and what level of escalation each one represents. Following are some examples:

- *Loss of password (Level One incident)*—The on-duty supervisor should be notified within 24 hours. He or she determines whether a change of password is necessary.

- *Burglary or other illegal building access (Level Two incident)*—If an unauthorized person is discovered on the premises, notify your immediate supervisor, who determines whether police need to be notified and who the incident should be escalated to, if at all. If the incident is serious enough to warrant it, the supervisor notifies the appropriate people in the escalation chain, such as the CSO, IT manager, or security administrator (SA). The person should be escorted out of the building, either by the authority to whom the incident was reported or escalated or by police. The responsible party specified in the security policy then writes an incident report.

- *Property loss or theft (Level Two or Level Three incident)*—If company property has been stolen, the human resources director or the on-duty supervisor should be notified immediately. They escalate the incident to the CSO and local law enforcement, if needed.

Including Worst-Case Scenarios

Worst-case scenarios are descriptions of the worst consequences that befall an organization if a threat happens. These scenarios might be unlikely, but they can help you determine the value of a resource at risk. Values are derived from reasonable consequences of files, computers, and databases being unavailable for specified periods. You might prepare scenarios that account for several time frames, such as a few minutes or several months.

CAUTION

Some security professionals don't recommend using the worst-case scenario approach to valuing assets because it can be extremely unlikely in the real world and can easily be used to distort a situation.

Another way to quantify the impact of financial loss or interruption of business activities is to assign a numeric value to an asset based on a range of dollar amounts. If the loss is estimated at $100 or less, the number 1 is assigned to the loss; if the loss is between $100 and $1000, the number 2 is assigned, and so on.

Updating the Security Policy

Based on the security incidents reported as a result of your ongoing security monitoring and any new risks your company faces, you should update the security policy. Any changes to the

2

policy should then be broadcast to the entire company by e-mail or by posting the changes on the company's Web site or intranet.

The goal of changing the security policy is to change employees' habits so that they behave more responsibly. Ultimately, a security policy should result in actual physical changes to the organization's security configuration. A call for redundant systems in the security policy might result in major expenditures for a new firewall or server to act as a failover device, for instance. The need to review security logs daily, as prescribed in a security policy, might mean investing in log file analysis software to make IT employees' jobs easier. Better protection means fewer internal or external incidents (attacks, viruses, intrusions, and so forth), which enables the company to focus on its primary mission.

Conducting Routine Security Reviews

After a security policy has been in place for a while, the security policy group should decide on a routine reassessment of risks to the company and its assets. You might not need to examine every asset in the company each time this reassessment is done; for example, you might decide to focus on only the most urgent security risks or any new risks that have cropped up as a result of changes in the company.

When reevaluating the organization's security policy, keep the following in mind: the need to make these reviews routine; the need to work with management to accept the ongoing risk analysis–security policy cycle; the need to respond to security incidents as they occur; and the need to revise the security policy as a result of incidents and other identified risks.

An effective security policy not only describes immediate steps to take when an intrusion is detected, but can also specify how often risk analyses should be conducted. A section of the policy that describes ongoing security reviews should identify the people who conduct risk analysis and then describe the circumstances under which a new risk analysis is required. For instance, when new equipment is purchased, these people can be notified so that they can determine whether new security policy statements need to be written or whether new measures should be taken.

Even though the security policy might specify conducting a risk analysis routinely every six months or every year, the policy should be flexible enough to allow "emergency" reassessments as needed. For instance, any attacks to partner businesses or offices of employees who work off-site should prompt the security policy group to reassess risks for the organization; in addition, news of any major security attacks on Internet servers or viruses circulating on the Internet should prompt risk reassessment.

CHAPTER SUMMARY

- A security policy provides a foundation for an organization's overall security stance and gives employees guidelines on how to handle sensitive information and IT staff instructions on defensive systems to configure; in addition, it reduces the risk of legal liability for the company and its employees.

- To protect overall security, it's important to formulate a clear policy that states what rights employees have and how they should handle company resources responsibly.

◻ Because risk can't be eliminated, businesses are turning to cyber risk insurance to offset losses. A security policy can help when applying for insurance and identifying what needs to be insured and from what threats.

◻ A good security policy is based on risk assessment, covers acceptable use of system resources, sets priorities for critical resources that need to be protected, and specifies the use of network resources by administrators and security staff.

◻ Legal liabilities should be covered in a security policy. Statements of acceptable and unacceptable use must be included, and guidelines for violations and punishments must be covered. This information helps the company avoid litigation from employees fired for misuse of systems.

◻ If an incident turns out to be a criminal offense, it's important to understand your legal obligations and how to protect yourself from litigation. After an investigation is turned over to the police, Fourth Amendment protections for search and seizure apply, and failure to respect those protections can result in being named in a lawsuit. You must understand the implications of a criminal investigation and aid police if ordered to do so by a subpoena or officers arrive to carry out a search warrant.

◻ Often a security policy is formulated as a series of specific policies rather than one long document. There are seven steps in creating a security policy: forming a security policy group; determining the overall security approach; identifying assets to protect; specifying auditing procedures; listing security risks; defining acceptable use; and creating the specific policies, such as user account, password protection, Internet use, and remote access policies.

◻ You need to present the proposal to management and gain approval to proceed with the project. This process involves explaining the expected ROI and calling attention to other costs associated with security incidents, such as loss of productivity, loss of morale or customer confidence, and possible legal costs.

◻ A security policy should describe in detail who responds to security incidents, what needs to be done, and why these procedures need to happen. Collectively, this information is called the incident response section of the security policy. It defines the response and escalation for incidents of varying severity and contains contact information for anyone who might need to be notified of an incident. Organizations often designate a security incident response team (SIRT) to take countermeasures when an incident is reported.

◻ An escalation procedure should be defined to determine who should be notified for each type of incident. Different incident levels can be defined, such as minor, moderate, major, and catastrophic. As the level of severity increases, so does the seniority of personnel responding.

◻ Security policies should be reviewed and updated regularly. They should also be modified if intrusion attempts or actual intrusions occur or when personnel changes and equipment purchases take place.

KEY TERMS

acceptable use policy — A policy that establishes what constitutes acceptable use of company resources and offers specifics on what's considered unacceptable use.

auditing — The process of reviewing records of network computers' activities; these records include who is connecting to a computer, what resources are being requested, and whether access is granted or blocked.

cyber risk insurance — A type of insurance policy that protects businesses from losses resulting from attacks, viruses, sabotage, and so on. It typically has specific coverages and exclusions like any insurance policy.

due process — A legal concept that ensures the government respects a person's rights or places limitations on legal proceedings to guarantee fundamental fairness, justice, and liberty.

escalation procedure — A set of roles, responsibilities, and measures taken in response to a security incident.

extranet — A private network a company sets up as an extension of its corporate intranet for the purpose of allowing outside entities (contractors, suppliers, partners, and so on) access to only a limited portion of the network infrastructure.

Fourth Amendment — The Fourth Amendment in the U.S. Bill of Rights provides constitutional protection from illegal search and seizure and guarantees the right to due process. It also implies an expected right of privacy, even though no such right is stated specifically.

Internet use policy — A policy that defines how users can access and use the Internet and specifies what rules apply to e-mail and other communications, such as instant messaging.

network security policy — A policy that defines and establishes responsibility for protecting the network and the information processed, stored, and transmitted on the network.

privileged access policy — A policy detailing additional access, functions, and responsibilities of users with privileged (administrative or root) access to resources.

remote access and wireless connection policy — A policy that defines what security measures need to be in place on a remote desktop or wireless connection before connecting to the organization's network.

role-based authentication — A method of authentication that grants users limited access based on the role they are assigned in the company and defines what resources the role is allowed to use.

search warrant — A legal document issued by the court allowing a search of a specified place for specific evidence. The warrant must detail what the search is seeking and where law enforcement is permitted to look for it.

security incident response team (SIRT) — A group of people designated to take countermeasures when an incident is reported.

security user awareness program — A training program designed to educate users about security topics, answer their questions about security, and prepare users to accept changes made for security purposes.

server security policy — A policy that regulates IT staff who have privileged access to company servers. This policy should cover all servers, including Web and database servers.

subpoena — A legal document requiring a person to appear, provide testimony, or cooperate with law enforcement. Testimony consists of written or oral declaration of fact under penalty of law.

tunneling protocols — Network protocols that encapsulate (wrap) one protocol or session inside another.

two-factor authentication — Authentication requiring at least two forms of verification from a user to be granted access. Verification requires something the user has, knows, or is.

worst-case scenarios — Descriptions of the worst consequences that befall an oganization if a threat occurs.

REVIEW QUESTIONS

1. What general best practices should you follow when developing a security policy? List at least five guidelines discussed in this chapter.

2. What can occur if a security policy is so rigidly formulated that too little trust is placed in network users? (Choose all that apply.)
   a. Network resources can be compromised.
   b. Productivity can be reduced.
   c. Employees might quit and go to other companies.
   d. Employees will find ways to circumvent security systems.

3. Which of the following sections of a security policy affects the most people in an organization?
   a. incident-handling policy
   b. privileged access policy
   c. acceptable use policy
   d. remote access policy

4. Which of the following security incidents is considered the most severe (Level Three)?
   a. An employee loses her password, which requires a change of password.
   b. An unauthorized person is discovered in the company building.
   c. The HR director's laptop computer containing 10,000 personnel records is stolen from his car.
   d. The door to the computer facility is found unlocked.

5. What is an escalation procedure? (Choose all that apply.)
   a. It describes how network security can be improved in stages.
   b. It describes how a virus can multiply and affect more assets.
   c. It describes different levels of response based on incident severity.
   d. It describes employees who should be involved in the response.

6. Having a security policy can help with what aspect of acquiring cyber risk insurance coverage?

   a. The security policy tells the insurance company how many employees you have.

   b. The security policy contains detailed information about safety records.

   c. Many security configurations specified in the security policy provide information for insurance applications.

   d. Auditing network use provides information about hardware coverage needs.

7. Which of the following policies should contain the statement "Network administrators are the only staff authorized to have root or domain administrator status"?

   a. user account policy

   b. acceptable use policy

   c. privileged access policy

   d. Internet use policy

8. Which of the following, if worded correctly, can protect companies from wrongful termination lawsuits?

   a. nondisclosure clauses

   b. acceptable use policies

   c. penalty clauses

   d. punishment clauses

9. A security policy can spell out simple but important information that an administrator would otherwise have to convey personally, such as:

   a. Users are not allowed to share accounts with each other.

   b. Users are not allowed to use password-protected screen savers.

   c. Users may install software on their own computers.

   d. Users are authorized to make copies of office software to install on their home systems.

10. Why is an acceptable use policy usually listed first in a security policy? (Choose all that apply.)

    a. It can generate controversy.

    b. It affects the most employees.

    c. It can get employees in trouble.

    d. It is the basis for terminating troublemakers.

11. Why is it helpful to speak in terms of "user accounts" rather than "full-time employees" in a security policy? (Choose all that apply.)

    a. User accounts apply to all employees, not just full-time employees.

    b. User accounts include freelancers and business partners.

    c. User accounts cover password use.

    d. User accounts are the most important aspect of network security.

12. A password policy might specify which of the following attributes for password selection?

    a. length requirements

    b. complexity requirements

    c. frequency for changing passwords

    d. all of the above

13. A password policy should be established in the _____ and enforced by _____ whenever possible.

    a. risk assessment process, management

    b. company Web site, network administrators

    c. security policy, software

    d. company employee handbook, security guards

14. Which of the following can be used to authenticate users for access to sensitive information? (Choose all that apply.)

    a. public or private keys

    b. password-based authentication

    c. role-based authentication

    d. two-factor authentication

15. E-mail hoaxes don't cause damage; they are only a nuisance. True or False?

16. Organizations with employees who connect remotely should consider which of the following security concerns?

    a. possibility of theft of mobile devices

    b. virus infections spreading from home and mobile systems or storage to corporate systems

    c. the use of up-to-date, effective antivirus and firewall software on mobile devices or home systems connecting to the network

    d. all of the above

17. Which of the following instructs employees formally about the organization's security strategy?

    a. acceptable use policy

    b. risk assessment

    c. strategy meeting

    d. security user awareness program

18. When should a security policy be revised or updated? (Choose all that apply.)

    a. every month

    b. only if your company merges with another company

    c. every six months to a year

    d. when a large number of employees are laid off

19. A good security policy is based on identifying assets to be protected and taking steps to secure them. True or False?

20. How can you convince managers to support a security policy?
    a. Tell them how a security policy can help reduce legal liabilities.
    b. Tell them it won't cost anything.
    c. Provide information about potential costs of doing nothing, such as loss of productivity or customer confidence or damage to the company's image.
    d. Reassure them that it won't be difficult or take much time.

21. What protects U.S. residents from illegal search and seizure?
    a. Fourth Amendment
    b. state and local ordinances
    c. U.S. Patriot Act
    d. First Amendment

HANDS-ON PROJECTS

HANDS-ON PROJECTS

Hands-On Project 2-1: Conducting Security Policy Analysis

Time Required: 20 minutes

Objective: Evaluate security policy clauses, identify deficiencies, and update policies in response to events or changes.

Description: Security policies should be revised to address security breaches or new threats. In this project, you evaluate an incident involving theft of proprietary information and identify some obvious security policy deficiencies. Then you recommend changes to the security policy to prevent similar incidents from reoccurring.

A local branch office of a major national stock brokerage had no policy requiring the termination of user ID and password privileges after employees leave. A senior trader left the brokerage and was hired by a competing brokerage. Shortly thereafter, the first brokerage lost two clients who said they were moving to a competing firm; their personal data files disappeared mysteriously from the company's databases. In addition, a year-end recommendations report the senior trader had been preparing was released two weeks earlier by the competing brokerage. An investigation of the company's access logs revealed that the employee records file had been accessed by someone outside the company. The job records, however, didn't reveal whether the report had been stolen because they had not been set up to record object accesses in a log.

The existing security policy states the following:

"On termination, employees shall surrender any laptops, disks, or computer manuals they have in their possession. They are no longer authorized to access the network, and they shall not take any hardware or software when they leave the office."

1. What changes would you make to the existing security policy so that it improves security after employees are terminated?

    _____

    _____

    _____

    _____

2. Brainstorm ideas for a security policy clause that covers access of company records and helps track when files are accessed.

    _____

    _____

    _____

    _____

CASE PROJECTS

CASE
PROJECTS

Case Project 2-1: Mapping Risk Analysis to a Security Policy

Six months after a security policy has been formulated and put into place, your company decides to do a risk analysis. The data in Table 2-3 presents some of the findings. Suggest ways in which you could modify the security policy to cover the new threats.

Table 2-3   Modifying a security policy

Asset	Threat	Probability	Consequences	Risk assessment	Change
Web server	High	Medium	Serious	Critical	The Web site went online
Office computers	Low	Low	Significant	Medium	Unchanged
Customer data	Medium	High	Damaging	High	Two employees in customer service were laid off and expressed anger
Job records	High	High	Serious	Critical	A laptop was lost or stolen while the VP of Marketing was in the airport

Case Project 2-2: Drafting a Security Policy

In this project, you continue developing a secure network for Green Globe R&D, Inc., the environmental research and design company for which you performed a risk assessment in Chapter 1. Using the information in the risk assessment and what you have learned in this chapter, produce a draft security policy containing the following:

- Title page
- Table of contents
- Introduction
- Scope and definitions
- Violations and penalties
- Acceptable use
- Unacceptable use
- Responsibilities (make up your own names and contact information) for the following:
    - Departmental (IT, Human Resources, and so on)
    - Management
    - Employees
- Internet and e-mail use, including
    - File downloads
    - Attachments
    - Objectionable content
    - Spyware, adware, and cookies
- Privileged access policy
- Extranet policy
- Remote access and wireless connection policy
- User accounts and passwords
- Physical and facility security (*Hint*: Remember to use the facility diagram)
- Server security

- Illegal activities:
    - Spam
    - Objectionable content
    - Theft of intellectual property and copyright infringement
    - Unauthorized entry into systems, corporate or otherwise, from corporate equipment
- Contact information (again, make up your own names and contact information) for the following:
    - Incident response team
    - Escalation procedures
- Security user awareness program, including
    - Methods
    - Responsible parties
- Employee acknowledgement (signature page)
- Appendixes:
    - Network diagram (from Chapter 1)
    - Facility diagram (from Chapter 1)
    - Risk analysis report and data (from Chapter 1)
- Change control and revision history
- References

This project might look like a tremendous task, but reviewing the information security policy document you downloaded from TechRepublic should be helpful. As you'll see, many sections of the policy are only a few sentences.

You can organize the information in whatever sequence you like and add items as needed. You can also use whatever resources you want, as long as you don't infringe copyrights and trademarks or violate your school's plagiarism policy. Any sections you don't understand can be clarified by Internet research. Using free templates (not copyrighted) and modifying them is strongly recommended. In the real world, you wouldn't be required to write the policy from scratch, and saving time means saving money the company is paying you for this task. The only rule is to cite your sources. Your grade won't be affected by using a template.

Remember, this is a draft policy, meaning you'll be adding to it, changing items that don't work, and revising based on changes in the environment, just as you would in a real security policy development and management cycle. When you're finished, proofread your work carefully and turn it in to your instructor.

3

PENETRATION TESTING TECHNIQUES

After reading this chapter and completing the exercises, you will be able to:

♦ Describe the process of network reconnaissance

♦ Describe common network attack techniques

♦ Explain types of malicious code attacks

This chapter examines techniques for attacking computers and networks. Attackers begin by gathering information about targets to discover job positions and contact information, corporate structure and security levels, and basic IT system architecture, for example. By learning how network reconnaissance is done, you can protect your network against information-gathering techniques.

The most vulnerable aspect of network security has always been people, however, so any effective security plan must address employee training to raise awareness. Attackers have sophisticated tools at their disposal, but they also use social engineering, which relies on people's natural desire to be helpful. By training employees, you can reduce this risk, but it can never be eliminated. Security is best achieved by using a variety of methods to build layers of defense around network systems.

Finally, you learn about network attack techniques and problems associated with the Internet. Passwords are generally the first line of defense for networks; however, many password-cracking tools are freely available. In addition, malicious code can damage systems and corrupt data. New viruses and worms emerge almost daily, so network administrators must know how to protect against them.

NOTE The Strategic Infrastructure Security (SIS) Exam SC0-471 uses the term "ethical hacking" in Domain 4.0. The more common and generally accepted term is "penetration testing," which is used throughout this book. This change in terminology has developed to more clearly differentiate between illicit network intrusion (hacking) and legitimate network intrusion (testing).

NETWORK RECONNAISSANCE

Network reconnaissance, the first step in attacking a network or computer, involves gathering as much information as possible about a potential target system. If the target is well defended, attackers usually seek an easier target unless they have a specific reason to compromise that target. On the other hand, if network reconnaissance shows that the target isn't defended well, attackers can use whatever means are available to gain access to the target. Generally, there are three steps to gathering information on target systems, discussed in more detail in the following sections:

- Footprinting
- Scanning
- Enumeration

NOTE Social engineering, another method of network reconnaissance, is covered in detail in "Social-Engineering Techniques" later in this chapter. Because securing people is the most difficult task, social engineering is a special problem and warrants its own section.

Footprinting

In the footprinting phase, attackers attempt to create a profile of a target organization. **Footprinting** involves using simple tools to determine an organization's security level. Attackers gather information such as the organization's Domain Name System (DNS) and e-mail servers, network IP address range, employee names and e-mail addresses, business contacts, and department information. For example, attackers might try to locate phone numbers and names of the organization's support staff. With this information, they try to gain more information from unsuspecting users who could, for example, be tricked into giving out passwords to an attacker posing as support staff. Most corporate management contact information is readily available online.

ACTIVITY

Activity 3-1: Footprinting an Organization

Time Required: 30 minutes

3

Objective: Conduct a footprinting experiment to see how attackers gather information.

Description: Gathering information involves a number of tools. In this activity, you perform footprinting on your school or another organization of your choice.

1. Start a Web browser and go to **http://samspade.org/**.

   If the Sam Spade site is down for maintenance, try Whois.com for DNS, IP, and URL searches.

NOTE

2. Scroll to the bottom of the page and click **Show Descriptions**. Scroll to the Reverse DNS tool, and enter a random IP address. (*Hint:* If you get stuck, try 63.0.0. 0.) Click **Scan rDNS**. The SamSpade.org Tools window reloads, with the address you entered in all the boxes. Click **Do Stuff**, and examine the results. Who owns the address block you entered? Try other tools available at this site, and see what happens.

   _____

3. Choose a site such as your school's Web site, but make sure to get your instructor's permission first. Next, see what information you can acquire by entering the site's URL at the Sam Spade page. For example, entering the fully qualified domain name in the IP Whois text box returns at least the IP address and sometimes even more information. Write down your findings:

   _____

   _____

   _____

   _____

4. How would you use this information to find out more about your target?

   _____

   _____

   _____

5. Exit your browser and leave your system running for the next activity.

Other methods of finding information on the Web include reverse phone number searches at *www.phonenumber.com* or using reconnaissance and security tools at Web sites such as *www.majorgeeks.com* and *www.snapfiles.com*. Searching newsgroups is another way to get information about a network. Administrators seeking help in solving network problems sometimes reveal information about their networks when posting messages to newsgroups. Even Google or Lycos search engines can provide a lot of information about an organization.

Scanning

Attackers use network **scanning** to identify active hosts on a network for the purpose of attacking them. Security specialists also use scanning to assess network security. Scanning methods, such as ping sweeps and port scans, return information about which IP addresses map to active hosts and the services those hosts offer.

A basic scan makes use of Internet Control Message Protocol (ICMP) packets to determine whether a target IP address is active by sending ICMP Echo (type 8) packets to the target host, and then waiting to see whether an ICMP Echo Reply (type 0) is received. If an ICMP Echo Reply is received, the target is active; no response means the target is down or the administrator has blocked Echo Reply packets. Network administrators often use the Ping command to test network connectivity and test whether a host is active. Figure 3-1 shows the output of a simple Ping command. Notice that the command is repeated with the addition of the -a switch (C:\>ping -a 192.168.1.19) to resolve the IP address to the target hostname (a computer named XP01).

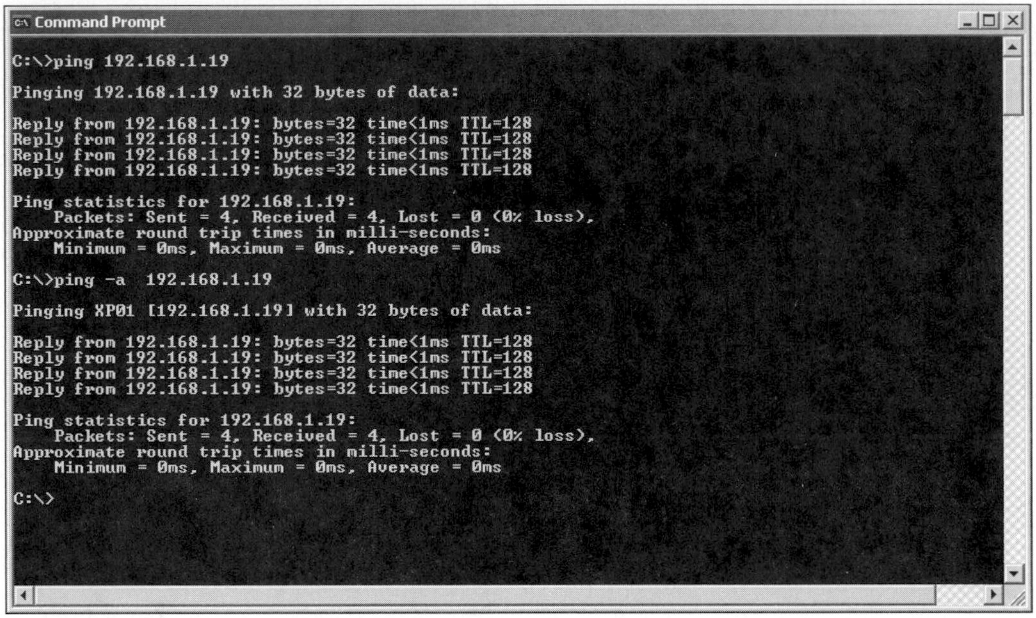

```
Command Prompt                                                        _ □ ×

C:\>ping 192.168.1.19

Pinging 192.168.1.19 with 32 bytes of data:

Reply from 192.168.1.19: bytes=32 time<1ms TTL=128
Reply from 192.168.1.19: bytes=32 time<1ms TTL=128
Reply from 192.168.1.19: bytes=32 time<1ms TTL=128
Reply from 192.168.1.19: bytes=32 time<1ms TTL=128

Ping statistics for 192.168.1.19:
    Packets: Sent = 4, Received = 4, Lost = 0 (0% loss),
Approximate round trip times in milli-seconds:
    Minimum = 0ms, Maximum = 0ms, Average = 0ms

C:\>ping -a  192.168.1.19

Pinging XP01 [192.168.1.19] with 32 bytes of data:

Reply from 192.168.1.19: bytes=32 time<1ms TTL=128
Reply from 192.168.1.19: bytes=32 time<1ms TTL=128
Reply from 192.168.1.19: bytes=32 time<1ms TTL=128
Reply from 192.168.1.19: bytes=32 time<1ms TTL=128

Ping statistics for 192.168.1.19:
    Packets: Sent = 4, Received = 4, Lost = 0 (0% loss),
Approximate round trip times in milli-seconds:
    Minimum = 0ms, Maximum = 0ms, Average = 0ms

C:\>
```

Figure 3-1   Ping command output

Pinging every suspected IP address on a network is too time consuming, even for an attacker with nothing better to do. To speed up the process, attackers or network administrators use a **ping sweep**, which sends ICMP Echo packets to multiple targets in an IP address range. Ping sweeps are one of the first steps novice attackers use in mapping out a network, so administrators usually disable them by blocking ICMP Echo Requests from addresses outside the internal network. A ping sweep is generally "noisy," so experienced attackers use more stealthy means to determine whether a host is present. Ping sweep tools are easy to find on the Internet, are available in GUI and command-line formats, and range from free to expensive. One well-known program is Fping (available at *www.fping.com* by clicking the latest Version link, not the Download fping link).

According to the System Administration, Networking and Security (SANS) Institute, even common firewall procedures can help attackers find the information they seek. Typically, firewalls and routers don't respond to a ping response packet if the target address exists on the network, but they do respond with an ICMP Destination Unreachable signal if the target isn't available. The absence of a response enables attackers to guess which IP addresses in an address range map to live hosts.

 Attackers might also perform passive or active scanning by using network-mapping tools, such as Nmap or LANmap. Network mapping is discussed further in Chapter 4.

NOTE

Enumeration

Enumeration takes footprinting a step further by trying to discover host computers or other devices on a network. Protocols such as ICMP and Simple Network Management Protocol (SNMP) are used to gather information or scan ports on remote hosts and look for well-known services in an attempt to identify a remote host's function. Tools such as SuperScan 4.0 (*www.foundstone.com*) enumerate hosts by using methods such as ICMP Echo packets, timestamp requests, and scans for open TCP or UDP ports. Typically, enumeration is used to find information on valid account names, network resources, shares, and applications. Although some information gathered through enumeration techniques might seem harmless, cracking passwords or finding vulnerabilities in OSs, network shares, or applications is possible.

Social-Engineering Techniques

The easiest and often the first method attackers use to penetrate network defenses is simply asking for information, whether by phone or e-mail or in person. **Social engineering** is the term for how attackers trick users or support desk staff into revealing valuable information, including passwords. Some information might seem worthless, but it can be used to gather more information from a different source. Social engineering relies on people's willingness to help others and their lack of training in social-engineering techniques. Users can still be tricked into giving out company information or passwords, even when they have been warned not to. For example, they receive a call from someone they believe to be from the support desk. Thinking they are helping the company solve a problem, they're all too eager to give the caller their passwords or a supervisor's name and phone number. With this information, the caller can get even more information from a supervisor and eventually learn passwords, account names, or details about the network configuration.

Dumpster diving is another form of social engineering that relies on people's lack of training in attack methods. The workplace is often thought of as a secure environment, and little thought is given to throwing proprietary documents into a trash container. When employees' names and phone numbers, network configurations, and even security policy documents are updated, users often just throw the old documents into the nearest trash container instead of disposing of them securely. An attacker looking for information can learn a lot by going through the trash, so developing methods for secure document disposal is wise. Methods include shredding or incinerating documents; some organizations out-source the job to a professional document disposal company.

Some brazen attackers even visit a company in person with the intent of gathering information. They might pose as a contractor, telephone technician, or potential customer—whatever seems least suspicious and helps them gain the most information. In this situation, attackers attempt to win the victim's trust to gather information.

For example, an attacker, Bob, is conducting reconnaissance on ABC Company. He's learned that ABC has a dedicated T-1 line for Internet access leased through WiggleStar Telecom. He also found out that the IT Department manager's name is Fred A. Stair and he's normally off on Thursday afternoons. Next, Bob visits a WiggleStar branch office to see how the technicians dress and whether they wear name badges. He then purchases similar clothing and pays a visit to ABC on Thursday afternoon. He arrives shortly before 5 p.m. because he knows that most employees, including the receptionist, leave at that time.

Bob greets the receptionist warmly and asks to see Fred Stair in the IT Department. The receptionist, Wilma, tells him Fred isn't in and asks whether she can leave him a message. Bob says, "Darn. I'm with WiggleStar Telecom, your network communications line provider. Fred called us yesterday afternoon about a problem with the outbound data access. Do you expect him in soon?" Wilma tells him that Fred won't be in until the next morning. Bob says, "If you could let me into your telecom room, I could probably have it fixed in a jiffy." Wilma says she doesn't know how to do that, but she offers to call the manager on duty, George Smith, to help Bob.

George comes to the front desk, takes Bob to the server room, and lets him in. Because it's the end of the day, George asks Bob how long he will be and whether he needs anything else. George explains that he's supposed to prepare a daily report and lock up the building. Bob says no, he'll be fine, and tells George to go ahead and take care of his work. By using the information he's gathered, Bob has gained full, unsupervised physical access to the company's server room. He can now access the company network, steal whatever information he wants, and create a backdoor for later use. Remember: If attackers have access to your systems, they own them.

Security Awareness Training

To reduce the risk of social-engineering techniques being successful, organizations should institute a security user awareness program. As you learned in Chapter 2, this program involves using memos, seminars, presentations, checklists, and other means of educating users about information security. Make sure all employees read and understand the company security policy, conduct training seminars on social-engineering tactics, and enforce strict controls on what type of information can and can't be given out. Also, make sure your company follows secure document disposal procedures. You might also consider extra training for people on the front lines, such as receptionists, help desk staff, phone operators, and other employees who make initial contact with the public. If these people are trained to recognize and deal with a possible social-engineering attempt, the attempt probably won't succeed.

NETWORK ATTACK TECHNIQUES

Most network attack techniques are based on the information-gathering procedures discussed in the previous section. Attackers rarely attempt to access systems they know nothing about. One reason is that if they don't know a network's security and logging measures, the risk of being caught increases. In addition, causing damage or stealing data while accessing systems without permission is considered trespassing, vandalism, and theft, which increases the stakes if attackers are caught. Therefore, attackers try to find as much information as possible before launching an attack. If you're monitoring, logging, and auditing your network, you have a chance of discovering information-gathering activities before an attack happens.

Attackers don't always leave tracks, however, so you need to understand what types of attacks are commonly used so that you can recognize one in progress. It's better to prevent an attack, but if one is under way, you can still prevent damage and possibly gather enough data to capture and prosecute the attacker. At the very least, if an attack happens that you're unaware of, you should still be able to discover it afterward, assess any damage, and close the security hole so that it can't be used again. You could also choose to leave the hole open with the intent of capturing intruders if and when they return. After attackers find an open target, they are likely to return. A word of caution: Make sure you consult the organization's security policy and operations manual before allowing an attack in progress to proceed. You should also consult with your company's Legal Department and, at a minimum, get your supervisor's signed permission.

CAUTION

Also, you should *never* perform penetration testing without explicit written permission from the system owner or a manager with the authority to allow this activity. Even if you're the administrator of a system, get your employer's written permission first. It's also wise to include details of the test, explaining what the program does, how it works, what it can reveal, and the purpose of running it. If you have a permission form with this information that's signed by someone with the proper authority, you're usually protected from termination or litigation.

Privilege Escalation and Unauthorized Access

Privilege escalation is exploiting a bug in software to gain access to protected resources. Many OS services require special privilege levels to function. For example, Windows services are usually configured to run with local administrator rights. A vulnerability such as a buffer overflow (discussed in the following section) could be used to run arbitrary code with elevated security privileges at the local system level. The net result is that the application operates with administrative rights, and the resource can be accessed and used in ways the developer or security administrator didn't intend.

Privilege escalation usually involves authorized users who have legitimate access with lower privileges gaining higher-level access to resources than they are supposed to have. This escalated privilege can go unnoticed for some time, but if attackers discover the bug, they'll take full advantage of the situation. This technique can also apply to attackers who have gained unauthorized access with lower-level privileges on the system. Attackers might discover credentials that give them access or find a vulnerability that allows them to access the system without authenticating, which can cause more problems.

Buffer Overflow Attacks

A **buffer overflow** is one of the most common mistakes novice programmers make. The buffer is simply a storage area in memory where data or instructions wait until the computer is ready to process them; this storage area is a specified size defined in an application. For example, if a program defines a buffer size of 100 MB (the total amount of memory the program is supposed to use), and the program writes data over the 100 MB mark without triggering an error or preventing the overwrite, a buffer overflow occurs. In a buffer overflow attack, an attacker finds this vulnerability in poorly written code that doesn't check for a defined amount of space utilization.

The problem happens because the computer can't tell the difference between data and instructions; it just does whatever it's told. If an attacker slips in malicious instructions along with a chunk of data that's too large for the buffer, the "overflow" code could run the commands in the attacker's code. Because the buffer capacity hasn't been defined correctly, an attacker is able to write code that overflows the buffer. The trick is not to fill the overflow buffer with meaningless data but to fill it with executable program code. That way, the OS runs the code, and the attacker's program does something harmful. Usually, the code elevates the attacker's permissions to that of an administrator or gives the attacker the same privileges as the creator of the poorly written program.

Keystroke Logging

Keystroke loggers, which range from freeware programs to hardware devices that attach directly to a computer's keyboard port, record everything typed at a computer terminal. They are often advertised as tools for preventing accidental data loss or for monitoring children's Internet use. Although both are valid uses, attackers often use keystroke-logging programs or devices to record passwords and other sensitive data. New versions are actually built into a standard keyboard and can't be detected through visual inspection. Keystroke loggers can work in stealth mode, meaning they're invisible to a computer user yet easily accessible to anyone who knows the device or program has been installed.

Perfect Keylogger Lite (*www.blazingtools.com/bpk.html*) is a freeware keystroke-logging tool. It doesn't support absolute stealth mode or remote installation but does log all keystrokes, including instant messages. Perfect Keylogger Lite isn't displayed in Task Manager and supports HTML log formats and log file encryption.

The full version can be installed in stealth mode and log keystrokes from many applications and e-mail log files to a specified address for review. This version also records mouse clicks, tracks Web site history, and can be installed and managed remotely.

Many keystroke loggers are available, and they can be handy tools. Be careful of legal liabilities when using them, however. Because keyloggers are technically spyware, antispyware scanners might detect them.

Denial-of-Service Attacks

After attackers have gained control of a computer, their goal might not be to steal files stored on it. Instead, they might use the compromised machine as a launching point for a **denial-of-service (DoS) attack** against a network server. By gaining control of someone else's computer, attackers protect their own identities from being traced. A DoS attack is successful only if the attacker is able to gain control of dozens or even hundreds of computers that can flood the target server with access requests.

In a DoS attack, a server is flooded with more requests than it can handle at any one time. This attack can be likened to a telephone switchboard flooded with so many incoming calls at one time that no calls can be handled. The server is so busy sending response messages to requests resulting from the DoS attack that it's unable to process legitimate requests, so the network is effectively brought to a halt and rendered nonfunctional. Numerous types of DoS attacks exist; the more common varieties—ping of death attacks, SYN floods, and address spoofing—are discussed in the following sections.

Ping of Death Attacks

The **ping of death** is a type of DoS attack used in the mid-1990s. By the end of 1997, most OSs had been patched to prevent it. According to Network Working Group Request for Comments (RFC) 719, the maximum allowed packet size is 65,535 bytes. To carry out a ping of death, an attacker creates an ICMP packet larger than the allowed maximum and sends it to the target system. The large packet is fragmented into smaller packets and reassembled at its destination. The target system at the destination point can't handle the reassembled oversized packet, thereby causing the system to hang, reboot, or crash.

SYN Flood Attacks

A **SYN flood** is a type of DoS attack that takes advantage of the TCP/IP three-way handshake. The attacker sends a TCP packet to the target with the SYN flag set, and then the target responds by sending a TCP SYN/ACK packet. Next, instead of sending an ACK back to the target, the attacker simply ignores the communication. The target is left with a half-open session. If the target is flooded with half-open sessions, its resources are depleted and it can't respond to legitimate traffic. This process is shown in Figure 3-2.

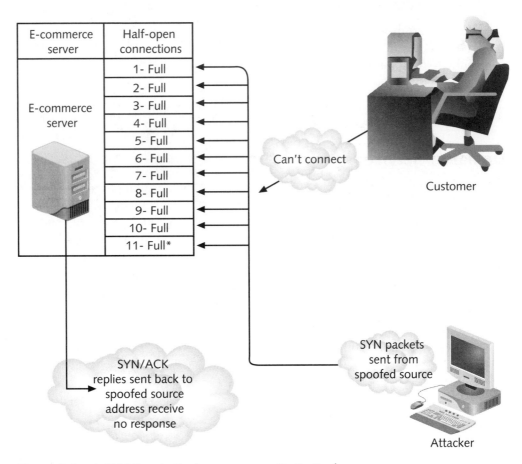

Figure 3-2   A SYN flood attack can cause a DoS attack

A SYN flood often involves hundreds of open sessions.

NOTE

Address Spoofing

Not usually thought of as a DoS attack, **address spoofing** can also cause a server to crash. To carry out this attack, attackers must first find an open port on the target and learn its IP address, and then send a packet to the target containing the target's address. Because the packet contains the same address and port as the target, the target could crash. A simple fix for this problem is to have your firewall's filtering rules drop this type of packet.

Your firewall should always drop inbound packets that contain source addresses matching your internal network.

TIP

Distributed Denial-of-Service Attacks

A **distributed denial-of-service (DDoS) attack** begins with attackers compromising hundreds or even thousands of computers connected to the Internet. After attackers have control of these **zombie** computers (also known as "bots"), they install some type of DDoS software. Several programs are readily available on the Internet with instructions on how to compromise a target system. One of the first well-known DDoS attack programs, Trinoo, was used in a two-day attack against the University of Minnesota in 1999. Three years later, attackers found a Remote Procedure Calls (RPC) for Distributed Component Object Model (DCOM) vulnerability in Windows, which allowed them to compromise 20,000 computers; the attackers then used these computers to launch an attack on the eBay site.

Activity 3-2: Learning More About DDoS Tools

ACTIVITY

Time Required: 30 minutes

Objective: Conduct research on well-known DDoS tools.

Description: DDoS attacks have become common in recent years and caused a lot of financial damage to companies. In this activity, you explore several DDoS tools and analyze defenses against them.

1. Start a Web browser and go to your favorite search engine. Type in the following names and find information on ways to defend against each type of attack: **Stacheldraht**, **Tribe Flood Network (TFN)**, **Shaft DDoS**, **Mstream**, and **Omega DDoS**.

2. Take notes as you examine each link and tool.

3. What are your recommendations for preparing for an attack by one of these tools? (*Hint*: These flood attack tools can also be used to defend against attacks.)

_____

_____

_____

_____

4. How could you prevent your systems from being used to carry out a DDoS attack on someone else?

_____

_____

_____

5. Close any open windows, and leave your system running for the next activity.

Password Exploitation

After educating users, passwords are considered the first line of defense for most networks. Users are responsible for selecting and protecting passwords they use to access resources, which presents a problem. Users don't always voluntarily adhere to recommended best practices for passwords, so you should adopt a three-pronged approach to password security. First, develop and enforce a strict password policy in your organization's security policy. Second, configure and enforce the use of strong passwords in your OS. Third, start a training campaign to teach users how to select and protect strong passwords, and make sure users know why strong passwords and strict handling of passwords are important.

The next sections discuss the weaknesses of password security and how to design a solid password scheme. Then you learn about password-cracking tools and Microsoft Security Baseline Analyzer, a free tool that scans computers for security vulnerabilities, including weak or missing passwords.

Password Weaknesses

Sometimes the most difficult part of strengthening your password design is determining where the weaknesses are. The best way to find out is by using penetration-testing techniques to pinpoint problem areas. You have two choices. You can test for weaknesses from the outside, attempting to find a vulnerable point as an attacker would, or you can test from the inside as an authenticated user or administrator. Both techniques have the potential to reveal valuable information, but to fine-tune your password design, you should do both.

If you want to simplify matters, you can run a password-cracking tool on the servers or computers you want to check, but this approach doesn't tell you much about the computers you don't test. The best way to cover all your bases is to conduct both internal and external testing.

3

Internal testing involves running password-cracking tools on one or more internal hosts. Pay particular attention to machines on the network perimeter because they're more exposed than those on the protected internal network. Testing internal hosts tells you what anyone authorized to access network resources can see. When conducting tests on the internal network, be sure to check the following types of passwords:

- Domain accounts
- Local accounts
- Service accounts
- Password files (.pwl extension in Windows 9.x)
- Passwords stored or transmitted in cleartext
- File protection passwords
- Shared resources
- Protected storage (cached passwords, browser auto-complete passwords, and so on)

External testing gives you a different perspective. When conducting external testing, you're attempting to crack passwords as an attacker would so that you know exactly how your system appears to the outside world. In external testing, you look for the passwords listed previously as well as the following types of passwords:

- Terminal services
- Remote desktop connections
- SQL Server
- IIS, Apache Web Server, and other Web applications
- Any third-party remote access software (even if you don't have any you're aware of, users sometimes install rogue programs)
- E-mail and any other communications software (Voice over IP, instant messaging, and so on)
- Virtual private network (VPN) access

Password Design

Designing and enforcing a comprehensive password policy is critical, as a username and password are often all that stands between an attacker and access. The details of a password policy depend on your organization's needs, but there are some general best practices you should follow. Different types of passwords might require unique security based on the access level they allow. For example, an administrative password that grants the administrator full access to all systems requires additional security measures.

An organization's password policy should include the following:

- Change passwords regularly on system-level accounts, according to the organization's security policies.

- Require users to change their passwords regularly (at least quarterly).

- Require password length of at least eight characters.

- Require complexity—passwords must include letters, numbers, and symbols and preferably should have both uppercase and lowercase letters.

- Passwords can't be common words or words found in the dictionary (the basis of a dictionary attack).

- Passwords must not identify a particular user, such as birthdays, names, or company-related words.

- Passwords should not be a word in any language, slang, jargon, or dialect. A dictionary attack can easily crack these passwords.

- Instruct users never to write a password down or store it online or on the local system.

- Instruct users not to reveal passwords to anyone over the phone, in e-mail, or in person, or hint at the password.

- Train users to use caution when logging on to ensure that no one can see them entering passwords.

- Limit reuse of old passwords and disable unused passwords (former employees, for example).

In addition to these guidelines, administrators can configure domain controllers to enforce password age, length, and complexity and to determine actions for failed logon attempts. A Windows Server 2003 domain controller, for example, can enforce many aspects of a password policy through Group Policy settings, such as the following:

- *Account lockout threshold*—Sets the number of failed logon attempts before the account is disabled temporarily. The value for this setting can range from 0 to 999 failed attempts. If it's set to 0, the account is never locked out, no matter how many failed attempts occur.

- *Account lockout duration*—Establishes the period of time the user account is locked out after a specified number of failed logon attempts. This value can range from 0 to 99,999 minutes. If it's set to 0, the account remains locked until an administrator unlocks it manually.

- *Reset account lockout counter after*—Determines the length of time the account lockout counter remembers failed logon attempts, ranging from 1 to 99,999 minutes.

- *Minimum password age*—Requires users to use their passwords for a minimum length of time (0 to 998 days) before they're allowed to change them. A setting of

0 means users can change their passwords at any time. If this setting is configured, it must be set to a shorter duration than the maximum password age setting.

- *Maximum password age*—Forces users to change their passwords after a set number of days, ranging from 1 to 999 days.

- *Minimum password length*—Requires a password to be at least a specified number of characters.

- *Enforce password history*—Keeps a record of users' previous passwords and doesn't allow reusing a password stored in the history. The value for this setting can range from 0 to 24 passwords remembered.

- *Store passwords using reversible encryption*—Discards the default encryption levels of Active Directory and applies reversible encryption instead. This setting should be avoided unless an application requires it, such as IIS, which uses Digest Authentication and requires enabling this setting.

Another important setting in Windows Server 2000/2003 and XP Professional is "Password must meet complexity requirements." Complexity requirements state that the password must follow these rules:

- Cannot contain any part of the username

- Must contain at least one uppercase alphabetic character (A–Z)

- Must contain at least one special character, such as $, @, &, #, and so on

- Must contain at least one lowercase alphabetic character (a–z)

- Must consist of at least six characters, unless the Minimum password length setting requires more

If Active Directory is used with Group Policy settings regulating password policies, setting password requirements at the root of the domain is best so that they apply to all users and groups. For a local machine, these settings are accessed via Control Panel. In Hands-On Project 3-2, you explore the Password Policy settings on your Windows XP Professional workstation. (These settings are the same in Windows Server 2000/2003 and Windows 2000 Professional, so you can access and configure them the same way as in XP Professional.)

Password-Cracking Techniques

Despite the best efforts to promote security through strong passwords and enforcement of a password policy, it's still entirely possible that passwords can be cracked. With enough time and processing power, most passwords can be cracked, in fact. Password cracking can be accomplished in several ways, from social engineering to brute-force attacks. It can be as easy as guessing someone's favorite football team or as sophisticated as using a network sniffer to detect passwords as they traverse the network.

A number of password-cracking tools are available for attackers to download and use. This section discusses one of the fastest, most effective password-cracking tools: John the Ripper (*www.openwall.com/john/*). This open-source product has versions for UNIX, DOS, and

Windows. It offers support for Kerberos and for Windows NT/2000/XP LAN Manager hash functions, and patches are available for others. John has several basic cracking modes, and you can also define custom modes (although that advanced technique is beyond the scope of this book). These are the most common modes:

- *Wordlist*—In this mode, you specify a text file containing one word per line (a word list), and John the Ripper tries each word in order. If you enable word-mangling rules, John tries each word in the list and "mangles" them to produce other likely password candidates so that each source word is tried along with multiple similar words.

- *Single crack*—This mode uses logon names and users' home directory names as candidate passwords along with word-mangling rules. This mode uses information against the account it was taken from and is much faster than wordlist mode. Cracked passwords are tried against all loaded password hashes in case other users have the same password.

- *Incremental*—This mode tries all possible character combinations as passwords. Because the possible combinations are practically endless, you need to define password length limits and character sets to use. Several mode definitions are predefined, such as All, Alpha, Alnum, and Digits, or you can set up a custom definition.

ACTIVITY

Activity 3-3: Downloading and Using Password-Cracking Tools

Time Required: 30 minutes

Objective: Learn to use password-cracking tools to see the vulnerability of most passwords computer users choose.

Description: In this activity, you download and install John the Ripper, and then use it to test the strength of different passwords.

1. Start Notepad and open a new text file. Type the following hashed passwords *exactly* as shown; include all the colons and don't insert any spaces. Later, you use John the Ripper to test the strength of these passwords.

```
Account01:1029:56DF280A5197FC62AAD3B435B51404EE:
0B6C1DD95A1F902BDD77F8A5F5045793:::
Account02:1030:B2BEF1B1582C2DC0AAD3B435B51404EE:
001D37F34602469CD641614761D378E6:::
Account03:1031:46BD192AD422C4A4AAD3B435B51404EE:
527F1CE6460E624A7A24D399C217BCFC:::
```

2. Save this file as **passfile.txt** in a location of your choosing, and exit Notepad.

3. Start your Web browser and go to **http://www.openwall.com/john**.

4. Click the most recent Windows binaries link for John the Ripper, and save the file to a folder named **John17**.

5. Close your Web browser, extract the files to the John17 folder, and navigate to the **run** folder inside the John17 folder. Copy the passfile.txt file you created in Step 2 to this folder.

6. Open a command prompt window and change to the **run** folder. Type **john–386 passfile.txt** and press **Enter**. Figure 3-3 shows the results of running this command against the three password hashes in passfile.txt.

NOTE

Simple passwords such as dictionary words can be cracked almost instantly, but more sophisticated passwords can take hours or even days to crack.

7. Close any open windows, and leave your system running for the next activity.

```
C:\WINDOWS\system32\cmd.exe                              _ □ ×

C:\>cd john17\run

C:\John17\run>john-386 passfile.txt
Loaded 3 password hashes with no different salts (NT LM DES [32/32 BS])
1A2B3C          (Account03)
3455            (Account01)
1234A           (Account02)
guesses: 3  time: 0:00:00:04 (3)  c/s: 660840  trying: Q, - 12341

C:\John17\run>_
```

Figure 3-3   Passwords cracked by John the Ripper

Tools for Pinpointing Password Vulnerabilities

Microsoft Baseline Security Analyzer (MBSA) isn't a password-cracking tool, but it scans your Windows system and pinpoints vulnerabilities, such as accounts with no password set, missing updates, or other potential security problems. This free Microsoft tool is quite useful. In Activity 3-4, you see what information you can find with it.

Activity 3-4: Downloading and Using MBSA

Time Required: 30 minutes

Objective: Use Microsoft Baseline Security Analyzer to find potential security vulnerabilities.

Description: MBSA provides a wealth of information, including account, system, and configuration errors; missing updates; and other possible problems. For this activity, you need a Windows XP workstation and Internet access.

1. Start a Web browser and go to **www.microsoft.com/technet/security/tools/ mbsa2/default.mspx**.

 Thess steps are written for version 2.0. If you download a newer version, the steps and screens might differ slightly.

NOTE

2. Click the **Download Now** link. Select a language, and click **Continue** to proceed with the product validation process. Follow the instructions to validate your Microsoft product, which must be completed successfully to download MBSA.

3. When the product validation is finished, you're returned to the download page. Scroll down the page to the Files in This Download box, and click the MBSASetup-EN.msi file's **Download** button. If a security warning appears, click **Save**. Select your desktop or another location for saving the file, and then click **Save**.

4. When the download is finished, click **Run** in the Download Complete dialog box to begin the installation. If a security warning appears, click **Run** to proceed. (If your download box closes when the download is finished, browse to the file's location on your hard drive and double-click the **MBSASetup-EN** Windows installer package to start the installation.)

5. When the MBSA Setup window opens (see Figure 3-4), click **Next** and follow the instructions to install the application. Read and accept the license agreement, and accept all default settings for the installation.

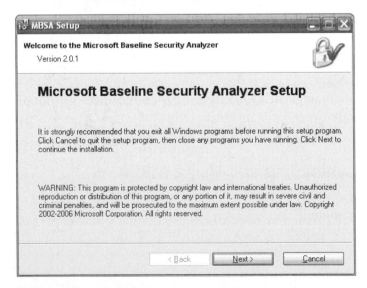

Figure 3-4 The MBSA Setup window

6. When the installation is finished, click **Start**, point to **All Programs**, and click **Microsoft Baseline Security Analyzer 2.0** to start MBSA. The MBSA main window opens, as shown in Figure 3-5.

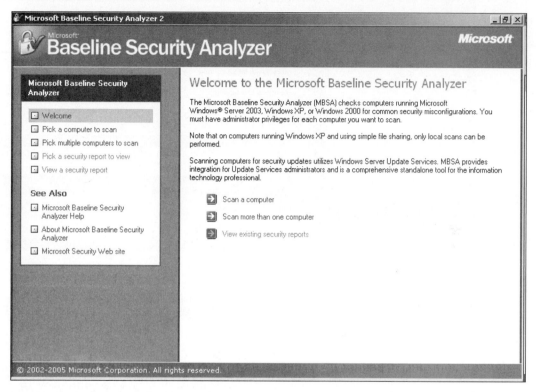

Figure 3-5   The MBSA main window

7. In the main window, click the **Scan a computer** link. Enter your computer name or IP address, if necessary, and click **Start scan**.

NOTE   Your computer name should already appear by default, but you can enter your IP address, if you want. Entering a security report name isn't necessary, however.

8. When the scan is finished, a results page is displayed (see Figure 3-6). Results will vary, depending on the computer being scanned.

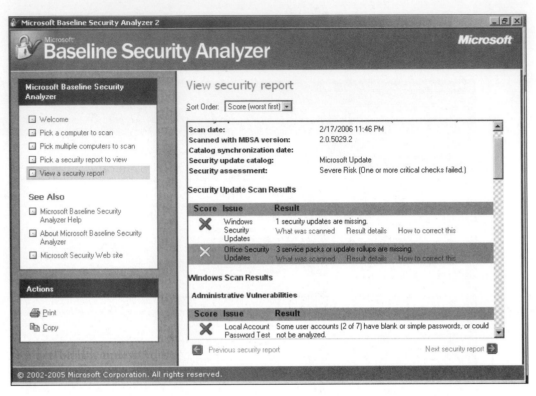

Figure 3-6   MBSA scan results

9. Examine your results. What did the scan find? Did the scan report any severe risks (denoted by a red X)? (Use an additional piece of paper for your answers, if needed.)

_____

_____

_____

_____

_____

_____

10. Did you expect these results, or were there vulnerabilities that surprised you?

_____

_____

11. For each severe risk, click the **How to correct this** link, and read the information about the problem and the instructions for correcting it. With your instructor's permission, correct the severe risks.

12. After the severe risks have been corrected, run the scan again. Note the changes that resulted because of your corrections. (Use an additional sheet for your answers, if needed.) If time permits, continue to scan and correct problems until your system is secured.

_____

_____

_____

_____

_____

_____

TIP

You should develop a security toolbox suited to your environment that includes password-cracking and recovery tools, protocol analyzers, traffic analyzers, forensics tools, and any others needed to maintain security on your network. To find more tools, use your favorite search engine, or visit *www.majorgeeks.com* and *www.snapfiles.com*, mentioned earlier. These sites are helpful starting points for a variety of security, Internet, optimization, and other handy tools.

MALICIOUS CODE ATTACKS

Malicious code, or **malware**, is software designed to prevent a computer or business from operating. Malware can be a virus, worm, Trojan program, or other type of program created with the intent of destroying or corrupting data or shutting down a computer or network. The following sections examine malware in more detail.

Viruses

A virus is a software program created to do harm instead of be productive. However, unlike most programs, it can't stand on its own; it must attach itself to some type of executable file to work. After it's attached to a host program, the virus can replicate to other computers by sharing the program on floppy disks, jump drives, or CDs, or it can be replicated as an attachment to an e-mail. When the virus has infected a computer, it carries out whatever instructions the programmer wrote into the code. The only solution is to prevent the virus from infecting the computer in the first place.

The good news is that pure data files, such as .jpg, .gif, .mp3, and .txt, are fairly safe in terms of not spreading a virus infection. The bad news is that recent developments in technology have made these files vulnerable (such as variations of the W32/Perrun-A viral strain). There's no way to completely prevent a virus from infecting your computer. Dozens of antivirus software companies create helpful products, but none can guarantee that you'll never get a virus. The problem is that antivirus software uses a **virus signature file** to compare against known viruses. Because new viruses are created every day, antivirus software is constantly outdated, so updating your virus definitions regularly is critical. For large companies, network administrators should consider using an enterprise edition of antivirus software so that they can "push" updates to computers throughout the organization.

Worms

Similar to a virus, a worm is a small piece of computer code designed to do harm, but it doesn't require a host program to work. It replicates throughout a network by looking for computers with a specific vulnerability, and then copying itself to the new machine and starting the process all over. The speed at which a worm can infect computers is staggering. In July 2003, Microsoft issued a security bulletin advising users of a buffer overflow vulnerability in the Windows 2000, XP, and 2003 RPC interface. A patch was released to correct this vulnerability. In August 2003, the MSBlaster worm (also known as Lovsan, MSBlast, and Blaster) exploited the RPC vulnerability to infect hundreds of thousands of computers in its first few days. Had those systems been patched in time, this worm would not have been so damaging—another example of why keeping systems up to date is critical.

Security professionals are also working to protect automatic teller machines (ATMs) from worm attacks, such as the Slammer and Nachi worms. Cyberattacks against ATMs are a serious concern for the banking industry and law enforcement agencies worldwide.

Trojans

A Trojan program, like its namesake, pretends to be something it's not. Often disguised as a game or helpful utility, a Trojan is actually malicious code designed to install a **backdoor** or rootkit on a computer. A backdoor or rootkit is simply a software tool that allows an attacker to access and use the computer, again without the user's knowledge. Unlike a virus, Trojans are standalone programs. After a Trojan runs and the rootkit is installed on a computer, the attacker can access the computer remotely across the network or Internet. Most rootkits hide within other OS tools and are difficult to detect.

Back Orifice, a Trojan program created in 1999, is still one of the most widely used. The program's new release is now marketed as an administrative utility similar to Windows XP Remote Desktop. The main difference is that Back Orifice works without users being aware of anyone accessing their computers.

A popular way of controlling computers is through Internet Relay Chat (IRC), which uses TCP port 6667. Because a compromised computer running IRC keeps a static connection to the remote IRC server, a simple Netstat command shows this connection. At a Windows command prompt, enter the netstat -an | find ":6667" command. A noninfected computer simply returns a command prompt, but an infected computer returns something similar to "TCP 192.168.1.23:1026 116.130.15.85:6667 ESTABLISHED." Most firewalls should be able to identify traffic using nonstandard ports, but many Trojan programs use common ports that are harder to detect. In addition, some home users and companies don't use firewalls at all, which leaves their computers open to even the simplest attacks.

Spyware

Spyware is software that gathers information from users' computers without their knowledge and sends it to a third party on the Internet. Spyware usually gathers information about users' Internet surfing habits, but it can also gather information such as e-mail addresses, credit card numbers, and passwords. Similar to a Trojan program, spyware is usually installed because users think they are getting a useful tool or program. In fact, many Web sites that advertise spyware removal are actually installing spyware on your computer.

Macros

A macro is a shortcut key that represents a list of commands or keystrokes. For example, instead of Ctrl+A to highlight the contents of a document, Ctrl+C to copy the selected data to the Clipboard, and Ctrl+V to paste the data to a different document, a macro can carry out all these commands at once. Programs such as Microsoft Word and Excel have built-in macro languages that you can use to create powerful macros. These macros can be embedded in the document and run when the document is opened. Although these helpful macros save time, macros can also be created for destructive purposes. The Melissa virus is one example. When a user opened a document infected with this virus, the document was sent as an e-mail message to the first 50 entries in the computer's address book.

Reducing Malware Risks

Malicious code attacks can be devastating. Some infamous malicious code attacks, such as the I Love You worm, have cost businesses millions of dollars in lost productivity caused by computer downtime and time spent recovering lost data, reinstalling programs and OSs, and hiring or contracting IT personnel. Although some estimated costs are available, no accepted or valid metrics are available to measure this cost. It isn't likely one will emerge because most companies are more concerned with preventing infections than with counting the cost; it certainly makes more sense to prevent damage than assess it after the fact. Also, companies don't want to advertise to their customers that they had systems that were left vulnerable.

Because a malware attack can be so damaging and the risk can't be prevented completely, taking a proactive approach to preventing infection is important. The most essential preventive measure is to use antivirus software and keep it updated. Because new viruses appear almost daily, keeping antivirus software updated with the most current virus signature files is critical.

Make sure that antivirus software is loaded, updated, and running on perimeter network devices, workstations, and particularly e-mail servers. Scan all incoming e-mail, and remove potentially harmful attachments. Disable autopreview in e-mail clients, make sure any instant messaging (IM) applications are monitored, and do not allow file downloads. Several excellent enterprise IM applications are available that offer monitoring and management controls not available with standard IM applications, such as AOL Instant Messenger (AIM) or Yahoo! Messenger.

Even with these precautions, your network can still be infected. The next most important step to prevent malware infection is end-user training. Make sure users are aware of the potential for infection. Because most viruses and worms use e-mail to propagate, users must be savvy enough to avoid opening e-mail attachments that could be harmful. Some companies create presentations, flyers, memos, or other guidelines for users to help them understand the risks and educate them on how they can help prevent infection.

CHAPTER SUMMARY

- Network reconnaissance involves gathering information about a potential target system. Reconnaissance involves three primary activities: footprinting, network scanning, and enumeration.

- In footprinting, an attacker attempts to build a profile of an organization. Scanning is used to identify active hosts on a target network. Enumeration takes footprinting a step further to discover host computers or other devices on a target network.

- Social engineering takes advantage of the natural desire people have to be helpful and aids attackers in reconnaissance efforts on a target network. It also uses techniques such as dumpster diving to gain access to vital corporate information.

- Security awareness training should be used to reduce the risk of social-engineering techniques being successful.

- Most network attack techniques are based on information gathered in the reconnaissance phase. Attack techniques include privilege escalation, denial-of-service, distributed denial-of-service, and buffer overflow attacks.

- Privilege escalation is exploiting a bug in software to gain access to protected resources. Denial-of-service attacks include address spoofing, SYN floods, and the ping of death.

- Passwords are usually the first line of defense. Because passwords are secure only if users keep them secure, a strictly enforced password policy is essential. A solid password policy should include guidelines for creating strong passwords and specify what constitutes weak passwords.

- To discover password weaknesses in your organization, you should conduct internal and external password security testing. Testing includes running password-cracking software to check for weak or missing passwords.

- Domain controllers can enforce certain aspects of password security through password policy settings. These settings are also available for local systems.

- Many password-cracking tools, such as John the Ripper, are available. John the Ripper has several basic cracking modes useful for different purposes, resource limitations, and time frames.

- Microsoft Baseline Security Analyzer is a free vulnerability assessment tool that can check for missing updates, weak or missing passwords, and other security vulnerabilities and configuration problems.

❑ Malicious code (malware) is a serious threat that includes viruses, Trojan programs, macros, and worms. Spyware, although not always malicious, can reduce productivity, consume resources, and reveal private information.

KEY TERMS

address spoofing — A type of attack that uses a packet with the target's IP address and port. Because the source address and port are the same as the target destination, the target could crash.

backdoor — A set of software tools that allows an attacker to access and use a computer without the user's knowledge by hiding running processes, files, or system data. Also known as a "rootkit."

buffer overflow — An attack method that takes advantage of poorly written programming code to overflow a system buffer with executable program code. If a maximum buffer size is defined, but the program is allowed to write more than the maximum to the buffer, an error condition exists that could allow a buffer overflow attack.

denial-of-service (DoS) attack — An attack that floods a host with more requests than it can handle, effectively preventing the host from responding to legitimate requests.

distributed denial-of-service (DDoS) attack — A DoS attack that uses multiple computers to attack a single target.

dumpster diving — A form of social engineering that involves using a company's carelessly discarded trash to find information. Security policies, employee personal information, and bills are valuable sources of information in gaining access to a system.

enumeration — A method for obtaining information on valid account names, network resources, shares, and applications; uses protocols such as ICMP and SNMP to scan remote hosts. Enumeration can also provide information about well-known services that identify the function of a remote host.

footprinting — A method attackers use to create a profile of a target system, including the organization's security level, DNS architecture and server names, e-mail system, IP addresses, contact information for employees, and so on.

keystroke loggers — Devices or computer programs used to capture keystrokes on a computer.

malware — Executable code designed to damage target systems. Malware can be a virus, worm, Trojan program, or macro.

network reconnaissance — The process of gathering as much information about a potential target system as possible, using scanning methods, ping sweeps, social engineering, packet capture and analysis, and other means.

ping of death — A DoS attack that sends an oversized packet to the target system, causing the target to crash, reboot, or hang. Most systems are patched to prevent this type of attack, but it was a successful method in the mid-1990s.

ping sweep — A tool that sends ICMP Echo packets to multiple targets, identified by a range of IP addresses, to build a map of a target network.

privilege escalation — A type of attack that exploits a software bug to gain access to resources that would normally have been protected.

scanning — A method attackers use to identify active hosts on a network. Also used by security personnel to identify vulnerable hosts.

social engineering — A method attackers use to gain information or access to a system by tricking users into voluntarily giving them the requested information. Social engineering can be done over the phone or in person.

spyware — Software that gathers information from users' computers about their Internet surfing habits. Spyware can also gather personal information, such as credit card numbers, e-mail account information, passwords, or logon names. Spyware is usually installed without the user's knowledge or permission.

SYN flood — A type of DoS attack that takes advantage of the TCP three-way handshake by sending multiple packets with the SYN flag set to a target. The target responds by sending a SYN/ACK packet, which the attacking system ignores, leaving the session half-open. The target system is eventually overwhelmed with half-open sessions and can't respond to legitimate requests.

virus signature file — A file prepared by antivirus software vendors that contains patterns of known viruses. Antivirus software uses these files to identify known viruses.

zombie — A computer that has been compromised and can be used to attack another computer; also known as a "bot." Usually, an attacker compromises hundreds or thousands of computers to launch an attack.

REVIEW QUESTIONS

1. Network reconnaissance can involve which of the following?
   a. buffer overflow attacks
   b. SYN floods
   c. footprinting
   d. privilege escalation

2. What type of attack takes advantage of the TCP three-way handshake?
   a. ping of death
   b. keystroke logging
   c. SYN flood
   d. address spoofing

3. Which of the following is used to identify active hosts on a network for the purpose of attacking them?
   a. footprinting
   b. ping of death
   c. scanning
   d. social engineering

4. Which of the following involves using presentations, memos, checklists, seminars, and other means to educate users about security?

   a. security boot camp

   b. security user awareness program

   c. security fundamentals training class

   d. social engineering test

5. Exploiting a bug in software to gain access to resources that would otherwise be protected with higher security controls is called which of the following?

   a. programming exploitation

   b. malicious code attack

   c. privilege escalation

   d. access rights augmentation

6. Which of the following is made possible by a coding error that doesn't define the maximum memory a program is allowed to use?

   a. buffer overflow attack

   b. page fault attack

   c. denial-of-service attack

   d. SYN flood

7. Which statement about a SYN flood is true?

   a. A SYN flood is a type of privilege escalation.

   b. A SYN flood exploits the TCP ACK flag.

   c. A SYN flood sends multiple packets with the SYN flag set.

   d. A SYN flood sends multiple packets with the SYN/ACK flags set.

8. Your firewall should always drop outbound packets that have source addresses matching an internal network host. True or False?

9. To launch a DDoS attack, an attacker gains control over hundreds or thousands of other computers, called _____ , and uses them in the attack.

   a. drones

   b. zombies

   c. slaves

   d. snoopies

10. Which of the following guidelines is recommended to help ensure strong passwords? (Choose all that apply.)

    a. Passwords must be longer than 10 characters.

    b. Passwords should be random combinations of symbols, uppercase and lowercase letters, and numerals.

    c. Passwords should be changed weekly.

    d. Passwords shouldn't identify a particular user.

11. Password complexity requirements in Windows include which criteria? (Choose all that apply.)

    a. Passwords must contain two uppercase characters.

    b. Passwords must not contain special characters.

    c. Passwords must contain at least one lowercase letter.

    d. Passwords must be at least six characters.

12. Which of the following is a basic cracking mode in John the Ripper? (Choose all that apply.)

    a. wordlist

    b. single crack

    c. brute force

    d. dictionary

13. Antivirus software uses a virus _____ file to compare scanned files with known viruses.

    a. signature

    b. classification

    c. blueprint

    d. design

14. A hidden program that gives an attacker access to your computer is called which of the following?

    a. stealth file

    b. doorway

    c. backdoor

    d. failsafe

15. What are some recommended ways to protect against malware? (Choose all that apply.)

    a. Load antivirus software and keep it updated monthly.

    b. Disable autopreview of e-mail.

    c. Scan all incoming e-mail.

    d. Don't allow any e-mail attachments.

3

16. Malware that can spread without the use of another program or file or any user action is called which of the following?

   a. virus

   b. Trojan

   c. macro

   d. worm

17. When conducting internal network security testing for password weaknesses, what types of passwords should you check? (Choose all that apply.)

   a. remote desktop

   b. service accounts

   c. VPN access

   d. shared resources

18. To carry out an address spoofing attack on a host, what information must the attacker find out?

   a. computer name

   b. local service account password

   c. IP address

   d. open port

19. The most important part of network security, and the hardest part to secure, is which of the following?

   a. applications

   b. workstations

   c. e-mail

   d. people

HANDS-ON PROJECTS

HANDS-ON PROJECTS

Hands-On Project 3-1: Using MBSA to Scan Multiple Computers

Time Required: 30 minutes

Objective: Use MBSA to scan a range of IP addresses.

Description: In this activity, you use MBSA to scan a group of computers. The ability to scan multiple computers remotely saves time, one of the most valuable assets an IT security administrator has. By using this tool to assess security vulnerabilities on multiple computers simultaneously, you can evaluate what changes are necessary to secure them, design a solution, and test it thoroughly before making any actual changes.

1. Click **Start**, point to **All Programs**, and click **Microsoft Baseline Security Analyzer 2.0**.

2. Click **Scan more than one computer**, and enter the IP address range of your classroom network in the next window. (Your instructor will provide the addresses to use.) Remember that the more machines you select to scan, the longer the scan takes, so scanning no more than five computers is best.

3. When the scan is finished, examine the results for each computer, and discuss the results with your classmates.

If you have access to a printer, you might find it easier to print the results for comparison and discussion.

TIP

4. How could an attacker gain entry into your classroom network? How would you exploit the vulnerabilities MBSA found? Discuss ways the security problems MBSA found could result in unauthorized access, damage to systems, or other harmful activities.

_____

_____

_____

_____

_____

_____

Hands-On Project 3-2: Exploring Windows Password Policy Settings

HANDS-ON PROJECTS

Time Required: 10 minutes

Objective: Explore the Password Policy settings in Windows XP Professional.

Description: Because users can't be relied on to adhere to password security, most administrators use software features that require users to use passwords securely. In this activity, you see how password security works on your XP Professional workstation.

1. Click **Start**, **Control Panel**, click the **Performance and Maintenance** link, and then click **Administrative Tools**.

2. Double-click **Local Security Policy** to open the Local Security Settings window (see Figure 3-7).

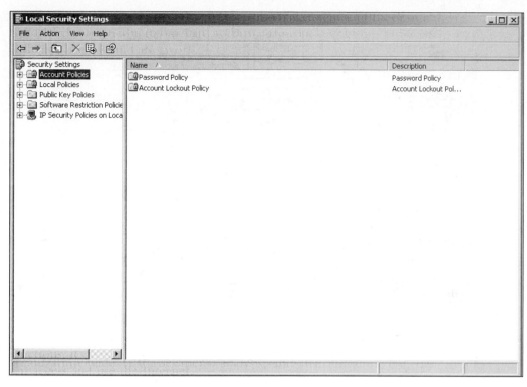

Figure 3-7   The Local Security Settings window

3. Click to expand **Account Policies** in the left pane, and then click **Password Policy**. Your window should look similar to the one in Figure 3-8.

4. Double-click each policy in the right pane, and inspect the available settings.

5. In the pane on the left, click **Account Lockout Policy**. As you can see in Figure 3-9, this is where you set up the account lockout options discussed previously.

6. Close all open windows, and leave your system running for the next activity.

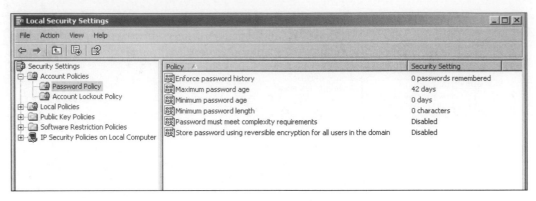

Figure 3-8   Viewing Password Policy settings

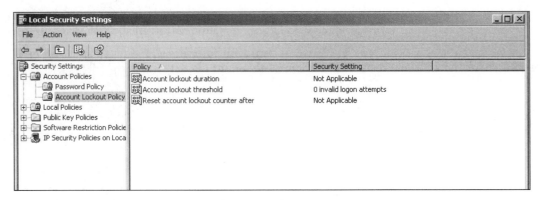

Figure 3-9   Settings for account lockouts

Hands-On Project 3-3: Identifying the Slammer Worm

Time Required: 15 minutes

Objective: Examine the Slammer worm.

Description: The Slammer worm wreaked havoc on networks in January 2003. As a network security professional, you should be aware of past attacks because history often repeats itself, and past viruses continue to circulate and infect computers for years after their release.

1. Start your Web browser and go to **www.cert.org**.

2. Type **Slammer Worm CA-2003-04 MS-SQL** in the Search text box and press **Enter**.

3

NOTE

When you have a few minutes, exploring *www.cert.org* for security information is time well spent. This federally funded research center specializing in Internet security is an excellent place to research current vulnerabilities and security alerts.

3. What vulnerability did the worm exploit?

_____

_____

_____

4. What port did Slammer use to connect to the attacked server?

_____

5. What impact did Slammer have?

_____

_____

_____

6. When was a patch for the vulnerability exploited by the Slammer worm?

_____

_____

7. Close your Web browser.

CASE PROJECTS

CASE
PROJECTS

Case Project 3-1: Designing Password Security for Green Globe

Passwords are generally the first line of defense for network security, and people are the key to making them work. After you have conducted a risk assessment and drafted an overall security policy, it's time to nail down some specifics.

First, you must design an effective password security policy for Green Globe R&D. Start by visiting Web sites of some well-known security organizations, colleges, and businesses to examine their policies. This step should give you a good idea of what your policy should include. You can find some helpful samples at *www.sans.org/resources/policies/Password_Policy.doc* and *http://its.psu.edu/policies/password.html*. Reading the article on password policy don'ts at *http://searchsecurity.techtarget.com/tip/1,289483,sid14_gci916934,00.html?track=sap805* is also recommended.

After developing a password policy, you must decide how to train users to follow it. Create a security user awareness program to educate Green Globe R&D employees on the password policy. The program can be any combination of methods or approaches you choose and might include the following:

- A PowerPoint presentation explaining the policy and its importance
- An interoffice memo about the policy
- A game or quiz with reward incentives for "superachievers" in policy comprehension and security practices
- Random tests to see whether employees can be tricked into revealing their passwords and whether they recognize the attempts

4

ANALYZING PACKET STRUCTURES

After reading this chapter and completing the exercises, you will be able to:

♦ Explain the Common Vulnerabilities and Exposures (CVE) standard

♦ Describe how signature analysis is used in examining network traffic

♦ Detect normal and suspicious traffic signatures

♦ Describe packet capture and analysis

♦ Explain ways to identify suspicious events

At its most basic level, securing network traffic comes down to a simple principle: allowing the traffic you want to pass through your network gateways and blocking all the traffic you don't want. The challenge is to separate the two types of network traffic by using a combination of firewalls, router access lists, intrusion detection system (IDS) filtering, antivirus software, and other security tools. For these devices to determine whether traffic is normal, administrators must tell them which is which. After a device can accurately tell the difference, it must then know how to respond, if it's capable of doing so.

This chapter examines the Common Vulnerabilities and Exposures (CVE) standard for recording information on attack signatures and explains signature analysis and how it's used in network security. You learn some techniques for identifying normal and abnormal network traffic and how to identify and analyze suspicious events. Finally, you learn how to capture packets for inspection and analyze traffic signatures, both normal and suspicious. Administrators use packet capture and analysis to monitor their network's performance or look for security violations, among other uses. Attackers can also capture packets being transmitted but are generally looking for passwords or gathering network data for later use.

EXAMINING THE COMMON VULNERABILITIES AND EXPOSURES STANDARD

One way to prevent attacks is to make sure security devices can share information and coordinate with one another. A network perimeter usually has a variety of hardware and software devices that provide security and need to work cooperatively with one another. You might have a router from one vendor, a firewall from another, and an IDS from a third. Unfortunately, the way they interpret signatures might differ. They probably address the same attacks but give them different names and describe their characteristics differently. The **Common Vulnerabilities and Exposures (CVE)** standard enables these devices to share information about attack signatures and other vulnerabilities so that they can work together.

How the CVE Standard Works

The CVE standard enables hardware and security devices to draw from the same databases of vulnerabilities, which are in the same format. For instance, a **scanner** (a device that scans a network for open ports or other potential vulnerabilities) that supports CVE compiles a report listing weak points in the system. When an alarm message is transmitted by an IDS that supports CVE, the attack signature can be compared to the report of current vulnerabilities to see whether an attack has actually occurred (see Figure 4-1).

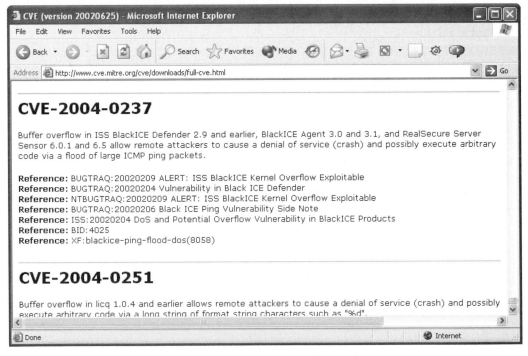

Figure 4-1   CVE enables security devices to share information

In Figure 4-1, the CVE standard has an impact on many different parts of a network:

1. An IDS sensor detects a possible attack.

2. The signature is checked against the database of known attack signatures available to the IDS to search for a match. If the IDS supports CVE, the attack report contains information on known network vulnerabilities associated with the attack signature.

3. The list of vulnerabilities is compared against a database of current vulnerable points in the system that have been compiled and stored by a CVE-compliant scanner to determine whether this possible attack can have an impact on the network.

4. Periodically, the list of vulnerabilities is updated with new entries from the CVE vulnerability Web site.

5. The manufacturers of CVE-compliant applications generate patches and updates for vulnerabilities, which can be installed on network applications.

Benefits such as stronger security and better performance result from all security devices on a network using information that complies with the CVE standard. If you're purchasing IDSs or other equipment for your organization, you should make sure the equipment supports CVE.

NOTE The CVE standard is a cooperative effort. The Mitre Corporation maintains the database of vulnerabilities at *http://cve.mitre.org*. Its work is funded by the U.S. Department of Homeland Security.

Scanning CVE Vulnerability Descriptions

You can go online to view current CVE vulnerabilities and even download the list so that you can review it at your convenience. Keep in mind, however, that as Mitre points out, the CVE list isn't a vulnerability database that can be used with an IDS. It's simply an informational tool. CVE listings are brief and just refer to listings in other databases; they don't contain IP addresses, protocol listings, or other characteristics of an event that qualify it as a signature. When you look at a CVE reference, you see the following:

- The name of the vulnerability

- A short description

- References to the event in other databases, such as BUGTRAQ

The number associated with a CVE listing tells you when the listing was made. For instance, CVE-2004-0221 tells you this listing was made in 2004 and was number 221 that year. The listing in Figure 4-2 was the 237th listing for 2004.

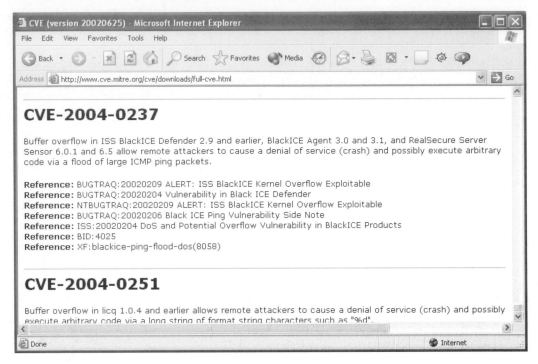

Figure 4-2   A CVE listing for a buffer overflow vulnerability that affects IDS software

The listing in Figure 4-2 indicates that vulnerabilities can affect IDS software as well as other types of applications. A **CAN** is a candidate for inclusion in the CVE list and follows the same naming format as CVE. The CVE Editorial Board must review and accept CANs before they can be added to CVE. The CVE numbering system, updated in October 2005, replaces the CAN prefix with a CVE prefix and includes a status line indicating whether the CVE name has a Candidate, Entry, or Deprecated status. Only the status line is updated when new CVE versions are released. You can view vulnerability listings at *http://cve.mitre.org/cve/downloads/* or use CVE's search engine to look for specific vulnerabilities.

Activity 4-1: Discovering Traffic Signature Vulnerabilities

Time Required: 30 minutes

Objective: Use the CVE Web site to discover traffic signature vulnerabilities.

Description: In this activity, you search the CVE Web site for traffic signature vulnerabilities so that you can determine whether your traffic analysis is susceptible to flaws.

1. In Windows XP Professional, start your Web browser and go to **http://cve.mitre.org**.

2. On the Common Vulnerabilities and Exposures (CVE) home page, click the **SEARCH** link at the upper right.

3. In the Search CVE dialog box, type **traffic signatures** in the Keyword(s) text box, and click **Search**. How many CVE entries did you find?

_____

4. Click **CVE-2000-0113** and read the information about the SyGate Remote Management program. Should all SyGate users be concerned about this candidate?

_____

_____

5. Click the browser's **Back** button to return to the page of entries, and click **CAN-2004-0593**. What significance does it have, if any, for the internal network?

_____

_____

6. If time permits, read other CVE or CAN entries. When you're finished, close your Web browser.

UNDERSTANDING SIGNATURE ANALYSIS

A **signature** is a set of characteristics—such as IP numbers and options, TCP flags, and port numbers—used to define a type of network activity. Besides TCP/IP packet attributes, a signature can also consist of a sequence of packets or other events, such as logons to a network.

Some IDSs assemble databases of "normal" traffic signatures. As traffic is detected, it's compared with the database, and any deviations from normal signatures trigger an alarm. Other IDSs refer to a database of well-known attack signatures. Any traffic that matches one of the stored attack signatures triggers an alarm. Understanding normal and suspicious traffic signatures helps you configure IDSs to work more effectively—to minimize the number of false positives (false alarms) and maximize detection of genuine attacks.

The following sections introduce you to **signature analysis**, which is examining TCP/IP communications to determine whether they are legitimate or suspicious. TCP/IP packets that are judged to be suspicious fall into several categories: bad header information, suspicious data payload, single-packet attacks, or multiple-packet attacks.

Bad Header Information

Packets are often altered by changing their header information, and packet filters usually scan for these alterations. Suspicious signatures can include malformed data that affects some or all of the following:

- Source and destination IP address
- Source and destination port number
- IP options

- IP fragmentation flags, fragmentation offset, or fragment identification
- IP protocol
- IP, TCP, or UDP checksums

A checksum is a simple error-checking procedure for determining whether a message has been damaged or tampered with while in transit. The number of data bits in a message is processed by using a mathematical formula. A numeric value (the checksum) is then calculated. The receiving computer applies the same formula to the message; if a different checksum is found, the receiving computer determines that the message has been tampered with or corrupted in some way and drops it.

Attackers can use software for generating packets set to their specifications to forge IP addresses or other types of header information. For instance, a packet can be divided into chunks and sent in a series. The initial chunk in the series can be eliminated from the set, which makes the receiving computer unable to reassemble the packets; in this way, a packet filter can be circumvented. More or fewer packets than indicated in the initial packet can be sent, which can disable a server that can't process more or fewer packets than it expected to receive.

Suspicious Data Payload

The payload (data) part of a packet is the actual data sent from an application on one computer to an application on another. Sometimes attacks can be detected by an IDS that matches a text string to a set of characters in the payload. For instance, a Trojan program called Hack'a'Tack sends a UDP packet that uses source port 31790 and destination port 31789. Originally designed as a remote administration tool for Windows 9x systems, Hack'a'Tack can be used for a variety of attacks, such as installing other programs, logging passwords, and restarting the system. The key to defending against this attack is detecting the string "A" in the payload.

NOTE   UDP ports 31791 and 31787 and TCP port 31785 are also known Hack'a'Tack ports. For more information on this Trojan program, do an Internet search. G-Lock Software (*www.glocksoft.com/trojan_list/Hack_a_Tack.htm*) has technical details about Hack'a'Tack and some helpful tools, such as the AAtools port scanner.

In another type of attack, the UNIX Sendmail program is exploited by adding codes to packet contents. Codes such as VRFY and EXPN are used to uncover account names on the Sendmail server. By adding the code EXPN DECODE in a packet's payload, attackers attempt to establish a connection with an alias called "decode." If a connection is made, attackers can use it to place malicious files on the exploited system. To defend against this type of attack, a network administrator should remove the "decode" alias line, which is installed by default with many UNIX/Linux systems in the /etc/mail/aliases file.

TIP Running an Internet search yields a wealth of tools and information, but be careful of downloading files. You might end up downloading the malicious software you're trying to avoid! Create a folder to store the files, unzip into that folder if necessary, and then run a virus scan on the folder. Any known malware signature will be recognized (provided you keep your antivirus software updated), and you can usually remove the files without harm. There's still a risk, but you can reduce it with some common sense and basic security protocols.

4

Single-Packet Attacks

A **single-packet attack** (also called an "atomic attack") can be completed by sending a single network packet from client to host. Because only a single packet is needed, a connection doesn't need to be established between the two computers. Many changes to IP option settings can cause a server to freeze up because it doesn't know how to handle these packets. IP option settings are shown in Table 4-1.

Table 4-1 IP option settings

Option number	Option name
0	End of Options
1	No Operation
2	Security
3	Loose Source and Record Routing
4	Internet Timestamp
7	Record Return Route
8	Option has been deprecated
9	Strict Source and Record Routing

As an example of IP options processing, suppose an Internet Control Message Protocol (ICMP) Echo Request (or "ping") packet is sent from a host to a server with Option 7 set. The Echo Reply response from the server might spell out the route the request takes to return from the server, thus revealing the IP addresses of hosts or routers on the network that the attacker can target. Option 4 can be used with Option 7 to record the time the Echo Reply packet spends between "hops" on the network. (A **hop** is the movement of a packet from one point on the network to another.) This information is valuable to attackers because it indicates how many routers are on the network.

Multiple-Packet Attacks

In contrast to single-packet attacks, **multiple-packet attacks** (also called "composite attacks") require a series of packets to launch an attack. These attacks are especially difficult to detect. They require a system, such as Cisco Secure IDS, to have multiple attack signatures on hand for reference. In addition, the sensor needs to maintain state information about a connection after it has been established, and it needs to keep that state information on hand for the entire length of an attack.

Denial-of-service (DoS) attacks are obvious examples of multiple-packet attacks. A type of DoS attack called an ICMP flood occurs when multiple ICMP packets are sent to a single host on a network. The result of this flood is that the server is so busy responding to the ICMP requests that other traffic can't be processed.

Components of a Packet Capture

A **packet sniffer** is software or hardware that monitors traffic going into or out of a network device. A packet sniffer captures information about each TCP/IP packet it detects. You can use one to study packets and identify characteristic features that tell you what type of connection is under way and whether the transmission is legitimate or suspicious.

Capturing packets and studying them can help you better understand what makes up a signature. Figure 4-3, for instance, shows a packet sent from one computer to another as part of a simple Echo Request.

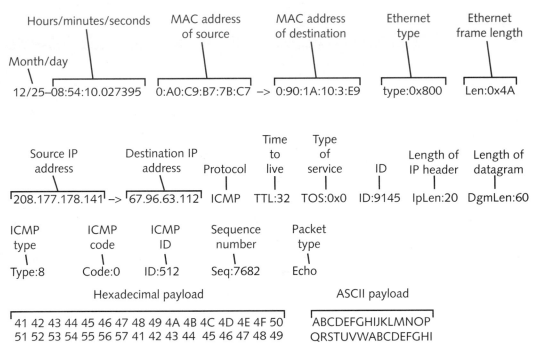

Figure 4-3 A single ICMP Echo Request packet capture

The lines of the packet capture have been separated so that they're easier to read and label. Normally, the lines are more crowded. The following list describes the elements in this ICMP packet:

- *Month/day*—The month and day the packet was captured; in this example, it's 12/25.

- *Hour:minute:second*—The hour, minute, and second the packet was captured. This packet-capturing software (Snort) breaks seconds down into milliseconds, as you can see in the entry 08:54:10.027395; not all software does.

- *Media Access Control (MAC) address of source computer*—The MAC address (0:A0: C9:B7:7B:C7, in this example) of the source computer identifies a hardware device on a network.

- *Media Access Control (MAC) address of destination computer*—The MAC address of the computer being "pinged" (in this case, 0:90:1A:10:3:E9).

- *Ethernet type*—The type of Ethernet used on this Internet connection. (*Note*: There are hundreds of Ethernet types. You can look up the type at *www.cavebear. com/archive/cavebear/Ethernet/type.html*.)

- *Frame length*—Ethernet transmits data in fixed-length segments called frames. This value describes the length of the frame used on this network.

- *Source IP*—The IP address of the computer making the connection request.

- *Destination IP*—The IP address of the computer being contacted.

- *Protocol*—The protocol used; in this case, it's ICMP, which is used to do IP error checking and verify that computers are present on the network.

- *Time to live (TTL)*—The **time to live (TTL)** value in this example is 32 hops. Both 32 and 128 are values commonly used by Windows systems, so this TTL value indicates that the source computer is using Windows.

- *Type of service (TOS)*—The **type of service (TOS)** is a part of the packet header used to express the packet's precedence—whether it should have low delay, whether it needs high reliability, and so on. No special precedence is being requested in this packet.

- *ID*—Every packet is assigned an identifying number when it's created. The **ID number** can be used to reassemble a packet in case it's divided into fragments. Looking at a sequence of packets to see how ID numbers increment from one to another can indicate the type of computer being used. ID numbers moving from packet to packet in an increment of one (from 9144 to 9155, for example) point to a Windows computer.

- *Length of IP header*—The IP length is set at 20 bytes, a length consistent with both Linux and Windows systems.

- *Length of datagram*—The length of the datagram (or packet) is 60 bytes, a value consistent with Windows systems. The minimum size is 21 bytes.

- *ICMP type*—ICMP has different types of messages (Echo Request, Redirect, Source Quench, and so on). Type 8 indicates an Echo Request packet.

- *ICMP code*—An 8-bit value that provides information about some types of ICMP packets.

- *ID*—The ICMP ID number (as opposed to the packet ID number) helps identify the ICMP packet so that the originating computer can make sure the response came from its original request.

- *Seq*—The ICMP sequence number identifies the ICMP packet in a sequence of packets.

- *Echo*—The type of ICMP packet being sent, based on the ICMP type number.

- *Hexadecimal payload*—The **hexadecimal payload** is the actual data the packet is transmitting, expressed in hexadecimal format.

- *ASCII payload*—The **ASCII payload** is the actual data part of the packet, given in ASCII format.

The information in a TCP packet contains elements that don't appear in an ICMP packet. The parts of a TCP packet that are different from the preceding ICMP packet are shown in Figure 4-4. The following list describes the TCP-specific elements in the packet. Some values shown in Figure 4-4 are in hexadecimal format, such as the sequence and acknowledgement numbers.

- *Source IP address:port/Destination IP address:port*—In a TCP packet, the port being used appears after the IP address, separated by a colon.

- *Protocol*—The protocol used is TCP.

- *Flags*—In the packet shown in Figure 4-4, two TCP flags, ACK and PSH, are used together. The ACK (acknowledgement) flag indicates that a connection has been established. The PSH (push) flag indicates that data is being sent from a memory buffer to the destination computer. (The information isn't being held in a buffer—it's sent immediately.)

- *4-byte sequence number*—This value gives the packet's sequence number.

- *4-byte acknowledgement number*—This number acknowledges receipt of the previous packet in the sequence.

- *Window size*—This value indicates the size of the window (buffer size) on the source computer so that the recipient can determine how many packets can be sent at one time.

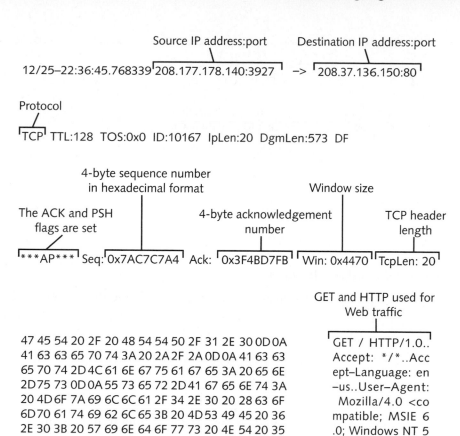

Figure 4-4   A TCP packet capture

- *TCP header length*—This value is the overall length of the TCP header plus options, if there are any.

- *GET and HTTP*—The GET method and the HTTP protocol in the ASCII payload indicate that a Web server is being contacted. The HTTP headers Accept-Language, User-Agent, and Host also appear in the ASCII payload.

The information in IDS signatures resembles the information in a packet capture. For instance, the Hack'a'Tack Trojan program mentioned previously corresponds to the signature shown in Figure 4-5. You can determine that the capture is a Trojan program because it's a recognized signature.

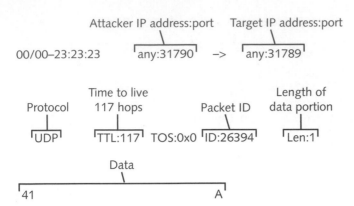

Figure 4-5   A Trojan program signature

The following list analyzes this information:

- *00/00*—A generic designation of the month and date the packet was captured.

- *23:23:23*—A generic designation of the hour, minute, and second the packet was captured. Additionally, some devices break seconds down into milliseconds.

- *attacker:31790—> target 31789*—The attacker uses port 31790 and targets the port 31789 on the destination computer.

- *UDP*—The protocol used.

- *TTL*—The TTL value represents the number of hops from one router or device to another.

- *TOS*—The type of service.

- *ID*—The ID number used by this packet; an attacker can manufacture an ID number along with other packet header information.

- *Len*—The length of the data part of the packet—only one byte, in this example.

The last line is the actual data part of the packet. In this case, the suspicious packet is indicated by the string "A" in the payload.

A variety of software tools can be used to capture packets that pass through a computer's network interface card (NIC). Later in this chapter, you learn how to use Ethereal, which is available in Windows and Linux versions. The IDS program Snort can also be used to capture packets in real time. Activity 4–2 walks you through downloading and installing Snort.

Activity 4-2: Downloading and Installing Snort

Time Required: 30 minutes

Objective: Download and install the open-source IDS program Snort.

Description: Snort is a freeware IDS program developed by Brian Caswell and Martin Roesch that's available for both Linux and Windows. In this activity, you download and set up the program in Windows XP. You use Snort later in this chapter as a packet-capturing tool.

4

NOTE

For the version of Snort used in these activities to work correctly, you must have WinPcap 3.0 installed first. If you have another version installed, uninstall it, and then install WinPcap 3.0. At the time of this writing, you can download WinPcap 3.0 from *www.winpcap.org/archive/*. Scroll down and click the 3.0 WinPcap.exe link. Follow the instructions, accepting the defaults, to finish the installation.

1. Start your Web browser and go to **www.snort.org**.

2. Click the **Get Snort** link at the left. In the Latest Production Snort Release (STABLE) list, click the **Click to view binaries** link. Click the **win32/** link and then the **old/** link. Scroll down the list of files on the page, and click **Snort-2_0_0.exe** to download a version for Windows.

NOTE

The Snort version you're downloading isn't the latest version, but it doesn't need to access a database program; in addition, it works with a GUI front-end program for testing purposes.

3. When the File Download-Security Warning dialog box opens, click **Save**. Create a folder called **Snort** at the top level of your drive (for example, C:\Snort or D:\Snort) where you can install the files and run them later. Then click **Save** to begin the download.

4. When the download is finished, double-click the icon for the file you downloaded. The InstallShield Wizard starts. If an Open File-Security Warning dialog box opens warning you that the publisher of this file couldn't be verified, click **Run** to proceed.

5. In the next window, read the license agreement, and then click **I Agree**.

6. In the Installation Options window, leave the defaults and click **Next**.

7. In the Choose Components window, accept the defaults, and then click **Next**.

8. In the Choose Install Location window, click to select the Snort folder you created in Step 3, and then click **Install**.

9. When the installation is finished, click **Close** in the Installation Complete window. If you see a dialog box warning you that WinPcap is required, click **OK** and close any open windows.

10. To test that the installation worked, click **Start**, point to **All Programs**, point to **Accessories**, and click **Command Prompt**.

11. At the command prompt, type **C:\Snort\bin\snort.exe –V** (substituting the path to Snort.exe on your computer, if necessary) and press **Enter**. If the installation was successful, you see a message with the version and Snort author's name, similar to the following:

```
-*>Snort!<*- Version 2.0.0-ODBC-MySQL-WIN32 <Build 72> By
Martin Roesch...".
```

12. Leave your system running for the next activity.

When Snort starts, it begins to capture packets as they connect with your NIC. When you stop the real-time packet capture by pressing Ctrl+C, the program displays a brief summary of what it found (see Figure 4-6).

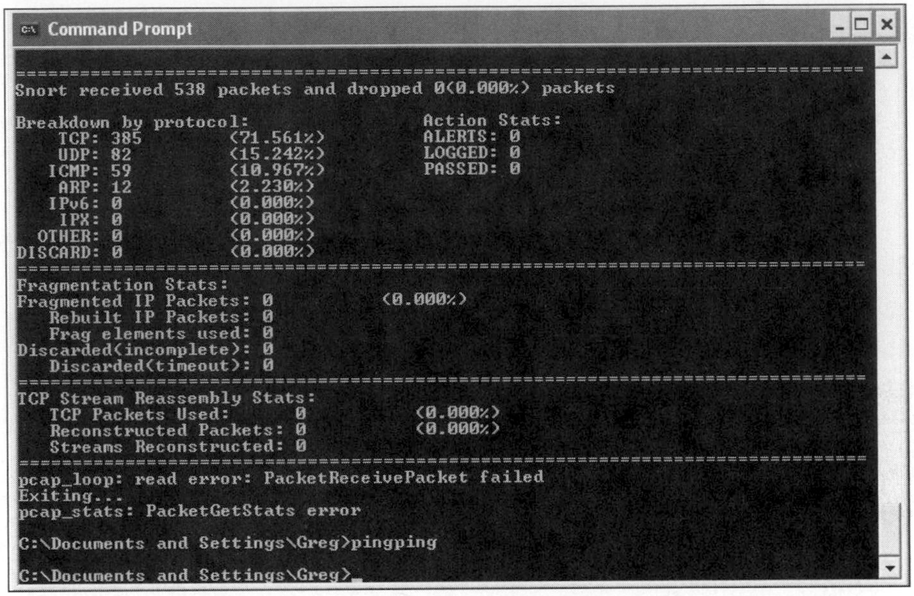

```
==================================================================
Snort received 538 packets and dropped 0(0.000%) packets

Breakdown by protocol:              Action Stats:
     TCP: 385        (71.561%)      ALERTS: 0
     UDP: 82         (15.242%)      LOGGED: 0
    ICMP: 59         (10.967%)      PASSED: 0
     ARP: 12         (2.230%)
    IPv6: 0          (0.000%)
     IPX: 0          (0.000%)
   OTHER: 0          (0.000%)
 DISCARD: 0          (0.000%)
==================================================================
Fragmentation Stats:
Fragmented IP Packets: 0            (0.000%)
   Rebuilt IP Packets: 0
    Frag elements used: 0
Discarded(incomplete): 0
   Discarded(timeout): 0
==================================================================
TCP Stream Reassembly Stats:
    TCP Packets Used:      0        (0.000%)
   Reconstructed Packets: 0         (0.000%)
   Streams Reconstructed: 0
==================================================================
pcap_loop: read error: PacketReceivePacket failed
Exiting...
pcap_stats: PacketGetStats error

C:\Documents and Settings\Greg>pingping
C:\Documents and Settings\Greg>_
```

Figure 4-6   Using Snort to capture TCP and UDP packets

One problem with using Snort as a packet-capturing tool is that unless you have logging enabled, Snort doesn't retain more than a few dozen packets at a time. The packets come across the network interface so quickly that you can easily miss them and, therefore, can't analyze them. Ethereal captures far more packets and stores them so that you can review them. The advantage of using Snort, however, is that you can set up intrusion alerts and block network traffic.

DETECTING NETWORK TRAFFIC SIGNATURES

Now that you have learned the basics of packet captures, you need to be able to determine whether traffic is normal or suspicious. You're probably familiar with the concept of **network baselining**, which is the process of determining what's normal for your network so that you can identify anomalies. The following sections explain how to tell the difference between normal traffic and suspicious activity.

Normal Traffic Signatures

To detect suspicious traffic signatures, being able to recognize normal traffic signatures is important. One aspect of normal TCP signatures that's easiest to identify is the use of TCP flags, as described in the following list:

- *SYN (synchronize) flag (0x2)*—This flag is sent from one computer to another when a connection is initiated; the two computers are attempting to synchronize a connection.

- *ACK (acknowledgement) flag (0x10)*—This flag is sent when the connection has been made.

- *PSH (push) flag (0x8)*—This flag indicates that immediate data delivery is required and to forward all the queued (stored in the buffer) data immediately to the destination.

- *URG (urgent) flag (0x20)*—This flag is used when urgent data is being sent from one computer to another.

- *RST (reset) flag (0x4)*—This flag is sent if one computer wants to stop the connection when there's a problem with it.

- *FIN (finished) flag (0x1)*—This flag lets one computer know that the other is finished when sending data.

- *Numbers 1 and 2*—These numbers are used for two reserved data bits.

The placement and use of these flags are strictly defined, and deviations from normal use mean that the communication is suspicious. For instance, the SYN flag should appear at the beginning of a connection; the FIN flag should appear only at the end. Both SYN and FIN flags in the same packet indicates suspicious network activity. However, the ACK and PUSH flags can be used together when data is sent from one computer to another.

Ping Signatures

In the previous section, a single ICMP Echo Request packet was analyzed. The sequence of packets in Figure 4-7 shows a signature of ICMP Echo Request packets captured by Snort when packets are sent that "ping" two different target computers. If you examine the first line of each echo, you can see that all three packets were sent from the same computer. Two of the requests were sent to the same machine, and the third targeted a different machine. This information is easy to determine from the MAC addresses of the sending (0:A0:C9: B7:7B:C7) and receiving computers (0:90:1A:10:3:E9 and 0:10:B5:50:33:A2).

The Echo Request packets received didn't cause a response to be sent, however. (The host computer had a firewall installed that prevented it from responding to Echo Request packets.) Figure 4-8 shows the packets exchanged when a computer *does* respond success-fully to an Echo Request with Echo Reply packets. Notice that both computers exchanging packets have a unique set of sequence numbers.

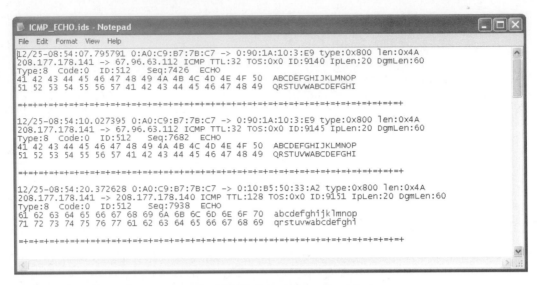

Figure 4-7   Normal signatures for ICMP Echo Request packets

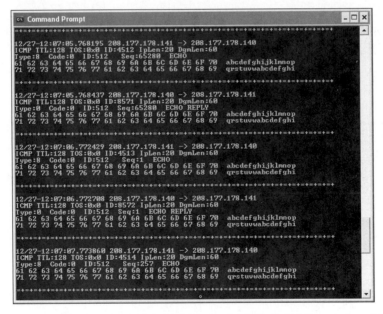

Figure 4-8   A successful exchange of ICMP Echo Request and Echo Reply packets

An analysis of the first four packets in Figure 4–8 shows the following:

1. The first packet shows the computer at IP address 208.177.178.141 sending an Echo Request packet (ICMP type 8) to 208.177.178.140 with the sequence number 4512 (shown in the figure as ID: 4512).

2. The second packet shows the computer at IP address 208.177.178.140 responding with an Echo Reply packet (ICMP type 0) with sequence number 8571.

3. The third packet shows the computer at IP address 208.177.178.141 responding with another Echo Request packet with sequence number 4513—only one number higher than the previous packet it sent.

4. The fourth packet shows the computer at IP address 208.177.178.140 responding with another Echo Reply packet with sequence number 8572.

You can also tell from examining the packets that two Windows computers are involved, as indicated by the TTL of 128, the IP length (IpLen) of 20, and the datagram length (DgmLen) of 60. A TTL of 64 and a datagram length of 84 are part of a Linux computer's signature. In addition, ICMP Echo Request packets start with a sequence number of 0 on a Linux computer.

TIP   In Windows, the ASCII payload section of an ICMP packet consists of a sequence of alphabetic characters; in Linux, the data payload is a string of characters followed by 0 through 9 (for example, !"#$%&'()*+,-./ 0123456789).

ACTIVITY

Activity 4-3: Using Snort to Capture ICMP Packets

Time Required: 15 minutes

Objective: Use Snort to capture ICMP packets for examination.

Description: For this activity, you need two computers connected to each other through a network or on the Internet. One student should sit at one computer with Snort installed (as described in Activity 4-2) to capture packets. The other should sit at the second computer to send Echo Request packets. Both computers can use Linux or Windows XP. Make sure no firewall rules are set up that block ICMP traffic (such as the ICMP rules applied by Windows XP's built-in Windows Firewall). Remember that command-line switches are case sensitive.

1. Both students should open a command prompt window. (In Linux, click the **Red Hat** icon, click **System Tools**, and click **Terminal**.)

2. Both students should type **ipconfig** (**ifconfig** in Linux) at the command prompt and press **Enter**.

3. Each student should write down the IP address of his or her computer and exchange it with the other student.

4. Student 1 (at the computer with Snort installed) should locate the Snort.exe program and write down the path to it. (These steps use C:\Snort\bin\snort.exe as an example.)

5. At the command prompt, Student 1 should type **C:\Snort\bin\snort.exe –v –d** (substituting his or her path to Snort.exe, if necessary) and press **Enter**. (*Note*: Be sure to leave a blank space before each hyphen in the command.)

6. Student 2 should make sure Student 1 is ready, and then type **ping** *IPaddressofStudent1'scomputer* and press **Enter**.

7. When packets begin to appear in the command prompt window, Student 1 should press **Ctrl+C** quickly to stop them. Ideally, Student 1 should stop the packet capture after only a few packets have crossed the NIC so that they can be reviewed from the beginning. (*Note*: If packet captures don't appear, try removing and reinstalling WinPcap.)

8. If necessary, repeat Steps 6 and 7 to stop the packet capture near the beginning of the communication. What are the sequence numbers of the packets the two computers exchanged?

_____

9. Close the command prompt window, and leave your system running for the next activity.

FTP Signatures

If your organization operates a public FTP server, you should review the signatures of packets that attempt to access that server. You need to determine whether the computer making the connection attempt is allowed to access the server in accordance with your packet-filtering rules.

The signature of a normal connection between a client and an FTP server includes a three-way handshake. Three separate packets contain different TCP flags that enable you to keep track of the connection, as shown in Figure 4-9.

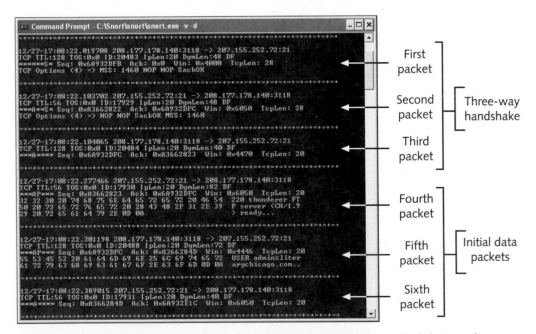

Figure 4-9   An FTP session's three-way handshake followed by initial data exchange packets

The packets shown in Figure 4-9 can be analyzed as follows:

1. In the first packet, the computer at IP address 208.177.178.140, port 3118 attempts to connect to the FTP server at 207.155.252.72, port 21. The third line shows that the packet has the SYN flag (S) set because a synchronization request is being made to the remote server. In the fourth line, the TCP option code 4 (maximum segment size, MSS) is set at 1460 bytes. This code tells the FTP server the maximum IP packet size it can handle without fragmenting the packet.

2. In the second packet, the FTP server responds to the client by sending a packet with the ACK flag (A) as well as the SYN flag (S) set.

3. In the third packet, the client responds with a packet that has the ACK flag (A) set.

4. In the fourth packet, the ACK and PSH (A and P) flags are set, and the client and server identify one another. In the packet's ASCII payload section, the server identifies itself as ready.

5. In the fifth packet, the user's logon name appears in clear text in the ASCII payload section.

6. In the sixth packet, the FTP server responds with the ACK flag (A), and the connection is established.

The MSS is specified early in the handshake between the client and server—specifically, as part of the SYN or SYN/ACK packets that are part of the three-way handshake. The MSS option in an ACK or ACK/PSH packet is a warning sign of a falsified packet. The NOP (no operation) TCP option provides several bytes worth of padding (unused space) around other options. A Selective Acknowledgement OK (SackOK) message at the end of line 4 means that **selective acknowledgements** (acknowledgements that certain packets in a sequence have been received) are permitted during this connection.

When data is actually exchanged between client and FTP server, the original ports aren't used. In this case, the server port 21 and client port 3118 are ports that initiate a **control connection** (an initial FTP connection). The data is transferred over a new connection using server port 20 and a client port, such as 5005, as shown in Figure 4-10.

Figure 4-10   An FTP data connection

The options in FTP handshake packets are the same, but they're presented in a different order. That's not, however, an indication of a malformed packet; TCP options can be presented in any order.

NOTE

ACTIVITY

Activity 4-4: Analyzing an Echo Request

Time Required: 15 minutes

Objective: Analyze captured Echo Request packets to determine information about the sending computer.

Description: Your firewall regularly receives a series of Echo Request packets from a computer at 67.118.23.141. You capture the packets with a packet-sniffing tool and notice the following information: DgmLen 84, ID 0, TTL 64. Answer the following questions:

1. What kind of computer is being used to send Echo Requests to your network?

   _____

   _____

2. What other criteria could you use to identify the computer being used?

   _____

   _____

   _____

   _____

Web Signatures

Most of the signatures you see in log files you analyze are Web related, which means they consist of packets sent back and forth from a Web browser to a Web server as a connection is made. A signature of a normal handshake between two Web browsers consists of a sequence of packets distinguished by their TCP flags. As mentioned, normal TCP traffic makes use of several TCP flags to control the connection. Being aware of these flags and where they're used can help you determine whether a signature is normal or part of a possible intrusion attempt.

In Figure 4-11, you see four packets that represent part of the handshake between the Web browser at IP address 208.177.178.140 using port 3927 and the Web server at 208.37.136. 150 using HTTP port 80.

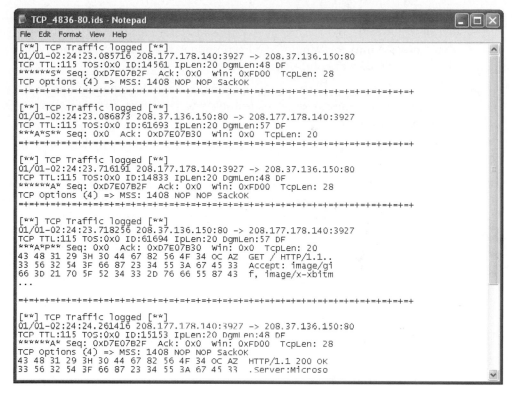

```
TCP_4836-80.ids - Notepad
File  Edit  Format  View  Help
[**] TCP Traffic logged [**]
01/01-02:24:23.085716 208.177.178.140:3927 -> 208.37.136.150:80
TCP TTL:115 TOS:0x0 ID:14561 IpLen:20 DgmLen:48 DF
*******S* Seq: 0xD7E07B2F  Ack: 0x0  Win: 0xFD00  TcpLen: 28
TCP Options (4) => MSS: 1408 NOP NOP SackOK
=+=+=+=+=+=+=+=+=+=+=+=+=+=+=+=+=+=+=+=+=+=+=+=+=+=+=+=+=+=+=+=+

[**] TCP Traffic logged [**]
01/01-02:24:23.086873 208.37.136.150:80 -> 208.177.178.140:3927
TCP TTL:115 TOS:0x0 ID:61693 IpLen:20 DgmLen:57 DF
***A*S** Seq: 0x0  Ack: 0xD7E07B30  Win: 0x0  TcpLen: 20
=+=+=+=+=+=+=+=+=+=+=+=+=+=+=+=+=+=+=+=+=+=+=+=+=+=+=+=+=+=+=+=+

[**] TCP Traffic logged [**]
01/01-02:24:23.716191 208.177.178.140:3927 -> 208.37.136.150:80
TCP TTL:115 TOS:0x0 ID:14833 IpLen:20 DgmLen:48 DF
*******A* Seq: 0xD7E07B2F  Ack: 0x0  Win: 0xFD00  TcpLen: 28
TCP Options (4) => MSS: 1408 NOP NOP SackOK
=+=+=+=+=+=+=+=+=+=+=+=+=+=+=+=+=+=+=+=+=+=+=+=+=+=+=+=+=+=+=+=+

[**] TCP Traffic logged [**]
01/01-02:24:23.718256 208.37.136.150:80 -> 208.177.178.140:3927
TCP TTL:115 TOS:0x0 ID:61694 IpLen:20 DgmLen:57 DF
***A*P** Seq: 0x0  Ack: 0xD7E07B30  Win: 0x0  TcpLen: 20
43 48 31 29 3H 30 44 67 82 56 4F 34 0C AZ   GET / HTTP/1.1..
33 56 32 54 3F 66 87 23 34 55 3A 67 45 33   Accept: image/gi
66 3D 21 70 5F 52 34 33 2D 76 66 55 87 43   f, image/x-xbitm
...

=+=+=+=+=+=+=+=+=+=+=+=+=+=+=+=+=+=+=+=+=+=+=+=+=+=+=+=+=+=+=+=+

[**] TCP Traffic logged [**]
01/01-02:24:24.261416 208.177.178.140:3927 -> 208.37.136.150:80
TCP TTL:115 TOS:0x0 ID:15153 IpLen:20 DgmLen:48 DF
*******A* Seq: 0xD7E07B2F  Ack: 0x0  Win: 0xFD00  TcpLen: 28
TCP Options (4) => MSS: 1408 NOP NOP SackOK
43 48 31 29 3H 30 44 67 82 56 4F 34 0C AZ   HTTP/1.1 200 OK
33 56 32 54 3F 66 87 23 34 55 3A 67 45 33   .Server:Microso
```

Figure 4-11   A normal exchange of packets between a Web browser and a Web server

The packets you see in Figure 4-11 can be analyzed as follows:

1. The first packet has the SYN flag set (the S in the third line), as the browser asks to synchronize a session with the server.

2. The second packet has the ACK flag set, as the server acknowledges the connection with the browser. In addition, the SYN flag is sent back to the browser as the server seeks to synchronize the connection with the browser.

3. In the third packet, the ACK flag is exchanged to acknowledge that a connection has been made.

4. In the fourth packet, the PSH flag is used with the ACK flag to indicate that data is going to be sent (or pushed) from memory storage areas called buffers.

Activity 4-5: Capturing a Web Site Handshake

Time Required: 20 minutes

Objective: Use Snort to capture a Web site connection handshake for examination.

Description: Capturing the sequence of a Web site connection with Snort enables you to inspect HTTP headers in each packet and the TCP flags exchanged during the handshake. You can use a Linux or Windows XP computer; this activity assumes you have Snort installed and an Internet connection.

1. Open a command prompt or terminal window. At the command prompt, type **C:\Snort\bin\snort.exe −v −d** (substituting your path to Snort.exe, if necessary) and press **Enter**.

2. When you see a message stating that Snort is initializing, start your Web browser and go to **www.course.com**.

3. Quickly switch back to the command prompt window and press **Ctrl+C** to stop the packets from being captured. Snort should display a report of the packets captured so far. Besides TCP packets, what sorts of packets were captured?

   _____

   _____

4. Scroll to the top of the packets shown in the command prompt window, and look for the SYN, SYN/ACK, ACK three-way handshake. (If you don't see it, you might need to connect to a different Web site and repeat Steps 2 and 3.)

5. Close any open windows, and leave your system running for the next activity.

Now that you know something about capturing normal traffic, you can look at analyzing abnormal signatures.

Abnormal Traffic Signatures

As IDSs become more sophisticated, the techniques attackers use to circumvent them have multiplied and become more complex. Illegal combinations of TCP flags and private IP addresses in packets are fairly easy to identify as abnormal compared with attacks that work by using a range of packets. Abnormal or suspicious traffic signatures can fall into these categories:

- *Informational*—This traffic might not be malicious but could be used to verify whether an attack has been successful. Examples include ICMP Echo Request packets or TCP packets sent to a specific port on a system.

- *Reconnaissance*—This traffic could represent an attacker's attempt to gain information about a network as a prelude to an attack. Examples include ping sweeps and port scans.

- *Unauthorized access*—This traffic might be caused by someone who has gained unauthorized access to a system and is attempting to retrieve data from it. Examples include the Back Orifice attack and the Internet Information Services (IIS) Unicode attack.

- *Denial of service*—This traffic might be part of an attempt to slow or halt all connections on a network device, such as a Web server or mail server. DoS examples include the ping of death and Trinoo attacks.

Some common examples of suspicious traffic—ping sweeps, port scans, random backdoor scans, and Trojan scans—are described in the following sections along with their signatures.

NOTE   If you need to review specific attacks or attack methods, such as Back Orifice, IIS Unicode, ping sweeps, port scans, and ping of death attacks, use an Internet search engine. Reviewing these attacks is a good idea because variations sometimes surface.

Ping Sweeps

To gain access to specific resources on an internal network, an attacker needs to determine the location of a host. One method is to conduct a ping sweep (also called an ICMP sweep) to send a series of ICMP Echo Request packets in a range of IP addresses. Usually, the messages come in quick succession (multiple packets can be detected in a second), indicating an automated tool being used. An example of a ping sweep is shown in Figure 4-12. Be sure to examine the ping times in the first line; this sweep took place in about 14 seconds.

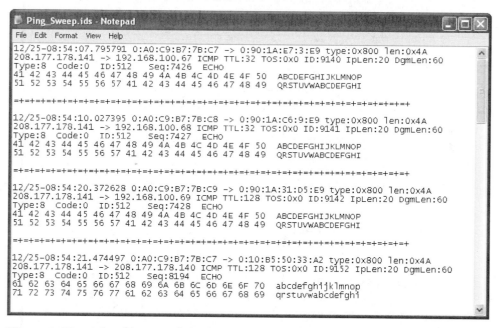

Figure 4-12   A log file record displaying the signature of an automated ping sweep

The ping sweep alone doesn't cause harm to computers on your network. The prudent response is to make note of the IP address in the ping sweep to track further activity. An IDS could be configured to transmit an alarm if that IP address attempts to connect to a specific host on the network, for instance.

Port Scans

If an attacker can determine any legitimate IP addresses on an internal network, the next step is to target one of those addresses and do a **port scan**—an attempt to connect to a computer's ports to see whether any are active and listening. Typically, the signature of a port scan includes a SYN packet sent to each port on an IP address, one after another, as shown in Figure 4-13.

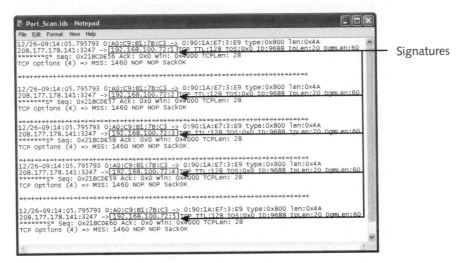

Figure 4-13   A log file record displaying the signatures of a port scan

In the example in Figure 4-13, the source port (3247) doesn't change from packet to packet. This indicates that the attacker isn't expecting the target computer to establish a full three-way connection but wants to find out whether the IP address is being used. In another type of port scan, the source *and* destination ports change with each packet because a full three-way connection is expected.

Random Backdoor Scans

As you learned in Chapter 3, a backdoor is an undocumented or unauthorized hidden opening (such as a port) through which a computer, program, or other resource can be accessed. One type of port scan probes a computer to see if any ports are open and listening that are used by well-known Trojan programs. Some Trojan programs are so well known that the backdoor ports on which they operate can be probed one after another to see whether those programs are already present. For example, a random backdoor scan might target certain ports and seek to exploit the programs listed in Table 4-2.

Table 4-2   Well-known Trojan programs and ports

Trojan program name	Port	Description
SubSeven	1243	Disables antivirus or firewall protection
NetBus	1245	Gives the Trojan program author remote access to the user's computer
Back Door	1999	Gives the Trojan program author remote access to the user's computer
KeyLogger	12223	Copies user keystrokes and sends information about the user's OS and passwords back to the Trojan program's sender
Whack-a-mole	12361	Gives the Trojan program author remote access to the user's computer
Back Orifice	31337, 31338	Records keystrokes and sends passwords back to the Trojan program's sender; can also be used to run programs on a computer

A random **Trojan scan** involves an attacker searching for any Trojan programs on a target computer to save the effort of installing these programs. Each SYN packet that's sent attempts to contact a different port used by a Trojan, such as the sequence of packets shown in Figure 4-14. (The ports being probed are indicated in the figure.) If you see this type of scan in your log files, you need to take action quickly to block the source IP address because it's likely that specific attacks will take place in the near future.

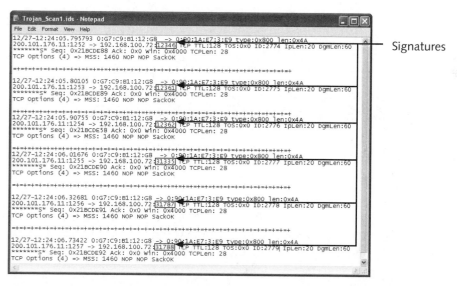

Signatures

Figure 4-14   A log file record showing the signatures of a backdoor scan

NOTE

For more information on blocking specific IP addresses, subnets, or address ranges with firewalls, see *Guide to Tactical Perimeter Defense: Becoming a Security Network Specialist* (Course Technology, 2008, ISBN 1428356304).

Specific Trojan Scans

Port scans can be performed in several ways. In a **vanilla scan**, all ports from 0 to 65535 are probed one after another. In another type called a **strobe scan**, an attacker scans only ports commonly used by specific programs in an attempt to see whether a certain program is present and can be used.

One common type of strobe scan searches IP addresses on a network for a specific Trojan program. If attackers can find a Trojan program that has circumvented the firewall and IDS and is already operating, they can save the time and effort of installing a new Trojan program. For instance, in Figure 4-15, a series of IP addresses is being scanned on port 31337. This port is used by the notorious Back Orifice Trojan program as well as other Trojans, such as ADM worm, Back Fire, and BlitzNet.

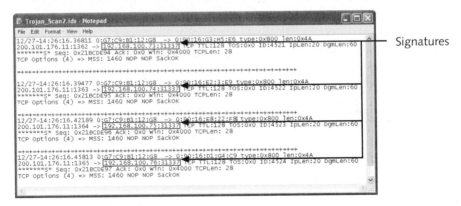

Figure 4-15   A log file record indicating a scan for the Back Orifice Trojan program

The type of scan shown in Figure 4-15 isn't necessarily dangerous, but it's of some concern because it's so specific. Attackers usually start with a general scan of IP addresses and get more specific as they look for ports, backdoors, or applications. If attackers have an indication from another method (such as an exchange of e-mails) that Back Orifice might be on the network, they might locate Back Orifice and launch an attack using it. You should immediately scan all computers on your network for viruses and Trojans and make sure your antivirus, firewall, and IDS Trojan signatures are up to date.

Antivirus software and many IDSs look for known virus and attack signatures. In addition, they require up-to-date signature files to operate at peak efficiency.

Another specific Trojan scan might target port 12345, which is used by the NetBus Trojan program. Like port 31337, it's familiar to security professionals because it appears so often in security alerts and lists of frequently used Trojan ports.

Nmap Scans

Network Mapper (Nmap) is a popular software tool for scanning networks, and you should be able to recognize the common types of scans it enables attackers to perform. With Nmap, attackers can send packets that circumvent the normal three-way handshakes two computers use to establish a connection or send packets for which an IDS might not be configured to send an alarm. The IDS might see a combination of TCP flags that it doesn't recognize, and because no rule exists for the combination, an alarm might not be triggered. Examples of Nmap scans include the following:

- *SYN scans*—The attacker sends a progression of packets with only the SYN flag set. The targeted computer responds with packets that have the ACK flag set, but the originating computer simply keeps sending SYN packets.

- *FIN scans*—The attacker sends only packets with the FIN flag set; a SYN flag is never sent.

- *ACK scans*—The attacker sends only packets with the ACK flag set; a SYN or FIN flag is never sent.

- *Null scans*—The attacker sends a sequence of packets that have no flags set. An IDS is likely to ignore packets with no flags set.

In each type of scan, a three-way handshake can never be established with the computer attempting to make a connection. The attacker is probably attempting to determine whether an application is active on a certain port: Each packet has an identical source port number and a seq (sequence) number that's set to zero and never changes, in violation of the standard rules of TCP communication. Figure 4-16 shows a FIN scan with the seq numbers, source port numbers, and F (FIN) flags enclosed in boxes to indicate the elements you should look for in this Nmap signature. In this example, the constant source port numbers, seq numbers, and F flag in every packet point to the use of Nmap in crafting these packets.

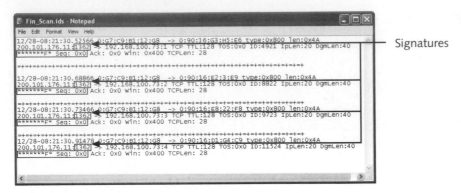

Figure 4-16   The signatures of a FIN scan conducted with Nmap

Activity 4-6: Identifying an Nmap Scan

Time Required: 10 minutes

Objective: Analyze a situation to identify the characteristics of an Nmap port scan.

Description: Normally, you review IDS logs for intrusion attempts by setting your IDS to log connection attempts that were blocked or for which an alarm was issued. By mistake, someone on your IT staff sets the IDS to log connection attempts that were allowed, too, so the log file you need to review is huge. To reduce the file size, you sort out traffic from computers on your network and from the DNS server. When you review the remaining entries, you notice a series of hundreds of packets that were sent in sequence and have no flags set. The IDS didn't detect these packets because apparently they're of no value in making a network connection. Answer the following questions:

1. What clues would you look for in these packets to determine whether they're evidence that an attacker is attempting to gain information about open ports on your network?

    _____

    _____

2. What should you do if you determine that this attempt has been made?

    _____

    _____

    _____

    _____

You can learn more about using Nmap to scan a network at *http://insecure. org/nmap*.

4

Understanding Packet-Capturing Techniques

Packet analysis, protocol analysis, and traffic analysis are basically the same tasks. Network administrators use **packet capture and analysis** to monitor network traffic and performance, identify and locate communication problems, and look for excessive traffic and security violations. Attackers can also analyze traffic but for different reasons. They are generally looking for passwords, reading confidential information, or gathering network data for later use.

Using Packet-Capturing Tools

Protocol analyzers were designed for packet decoding and network diagnosis to help network administrators troubleshoot network problems. With real-time packet capture and accurate data analysis, administrators can monitor bandwidth use and detect attacks when they begin. Attackers can also use protocol analyzers (sometimes called packet-sniffing tools) to gain valuable information about your network, including passwords.

The risk of attackers using packet sniffing can be reduced in a number of ways. You can deploy a switched infrastructure so that the only packets attackers can sniff are limited to the switch port or virtual LAN (VLAN) they're connected to. Use encryption to prevent intruders from being able to read captured packets. Encrypt sensitive data, and make sure authentication credentials aren't sent in cleartext unless the infrastructure can't support sending encrypted data over the network. Install antisniffing software or hardware if the risk is high or your data is extremely sensitive. In a high-security environment, segregate highly sensitive data from all external access and configure tight controls on internal access. Remember to pay attention to physical security, too. Install software that allows administrative disabling of promiscuous mode for NICs. Make sure attackers can't gain access to workstations, cabling, or connectivity devices, such as switches, hubs, and routers.

Finally, be aware of what's normal for your system and traffic patterns so that you can recognize abnormal behaviors. Capture and examine traffic traveling across your network at different times to get a good baseline for your network. You should also know what an abnormal packet looks like. For example, if a SYN flood is launched on your network, you must be able to recognize the pattern and read the packets. Several open-source, freeware, and commercial packet-capturing tools are available. The key is to pick one and learn it well instead of jumping around from one program to another. The differences in tools are mainly in the number of protocols they support and the user interface. Some popular products are Ethereal, EtherPeek, Network Associates SnifferPro, and Windows Network Monitor. Your goal is to learn how to read packets to identify their type, source, and purpose; the next section focuses on Ethereal because it's free and gives you practice in capturing and analyzing packets.

Ethereal

Ethereal is open source, so you can download it free and run it on several different platforms. Ethereal can capture data in real time as well as read from a capture file. It can even read capture files from SnifferPro, EtherPeek, Tcpdump, Windows Network Monitor, and more. In the following activity, you download and install Ethereal.

ACTIVITY

Activity 4-7: Downloading and Installing a Packet Capture and Analysis Tool

Time Required: 30 minutes

Objective: Download and install Ethereal, an open-source packet capture tool.

Description: You can learn a lot from analyzing packets traveling across your network, but you need specialized tools to capture and analyze packets. In this activity, you download and install Ethereal. If you didn't do so in Activity 4-3, you need to download and install WinPcap 3.0 to run Ethereal.

1. Start your Web browser and go to **www.ethereal.com**.

2. Click **Download** to go to the Ethereal: Download page.

3. Click the **Windows: Download Now** link.

4. When the File Download dialog box opens, click **Open** or **Run**. If you see a security warning about an unknown publisher, click **Open** or **Run** again. The file is downloaded to a temporary folder on your computer, and the Ethereal setup wizard starts automatically. Click **Next** to begin the installation.

5. In the Ethereal Setup: License Agreement window, click **I Agree**.

6. In the Choose Components window (see Figure 4-17), accept the defaults, and then click **Next**.

7. In the Select Additional Tasks window, accept the defaults and click **Next**.

8. In the Choose Install Location window, click **Browse**, navigate to and click the folder where you want to install the software, and then click **Next**.

9. In the Install WinPcap? window, click to clear the **Install WinPcap 3.1** check box (see Figure 4-18), and then click the **Install** button.

10. The Installing window displays messages about the installation progress. When you see the "Completed" message, click **Next**, and then click **Finish**.

11. Exit your Web browser, and leave your system running for the next activity.

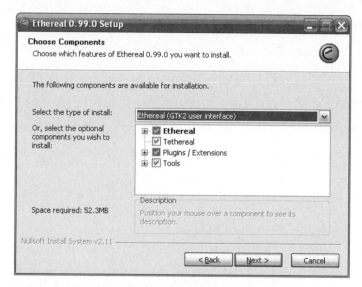

Figure 4-17   The Choose Components window

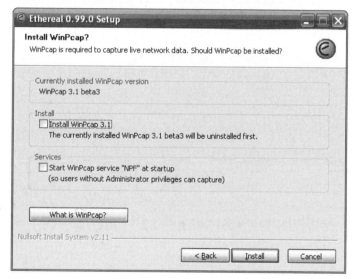

Figure 4-18   The Install WinPcap? window

Analyzing Captured Packets

Now that you have a tool to capture packets, you're ready to learn how to read them. The next activity walks you through capturing packets for analysis.

ACTIVITY

Activity 4-8: Using Ethereal to Capture and Analyze Packets

Time Required: 30 minutes

Objective: Use Ethereal to capture and analyze packets.

Description: In this activity, you use Ethereal to capture packets so that you can learn how to identify an attack in progress, pinpoint where the attack is coming from, and determine what type of attack it is. You might also need to analyze packets to identify a malfunctioning NIC or another source of traffic abnormalities.

1. Click **Start**, point to **All Programs**, point to **Ethereal**, and click **Ethereal**. The Ethereal Network Analyzer window opens.

2. Click **Capture**, **Options** from the Ethereal menu. In the Ethereal: Capture Options dialog box (see Figure 4-19), click the **Interface** list arrow, and click your NIC in the drop-down list. Click **Start** to begin capturing packets.

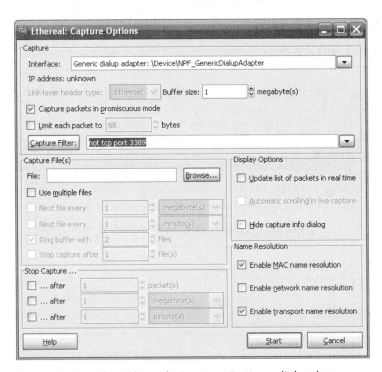

Figure 4-19   The Ethereal: Capture Options dialog box

3. The Ethereal: Capture dialog box opens with a series of 0% readings, reporting that no data has been captured yet (see Figure 4-20).

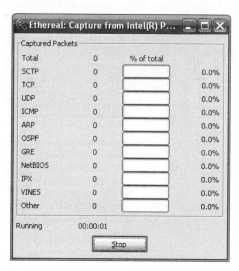

Figure 4-20   Viewing results of a packet capture

4. Open a command prompt window, type **ping *IPaddress*** (substituting the IP address of your partner or another lab computer), and press **Enter**.

5. Click **Stop** at the bottom of the Ethereal: Capture dialog box. You should see information about packets that have passed through your network gateway in the main Ethereal window. One of the first lines contains information about your ping request. Write down what protocol is listed, and explain what the abbreviations mean. (*Hint*: Click the IP address you just sent the ping request to and look at the middle section of the Ethereal window, where detailed information about the packet is displayed.)

_____

_____

_____

6. Type **exit** and press **Enter** to close the command prompt window.

7. Click **File**, **Quit** from the Ethereal menu, and then click **Continue without saving** to close the Ethereal window and return to the Windows desktop. Leave your system running for the projects at the end of the chapter.

For additional practice in using Ethereal, visit the sites listed in Appendix B.

NOTE

IDENTIFYING SUSPICIOUS EVENTS

You've learned about well-known attack signatures you might encounter when inspecting IDS log files. Unfortunately, attackers often avoid launching well-known attacks. Instead, they use more subtle means to try to gain unauthorized access to computers in your network. For instance, instead of the sequence of FIN packets described previously, you might see only a single FIN packet sent to a port on a computer. Other "orphaned" packets might follow, but only after an interval during which several legitimate packets have passed through. The interval acts as a distraction during which stages of the attack are separated, so an administrator might not realize that they're part of the same attack.

These attacks can be extremely difficult to detect by reviewing log files manually. It's your responsibility to respond to alarms and determine what they mean, however, so you must examine logs regularly. Log files can fill up quickly with so many entries that they are overwhelming to review, and you might miss important entries. Fortunately, there are ways around the tedious chore of poring through thousands of log entries looking for known attack signatures or other abnormal signatures. Instead, you need to depend on an extensive database of signatures that includes these events.

This section describes events and characteristics of network communication that you need to identify as suspicious events after your IDS has responded to them by transmitting an alarm. The discussion includes packet header discrepancies, advanced IDS attacks, and Remote Procedure Calls (RPC) abuses.

CAUTION

IDS alarms for the suspicious events described in this section might indicate that your packet filter isn't working effectively (because it has let suspicious packets through to reach the IDS). As a result, the packet filter's rule base needs to be revised. You can also fine-tune how an IDS responds to events. Advanced IDS configuration is covered in *Guide to Tactical Perimeter Defense: Becoming a Security Network Specialist* (Course Technology, 2008, ISBN 1428356304).

Packet Header Discrepancies

Discrepancies you see in TCP, IP, ICMP, or UDP packet headers can provide warning signs that an attacker has crafted the packet (purposely manufactured or altered it). However, instead of seeing these discrepancies on a well-defined and lengthy succession of packets, you might see only a single packet with a falsified IP address, falsified port number, illegal TCP flags, TCP or IP options, or fragmentation abuses.

Falsified IP Address

Your IDS might send alarms for violations of IP header settings, as specified in RFC 791, "Internet Protocol." For example, an IP address shouldn't appear in one of the three reserved ranges (10.0.0.0 to 10.255.255.255, 172.16.0.0 to 172.31.255.255, and 192.168.0.0 to 192.168.255.255). Using addresses in the reserved ranges is limited to private networks. If you do see one in a packet, the reason might be that a router or other device has been misconfigured or is malfunctioning. On the other hand, the packet might show one of these private addresses because an attacker has used **IP spoofing** (inserted a false address into the IP header to make the packet more difficult to trace back to its source).

> For more information on the correct use of private IP addresses, see RFC 1918, "Address Allocation for Private Internets," at *www.faqs.org/rfcs/ rfc1918.html*.

TIP

A land attack is an example of a falsified IP address used to cause a server to malfunction. It occurs when an IP packet is detected that has an invalid IP address setting in which the source and destination IP/port addresses are the same. Another attack that uses an invalid IP address, the localhost source spoof, should trigger an alarm if the local host source address of 127.x.x.x occurs in a packet.

Falsified Port Number or Protocol

Protocol numbers can also be altered to elude an IDS. TCP and UDP headers should never have the source or destination port set to 0 because this number is reserved by the Internet Assigned Numbers Authority (IANA). IANA assigns protocol numbers in addition to port numbers. The Protocol field (in IPv4; in IPv6, the field is Next Header) is an 8-bit field for specifying the Transport-layer protocol, such as ICMP (#1), TCP (#6), or UDP (#17). Currently, the protocol number can't be set higher than 137. The numbers 138 to 252 are unassigned, 253 and 254 are used for experimentation and testing, and 255 is reserved. Using undefined protocol numbers might indicate an attacker's attempt to establish a proprietary communication channel, which is a channel that's known to and used only by that person.

Illegal TCP Flags

As you learned in "Normal Traffic Signatures" earlier in this chapter, the TCP flags SYN and ACK are exchanged to establish a connection between computers. The PSH flag is used when data is being sent, and the FIN flag is used when a connection is finished. Other normal TCP flag rules include the following:

- Every packet in a connection should have the ACK bit set, except for the initial SYN packet and possibly an RST packet used to terminate a connection.

- Packets during the "conversation" portion of the connection (after the three-way handshake but before the teardown or termination) contain only an ACK flag by default. They can also contain PSH and URG flags.

- FIN/ACK and ACK are used during normal teardown of an existing connection. PSH, FIN, and ACK might also be seen near the end of a connection.

- RST or RST/ACK can be used to terminate a connection immediately.

One way to detect an abnormal packet signature is to look at the TCP flags for violations of normal use. A packet with the SYN and FIN flags set shouldn't exist in normal traffic; however, an attacker might set both flags to cause the destination computer to crash or freeze because it doesn't know how to respond. After the server is disabled, the attacker can then attack a computer on the internal network with an IP address that has been detected earlier through network scans.

The following list summarizes signatures of malformed packets that misuse the SYN and FIN flags:

- SYN/FIN is probably the best-known illegal combination. Because SYN is used to start a connection and FIN is used to end a connection, it doesn't make sense to include both flags in a packet. Many scanning tools use SYN/FIN packets because in the past, some IDSs weren't configured to recognize or block them. However, most IDSs are configured to catch illegal combinations now. It's safe to assume that any SYN/FIN packets are created by attackers.

- SYN/FIN/PSH, SYN/FIN/RST, SYN/FIN/RST/PSH, and other variations on SYN/FIN are sometimes called XMAS attacks. Attackers who know that IDSs are looking for packets with just the SYN and FIN bits set sometimes use these SYN/FIN variations.

- Packets should never contain a FIN flag by itself. FIN packets are often used for port scans, network mapping, and other stealth activities.

- A SYN-only packet, which should occur only when a new connection is being initiated, shouldn't contain any data.

You might also encounter **null packets**—TCP packets with no flags set, which could cause a server to crash. A packet with no flags set violates TCP rules.

TCP or IP Options

TCP options in a packet can alert you to intrusion attempts and even enable you to identify the OS being used. For instance, only one MSS or window option should appear in a packet. MSS, NOP, and SackOK should appear only in packets with the SYN and/or ACK flag set. Additionally, TCP packets have two reserved bits. Any packet using either or both of the reserved bits is probably malicious. (RFC 793, the TCP Internet standard, says that the reserved field in the TCP header is for future use and must be zero.)

IP options were originally intended as ways to insert special handling instructions into packets that weren't dealt with in other header fields. However, attackers mostly use IP options now for attack attempts. Because of this vulnerability, many filters simply drop all packets with IP options set.

Fragmentation Abuses

Every type of computer network (for example, Ethernet or token ring) has its own **maximum transmission unit (MTU)**—the maximum packet size that can be transmitted. Packets larger than the MTU must be fragmented—divided into segments small enough for the network to handle.

After a packet is fragmented, each fragment receives its own IP header. However, only the first packet in a set includes a header for higher-level protocols. Most filters need the information in the higher-level protocol header to make the decision to allow or deny the packet. Accordingly, attackers send only secondary fragments (any fragment other than the first one). These packets are often allowed past the IDS, and filter rules are applied to first fragments only.

Fragmentation can occur normally. However, an IDS should be configured to send an alarm if it encounters many fragmented packets. Several different types of fragmentation abuses can occur. The following list describes some of the more serious ones:

- *Overlapping fragments*—Two fragments of the same packet have the same position in the packet, so the contents overlap. A correctly configured firewall should always drop this type of packet.

- *Fragments that are too long*—An IP packet can be no longer than 65,535 bytes. Packets that are larger than the maximum size after being reassembled from their fragments might cause some systems to crash and could indicate a DoS attack.

- *Fragments overwriting data*—Some early fragments in a sequence are transmitted along with random data. Later fragments overwrite the random data. If the packet isn't reassembled correctly, the IDS can't detect the attack.

- *Fragments that are too small*—If any fragment other than the final one in a sequence is less than 400 bytes, it has probably been crafted intentionally. This small fragment is often part of a DoS attack.

Advanced Attacks

Most attacks discussed so far have been protocol anomalies—violations of the protocol rules described in RFCs. Some complex attacks use pathnames, hexadecimal codes, and obfuscated directory names to fool an IDS into letting the packet through without triggering an alarm. Some advanced IDS evasion techniques include the following:

- *Polymorphic buffer overflow attacks*—These attacks are as complicated as they sound. A tool called ADMutate is used to alter an attack's shell code in such a way that the code differs slightly from the known signatures many IDSs use. After attacking packets elude the IDS and reach their intended target, they reassemble into their original form.

- *Path obfuscation*—A directory path statement in a packet's payload is obfuscated by using multiple forward slashes. For example, /winnt/. /. /. / is essentially the same as /winnt. However, because the signatures don't match exactly, an IDS might be unable to detect this attack. To evade IDSs configured to trigger alarms when they encounter multiple forward slashes, attackers might use the Unicode equivalent of a forward slash, %co%af.

- *CGI scripts*—A set of packets is sent to a series of well-known **Common Gateway Interface (CGI) scripts** (scripts used to process data submitted over the Internet). Examples include Count.cgi, FormMail, AnyForm, Php.cgi, TextCounter, and GuestBook. You can be certain someone is attempting to exploit your network if you don't actually have these files on your network, but packets attempt to locate them anyway. For more information on CGI scripts, visit *http://hoohoo.ncsa.uiuc.edu/cgi/overview.html*.

The only way to avoid these attacks is to keep your IDS signatures up to date and watch your log files closely.

Remote Procedure Call Attacks

Remote Procedure Calls (RPC) is a standard set of communication rules that allows one computer to request a service (a remote procedure) from another computer on a network. RPC uses the Portmapper service to maintain a record of remotely accessible programs and the ports they use; Portmapper converts RPC program numbers into TCP/IP port numbers. Because RPC can provide remote access to applications, attackers use it to gain unauthorized access to those applications. Here are some examples of RPC-related events that should trigger IDS alarms:

- *RPC dump*—A targeted host receives an RPC dump request, which is a request to report the presence and port use of any RPC services the system provides.

- *RPC set spoof*—A targeted host receives an RPC set request from a source IP address of 127.x.x.x.

- *RPC NFS sweep*—A target host receives a series of requests for the Network File System (NFS) on a succession of different ports.

RPC services, such as Network Information System (NIS), use a 4-byte service number because there are too many services to use a 2-byte port number. When an RPC service starts, it allocates a random TCP or UDP port for itself. It then contacts Rpcbind or Portmapper and registers its service number and TCP/UDP port. Portmapper and Rpcbind always run on port 111, for example. A client wanting to talk to a server contacts Portmapper first to get the port number, and then continues the exchange with the server. A client can bypass Portmapper and scan for services. There's no guarantee that a particular service will end up on a particular port.

NOTE

The Rpcbind daemon, a more recent implementation of Portmapper, includes all the functions of Portmapper plus added features.

CHAPTER SUMMARY

- Network security hardware and software should work cooperatively to share information. A standard called Common Vulnerabilities and Exposures (CVE) enables IDSs, firewalls, and other devices to share attack signatures and information about network vulnerabilities so that they can better protect networks. Mitre maintains a list of current vulnerabilities as an online database, and you can use the list to update your own CVE database and learn about new attacks.

- Interpreting the signatures of normal and abnormal network traffic can help prevent network intrusions. Recognizing the characteristics of a possible intrusion makes it possible to interpret and react effectively to log files and alert messages.

❑ You can adjust filter rules to reduce the number of false alarms you receive from an IDS. More important, you can prevent intrusions before they occur or keep intrusions that are under way from causing excessive damage.

❑ Analyzing traffic signatures is an integral part of intrusion prevention. A signature is a set of characteristics, such as IP addresses, port numbers, TCP flags, and options. Normal traffic makes valid use of these settings. Possible intrusions are marked by invalid settings, such as bad header information, suspicious contents in the data payload, IP options settings, and a succession of packets, such as a denial-of-service attempt.

❑ You can set up the open-source IDS Snort as a packet sniffer to capture packets and study their contents. Parts of the packet header, such as the datagram length, can indicate a Windows or Linux system. TCP flags are used in sequence to create a normal three-way handshake between two computers.

❑ By learning what normal traffic signatures look like, you can identify signatures of suspicious connection attempts. You can monitor suspicious events, such as ping sweeps, port scans, random backdoor scans, and Trojan scans. You should also be familiar with the characteristics of packets crafted with Nmap.

❑ You can use packet capture and analysis to monitor traffic, locate potential problems, and look for security violations. Many packet-capturing tools are available, such as Ethereal, Network Monitor, EtherPeek, SnifferPro, and Tcpdump.

❑ You can identify a variety of other suspicious network events, including "orphaned" packets, land attacks, localhost source spoofs, falsified protocol numbers, and illegal combinations of TCP flags, such as SYN/FIN.

❑ Advanced attacks are especially difficult to detect without a database of intrusion signatures or user behaviors. Some complex attacks don't match a known intrusion signature and elude IDSs. Others use confusing pathnames or other keywords in the data payload.

❑ Another advanced attack method might include attempts to connect with and abuse common CGI scripts or misuse Remote Procedure Calls, which enables remote users to access services on a computer.

KEY TERMS

ASCII payload — The actual data part of the packet, given in ASCII format.

CAN — A prefix the CVE Web site uses to identify candidate vulnerabilities. In October 2005, this prefix was replaced with "CVE," and a vulnerability's status is now noted as Entry, Candidate, or Deprecated.

Common Gateway Interface (CGI) scripts — Scripts used to process data submitted over the Internet.

Common Vulnerabilities and Exposures (CVE) — A standard that enables security devices to share information about attack signatures and other vulnerabilities so that they can work together to provide network protection.

control connection — An initial FTP connection between client and server.

hexadecimal payload — The actual data a packet is communicating, expressed in hexadecimal format.

hop — The movement of a packet from one point on the network to another.

ID number — For packets in general, it's an identifying number used to reassemble a packet that's divided into fragments. For ICMP packets, it identifies the ICMP packet so that the originating computer can make sure the response came from its original request.

IP spoofing — The process of inserting a false address into the IP header to make the packet more difficult to trace back to its source.

maximum transmission unit (MTU) — The maximum packet size that can be transmitted over a type of network, such as an Ethernet network.

multiple-packet attacks — Attacks that require a series of packets to be transmitted.

network baselining — The process of determining what's normal for your network so that you can identify anomalies.

null packets — TCP packets with no flags set.

packet capture and analysis — A procedure administrators use to identify problems, analyze and monitor traffic conditions, locate security violations, and perform other network-monitoring tasks. Attackers also use it to gather information about a network.

packet sniffer — Software or hardware that monitors network traffic and captures information about TCP/IP packets it detects.

port scan — An attempt to connect to a computer's ports to see whether any are active and listening.

Remote Procedure Calls (RPC) — A standard set of communication rules that allows a computer to request a service from another computer on a network.

scanner — A device that scans a network for open ports or other potential vulnerabilities.

selective acknowledgements — Acknowledgements that selected packets in a sequence have been received instead of acknowledging every packet.

signature — A set of characteristics—such as IP numbers and options, TCP flags, and port numbers—for defining a type of network activity.

signature analysis — The practice of examining TCP/IP communications to determine whether traffic is legitimate or suspicious.

single-packet attack — An attack that can be completed by sending a single network packet from client to host.

strobe scan — A type of port scan that probes ports commonly used by certain programs in an attempt to see whether the program is present and can be used.

time to live (TTL) — A value that tells a router how long a packet should remain on the network before it's discarded.

Trojan scan — A type of port scan that looks for Trojan programs that have already circumvented security measures and are running on the scanned system. If attackers can find one already installed, they can use it instead of having to install a new one.

type of service (TOS) — The part of a packet header used to express a packet's precedence—whether it should have low delay, whether it needs high reliability, and so on.

vanilla scan — A type of port scan in which all ports from 0 to 65535 are probed one after another.

REVIEW QUESTIONS

1. Security devices on a network process digital information, such as text files and Web pages, the same way. However, which of the following information might they handle differently?

   a. protocols

   b. TCP/IP headers

   c. attack signatures

   d. port numbers

2. In which of the following ways can the CVE standard improve coordinating intrusion information on a network? (Choose all that apply.)

   a. Attack signatures can be compared with the lists of known attack signatures on the CVE Web site.

   b. Attack signatures can be compared with current network topology.

   c. Installing application patches can thwart an attack report.

   d. Current network vulnerabilities can be used to generate application patches.

3. Which of the following can be included in a network traffic signature? (Choose all that apply.)

   a. logon attempts

   b. message digest

   c. TCP options

   d. Ethernet interface number

4. What is the name of an error-checking procedure that uses a formula to calculate a numeric value?

   a. check string

   b. one-way hash

   c. hexadecimal code

   d. checksum

5. How do attackers use fragmentation to circumvent network defenses? (Choose all that apply.)

   a. Fragments are too large or too small.

   b. The first packet is missing.

   c. Multiple initial packets are sent.

   d. The final fragment sent is less than 400 bytes.

6. Which of the following packets should never have a data payload?

   a. one with SYN/ACK flags set

   b. one with the ACK flag set

   c. one with the SYN flag set

   d. one with ACK/PSH flags set

7. Which of the following is not required for a single-packet attack? (Choose all that apply.)

   a. a source IP address

   b. a destination IP address

   c. an ICMP Echo Request

   d. an established connection

8. Which of the following is an example of a multiple-packet attack? (Choose all that apply.)

   a. ping of death

   b. ICMP flood

   c. false Internet timestamp

   d. a packet with SYN/FIN/ACK flags set

9. Which of the following time to live (TTL) values is commonly used by Windows computers? (Choose all that apply.)

   a. 128

   b. 64

   c. 32

   d. 60

10. What is the purpose of the 4-byte acknowledgement number in a TCP header?

   a. It acknowledges receipt of the previous packet in the sequence.

   b. It acknowledges that a connection has been made.

   c. It verifies that the source and destination IP addresses are correct.

   d. It acknowledges the ID number the packet is using.

11. Which of the following is the correct order in which TCP flags appear during a normal connection?

   a. SYN, ACK, FIN, RST

   b. SYN, PSH, ACK, RST

   c. SYN, ACK, ACK/PSH, FIN

   d. SYN, PSH, ACK, FIN

12. Which OS typically has the following as part of its signature: DgmLen 84, TTL 64, initial sequence number 0?

13. Which OS typically has alphabetic characters in its ASCII payload?

14. Which protocol uses different port numbers to establish a connection and to transfer data?

    a. TCP/IP

    b. FTP

    c. HTTP

    d. ICMP

15. Which of the following is an example of a reconnaissance traffic signature?

    a. Trojan program

    b. ping sweep

    c. denial of service

    d. ping of death

16. A Back Orifice attack falls into what category of suspicious traffic signatures?

    a. information

    b. reconnaissance

    c. denial of service

    d. unauthorized access

17. Which program keeps track of services and ports made available through Remote Procedure Call?

    a. Network Information System

    b. Network File System

    c. Network File Sharing

    d. Portmapper

18. What does the ASCII payload section of an ICMP packet in Linux contain?

19. The maximum packet size that can be transmitted on a type of network is known as which of the following?

    a. maximum fragment threshold

    b. maximum packet limit

    c. mandatory transmission unit

    d. maximum transmission unit

20. To avoid attacks that use advanced evasion techniques, such as confusing pathnames, hexadecimal codes, and CGI scripts, you must do which of the following? (Choose all that apply.)

   a. Watch your log files closely.

   b. Install additional IDS sensors.

   c. Keep your antivirus software updated.

   d. Keep your IDS signature files updated.

HANDS-ON PROJECTS

Hands-On Project 4-1: Researching the TCP and IP RFCs

Time Required: 45 minutes

Objective: Research RFCs to find technical protocol details.

Description: All too often, network administrators receive alerts from IDSs but don't know how to interpret the data. This chapter has given you some tips for analyzing normal and abnormal traffic signatures, but you should make sure you have a solid foundation in the specifications for TCP, IP, UDP, and ICMP traffic so that you know what constitutes a possible intrusion. In this project, you look up the RFCs for TCP and IP traffic and focus on information about possible intrusions.

NOTE   Although this book refers to the discrete chunks that make up TCP/IP communications collectively as "packets," the protocols you're about to examine refer to these chunks differently because each protocol depends on higher- or lower-level protocols for certain services. For example, TCP relies on IP for fragmentation and reassembly, so the details of how they happen isn't a concern. Therefore, chunks of data are called "segments" in TCP and "datagrams" in IP. RFC 793 (TCP) explains this concept.

1. Start your Web browser and go to **www.ietf.org/rfc.html**.

2. In the RFC number text box, type **793** and click **go**.

3. Read the RFC for TCP packets. The maximum segment size (MSS) must appear only in a TCP packet with which flag set?

   _____

4. Look at Figure 6 in this RFC. Which flags does it indicate might appear together?

   _____

5. Read page 27 of the RFC. What is being synchronized when a packet with the SYN flag is sent?

   _____

6. Go back to **www.ietf.org/rfc.html**. Type **791** in the RFC number text box and click **go**.

7. In the specification for Internet Protocol, scroll down to the part of the document titled "Fragmentation and Reassembly." How big should packet fragments be, and how many fragments can be in a packet?

_____

8. Go to page 12 of the RFC. In the section on flags, you see an explanation of DF, which appears in many packet headers. What does DF stand for?

_____

9. Close any open windows.

CASE PROJECTS

CASE PROJECTS

Case Project 4-1: Filtering Out Common Scans

You have determined that an Nmap null scan has been launched against a computer on your network, as described in Activity 4-6. You suspect that other scans might take place. What sorts of filter rules should you establish so that your IDS can send an alarm when one is detected?

CASE PROJECTS

Case Project 4-2: Researching Security Products

In Chapter 2's case project, you drafted a security policy for Green Globe R&D. During the remainder of the book, you'll be adding to that document. As in real life, information and technology seldom remain static, and your policies must adapt to these changes. You must also do research on tools, utilities, devices, and applications you can use to address new threats.

Network security devices and software enforce and support your security policies. By establishing a plan for each segment of your network and documenting the plan, you're laying the groundwork for effective and consistent security management practices. The chapter has covered information you'll use to secure networks, particularly how to review and monitor traffic logs for signs of intrusion or attack. Reviewing logs has some disadvantages, however. Even minimal logging can generate thousands of entries daily. Examining these entries manually is time consuming and tedious, and spending all day reviewing logs takes away from time you need to secure your network. Reviewing log files manually is also prone to errors, and log entries show you only what happened in the past, so they aren't useful for real-time monitoring. Finally, log files have a size limit, so when they reach that limit, they overwrite older entries, possibly deleting important information.

Fortunately, tools that monitor logs on a real-time basis are available. Most can send an alert if suspicious activity is detected, and some can even mount a defense under certain conditions indicating an attack. Using the Tool Comparison Chart your instructor gives you, locate several tools for analyzing logs, and record the required information. Many tools perform other tasks, too. An all-in-one tool is great from a budget standpoint. There are several factors to consider:

- *Compatibility*—Is the tool compatible with your existing systems? Refer to your hardware and software inventory to answer this question. Check the platform the tool runs on, programming languages required for the tool, and hardware the tool supports, such as IDSs, firewalls, servers, routers, and so on.

- *Scalability*—Can the tool support the company's projected growth for the next five years? Can the tool be upgraded or updated to keep up with new threats, attack signatures, and so forth?

- *Cost*—How much will the tool cost to set up? To maintain?

- *Vendor*—Is the vendor reputable and stable? What kind of long-term support can you expect?

- *Portability*—Can the tool be used with (ported to) different platforms and products?

- *Tracking*—Does the tool offer reverse DNS lookup, Whois, and other features for tracing attacks and connections?

- *Report format*—How does the tool organize and display reports? GUI or command-line interface?

- *Response and alerts*—Can the tool send alerts? Can you customize alerts (specify alert-triggering conditions and people to send the alert to) and configure a response if certain conditions are met?

- *Security flaws*—Does the tool have any known security flaws? For example, older versions of AWStats (a tool listed as an example in the Tool Comparison Chart) that use the CGI feature might allow attackers to run arbitrary commands by using permissions of your Web server user, usually nobody or wwwroot. Keep in mind that software is code, and code can have flaws.

- *Management and configuration*—How is the tool managed? Centrally? Remotely? Does configuration require editing one or many files? Does it use a GUI or command-line interface? Does it require knowing a programming language, script, or platform that's unfamiliar to support personnel?

As you progress through this book, keep these tools in mind and be thinking about how to integrate log file analysis, auditing, and ongoing maintenance and monitoring into your security policy and procedures. Use Internet search engines, your library, and other resources to find tool examples, and compile your list in a report to submit to your instructor. Remember to cite your sources and avoid plagiarism and copyright and trademark infringement.

5

CRYPTOGRAPHY

After reading this chapter and completing the exercises, you will be able to:

♦ Describe key events in cryptography history

♦ Explain components of cryptographic protocols

♦ Explain common cryptography standards

♦ Describe modern cryptanalysis methods

This chapter introduces you to the main concepts of cryptography. Cryptography has existed for centuries, and this chapter presents a brief survey of some key events in its history. You also learn about the components of cryptographic protocols: cryptographic primitives, encryption algorithms, hashing algorithms, and digital signatures. They are the building blocks of modern protocols, and each component works with others to achieve the main goals of cryptography: confidentiality, message integrity, and nonrepudiation. Key management is a major challenge in cryptographic applications, so you learn about private and public key exchange methods, too.

Next, this chapter reviews common implementations of cryptographic standards in information technology, including Data Encryption Standard, Advanced Encryption Standard, and the International Data Encryption Algorithm. You also learn about cryptographic applications used in wireless communication and on the Internet and the encryption components of Internet Protocol Security (IPSec). Finally, modern cryptanalysis is discussed, including common attacks against encryption algorithms and cryptographic protocols and ways to defend cryptographic systems against these threats.

Reviewing Historical Cryptography Techniques

Cryptography is the process of converting plaintext (readable text, also called cleartext) into ciphertext (unreadable text) by using an encoding function, such as an encryption algorithm or a secret list of substitution characters. This encrypted text can then be transmitted in many forms, including written messages and electronic data. Cryptography helps achieve two critical goals of information security: confidentiality of information and integrity of data.

Throughout history, the capability to prevent unwanted compromise of communications has been important in government, military, and business operations where secrecy is a competitive advantage and sometimes a survival tactic. The history of cryptography could fill several volumes easily. However, for the scope of this chapter, some major examples of classical cryptography and the use of cryptography during World War II are discussed to give you a historical overview.

TIP

For a timeline of developments in cryptography, visit *www.securetrust.com/ resources/cryptography-history/*.

Classical Cryptography

Throughout history, the need for secrecy in times of war or intrigue prompted people to find methods of concealing the content of communications. With the recent popularity of books such as *The Da Vinci Code*, there has been a renewed interest in the subject of classical cryptography.

NOTE

The earliest known use of cryptography is in hieroglyphs from Egypt's Old Kingdom, more than 4000 years ago. The hieroglyphs appeared to be for amusement or mystery instead of hiding information, demonstrating yet another use for secret codes.

In the era of classical cryptography, messages were usually sent in written documents via couriers. Because of the threat of these documents being intercepted, cryptographic techniques were developed to secure messages. Although these techniques are primitive by today's standards, they were fairly secure for that time.

The main forms of classical cryptography ciphers are substitution ciphers and transposition ciphers. A **substitution cipher** maps each character, such as a letter of the alphabet, to a different character to obscure the message text. A **transposition cipher** simply rearranges the order of characters in each word. The following sections discuss a few important instances of cryptography and cryptanalysis in classical history.

Atbash Cipher

The Atbash cipher, a simple substitution cipher, has been traced back to around 500 B.C. and is associated with mystic interpretations of Hebrew religious texts. It's believed to hide names of people and places in the Hebrew Bible. The key to cracking a substitution cipher is discovering the substitution pattern. In the Atbash cipher, the substitution is based on reversing the order of the alphabet, as shown in this example with the English alphabet:

```
Alphabet:     a b c d e f g h i j k l m n o p q r s t u v w x y z
Substitution: z y x w v u t s r q p o n m l k j i h g f e d c b a
```

Now that you know the substitution pattern, try examining an Atbash ciphertext to decrypt it. The following is an English sentence using the Atbash cipher method of encryption:

```
xibkgltizksb rh xllo
```

To decrypt it, substitute each ciphertext character with the corresponding letter of the alphabet to reveal the message:

```
cryptography is cool
```

The weakness of the Atbash cipher is obvious: Anyone who knows the alphabet of the language used can decrypt the message simply by reversing the alphabet.

Caesar Cipher

Like the Atbash cipher, the Caesar cipher is a substitution cipher, but it's based on shifting letters of the alphabet by a certain number of positions. Typically, Julius Caesar used three shift positions for encrypted messages. An example of the Caesar cipher using the English alphabet with three shift positions is shown here:

```
Alphabet:     a b c d e f g h i j k l m n o p q r s t u v w x y z
Substitution: d e f g h i j k l m n o p q r s t u v w x y z a b c
```

Here's a message encrypted with the Caesar cipher:

```
fubswrjudskb lp yhub frro
```

To decrypt, use the substitution key on the ciphertext to get the following:

```
cryptography is very cool
```

Like the Atbash cipher, the weakness of the Caesar cipher is its substitution scheme. The cipher depends on shifting positions of letters in an alphabet, making it susceptible to a brute-force attack.

Historical Cryptanalysis

Cryptanalysis is the study of breaking encryption methods. Historically, cryptanalysts used frequency analysis to examine the number of times certain letters appear in a message and extrapolate likely character substitutions. For example, letters such as E and T appear more frequently in the English language than Z and X. Because substitution ciphers use

monoalphabetic substitution, a one-for-one character substitution, they are vulnerable to frequency analysis.

Around 1467, Leon Battista Alberti developed a **polyalphabetic substitution** scheme that applies multiple substitution ciphers to different parts of a message, often to each plaintext character. The Vigenère cipher is one that uses polyalphabetic substitution.

NOTE   To see an example of decrypting ciphertext with frequency analysis, go to *http://en.wikipedia.org* and search on "frequency analysis (cryptanalysis)."

WW II Cryptography

In modern times, WW II illustrates the importance of cryptanalysis in gaining a military advantage against an enemy. Intercepting the enemy's communications can result in strategic and tactical advantages in military operations. However, intercepted communications are useless unless their encryption can be broken. Military intelligence analysts depend on cryptanalysts (code breakers) to decipher encrypted text and find the plaintext messages. After the message is readable, strategists can use the information to gain an advantage over the enemy. The following sections briefly describe some methods Nazi Germany, the Imperial Empire of Japan, and the United States used used to protect messages during WW II.

The Enigma Machine

The Wehrmacht Enigma was a type of electromechanical rotor machine used in Nazi Germany to generate encrypted messages. The Allied powers were able to decrypt this cipher and gather important intelligence information during the latter two years of the war. The Enigma machine used a set of rotating disks with electrical contacts to produce a fixed substitution for a letter. Unlike simple substitution ciphers, however, it used polyalphabetic substitution, so the substitution cipher changed for each letter in the message. This method of encryption is symmetrical, in that the same steps must be followed to encrypt and decrypt the message.

JN-25 and the Battle of Midway

The Imperial Japanese Navy used JN-25 as its primary encryption method. It was the 25th code that Allied cryptanalysts identified—hence its name—and was based on the use of codes and codebooks. Unlike polyalphabetic substitution ciphers that encrypt at the letter level, the code method encrypts based on a word or phrase's meaning. The codebook provides the method for encrypting a plaintext message into coded text. The recipient needs a copy of the codebook, too, to decrypt the coded text into a plaintext message. The following sentences are an example of this codebook method:

Coded text: The sparrow is flying high.

Codebook decryption: The carrier Ryujo has left port.

At the time, codes were probably more secure than cipher methods of encryption because codes don't reveal an easily detectable pattern, as substitution ciphers do. Additionally, changing the codebooks periodically helped ensure the confidentiality of messages.

However, if the codebook was broken before the next change occurred, message interceptors had a window of time during which they could decode messages easily, which is what happened with JN-25. The codebook was changed shortly before the attack on Pearl Harbor, so there was not enough time for cryptanalysts to break the code. However, later in the war, the U.S. Navy's signal intelligence command, under Commander Joseph Rochefort, broke this version of the codebook. The ability to read Japanese-encrypted traffic contributed to the U.S. Navy's military advantage and victory in the Battle of Midway.

Human Language: Codetalkers

The most effective method of message integrity in WW II was achieved by Native American codetalkers. The main language used in the Pacific Theater was Navajo, but Hitler knew about this practice from WW I and had German anthropologists study the Navajo language before WW II. For the European Theater, American troops used Comanche and Choctaw codetalkers. The languages weren't used in their natural spoken form; they were adapted so that even a native speaker couldn't understand the messages. A major advantage of using Native American languages is that they aren't found outside the United States, so they bear little resemblance to familiar languages. High-ranking military officers have stated that the United States wouldn't have won the Battle of Iwo Jima if not for the secrecy codetalkers made possible.

NOTE

You probably know something about WW II codetalkers from the movie *Windtalkers*.

Human language is much harder to break than mathematical algorithms, and becoming fluent in a language takes many years. Additionally, there's a distinct difference between someone who has spoken a language from childhood versus someone who learned it as an adult, making it difficult for an imposter to interject fake messages.

COMPONENTS OF CRYPTOGRAPHIC PROTOCOLS

Cryptographic systems used in computer security share common components combined into cryptographic protocols and standards. A cryptographic system (protocol) is a combination of cryptographic functions called **cryptographic primitives**, which are modular mathematical functions that work together as the basic building blocks of modern cryptography. They include encryption algorithms, hashing functions, pseudorandom number generators, and basic logical functions.

The details of the mathematical aspects of cryptographic design are beyond the scope of this book. For the purposes of this book, you need a rudimentary understanding of the underlying math, and enough information is offered to help you understand the basic structure of cryptographic protocols. Knowing the basics of how these protocols are structured can help you determine what types best serve your needs and understand their vulnerabilities and deployment requirements. If you're interested in learning more about the mathematical sciences used in cryptography, refer to *Algebraic Aspects of Cryptography* (Neal Koblitz et al, Springer, 2004, ISBN 3-5406-3446-1).

Cryptographic Primitives

Cryptographic primitives, used alone, can't provide data integrity, confidentiality, nonrepudiation, and authentication. A primitive can accomplish only one of these goals. Each primitive is designed to perform a specific task reliably, such as generating a digital signature for a set of data. To provide adequate security, primitives must be used with other primitives.

In some ways, a cryptographic primitive is like a programming language. Software engineers don't create a new programming language for every new program. They use existing, proven languages in a modular fashion to create a software application that performs a defined set of functions. The same principle applies to cryptographic primitives. A cryptographic system designer doesn't create new primitives, as doing so is complex and prone to errors, even for experienced experts.

Primitives aren't usually the source of security failures in cryptographic protocols. Security flaws result from mistakes in designing the protocol, such as an overall poor design, poorly chosen primitive combinations, or bugs introduced during the design process.

Each primitive in a cryptographic system handles one aspect of securing data. For example, the encryption algorithm performs encoding, thus providing message confidentiality but not message integrity or authentication. By combining the encryption algorithm with a hashing function, however, you can meet the requirement of message integrity. You can also add a digital signature for message authentication.

In the following sections, you examine cryptographic primitives common to modern cryptographic systems. From the most basic logical functions to more intricate encryption algorithms and key generation routines, you learn the fundamentals of how they work on their own and combined with others.

Exclusive OR Functions

The **exclusive OR (XOR) function** is used in cryptography as a linear mixing function to combine values. For example, the output of other primitive ciphers can be combined with an XOR function to produce a pseudorandom value on which another cipher performs additional operations. An XOR function is based on binary bit logic and results in a logical value of true if only one of the operands has a value of true. So, for example, if x and y are the same (both true or both false), the XOR output is 0 (false). If x and y are different, the XOR output is 1 (true). The truth table in Figure 5-1 shows input of x and y with the result of the XOR function in the far right column.

x	y	xXORy
0	0	0
0	1	1
1	0	1
1	1	0

Figure 5-1 An XOR truth table

The XOR function is useful as a cryptographic primitive because of its reversible property, as shown in the following example:

```
p XOR k = c
c XOR k = p
```

In this equation, p represents plaintext, k is the key, and c is ciphertext. The c resulting from p XOR k is reversible in the c XOR k statement.

Permutation Functions

Bit-shuffling **permutation functions**, often used in symmetric algorithms, reorder sets of objects randomly—for example, rearranging input bits, such as the binary input 010 into 001. A good analogy for a random permutation is shuffling a deck of cards, which ideally causes the deck to be dealt in a completely random order. Some variations of permutation functions are suitable for cryptographic use, but many aren't. One cryptographically notable variation is an expansion permutation, in which certain bits are used more than once. For example, the input 010 is rearranged and expanded into 0101.

Substitution Box Functions

A **substitution box (S-box) function** transforms a number of input bits into a number of output bits and produces a lookup table that can be fixed or dynamic, depending on the cipher. It's a basic component of symmetric key algorithms. The purpose of this function, as with permutation functions, is disguising the relationship of ciphertext to cleartext. An S-box function is usually described as n (input bits) × m (output bits), so a 6x4 S-box means that 6 input bits are transformed into 4 output bits.

Feistel Networks

Created in 1973, a **Feistel network** (shown in Figure 5-2) is a symmetric block cipher that's the basis of several symmetric encryption algorithms. A Feistel network's purpose is to obscure the relationship between ciphertext and keys (a shortcoming of symmetric algorithms). It does this by combining multiple rounds of repeated operations, such as processing cleartext input with XOR functions. A key schedule is used to produce different keys for each round. The advantage of a Feistel network is that its encryption and decryption operations are similar or even identical, which reduces the size of its code and the resources needed to use it. Feistel encryption works because the key schedule can be reversed, using keys in exact reverse order.

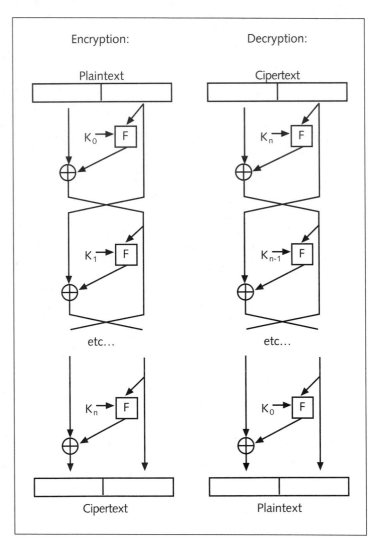

Figure 5-2   A Feistel network

Pseudorandom Number Generators

Pseudorandom number generators (PRNGs) are essential components of a cryptographic algorithm. A PRNG is an algorithm for generating sequences of numbers that approximate random values. To be considered a cryptographically secure pseudorandom number generator (CSPRNG), it must meet certain design principles and be resistant to known attacks. Many cryptographic functions require random values that serve as seeds for further computations, such as the following:

- *Nonces*—A nonce is a number or bit string (usually random) used to prevent generating the same ciphertext during subsequent encryptions of a message. Using nonces strengthens encryption and makes it more resistant to being broken.

- *One-way functions*—A one-way function is easy to compute but difficult and time consuming to reverse. Some one-way functions include integer factorization, discrete logarithms, and the Rabin function. They are considered one-way because no efficient inverting algorithm has been discovered, but new methods could prove these functions reversible.

- *Salts*—A salt consists of random bits used as input for key derivation functions and to pad values (hide the true contents). Initialization vectors, passwords, and passphrases are sometimes used as salts.

- *Key derivation (generation)*—A key derivation function generates secret keys from a secret value (usually a randomly generated value) and another piece of information, such as a password.

PRNGs can be hardware or software based. In general, hardware PRNGs offer sequences that are closer to being truly random, but the hardware can be expensive and cumbersome and is vulnerable to the same threats as any hardware security device. Several algorithms can produce random number sequences of high enough quality for cryptographic purposes, making hardware PRNGs unjustifiably expensive in most cases.

PRNG values aren't completely random because they are generated by a structured method based on fairly small initialization values called the PRNG's state. The state is generally measured in bits, and the initial state's size determines the maximum sequence length before it repeats, known as the PRNG's period. In modern computing, it's possible to provide a long enough state to ensure that the PRNG's period is longer than any computer could compute in a reasonable amount of time—say, 100 million years or so. If one bit is produced every picosecond, the PRNG's period with a 64-bit state is more than 140 million years.

There are still some problems with PRNGs, even ones considered cryptographically secure. One problem is that by providing a starting point for random number generation, the resulting value isn't truly random. Another problem is that the PRNG always produces the same values when initialized with a particular state. To be secure, mechanisms to prevent a PRNG from reusing an initializing state are necessary.

CSPRNGs produce values that are random enough to suit the intended use. In practice, there's no certain way to determine the output of a CSPRNG from truly random numbers without knowing the algorithm used and its initialization state. Because distinguishing between truly random or generated pseudorandom numbers isn't considered feasible, most algorithms and protocols using CSPRNGs are considered secure.

Hashing Functions

One method of verifying message integrity is by using **hashing functions**, which generate a hash value, also known as a message digest, from input. (Hashing algorithms, discussed later in this chapter, define the instructions for running hashing functions.) A hash value is a fixed-size string representing the original input's contents. If the input changes in any way (even adding a period at the end of a sentence), the resulting output has a different hash value.

With messages sent over the Internet, verifying message integrity and authenticating the source are critical. Source authentication verifies the sender's identity and prevents messages from fraudulent or spoofed sources from being accepted. Using a hashing function to verify message integrity is as simple as comparing the message digest the sender calculates with the message digest the receiver calculates. If the values are the same, the sender's message hasn't been altered during transmission.

Hashing functions are also used for error detection, as with Cyclic Redundancy Check (CRC), a commonly used method of verifying that a message wasn't altered by a transmission error, such as interference on the transmission medium.

Encryption Algorithms

To see how cryptographic primitives are combined to provide confidentiality, integrity, authentication, and nonrepudiation, understanding the basic mathematical concepts is helpful. As you know, an algorithm is a precisely defined set of instructions for carrying out a task. Computer algorithms, for example, provide exact instructions for which operations to carry out, which criteria change operations, how many times to perform an operation (called looping), and when to stop.

In algorithms, a strict order of operations is essential; in computer programs, this strict order of operations is called control flow. If a program processes the same input for the same purpose, but the instructions vary, the results would never match, nor would they be repeatable, reversible, and predictable. Output values change, of course, if the input varies, but the instructions for processing input must stay the same. For example, the instruction "Find the largest item in the list" generates different values depending on the list's contents but must always process the list exactly the same way to achieve consistency.

An **encryption algorithm**, like any other algorithm, is a set of precise instructions that provides an encoding function for a cryptographic system or generates output for use in additional operations. (Remember that some algorithms also double as CSPRNGs, such as stream and block ciphers.) In the simplest applications, it's a mathematical formula that works with a key to generate ciphertext from cleartext input. Encryption algorithms also combine with other primitives that perform integrity checking or authentication. A hashing function, for example, can be used to check data integrity or to generate pseudorandom numbers the encryption algorithm can use in encoding iterations. This process is repeatable and reversible.

Key Size in Encryption Algorithms

An encryption algorithm's strength is often tied to its key length. The longer the key, the harder it is to break the encryption. Longer keys offer more protection against brute-force attacks, in which every possible key is tried to decrypt a message. As computers have increased in processing power, however, attackers have been able to carry out brute-force attacks more quickly and break encryption keys. Therefore, to keep up with advances in processors, encryption key sizes had to increase.

So, for example, an encryption algorithm using a 256-bit key is stronger than one using a 128-bit key. However, this comparison shouldn't be made between symmetric and asymmetric algorithms. Asymmetric algorithms have longer keys but aren't necessarily stronger. For instance, to have the same cryptographic strength as a 128-bit symmetric algorithm, an asymmetric algorithm would have to be approximately 3000 bits.

Some encryption algorithms require large key sizes for adequate security. In addition, key sizes should be increased to match increases in computer processing speed, but often older applications aren't flexible enough to accommodate large key sizes. Recent advances in factoring mathematics and computing technology make cryptographic attacks more feasible, so using the correct key size is important to ensure the security of weaker algorithms.

Types of Encryption Algorithms

The two major types of encryption algorithms are block ciphers and stream ciphers. A **block cipher** encrypts groups of text at a time. For example, a block cipher encrypts the whole word *cat* instead of encrypting each letter. A **stream cipher** encrypts cleartext one bit at a time to produce a stream of encrypted ciphertext, so the letters c, a, and t in *cat* are encrypted separately.

Block ciphers and stream ciphers use keys differently, so they fall into two categories: symmetric and asymmetric. **Symmetric algorithms** use the same key to encrypt and decrypt a message. They are considered the workhorse of the encryption world and are a faster and more efficient method of encrypting data because they require fewer computing resources. Most encryption protocols in daily use are based on symmetric algorithms, and the majority of symmetric algorithms are block ciphers.

By contrast, **asymmetric algorithms** use a specially generated key pair. One key encrypts cleartext into ciphertext, and the other key decrypts ciphertext into cleartext. It doesn't matter which key of the generated pair is used to encrypt—only that the other key is used to decrypt.

Blowfish

Blowfish is a 64-bit block cipher composed of a 16-round Feistel network and key-dependent S-box functions. This unpatented cipher used worldwide has a variable key size, from 32 to 448 bits. The default key size is 128 bits. Blowfish is fast in encryption and decryption operations, but its 64-bit block size is now considered too short and makes Blowfish vulnerable to some attacks.

Notable for its public license status and excellent performance, Blowfish is still a widely used cipher, however, and is very fast except when changing keys. Its high memory requirements and slow key derivation functions aren't a problem for most desktop and laptop computers (even older ones) but make it unsuitable for smart cards or similar limited resource systems.

NOTE   Bruce Schneier developed Blowfish in 1993 as a replacement for Data Encryption Standard and International Data Encryption Algorithm. For more details, visit *www.schneier.com/paper-blowfish-fse.html*.

Twofish

Twofish, the successor to Blowfish, is a 128-bit symmetric block cipher composed of a 16-round Feistel network and key-dependent S-box functions. Twofish also has a complex key schedule and a variable key size of 128, 192, or 256 bits. Like Blowfish, it's publicly licensed but hasn't been used as much as its predecessor. Although some theoretical work on cryptanalysis methods against Twofish has been published, it hasn't been broken.

NOTE   Specific attacks against cryptographic systems are examined later in the chapter in "Modern Cryptanalysis Methods."

Rivest Cipher Family

Rivest Cipher 4 (RC4) is a stream cipher widely used in Web browsers using Secure Sockets Layer (SSL), Wired Equivalent Privacy (WEP), Wi-Fi Protected Access (WPA), and Transport Layer Security (TLS). RC4 uses an XOR function to combine a pseudorandomly generated stream of bits (the keystream) with the plaintext and produce ciphertext. To generate the keystream, the cipher uses a secret internal state composed of two parts: a permutation of all 256 possible bytes and two 8-bit index pointers. The permutation is initialized with a variable-length key, and then a pseudorandom stream of bits is generated with a PRNG. RC4 isn't recommended for new applications because of its weak use of keys and lack of nonces but is still used because of its speed and simplicity.

In addition to RC4, Rivest created other ciphers in the RC family. Notably, RC6 was developed for the Advanced Encryption Standard competition and selected as a finalist. It wasn't the winning algorithm, but it's still available for applications requiring encoding functions. It's not free, however, because it's a patented algorithm.

Rijndael

Rijndael is the encryption algorithm incorporated into the Advanced Encryption Standard (AES). It's a block cipher composed of 10 to 14 rounds of S-box and XOR functions but doesn't use a Feistel network. This symmetric algorithm specifies how to use 128-bit, 192-bit, or 256-bit keys on 128-bit, 192-bit, or 256-bit blocks. It applies 10 rounds for 128-bit keys, 12 rounds for 192-bit keys, and 14 rounds for 256-bit keys. The standard AES implementation of Rijndael has a fixed block size of 128 bits and uses keys of 128, 192, or 256 bits. In practice, the Rijndael algorithm can support larger key and block sizes than AES.

The difference between the number of rounds Rijndael uses (10, 12, or 14) and the number of rounds the best-known attacks against block ciphers use (7, 8, or 9) is fairly small, which has caused some concern among cryptographers. The major concern, however, centers on Rijndael's mathematical structure. Most ciphers don't have Rijndael's neat algebraic description, leading some cryptographers to speculate that a flaw in the mathematical structure could lead to successful attacks. The main point is that, like any other security measure, Rijndael will eventually fail. Although some attacks are theoretically possible now, none have succeeded in breaking it. However, you should stay abreast of new developments and threats.

 NOTE The name "Rijndael" comes from the names of its creators, the prominent cryptographers Vincent Rijment and Joan Daemen. The names "Rijndael" and "AES" are used interchangeably, but they aren't the same. Rijndael is the algorithm, and AES is the implementation.

Rivest, Shamir, Adelman

Rivest, Shamir, and Adelman developed RSA (the first letter of each creator's surname) for public key encryption. RSA uses a public key that's freely shared and a private key that's kept secret. If RSA is used with long enough keys and is kept updated, it's believed to be secure. RSA is widely used in e-commerce protocols and is the default encryption and signing scheme for X.509 certificates.

RSA keys are usually 1024 to 2048 bits, although larger (and smaller) keys are supported. Keys smaller than 512 bits can be broken quickly with modern computing resources. Even the security of 1024-bit keys has been called into question since 2003. Therefore, experts recommend keys that are 2048 bits or longer. As with any asymmetrical encryption system, key exchange is a challenge. Key distribution must be protected against man-in-the-middle attacks, usually by using Public Key Infrastructure (PKI) components, such as digital certificates, which are signed and can be authenticated with hashing functions.

RSA is also vulnerable to timing attacks, adaptive chosen ciphertext attacks, and branch prediction analysis. Timing attacks are a type of side channel attack, discussed later in

"Modern Cryptanalysis Methods." Adaptive chosen ciphertext attacks exploit flaws in the public key cryptography standard (PKCS) scheme to recover session keys; using newer PKCS versions with secure padding schemes is recommended. (PKCS is covered later in this chapter.) Branch prediction analysis takes advantage of processors that use a predictor to determine whether a conditional branch in a program's control flow is likely to be taken. The attack uses a spy process to determine the private key statistically.

Hashing Algorithms

Hashing algorithms are sets of instructions applied to variable-length input (the message) that generate a fixed-length message digest representing the input. The message digest is used for comparison to ensure message integrity. Hashing algorithms don't provide confidentiality because they don't encrypt the message contents, but they do provide verification that a message hasn't been altered. (Remember that hashing algorithms are mathematical formulas, and hashing functions are the process the computer uses to generate a hash value.)

When a message with a message digest is received, the hashing algorithm is run against the contents again. If the values match, the message is considered unaltered. If the values don't match, the message might have been tampered with or corrupted during transmission. Several hashing algorithms are available, but the most common are Message Digest 5 and Secure Hash Algorithm 1, discussed in the following sections.

Message Digest 5

Ronald Rivest devised **Message Digest 5 (MD5)** in 1991 as a replacement for MD4, which was not secure. It's used in many cryptographic applications, such as digital signatures and virtual private networks (VPNs). MD5 makes only one pass on data and generates a 128-bit hash value displayed as a 32-character hexadecimal number.

Methods have emerged that make generating collisions in MD5 easy, however. A collision occurs when computing the MD5 algorithm with two different initialization vectors produces the same hash value. To be considered secure, no algorithm should be initialized with the same state or produce the same results (a collision). Collisions can be used to determine the plaintext, and because MD5 is commonly used for password storage, the possibility of deciphering plaintext is a serious security risk. Also, rainbow tables have been posted on the Internet. These precompiled lookup tables of possible hash-plaintext combinations make successful brute-force attacks more likely. They can also be used to generate collisions and make password cracking easier. If one plaintext string generates the same hash value as another, the attacker can use the known information to determine the unknown values.

Secure Hash Algorithm

The National Security Agency designed **Secure Hash Algorithm (SHA)** as a successor to MD5. It was approved for federal government use, and SHA version 1 (SHA-1) is used in many cryptographic applications that require checking message integrity, including SSL, SSH, and IPSec (discussed later in "Internet and Web Standards").

The SHA standards include five algorithms: SHA-1, SHA-224, SHA-256, SHA-384, and SHA-512. SHA-1 is the most commonly used, and the other four are sometimes referred to collectively as SHA-2. SHA-1 generates a message digest of 160 bits, and the number added to the other four algorithms' names denotes the message digest's length. Table 5-1 summarizes SHA message digest and block sizes and how many rounds of computation are performed.

Table 5-1   Summary of SHA algorithms

Algorithm	Message digest length	Block size	Rounds of computation
SHA-1	160	512	80
SHA-224 and SHA-256	224/256	512	64
SHA-384 and SHA-512	384/512	1024	80

NOTE

You can learn more about SHA-1 in FIPS Publication 180-1 at *www.itl.nist.gov/ fipspubs/fip180-1.htm*.

Methods have been devised to decipher a message's original text based on hash values. The U.S. government has become so concerned about SHA-1 vulnerabilities that it has announced plans to phase out its use by 2010. A competition is under way, similar to the AES algorithm competition, to designate the next version, SHA-2, by 2012. However, although the effects of SHA-1 attacks in a lab environment are severe, no feasible attack methods outside the lab environment have proved successful in compromising SHA-1.

Until SHA-2 is selected, most cryptographic applications continue to use SHA-1 and MD5, but storing passwords is still a major concern. In some systems, the password isn't saved in the file system; instead, a hashed value of the password is stored. When the system carries out password validation for authentication, it takes user input and generates a hash value to compare with the stored value.

TIP

One method of reducing the vulnerabilities of hashing algorithms is to add a salt to plaintext before hashing. Another method called key strengthening involves applying the hashing function more than once. No method of reinforcement is 100% secure, but these methods can help improve the security of MD5 and SHA-1.

Message Authentication Code

Message Authentication Code (MAC), also known as Message Integrity Check (MIC), uses a shared secret key agreed on by the sender and receiver in the verification process to generate a MAC tag (a sort of enhanced message digest) for a message. The shared secret key adds a measure of security to the hashing algorithm.

Be sure not to confuse this abbreviation with Media Access Control (MAC), a common abbreviation in networking protocols.

TIP

The message and MAC tag are then sent to the receiver. The key is also sent to the receiver securely, usually separately from the message. The receiver goes through the same process of using the transmitted message and key to generate a MAC tag and compares this tag with the one received in the message to confirm the message's integrity and authenticity. The verification process is protected by secure communication of the key, which ensures that the sender and receiver generate the same MAC tag from the message. Figure 5-3 illustrates this process.

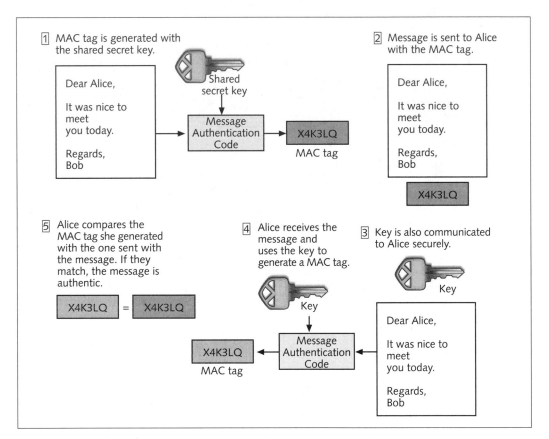

Figure 5-3 The MAC process

As with symmetric cryptography, MAC uses a single key in verifying message integrity, so the challenge is key management—how to securely communicate the secret key that sender and receiver use. If communication of the secret key is compromised, an attacker could forge a message between the sender and receiver without MAC detecting it. MAC can still be used, as long as care is taken to secure communication of the secret key with encryption.

Digital Signatures

Digital signatures use hashing algorithms with asymmetric encryption to produce a method for verifying message integrity and nonrepudiation. Nonrepudiation means ensuring that participants in a message exchange can't deny their roles in the process. This process is explained in the following example and illustrated in Figure 5-4.

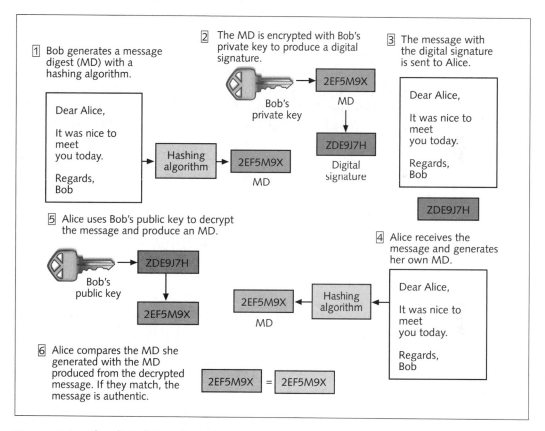

Figure 5-4   The digital signature process

Bob wants to send Alice a digitally signed message. He goes to the organization's directory to find Alice's public key certificate. He then digitally signs the certificate, and the process works as follows:

1. Using a hashing algorithm, a message digest of Bob's message to Alice is calculated.

2. The message digest is encrypted by Bob's private key. The resulting ciphertext is the digital signature of the message.

3. The digital signature with the message is sent to Alice.

4. Alice runs the message she receives through the same hashing algorithm Bob used to get a message digest.

5. Alice then decrypts the message's digital signature with Bob's public key, which produces the message digest calculated in Step 1.

6. Alice compares the message digest she calculated with the message digest Bob calculated to verify the message's integrity. If the message digests are the same, the message is authentic.

Nonrepudiation is achieved in this process because the signature is encrypted by Bob's private key (which only he owns and has access to), and the successful decryption by Bob's public key confirms his identity.

Digital signature security vulnerabilities are mostly associated with the IT infrastructure required to support interoperability. When a sender digitally signs a message, the receiver must have access to and trust the same certification authority (CA, discussed later in "Key Management") that issued the sender's credentials. Therefore, Internet users can't rely on digital signatures because not all users have the configuration to trust issuing CAs. Interoperability and political issues of recognized CAs among organizations as well as countries are a barrier to universal acceptance of digitally signed documents and messages. Cases are being tried worldwide to determine whether digital signatures can be recognized as a legally valid method for signing documents.

ACTIVITY

Activity 5-1: Examining Digital Certificates

Time Required: 20 minutes

Objective: Obtain and examine a digital certificate.

Description: In this activity, you visit a CA that issues digital certificates for personal use. You obtain a digital certificate and examine it. For this activity, you need a valid e-mail address and a workstation running Windows XP Professional.

1. Start your Web browser and go to **www.thawte.com/secure-email/personal-email-certificates/index.html**.

2. Click the **Click here** link and follow the instructions to get a personal e-mail certificate. It should take only a few minutes for your certificate to be issued.

3. When you receive an e-mail from Thawte that your certificate has been issued, return to your account page at Thawte (if necessary), click to expand **certificates** at the left, and then click **view certificate status**.

4. Click the link for your certificate under **Type**. Scroll to the bottom of the page, and click **fetch** to retrieve and install your new certificate.

5. To view your certificate, click **Tools**, **Internet Options** from the menu. Click the **Content** tab, and click the **Certificates** button. (These instructions are for Internet Explorer. Steps might vary in other browsers.)

6. Click the **Personal** tab, if necessary, click the **Thawte Freemail Member** certificate, and click the **View** button at the bottom. Examine your certificate. What signature algorithm is used? What is the public key type?

_____

5

7. Click **OK**. In the Certificates dialog box, click the **Untrusted Publishers** tab (see Figure 5-5). Note any untrusted publishers that are listed:

_____

_____

_____

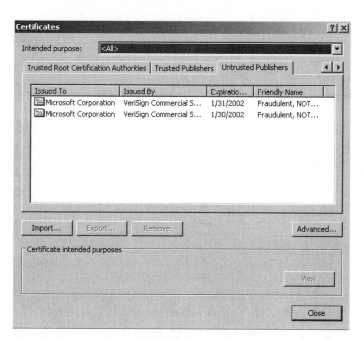

Figure 5-5   Untrusted certificate publishers

8. Click the **Trusted Root Certification Authorities** tab and locate Thawte's certificates. Who issued them? When does the Thawte primary root CA certificate expire?

_____

9. Close all open windows and leave your system running for the next activity.

Key Management

The major issue with cryptographic algorithms is secure key exchange. To prevent compromise of encrypted traffic, cryptographic systems change keys frequently and distribute them to all authorized parties. This process of changing and distributing keys is called **key management** and is difficult to carry out reliably.

Private Key Exchange

Private key exchange uses a symmetric cryptographic algorithm in the encryption process, in which the same key (also called a "shared key") is used to encrypt and decrypt a message. Therefore, the message is only as secure as the shared key. The following is an example of a private key exchange, shown in Figure 5-6:

1. Bob has a cleartext message for Alice. He uses a shared key to encrypt it into ciphertext to protect the message from unintended readers.

2. Bob sends the encrypted message to Alice.

3. For Alice to be able to read the message, she needs the shared key to decrypt the ciphertext. This key must be sent to Alice securely and separately to ensure the message's confidentiality. Sending it with the message defeats the purpose of encryption.

4. Alice receives the message and uses the shared key she received from Bob to decrypt it.

Public Key Exchange

Public key exchange uses asymmetric cryptography in the encryption process and generates a key pair: one to encrypt and the other to decrypt. To achieve key management when two keys are used, one key is labeled as the public key and the other as the private key. The public key is shared freely, but only the key owner knows the private key.

When an encrypted message is sent to the private key owner, the sender encrypts the message with the public key. The recipient then uses the private key to decrypt the message. Therefore, the keys have an inverse relationship to each other, with each key capable of reversing what the other has done. Confidentiality is ensured because the private key owner is the only person able to decrypt what the public key has encrypted. Encrypting and decrypting the message with the public key isn't possible.

NOTE

Many computer users use public key exchange in the form of SSL Web browser encryption and often don't realize it.

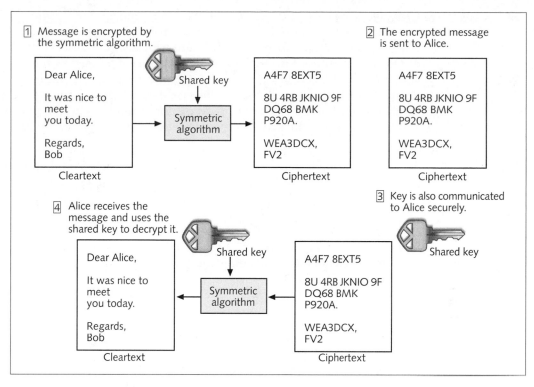

1 Message is encrypted by the symmetric algorithm.

2 The encrypted message is sent to Alice.

3 Key is also communicated to Alice securely.

4 Alice receives the message and uses the shared key to decrypt it.

Figure 5-6   The private key exchange process

The IT infrastructure to support asymmetric cryptography and public key exchange is more complex than symmetric cryptography and private key exchange. The following list describes components of an asymmetric cryptography system:

- *Certificates*—A certificate is a file containing information on the user (or service) and the assigned public key. It also contains information on the certification authority and its digital signature so that users can trust the public key's authenticity.

- *Certification authorities (CAs)*—These organizations issue public and private key pairs to people or services. A CA keeps track of issued credentials and manages revoking certificates, if needed. A CA also verifies that the public and private keys have indeed been issued legitimately and are trustworthy.

- *Registration authorities (RAs)*—Also called registrars, they serve as a front end to users for registering, issuing, and revoking certificates. For security reasons, users rarely contact CAs. Instead, they interact with an RA, which acts as an intermediary in the certificate-issuing process. Before an RA issues public and private keys to a user, identity verification is required to ensure that the certificate reflects the user's identity accurately.

- *Certificate revocation lists (CRLs)*—CAs track and publish listings of invalid certificates. CRLs should be checked to make sure certificates are legitimate; usually applications perform the check automatically, unless users have disabled this feature. If a certificate is listed on a CRL, the cryptography system gives users a warning that the certificate isn't valid. Certificates can be considered invalid for many reasons. A user might have been issued a new certificate, so the older certificate needs to be taken out of service, for example. A common reason is that a user is no longer affiliated with the issuing CA because he or she has been fired.

- *Message digests*—The recipient's message software compares the received message's hash value with the transmitted message's hash value to verify that the message is unchanged.

Putting all these components together, the following process takes place when issuing a certificate for use in public key exchange (see Figure 5-7):

1. Alice applies with an RA for a certificate. The RA works with the CA to issue certificate credentials containing the public and private keys. In this process, identity verification is carried out via the organization's standard operating procedure for issuing certificates. A copy of Alice's public key certificate is kept in the organization's directory along with issued certificates.

2. Bob wants to send Alice a message. He goes to the organization's directory to get a copy of her public key certificate. Each time the certificate is used, the CA is consulted to make sure the certificate isn't listed on the CRL.

3. Bob uses Alice's public key certificate to encrypt the message and then sends the encrypted text to Alice.

4. Alice, after receiving the message, uses her private key to decrypt it.

Although use of asymmetric cryptography is widespread for communicating symmetric keys safely and for security on the Internet, using asymmetric systems for everyday encryption of e-mail and digital signatures has met with mixed success. Asymmetric encryption systems, also known as Public Key Infrastructure (PKI), have been used in the U.S. Department of Defense and large corporations, but the complexity and cost of PKI systems have discouraged many organizations from adopting this technology.

Public Key Cryptography Standards

Created by RSA Labs to improve interoperability in public key cryptography, **public key cryptography standards (PKCSs)** aren't actual industry standards, but they have helped move modern information security cryptography, PKI in particular, toward standardization. Several PKCS designations have even moved into the standards track through the IETF, and others are used as de facto standards. Some PKCS designations have been withdrawn or made obsolete; for example, PKCS #2 and #4 were withdrawn, and PKCS #6 was made obsolete by a newer version of X.509. PKCS #13, Elliptic Curve Cryptography Standard, and #14, Pseudorandom Number Generation, are under development. (For a more detailed list of standards that are still valid, refer to Appendix B.)

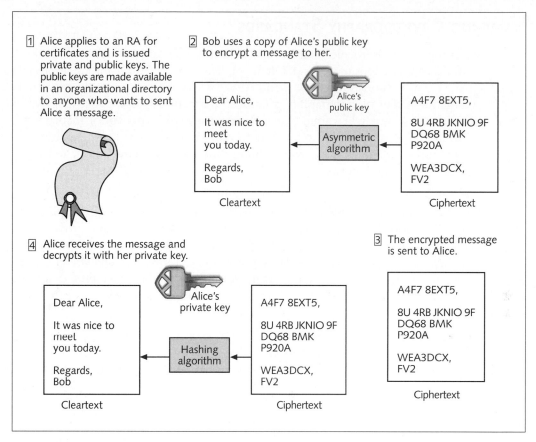

Figure 5-7   The public key exchange process

X.509

X.509 is an International Telecommunication Union standard for PKI developed in 1988 by the Internet Engineering Task Force's (IETF's) Public-Key Infrastructure Working Group (PKIX). X.509 specifies standard formats for public key certificates, a strict hierarchical system for CAs issuing certificates, and standards for CRLs. X.509 certificates use RSA for key generation and encryption and MD5 hashes to verify the certificate's integrity.

NOTE   X.509 is also the basis for modern directory services, such as Lightweight Directory Access Protocol used in Microsoft Active Directory. This topic is discussed in more detail in Chapter 8.

EXAMINING CRYPTOGRAPHY STANDARDS

Cryptographic protocols describe how algorithms should be used and specify the security requirements designs must meet. Often you hear the algorithm and the protocol that applies it used synonymously—Rijndael and AES, for example. Technically, they aren't the same. Remember that cryptographic primitives perform a single task reliably but can't be considered secure when used alone. A **cryptographic protocol** incorporates a detailed description of standardized requirements and guidelines for key generation and management, authentication, encryption, hashing functions, nonrepudiation, and other aspects of ensuring message security.

Some reasons for standardizing cryptographic protocols are interoperability, reliability, and scalability, as with most computer standards. Standardized cryptographic protocols and algorithms have another objective, perhaps even more important: attracting cryptanalysis attacks. Trying to attract attacks might seem strange, but primitives are proved secure through cryptanalytic efforts to break them. So the more cryptanalytic efforts expended on breaking a standard, the better. Standardization, in this case, provides more rigorous, independent study to verify whether a standard performs as expected and meets its requirements.

The following sections examine major cryptographic standards and some commonly used cryptographic protocols. Keep in mind that many of these systems are also used for remote access and VPN security, wireless security, authentication, and a host of other purposes.

As in most aspects of information security, choosing the most secure or expensive system isn't always the best option. Security must be matched to the organization's requirements and plans for the system's use. You should also consider the available budget, resources to handle the system life cycle, and existing infrastructure.

The Computer Security Resource Center (CSRC) at the National Institute of Standards and Technology is one of the primary agencies responsible for establishing cryptographic standards. For more information on these protocols, visit *http://csrc.nist.gov* and search on the protocol's name, such as AES or DES.

Data Encryption Standard

IBM submitted the **Data Encryption Standard (DES)** algorithm to the National Bureau of Standards, and it was selected in 1976 as a Federal Information Processing Standard (FIPS). FIPS is an important standard because federal laws mandate its use in certain government projects. DES was an effort to develop a standard way to secure business communication in the United States and was subsequently adopted internationally. It's composed of a 16-round Feistel network with XOR functions, permutation functions, 6x4 S-box functions, and fixed key schedules. Using these primitives, the DES algorithm generates 64 bits of ciphertext from 64 bits of plaintext by using a 56-bit key.

TIP Visit *www.itl.nist.gov/fipspubs/fip46-2.htm* for more detailed information on DES.

Triple DES

DES is not considered secure for current encryption purposes, however, mainly because of its 56-bit key size, which is short by cryptographic standards. For this reason, a more secure variation called **Triple DES (3DES)** is used now in which ciphertext goes through three iterations (rounds of encryption). Encrypting with a different key for each iteration increases security. As shown in Figure 5-8, three separate 64-bit keys are used to process the same bit of unencrypted text: The first key encrypts it, the second key decrypts it, and the third key encrypts it again. Using three keys strengthens encryption, but the problem is the time and resources needed to encrypt the information. It takes three times as long as DES does, which uses only a single key. It's also more processing intensive, making its use a trade-off.

TIP Visit *www.itl.nist.gov/fipspubs/fip46-2.htm* for more detailed information on 3DES.

Figure 5-8 3DES encryption

Although most modern computers are capable of using stronger encryption without intolerable performance degradation, encryption must be selected and managed carefully. Use stronger encryption to ensure confidentiality when needed and other forms of security, such as digital certificates, for authentication or integrity. In short, if you don't need to encrypt everything, don't.

Advanced Encryption Standard

The National Institute of Standards and Technology (NIST) approved the **Advanced Encryption Standard (AES)** protocol for U.S. government use on May 26, 2002. The Rijndael algorithm was selected for AES through a widely publicized international competition. AES is stronger than 3DES and works faster. As of 2006, it's the most widely used encryption method, no doubt because of its status as the accepted government standard and its perceived strength of security. AES is also approved for classified government information.

To date, the only successful attacks against AES have been side channel attacks, which target the underlying system rather than the cipher implementation. A theoretical attack, extended sparse linearization (XSL), has the potential to exploit weaknesses in AES, but to date, no such attack has happened, nor has the theory been proved correct. Side channel and XSL attacks are explained in "Modern Cryptanalysis Methods" later in this chapter.

TIP

For more information on AES, see *www.csrc.nist.gov/publications/fips/ fips197/fips-197.pdf* and *www.faqs.org/rfcs/rfc3268.html*. To learn more about U.S. government guidelines for using cryptography, read NIST Special Publication 800-21, Guideline for Implementing Cryptography in the Federal Government, at *http://csrc.nist.gov/publications/*.

International Data Encryption Algorithm

International Data Encryption Algorithm (IDEA) is a commonly used European symmetric algorithm that Xuejia Lai and James Massey designed in 1991. IDEA was developed as a replacement for DES and is derived from an earlier cipher called Proposed Encryption Standard (PES). It's a block cipher that encrypts in 64-bit blocks, with eight and a half rounds of modular addition/multiplication math and XOR functions, and it has a 128-bit key. IDEA is licensed worldwide by MediaCrypt and is free for noncommercial use.

TIP

For more information on IDEA, see *www.mediacrypt.com/_pdf/IDEA _Technical _Description_0105.pdf*.

Wireless Network Cryptography

Wireless networking has become an essential tool for many businesses, so several standards for wireless communication security have been developed. Wireless networks face special challenges because of the mobile nature of wireless devices and the basic signaling medium, radio waves. Because signals can be intercepted so easily, encryption is even more essential for ensuring confidentiality.

Wired Equivalent Privacy

Early wireless networking had only Wired Equivalent Privacy (WEP) for security. WEP was severely flawed and ridiculously simple to crack. It uses the RC4 algorithm with keys up to 128 bits. The 802.11 implementation uses a 40-bit or 104-bit key with a 24-bit initialization vector (IV) added to the beginning of the message. The IV initializes the keystream that RC4 generates and is transmitted in cleartext.

To understand WEP's inherent weaknesses, you need to understand IV vulnerabilities. An IV is part of the RC4 encryption key, so it gives attackers 24 bits of the key. The IV is a short stream by cryptographic standards, and reusing the same key results in the keys repeating after a short time. All users use the same key, so capturing enough packets to crack the key and decrypt transmissions isn't hard.

NOTE Because WEP is adequate only for very small networks with loose security requirements, it's not discussed further here. WEP should be configured as a preventive measure for casual or accidental intrusions, but any knowledgeable attacker can bypass it easily, so it should be used with more robust security measures. For more information on wireless networking and securing wireless networks, see *Guide to Tactical Perimeter Defense: Becoming a Security Network Specialist* (Course Technology, 2008, ISBN 1-4283-5630-4).

Wi-Fi Protected Access

As an emergency measure, Wi-Fi Protected Access (WPA) was released to address WEP's deficiencies. WPA replaced WEP encryption with Temporal Key Integrity Protocol (TKIP). TKIP is based on the same RC4 calculation mechanisms used in WEP but includes a method for generating new keys for each packet to address WEP's problem of repeating, static keys. TKIP also incorporates automatic synchronization of unicast encryption keys between wireless access points (APs) and stations, so not every machine has to be rekeyed manually, as in WEP.

In TKIP, different keys are used for authentication and encryption. Keys used between a pair of devices are called pairwise keys. After a station's credentials are accepted, the authentication server produces a master key for that session, and TKIP distributes this key to the station and AP. This pairwise master key (PMK) generates data encryption keys, data integrity keys, and session group keys for multicasts. It isn't used for any other purpose, which makes it less vulnerable to attack.

At the start of a session, the PMK is used to compute keys for encryption, data integrity, and authentication. The pairwise transient key (PTK) is the first key created from the PMK. It's actually four keys shared between the wireless AP and wireless client. PTKs are used in further key generation based on the cryptographic algorithm in use, whether it's TKIP or AES. Keys are transient, meaning they change in real time during a session, and a new key is generated dynamically for each packet.

To learn more about how TKIP, WPA, and the 802.11i standard work, search the Internet for articles. You can also download the 802.11i standard at *http://standards.ieee.org.*

TIP

WPA2/IEEE 802.11i

Wi-Fi Protected Access version 2 (WPA2) is based on the final ratified 802.11i standard; it uses AES for encryption and supports 802.1x or preshared keys for authentication. One notable difference from 802.11i is that WPA2 allows both TKIP and AES clients to communicate, whereas 802.11i recognizes only AES.

WPA and WPA2 are used in Personal Security and Enterprise Security modes of operation, which offer guidance on how to use WPA and WPA2 for different purposes. Personal Security mode is designed for single users or small office/home office (SOHO) settings, and Enterprise Security mode is designed for medium to large businesses and provides the highest level of security.

Table 5-2 summarizes the major wireless security standards.

Table 5-2   Wireless security standards

Type	Encryption	Authentication	Key length	Security level
WEP	WEP	Shared key	40–104 bits with a 24-bit IV	Low
WPA Personal Security	TKIP	Preshared key	128 bits	Medium
WPA2 (802. 11i) Personal Security	AES	Preshared key	128 bits	Medium to high
WPA Enter- prise Security	TKIP	802.1x	128 bits	Medium to high
WPA2 (802. 11i) Enterprise Security	AES	802.1x	128 bits	High

Internet and Web Standards

Because the Internet uses public lines, it's not secure, so methods of keeping messages private while being transmitted over public lines are constantly being developed, tested, broken, and upgraded. Several encryption standards, discussed in the following sections, are used to secure Internet browsing, e-commerce, e-mail, and more.

Secure Shell

Secure Shell (SSH) provides authentication and encryption of TCP/IP packets. It works primarily with Linux/UNIX systems (although Windows versions are available) and uses public key cryptography. When a client initiates an SSH connection, the two computers exchange keys and negotiate algorithms for authentication and encryption to create a secure connection at the Transport layer. The username and password transmitted to the server are encrypted. All data sent subsequently is encrypted, too. SSH is available free with the OpenSSH package (*www.openssh.org*).

5

Secure Sockets Layer

Netscape Communications Corporation developed Secure Sockets Layer (SSL) as a way of enabling Web servers and browsers to exchange encrypted information. SSL is a secure way to transmit data on the Web, such as credit card numbers used for online purchases. SSL uses asymmetric keys to start an SSL session and exchange keys. After the session is established, SSL uses dynamically generated symmetric keys for most of the transfer.

Transport Layer Security

Transport Layer Security (TLS) was designed to provide additional security for Internet communication. Although it's similar to SSL in operation and design, TLS adds some notable improvements. First, it uses a hashed message authentication code (HMAC) that increases security by combining the hashing algorithm with a shared secret key. Both parties must have the same shared secret key to authenticate the data. Second, TLS splits the input data in half, processes each half with a different hashing algorithm, and then recombines them with an XOR function. This method provides protection if one of the algorithms is proved vulnerable.

TLS provides authentication and encryption mechanisms. It supports certificate-based authentication, as SSL does, and the handshake process to establish a session is similar to SSL. For encryption, TLS can support a variety of symmetric and asymmetric ciphers and several hashing algorithms. TLS uses symmetric keys for bulk encryption and asymmetric keys for authentication and key exchange.

TIP

To learn more about the technical details of TLS, search at *www.ietf.org*. The first definition of TLS is in RFC 2246, and you can review the current approved version in RFC 4346. Many RFCs also deal with extensions of TLS.

Internet Protocol Security

Internet Protocol Security (IPSec) is a set of standard procedures the IETF developed for securing communication on the Internet. IPSec has become the standard set of protocols for securing tunneled communication, such as VPNs, for a number of reasons:

- IPSec works at Layer 3 and, therefore, provides a type of security not available with protocols that work at Layer 2.

- IPSec can encrypt an entire TCP/IP packet.

- IPSec was originally developed for use with IP version 6 (IPv6), although it also works with the current IPv4.

- IPSec authenticates source and destination computers before data is encrypted or transmitted.

Perhaps the biggest advantage of using IPSec is that it has gone through the process of standardization and is supported by a variety of hardware and software devices. In OSs such as Windows Server 2003 and XP, you can set up an IPSec connection with another IPSec-enabled Windows computer. You add IPSec security policy support as a snap-in to the Microsoft Management Console.

If you want more background on IPSec and related technologies, you can find links to the original RFC papers at *www.ietf.org/rfc/rfc2401.txt*.

When an IPSec connection is established between two computers, the computers authenticate one another and then establish the Security Association (SA) settings they use to communicate. An SA is a relationship between two or more parties that describes how they use security services to communicate and tracks details of a communication session. SAs are unidirectional, meaning that an SA is set up in each direction of a communication, forming two one-way SAs between parties.

Each IPSec connection can perform encryption, encapsulation, authentication, or a combination of the three. When determining which services to use, the parties in a connection must agree on the details, such as which algorithm to use for encryption. After completing that transaction, the parties must share session keys. These transactions take place in the background. However, in an OS environment, you need to decide whether IPSec is required for all connections to the host machine or whether the host requests an IPSec connection for computers or other devices that support it. If IPSec is not supported on the client machine, it isn't used. If you want to connect to another computer while requiring IPSec, you must adjust the packet-filtering rules; otherwise, your IPSec-enabled computer blocks all other connections by default.

IPSec Components

IPSec's many components provide encryption, encapsulation, key exchange, and authentication. These components include the following:

- *Internet Security Association Key Management Protocol (ISAKMP)*—ISAKMP enables two computers to agree on security settings and establish an SA so that they can exchange keys by using Internet Key Exchange.

- *Internet Key Exchange (IKE)*—This protocol enables computers to exchange keys to make an SA. By default, IKE uses UDP port 500 on both the client and server. Other configurations might use different ports.

- *Oakley*—This protocol enables IPSec to use the Diffie-Hellman encryption algorithm to create keys. (You can learn more about Diffie-Hellman encryption at *www.ietf.org/rfc/rfc2631.txt*.)

- *IPSecurity Policy Management*—This service runs on Windows computers. It retrieves IPSec security policy settings from Active Directory and applies them to computers in the domain that use IPSec.

- *IPSec driver*—This piece of software handles the tasks of encrypting, authenticating, decrypting, and checking packets.

Suppose you have configured a VPN connection between two computers and you want the connection to use IPSec. When one IPSec-compliant computer connects to the other, the following process occurs:

1. The IPSec driver and ISAKMP retrieve the IPSec policy settings.

2. ISAKMP negotiates between hosts, based on their policy settings, and establishes an SA between them.

3. The Oakley protocol generates a master key for securing IPSec communication.

4. Based on the security policy established for the session, the IPSec driver monitors, filters, and secures network traffic.

CAUTION IPSec isn't foolproof. For instance, if the computer running IPSec-compliant software has already been compromised, no communication from it, including IPSec communication, can be trusted. IPSec isn't a substitute for firewall, antivirus, and IDS software.

The two core IPSec components are the ones that protect TCP/IP packets exchanged in the connection: Authentication Header and Encapsulating Security Payload, discussed in the following sections.

Authentication Header

Authentication Header (AH) is an IPSec component that authenticates TCP/IP packets to ensure data integrity. With AH, packets are signed with a digital signature that tells other

IPSec devices the packet contains accurate IP header information because it originated from an IPSec computer. Digitally signing a packet indicates that it hasn't been tampered with or that the IP information in the header hasn't been spoofed. It ensures integrity but not confidentiality.

To authenticate all or part of a packet's contents, AH adds a header calculated by IP packet header and data values, essentially creating a message digest of the packet. Security is achieved by calculating the values with a hashing algorithm and a key known only to parties in the transaction. (Keys are exchanged when the SA is established.) An AH header doesn't change message contents; it simply adds a field following the IP header. The field contains the computed value of the IP header (except fields that change in transit, such as the time to live [TTL] field) and the data, as shown in Figure 5-9.

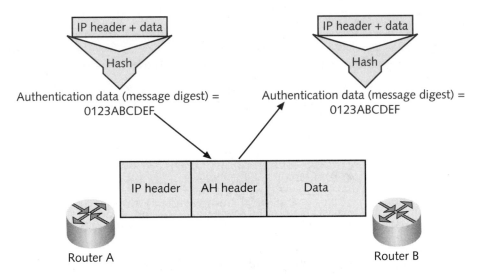

Figure 5-9   AH message exchange

AH works a little differently in the two IPSec modes: tunnel and transport (see Figure 5-10). In tunnel mode, AH authenticates the entire original header and builds a new IP header placed at the front of the packet. The only fields not authenticated by AH in tunnel mode are fields that can change in transit. In transport mode, AH authenticates the data and the original IP header, except fields that change in transit.

Encapsulating Security Payload

AH provides authentication and integrity for messages but not confidentiality. The confidentiality of data transmitted by using IPSec is ensured by means of Encapsulating Security Payload (ESP). ESP encrypts different parts of a TCP/IP packet, depending on whether IPSec is used in transport or tunnel mode.

In tunnel mode, ESP encrypts both the header and data portions of a packet. This encryption protects data, but because the IP header is encrypted, the data can't pass through a firewall that performs NAT because the firewall doesn't know how to interpret the IP source and destination information in its encrypted form. In transport mode, only the data

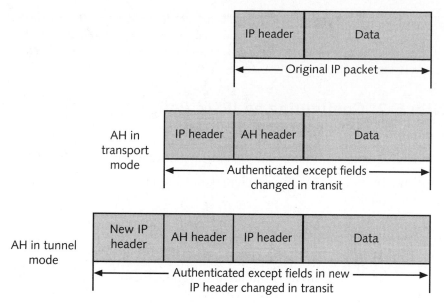

Figure 5-10 AH in tunnel and transport modes

portion is encrypted. As a result, if the connection passes through a firewall performing NAT, IPSec should be configured to work in transport mode. Figure 5-11 shows the difference the IPSec mode makes to ESP.

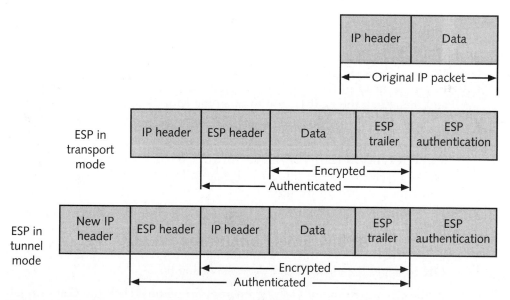

Figure 5-11 ESP in tunnel and transport modes

NOTE

Using AH and ESP together offers additional security, but you might not want to use ESP if another device or application is already providing encryption. ESP, like other forms of encryption, requires substantial processing resources and can slow the rate of data transfer.

ACTIVITY

Activity 5-2: Configuring an IPSec Policy

Time Required: 15 minutes

Objective: Configure an IPSec policy that includes strong encryption methods for security.

Description: In this activity, you configure your Windows XP Professional computer to use an IPSec policy.

1. Open Control Panel, click **Performance and Maintenance**, and then click **Administrative Tools**.

2. Double-click **Local Security Policy** to open the Local Security Settings window. Click to select **IP Security Policies on Local Computer**. Right-click **Client (Respond Only)** and click **Properties**.

3. Examine the security methods used for this policy, and then click the **Authentication Methods** tab. Notice that Kerberos is the default method.

4. Click the **Add** button. Click **Use a certificate from this certification authority (CA)**, and then click **Browse**. Examine the list. How could this capability be used in an enterprise network?

   _____

   _____

5. Click **Cancel** twice to return to the Edit Rule Properties dialog box.

6. In the Security method preference order list box, click **Encryption and Integrity**, and then click the **Edit** button to open the Modify Security Method dialog box. Click the **Custom** option button, and then click the **Settings** button.

7. In the Custom Security Method Settings dialog box, verify that the **Data integrity and encryption (ESP)** check box is selected. Under that check box, make sure **SHA1** is selected in the Integrity algorithm list box and **3DES** is selected in the Encryption algorithm list box.

8. In the Session key settings section, click the **Generate a new key every** check box on the right, and enter **7200** (2 hours) in the text box for seconds, as shown in Figure 5-12.

9. Click **OK** twice to return to the Edit Rule Properties dialog box, and then click **OK** to apply the changes and close the dialog box.

10. In the Client (Respond Only) Properties dialog box, click the **General** tab. Click the **Advanced** button, and examine the available key exchange settings. When you're finished, click **OK** twice.

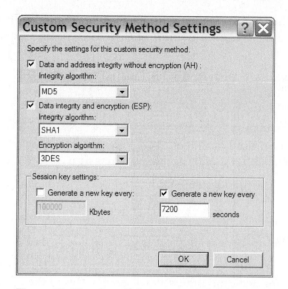

Figure 5-12   Specifying an interval for generating new keys

11. In the Local Security Settings window, right-click **Secure Server (Require Security)** and click **All IP Traffic**. Click the **Edit** button to open the Edit Rule Properties dialog box for the Secure Server option (see Figure 5-13).

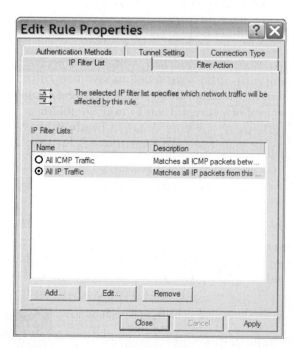

Figure 5-13   The Edit Rule Properties dialog box for the Secure Server option

12. Click each tab and examine the available settings. What function does the IP filter list serve? What is the default authentication method? What is the default filter action?

_____

_____

_____

13. To apply a policy, right-click it in the Local Security Settings window and click **Assign**. To deactivate it, right-click the policy and click **Unassign**.

14. Close all open windows and leave your system running.

MODERN CRYPTANALYSIS METHODS

Many attacks are aimed at cryptographic systems. Some are targeted at the encryption algorithm, some exploit flaws in a protocol, and others attack weaknesses in the hardware or software running cryptographic applications. New attacks emerge constantly, so security professionals must keep up to date on threats and countermeasures.

Cryptographic systems present a special challenge, however. Because the expertise to create algorithms or design protocols is based on advanced mathematics, most information security professionals lack the training to address bugs or design flaws. Instead, they must rely on the expertise of mathematicians who design algorithms and agencies, such as the NSA, that test and standardize them. Adhering to guidelines for using and managing cryptographic systems is crucial to maintaining security. The following sections discuss some common attacks against cryptographic systems. You learn the basics of how these attacks work and ways to defend your cryptographic systems from them.

NOTE

The mathematical underpinnings of each attack aren't explained because you don't need to know them for security purposes. You just need to know which algorithms are vulnerable and how to defend against attacks. If you're interested in learning more about the specific mechanisms in an attack (or any other aspect of cryptography), you can conduct an Internet search.

Side Channel Attacks

A side channel attack doesn't attack the cipher directly; instead, it attacks the underlying systems that leak information, which can be used to compromise the data being stored, processed, or transmitted. These leaks are unintentional signals (emanations) that could expose information being processed. Some types of side channels attacks include the following:

- *Timing attacks*—Attacks based on measuring how much time computations take to perform. For example, a timing attack might watch data move in and out of the

CPU or memory. Watching how long it takes to transfer key information can yield clues about key length or eliminate certain key lengths.

- *Power monitoring attacks*—Attacks that use hardware's varying power consumption during computations. Watching the power input to the CPU during computations reveals information that can be used to determine the algorithm.

- *Acoustic cryptanalysis*—Similar to power monitoring attacks, acoustic cryptanalysis exploits the sound computations produce. The current to power hardware produces heat, which is leaked into the atmosphere. The fluctuations of heating and cooling (thermodynamics) produce low-level acoustic noise that can be examined for clues about the underlying system.

- *Radiation monitoring*—Leaked radiation provides plaintext or other information that can be used to launch an attack. Electrical current fluctuations generate EM radiation waves, which can occur in patterns. The patterns can be recorded and analyzed to gain information about associated hardware, and sometimes bits of data can be captured.

- *Thermal imaging attack*—If the surface of the CPU can be seen, infrared images can be taken that provide clues about the code that's running.

Side channel attacks rely on emitted information, as in acoustic or radiation monitoring, and relational information, as in timing or power monitoring attacks. Countermeasures against side channel attacks include power conditioning and UPSs to control power fluctuations and emissions, shielding to prevent radiation leakage, and strong physical security to prevent acoustic recorders or other monitoring devices from being installed.

Obviously, launching these attacks requires a high level of expertise, which eliminates many potential attackers. As successful attacks emerge, however, automated scripts and instructions invariably appear, making it possible for less knowledgeable attackers to use the techniques.

Passive Attacks

In a passive attack, cryptanalysts simply observe data being transmitted. To gather information, they don't interact with parties exchanging information; they just eavesdrop on transmissions. Detecting this type of attack is difficult because attackers aren't transmitting anything. Therefore, countermeasures against passive attacks focus on using strong encryption so that attackers can't decrypt any data they intercept or crack keys.

Chosen Ciphertext and Chosen Plaintext Attacks

A chosen ciphertext attack selects a captured encrypted message (ciphertext) and decrypts it with an unknown key. It's sometimes done by using a decryption oracle, a device that decrypts ciphertext messages the attacker (or software) has selected. This attack is sometimes called a lunchtime or midnight attack because it involves the attacker gaining access to a decryption oracle left unattended during breaks or at night. Chosen ciphertext attacks can be prevented by using the correct cryptographic padding values or redundancy checks.

In a chosen plaintext attack, the attacker can select arbitrary plaintext messages to be encrypted to get the resulting ciphertext messages. Because encryption is carried out in both hardware and software and used in a wide variety of applications, a chosen plaintext attack is often possible.

Public key encryption algorithms that aren't randomized are vulnerable to chosen plaintext attacks. Countermeasures are based on randomized encryption, in which some mechanism (such as CSPRNGs and randomized padding) is used to produce randomized ciphertext messages that can't be looked up in a rainbow table. Any algorithm that's not vulnerable to chosen plaintext attacks is also considered secure against chosen ciphertext and known plaintext attacks.

XSL Attacks

An XSL attack is a method of block cipher cryptanalysis based on complex mathematical functions (multivariate quadratic equations) and uses an extended sparse linearization algorithm. The researchers who developed the XSL algorithm claim it can potentially break Rijndael (AES) as well as other block algorithms, such as Camellia and Serpent. If true, this claim is a cause for concern because AES is used in government agencies and many commercial organizations.

Most cryptanalysis methods require an unrealistically high number of known plaintext messages to perform cryptanalysis with any effectiveness. XSL attacks require far fewer known plaintext messages to recover a key, which is a major concern. The potential for the XSL algorithm to crack Rijndael is highly debated, but this method warrants further study, and security professionals should monitor new developments.

Random Number Generator Attacks

Modern cryptographic systems require random values for many operations, and hardware or software components that generate or use random numbers can be compromised if attackers can gain access to them via a random number generator attack. They can substitute predictable values and break the entire coding system. These attacks require only a single access to the system, so no further information needs to be sent, as with viruses or worms that obtain a key and then e-mail it back to the attacker. These are the major countermeasures against random number generator attacks:

- Combine hardware-generated random numbers with the output of a secure stream cipher. XOR functions are usually used for this method.

- Consider using open-source software for encryption systems. Vendors often don't explain how proprietary products generate random numbers or provide a method to audit the process. Without a way to audit the process, there's no way to assess its security.

- Make sure physical security for the system is strong.

- Use off-the-shelf hardware for security systems, and don't announce their intended use (such as in online help forums) to prevent potential attackers from knowing what equipment you're using.

- Use a true random source for password generation. Ideally, use a random password/passphrase generator instead of allowing users to choose their own. In practice, this method might be difficult, especially when users must remember their passwords. At a minimum, use the tools provided with your OS to enforce strong password policies and reduce the possibility of weak passwords.

5

Related Key Attacks

A related key attack is a form of cryptanalysis in which attackers can observe a cipher's operation by using several different keys. Initial values for these keys are unknown, but a mathematical relationship connecting the keys is known.

WEP is an important example of a cryptographic protocol that failed because of related key attacks. Each client in a WEP network uses the same key and the RC4 algorithm. WEP keys must be changed manually, so typically, this task isn't done often. Attackers can assume that all keys in WEP encryption are related by a known IV. With 24 bits for an IV, only about 17 million keys are possible. This number sounds high, but in practice, WEP's key schedule repeats in a short time. WEP's inherent weaknesses and certain weak keys in RC4 make recovering WEP keys used for encryption easy. In 2005, the FBI demonstrated that WEP could be broken and the WEP key recovered in under three minutes.

Preventing related key attacks on WEP networks isn't possible, given the protocol's weaknesses. To defend wireless networks against related key attacks (and other attacks), use WPA or 802.11i for security. To defend wired cryptographic systems against related key attacks or others that exploit weak key schedules, use a cryptographic protocol, such as AES, that incorporates a strong key schedule.

NOTE Some older NICs can't perform strong encryption methods, so you might need to upgrade NICs to support stronger encryption.

Integral Cryptanalysis

Integral cryptanalysis is applicable to block ciphers that use a substitution-permutation network, which includes Rijndael, Twofish, and IDEA, among others. This attack uses sets of chosen plaintext messages sharing a common constant. Each set of messages shares a constant value, and the remainder of each plaintext message is tried with all possible variables, much like a brute-force attack that checks all possible keys. In integral cryptanalysis, however, only part of the message is tested; the remaining bits are constant. For example, in a set of 256 chosen plaintext messages, each might vary by only 8 bits. In this attack, each set of plaintext messages has an XOR sum of zero, and the corresponding sets of ciphertext messages (generated from the plaintext messages) offer information about the cipher's operation based on the XOR variations.

Differential Cryptanalysis

Differential cryptanalysis applies mainly to block ciphers but can also be used against stream ciphers and hashing functions. Generally, it examines how differences in input affect the output. In block ciphers, it's used to discover where the cipher has nonrandom behavior. Predictable behavior in ciphers results in weaknesses attackers can use to gain information about the cipher's functions and then recover keys.

Differential cryptanalysis uses pairs of plaintext messages related by a constant difference. By computing differences in the corresponding ciphertext messages (called differentials), attackers might be able to find statistical patterns. Differentials depend on the nature of S-box functions used for encryption, so attackers analyze differentials for each S-box value to look for their frequency of use. This information reveals areas where the cipher displays nonrandom behavior.

Because predictable behavior makes a cipher more vulnerable to being broken, using secure PRNG methods is critical. The goal of cryptographers is to prevent or mask predictable behavior. Obviously, no algorithms are 100% random, but nonrandom functions can be disguised.

NOTE Remember the importance of staying informed on the cryptographic system you're using. Sign up for mailing lists and newsletters to keep up to date on emerging threats and new defenses. New versions to correct flaws are released often, so make sure your systems are patched and updated. Another useful place to find information about emerging attacks is hackers' sites. Often they're the first ones to report flaws in cryptographic systems.

CHAPTER SUMMARY

❏ Cryptography is the process of converting plaintext into ciphertext by using an encoding function, such as an encryption algorithm or secret list of substitution characters. Cryptanalysis is the study of breaking encryption methods.

❏ The main forms of classical cryptographic ciphers are substitution ciphers, which use monoalphabetic substitution, and transposition ciphers, which rearrange the order of characters. Polyalphabetic ciphers apply multiple substitution ciphers to parts of a message, with a keyword determining which substitution alphabets are applied to which parts.

❏ Cryptographic primitives are modular mathematical functions that are the basic building blocks of cryptographic systems. Each one is designed to perform a specific task reliably. Used alone, however, they can't ensure adequate security; they must be used with other primitives. Cryptographic primitives include exclusive OR (XOR) functions, permutation functions, substitution box (S-box) functions, Feistel networks, pseudorandom number generators, and hashing functions.

❑ An encryption algorithm is a set of instructions that provides the encoding function to a cryptographic system or generates output for use in additional operations. Algorithms are classified as block ciphers or stream ciphers. Block ciphers encrypt groups of text, and stream ciphers encrypt cleartext one bit at a time.

❑ Symmetric algorithms use a shared key in a private key exchange to encrypt a message and decrypt ciphertext. Asymmetric algorithms use two keys for encryption and decryption. Public key exchange is also used to exchange private keys for symmetric algorithms.

❑ Digital signatures use hashing algorithms with asymmetric encryption for verifying message integrity and for nonrepudiation.

❑ Public Key Infrastructure (PKI) components include certificates, certification authorities (CAs), registration authorities (RAs), certificate revocation lists (CRLs), and message digests.

❑ Cryptographic protocols describe how algorithms should be used and raise the security requirements designs must meet. Common protocols include DES, 3DES, AES, and IDEA.

❑ Wireless network cryptographic protocols include WEP, WPA, and 802.11i. For Internet security, SSL, SSH, and TLS are common. IPSec is another major cryptographic protocol used for Internet, VPN, and network security.

❑ Attacks on cryptographic systems include side channel attacks, passive attacks, chosen ciphertext and chosen plaintext attacks, random number generator attacks, and XSL attacks. In addition, integral and differential cryptanalysis attempt to discover patterns that might reveal nonrandom behaviors in a cipher.

KEY TERMS

Advanced Encryption Standard (AES) — The current U.S. government standard for cryptographic protocols, AES uses the Rijndael algorithm with key sizes of 128, 192, or 256 bits and a fixed block size of 128 bits.

asymmetric algorithms — A type of mathematical formula that generates a key pair: one key to encrypt cleartext and another key to decrypt ciphertext.

block cipher — A type of encryption algorithm that encrypts groups of cleartext characters.

cryptanalysis — The study of breaking encryption methods. Some common attack methods against cryptographic systems include differential and integral cryptanalysis, random number generator attacks, side channel attacks, and XSL attacks.

cryptographic primitives — Modular mathematical functions that perform one task reliably. They form the basic building blocks of modern cryptography.

cryptographic protocol — A detailed description that incorporates standardized requirements and guidelines for key generation and management, authentication, encryption, hashing functions, nonrepudiation methods, and other aspects of message security.

cryptography — The process of converting plaintext into ciphertext by using an encoding function.

Data Encryption Standard (DES) — An older protocol composed of a 16-round Feistel network with XOR functions, permutation functions, 6x4 S-box functions, and fixed key schedules. DES generates 64 bits of ciphertext from 64 bits of plaintext by using a 56-bit key.

digital signatures — A method of verifying nonrepudiation and integrity in messages.

encryption algorithm — A precise set of instructions that provides an encoding function for a cryptographic system or generates output for use in additional operations.

exclusive OR (XOR) function — This cryptographic primitive based on binary bit logic is used as a linear mixing function, combining values for use in further computations.

Feistel network — A cryptographic primitive that forms the basis of many symmetric algorithms. Feistel networks combine multiple rounds of repeated operations, such as processing cleartext input with XOR functions. A key schedule is used to produce different keys for each round.

hashing algorithms — Sets of instructions applied to variable-length input (the message) that generate a fixed-length message digest representing the input. Hashing algorithms don't provide confidentiality because they don't encrypt the message contents, but they do provide verification that a message hasn't been altered.

hashing functions — Processes a computer runs to verify message integrity by generating a hash value (also known as a message digest), which is a fixed-size string representing the original input's contents. Hashing functions are also used for error detection.

International Data Encryption Algorithm (IDEA) — A common European symmetric algorithm that uses 64-bit blocks and eight and a half rounds of modular addition/multiplication math and XOR functions. IDEA has a 128-bit key.

Internet Protocol Security (IPSec) — A set of standard procedures that the Internet Engineering Task Force (IETF) developed for enabling secure communication on the Internet.

key management — A way to prevent keys from being discovered and used to decipher encrypted messages. One method is changing keys frequently.

Message Authentication Code (MAC) — A hashing algorithm that uses a shared secret key to generate a MAC tag for a message.

Message Digest 5 (MD5) — A widely used hashing algorithm that produces a 128-bit hash value displayed as a 32-character hexadecimal number.

monoalphabetic substitution — A one-for-one character substitution scheme; this encryption method is vulnerable to frequency analysis.

permutation functions — Bit-shuffling cryptographic primitives that reorder sets of objects randomly.

polyalphabetic substitution — This encryption method applies multiple substitution ciphers to different parts of a message, often to each plaintext character.

private key exchange — In symmetric cryptography, the same key is used to encrypt and decrypt a message. Public Key Infrastructure is often used for private key exchange.

pseudorandom number generators (PRNGs) — Cryptographic primitives used to generate sequences of numbers that approximate random values.

public key cryptography standards (PKCSs) — A set of standards RSA developed to provide standardization guidelines for cryptography. Many of these 15 standards have moved into the IETF standards track.

public key exchange — In asymmetric cryptography, two keys are required: the public key and private key. The public key, used to encrypt the message, is shared freely. The private key, used to decrypt the message, is kept secret.

Rijndael — The encryption algorithm used in AES is a symmetric block cipher composed of 10 to 14 rounds of S-box and XOR functions. It supports 128-bit, 192-bit, or 256-bit keys and block sizes. Rijndael applies 10 rounds for 128-bit keys, 12 rounds for 192-bit keys, and 14 rounds for 256-bit keys.

Secure Hash Algorithm (SHA) — A hashing algorithm that the NSA designed as a replacement for MD5. SHA-1 produces a 160-bit message digest.

stream cipher — A type of encryption algorithm that encrypts one bit at a time.

substitution box (S-box) function — A cryptographic primitive that transforms a number of input bits into a number of output bits and produces a fixed or dynamic lookup table.

substitution cipher — A type of encryption method in which one character in the message is replaced with another character in a one-to-one substitution scheme.

symmetric algorithms — A type of mathematical formula in which the key for encrypting cleartext is the same key for decrypting ciphertext.

Transport Layer Security (TLS) — A protocol designed to provide additional security for Internet communication. TLS uses a hashed message authentication code (HMAC) to combine the hashing algorithm with a shared secret key. TLS splits input data in half, processes each half with a different hashing algorithm, and recombines them with an XOR function.

transposition cipher — A type of encryption method that rearranges the order of characters in each word of a message.

Triple DES (3DES) — An enhanced variation of DES that uses three 64-bit keys to process data. *See also* Data Encryption Standard (DES).

X.509 — An International Telecommunication Union standard for PKI that specifies standard formats for public key certificates, a strict hierarchical system for CAs issuing certificates, and standards for certificate revocation lists. X.509 certificates use RSA for key generation and encryption and MD5 hashes to verify the certificate's integrity.

REVIEW QUESTIONS

1. The Caesar cipher shifts letters of the alphabet by a certain number of positions, usually three. True or False?

2. Which of the following is a main form of classical cryptography methods? (Choose all that apply.)

   a. substitution ciphers

   b. polyalphabetic ciphers

   c. transformation ciphers

   d. transposition ciphers

3. How do polyalphabetic ciphers work?

   a. They apply multiple substitution ciphers to different parts of a message and are controlled by a codebook.

   b. They apply multiple substitution ciphers to different parts of a message and are controlled by a keyword.

   c. They apply multiple transposition ciphers to different parts of a message and are controlled by a keyword.

   d. They apply multiple substitution ciphers in multiple rounds to a message and are controlled by a keyword.

4. Define cryptographic primitives.

5. Which of the following is used as a cryptographic primitive? (Choose all that apply.)

   a. pseudorandom number generators

   b. hashing functions

   c. polyalphabetic ciphers

   d. side channels

6. Why are cryptographically secure pseudorandom number generators so important to cryptography?

7. What is the block size in the AES implementation of Rijndael?

   a. 128 or 256 bits

   b. 128, 192, or 256 bits

   c. variable

   d. 128 bits

8. Which of the following symmetric algorithms doesn't use a Feistel network?

   a. DES

   b. Blowfish

   c. 3DES

   d. AES

5

9. Which of the following issues public and private key pairs?

   a. certificate publisher

   b. certification authority

   c. certificate revocation list

   d. certificate store

10. Which of the following is used to check whether a certificate is still valid?

    a. certificate revocation list

    b. certification authority

    c. certificate publisher

    d. registration authority

11. Which of the following is a symmetric algorithm not considered safe for encryption use?

    a. AES

    b. Diffie-Hellman

    c. DES

    d. RSA

12. In digital signatures, which of the following values is compared to verify a message's integrity?

    a. public key

    b. message digest

    c. private key

    d. certificate

13. Using symmetric and asymmetric algorithms to encrypt the same amount of data, which of the following statements is correct?

    a. The symmetric algorithm encrypts data faster than the asymmetric algorithm.

    b. The asymmetric algorithm encrypts data faster than the symmetric algorithm.

    c. The symmetric and asymmetric algorithms work at the same speed to encrypt data.

14. A symmetric and asymmetric algorithm are used to apply the same level of encryption strength to the same amount of data. Which of the following statements about the required key size is correct?

    a. There's not enough information to determine the key size required for either algorithm.

    b. The symmetric algorithm requires a larger key size than the asymmetric algorithm.

    c. The asymmetric algorithm requires a larger key size than the symmetric algorithm.

    d. The key size is the same, regardless of which algorithm is used.

15. Which of the following combines a hashed message authentication code with a shared secret key, processes each half of the input data with different hashing algorithms, and recombines them with an XOR function?

    a. SSL

    b. SSH

    c. TLS

    d. WPA

16. Which of the following is a reason IPSec has become the standard protocol for tunneled communication? (Choose all that apply.)

    a. IPSec is fast and supported universally.

    b. IPSec supports IPv4 and IPv6.

    c. IPSec is implemented at Layer 2.

    d. IPSec can encrypt the entire packet.

17. Which of the following is a type of side channel attack? (Choose all that apply.)

    a. acoustic recorders

    b. emission testing

    c. power monitoring

    d. thermal imaging

18. Which of the following is the component that enables IPSec to use Diffie-Hellman to create keys?

    a. Internet Key Exchange

    b. Internet Security Association Key Management Protocol

    c. Oakley

    d. IPSec driver

19. Authentication Header verifies TCP/IP packets' integrity by signing packets with a digital signature. True or False?

20. In tunnel mode, Encapsulating Security Payload encrypts which of the following?

    a. packet header

    b. data

    c. both the header and data

    d. neither the header nor data

HANDS-ON PROJECTS

Hands-On Project 5-1: Using TrueCrypt for Virtual Volume Encryption

Time Required: 20 minutes

Objective: Use an open-source encryption tool on a designated volume.

Description: In this project, you download and install TrueCrypt, an open-source encryption tool. A wizard steps you through the process of encrypting a volume on your hard drive.

1. Start your Web browser, go to **www.truecrypt.org**, and download the most recent version of TrueCrypt for Windows.

2. Unzip the downloaded file and run the installation program. After TrueCrypt is installed, you can work through a short tutorial, if you like.

3. Start TrueCrypt, which opens to the main window shown in Figure 5-14. Click the **Create Volume** button to start the volume creation wizard.

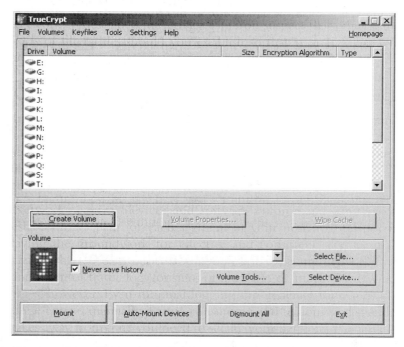

Figure 5-14   The main window in TrueCrypt

4. Click **Create a standard TrueCrypt volume**, and then click **Next**.

5. Click the **Select File** button to create a file-based volume. Browse to and select a location on your hard drive, and then enter a name of your choosing. Click **Save**, and then click **Next**.

6. In the Encryption Options window, click the different encryption algorithms, and read the available information. When you're finished, click to select **AES**. In the Hash Algorithm section, review the available types of hashing algorithms. Click to select **SHA-1**, and then click **Next**.

7. In the next window, enter **1 MB** for the size of the container for your encryption volume, and then click **Next**.

8. Enter a password, confirm it, and then click **Next**.

9. In the Volume Format Options window, click to select **FAT**, and then click **Default** for the cluster. Click **Format** to create the volume. When you see a message that the volume has been created successfully, click **OK**. Click **Exit** to finish.

10. The TrueCrypt main window should be open; if not, simply start TrueCrypt again. In the main window, click to select an unused volume drive letter to mount the volume. Make sure the location and filename you selected in Step 5 is displayed next to the blue Volume logo at the bottom. If it isn't, click the **Select File** button to find the file you created.

11. Click the **Mount** button. In the next window, enter the password you created in Step 8, and click **OK** to mount the volume.

12. In Windows Explorer, navigate to the drive letter you designated in Step 10, and view the encrypted volume. If you store information in this volume, it's encrypted automatically.

13. When another user logs on to this computer, how does TrueCrypt prevent him or her from seeing the confidential file?

_____

_____

_____

Hands-On Project 5-2: Using a Symmetric Algorithm in Word 2003

Time Required: 5 minutes

Objective: Explore the simple encryption used in Word 2003.

Description: In this project, you use Word 2003 to encrypt a document's contents and view the resulting ciphertext.

1. In a new Word document, type **The quick brown fox jumped over the lazy dog**.

2. Click **File**, **Save As** from the menu.

3. In the Save As dialog box, click the **Tools** list arrow at the upper right.

4. Click **Security Options** in the list to open the Security dialog box (see Figure 5-15). Click the **Advanced** button.

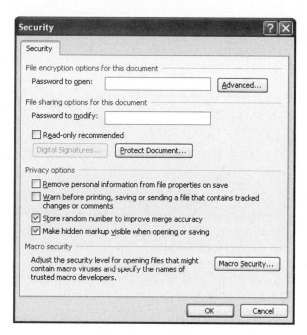

Figure 5-15   The Security dialog box

5. In the Encryption Type dialog box, click **RC4, Microsoft Enhanced RSA and AES Cryptographic Provider (Prototype)** in the list of encryption algorithms (see Figure 5-16), and notice that the key length is 128. Click **OK** to return to the Security dialog box.

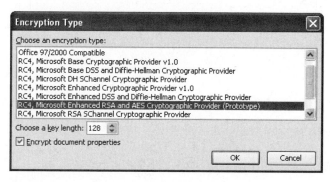

Figure 5-16   The Encryption Type dialog box

6. In the Password to open text box, type the password **Secret4Me**, and then click **OK**.

7. Type the password again in the Confirm Password dialog box, and then click **OK**.

8. In the Save As dialog box, type a filename and click **Save**.

9. Exit Word, start Notepad, and open the saved file. Can you read the original message? What is the shared key to decrypt this message?

CASE PROJECTS

Case Project 5-1: Investigating the Use of Encryption in Green Globe's Operations

CASE PROJECTS

Review the diagram of Green Globe's demilitarized zone (DMZ) in Figure 5-17, and write a report assessing the need for encryption in Green Globe's operations. Describe operations taking place in the DMZ that require encryption, and explain how encryption is used to secure the Web service. In your report, make sure you include the VPN gateway on the outer firewall, which provides Remote Access Service (RAS) for Green Globe's remote users. In addition, examine whether the FTP server is effective in ensuring confidentiality of transferred files, and recommend alternatives for encrypting FTP traffic.

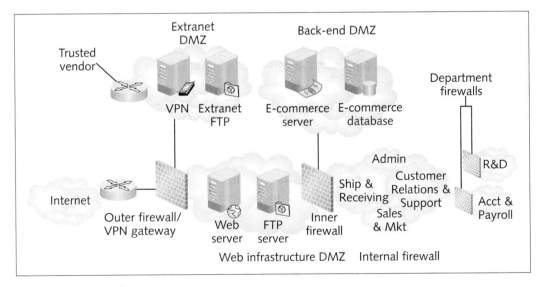

Figure 5-17   Green Globe's DMZ

6

INTERNET AND WEB SECURITY

After reading this chapter and completing the exercises, you will be able to:

♦ Describe weak points in the structure of the Internet

♦ Explain attack techniques against Web sites and Web users

♦ Explain methods for hardening Web and Internet resources

As use of the Internet becomes more prevalent, the number of attackers taking advantage of Internet users increases. In this chapter, you explore the infrastructure of Internet connectivity so that you can better understand weak points that attackers exploit.

You then explore several methods attackers use against Internet components, such as Web servers, Web browsers, and e-mail clients. Finally, you learn how to harden infrastructure points to improve network security and reduce the risk of critical information and data being compromised.

EXAMINING THE STRUCTURE OF THE INTERNET

The Internet has become a widely used tool. Government organizations use it to streamline services and communications, for example, and businesses use it to conduct transactions and marketing operations. For many organizations, the Internet is indispensable in today's competitive marketplace.

In the medium of the Internet, opportunists seek ways to exploit poorly designed systems. Whether the aim is political, criminal, greed, or just curiosity, there's a constant cycle of offense and defense: Attackers discover new exploits, and then hardware and software vendors distribute notifications and patches to defend against these exploits. In the following sections, you examine the structure of the Internet and see how administrators and users can minimize risks.

Understanding the Structure of the Internet

The Internet is a network of networks tied together to form an infrastructure for communication. Often the terms Internet and World Wide Web (WWW) are used interchangeably, but technically, they are quite different.

The Internet, a massive public broadcast medium established in the mid-1960s, is essentially an interconnected web of networks and computers that work together to provide worldwide communication—hence the term "a network of networks." The World Wide Web is just one of the services the Internet offers. Many other services are offered through this medium, such as e-mail, which uses Simple Mail Transfer Protocol (SMTP) for communication, and file transfer, which uses File Transfer Protocol (FTP). The Web is a method of accessing information through the Internet by using HTML hyperlinks. It makes use of Web servers, Web browsers, and Web pages to communicate information through the Internet network.

TIP

Think of the Internet as a bus and the Web as people on the bus. The bus is a means of conveyance for grumpy passengers, screaming babies, and people talking too loudly, which is a fairly accurate representation of a lot of the interaction on the Web.

The early Internet was based on the Defense Department's ARPANET infrastructure (the original Internet backbone) and later the National Science Foundation's NSFNET, both of which depended on the concept of interconnected Internet backbones that support a distributed mesh topology. This early network defined the hierarchy of networks that's still in operation today.

By the early 1990s, the National Science Foundation (NSF) decided to stop funding NSFNET and move toward commercialization of the Internet. Many of NSF's regional networks became commercial network service providers (NSPs), such as Netcom, UUNet/MCI Worldcom, and PSINet. Also known as backbone Internet service providers, these

NSPs expanded their backbone networks. To maintain their government funding, NSF required them to allow free flow of traffic from one backbone to the other.

Tier System

The Internet is a tier system that connects networks around the world. This system starts with a backbone network connected via network access points (NAPs) to regional ISPs. Regional ISPs service **point of presence (POP) ISPs** that connect to business, education, or home networks. The Internet is composed of a collection of backbones serviced by major carriers. The following sections explain NAPs and ISPs in more detail.

6

Routers and the Internet Communication Backbone

The Internet communication backbone is an interconnected network of backbones owned by businesses or NSPs. Much like an anatomical backbone, where nerve signals travel across the spinal cord, an Internet backbone provides a conduit for network communication between different points of Internet access.

Routers direct network traffic to its destination via routing tables and updates from routing protocols. Routers in NSP backbones differ from routers in a LAN in the high amount of traffic they are designed to handle and the routing protocols they use for the Internet backbone environment. The physical memory, CPU speeds, interfaces, and OSs of routers used in NSP backbones can support enormous amounts of traffic and large routing tables.

NOTE

For more information on routing, refer to *Guide to Tactical Perimeter Defense: Becoming a Security Network Specialist* (Course Technology, 2008, ISBN 1428356304).

Network Access Points

Network access points (NAPs) are highly secure public facilities in which backbones have interconnected data lines and routers exchanging routing and traffic data. They provide space, power, and network connectivity between several levels of the Internet's tier system, such as between a regional ISP and a POP ISP or between a backbone and a regional ISP.

Backbones exist in different regions of the world, and NAPs are positioned in each country for interconnectivity between these backbones. Each NSP backbone exchanges routing and traffic data in one of two ways: NAPs or private peering relationships (see Figure 6-1). Private peering relationships are contracts between commercial NSPs or ISPs that enable them to bypass the Internet backbone for data and route exchanges.

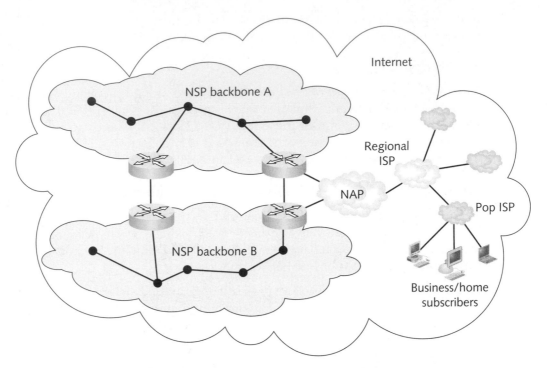

Figure 6-1   The Internet backbone: a network of NSP backbones

Internet Service Providers

An ISP provides access to the Internet in different levels depending on type. A local ISP or POP ISP provides Internet access directly to consumers or businesses. A regional ISP sells bandwidth to local or POP ISPs for their use or to organizations with high bandwidth requirements. A backbone ISP or NSP gives regional ISPs backbone access. An ISP, if large enough, might offer services at all these levels, from local/POP access to backbone ISP.

Domain Name System

The **Domain Name System (DNS)** is a name resolution service that translates hostnames to IP addresses used to identify host computers. Thirteen root servers named A through M and operated by commercial, educational, and government organizations are the foundation of the Internet DNS and are often targets of attack.

DNS is a hierarchical system, as shown in Figure 6-2. Root servers know which servers on the Internet are responsible for top-level domains (such as .org or .com). Each top-level domain has its own servers that delegate responsibility for domain name–to–IP address resolution to name servers lower in the hierarchy. In reality, most DNS information on the Internet is cached, so DNS lookups rarely have to go all the way up the hierarchy to root servers.

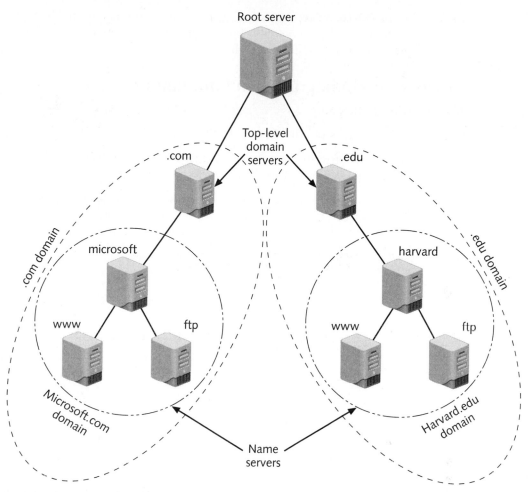

Figure 6-2 DNS hierarchy

The 13 root servers were located in the United States originally. However, servers C, F, I, J, K, and M are on other continents now, which is possible because they make use of **anycast addressing**. Unlike unicast and multicast addressing, anycast addressing enables a group of servers, even those in different locations, to act as a root server. It's a way of decentralizing DNS services, and balancing the load among several servers improves availability.

For a review of DNS and IP addressing, see Chapter 2 of *Guide to Tactical Perimeter Defense: Becoming a Security Network Specialist* (Course Technology, 2008, ISBN 1428356304).

At ISPs, a local DNS server replicates entries from higher servers in the DNS hierarchy and resolves DNS requests. This server also forwards queries up the hierarchy if it can't resolve a request with its own DNS table or cache.

Activity 6-1: Finding Domain Information

Time Required: 10 minutes

Objective: Find your network's DNS and ISP information.

Description: In this activity, you use network tools available at Network-Tools.com to discover domain information about your network.

1. Start your Web browser and go to **http://network-tools.com**. Figure 6-3 shows the interface for this tool.

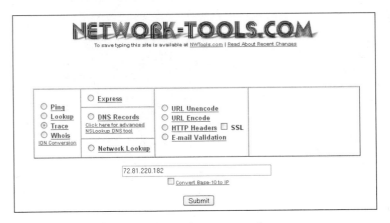

Figure 6-3   The Network-Tools.com interface

2. Click the **Lookup** option button, type your school's domain name (such as schoolname.edu) in the text box below the option buttons, and then click **Submit**. What is the IP address that corresponds to your school's domain name? What country and region are shown for this domain name?

   _____

   _____

3. Click the **Whois** option button, and then click **Submit**. Who is the contact for your school's domain name? What are the name servers listed for your school's domain?

   _____

   _____

4. Click the **DNS Records** option button, and then click **Submit**. What are the mail servers for your school's domain (MX records)?

_____

_____

5. Click the **Trace** option button, and then click **Submit**. Who are the ISP providers handling the school's Internet traffic?

_____

_____

6. Exit your browser, and leave your system running for the next activity.

Understanding Weak Points in the Internet's Structure

For all the usefulness the Internet offers, risks are inevitable when people and organizations operate in this environment. Attackers discover new ways of exploiting the Internet infrastructure constantly, and IT professionals are often in a catch-up game to stay ahead of attackers' exploits. In the following sections, you examine some techniques attackers use to exploit weaknesses in the Internet's structure.

IP Spoofing

Computers on the Internet are identified mainly by their IP addresses, which aren't authenticated by TCP/IP. As mentioned in Chapter 3, this lack of authentication makes IP spoofing possible. Attackers change the source IP address in the headers of malicious packets they're sending to match a trusted host's IP address. To find a legitimate IP address, attackers sometimes send ping packets into a network and wait for responses. IP spoofing is most often used in denial-of-service (DoS) attacks. Attackers don't care about receiving responses to their packets; they want to trick a network's defense systems into accepting packets so that they can flood the network with packets and cause it to crash. Attackers sometimes use IP spoofing to fool servers into sending responses to their forged addresses, however. Because IP spoofing is so widespread, it also makes accountability for malicious actions on the Internet difficult; anyone can claim that he or she was IP spoofed.

Modern network routers and firewalls offer software protection against known forms of IP spoofing. Packet filtering through routers is a major defense, for example. It includes ingress filtering to prevent spoofed IP source addresses from entering a network and perhaps egress filtering to prevent users inside a network from sending spoofed packets outside the network. Additionally, IPv6 will offer improvements to prevent IP spoofing, such as authenticated headers in each packet.

TIP

For more information on defending a network against spoofing attacks, visit *www.ietf.org/rfc/rfc4953.txt*.

Routing Security

The Internet network is linked by routers, and routing protocols, such as Border Gateway Protocol (BGP), are used to communicate information updates for routing tables. However, routing information isn't authenticated, so it's vulnerable to compromise. Attackers could send modified routing updates that misdirect data to a destination of their choosing. With this data, they could launch DoS attacks, use IP spoofing to intercept packets, or launch man-in-the-middle attacks, in which an attacker's computer or router is placed between the source and destination of a communication to intercept and steal information.

TIP

For more information on routing security, see Steven M. Bellovin's brief at *www.cs.columbia.edu/~smb/talks/routesec.pdf.*

DNS Security

DNS was originally designed as a public database for name resolution services, so checking the authenticity and integrity of information stored in name servers wasn't considered necessary. This lack of security has caused several problems for the Internet community.

One problem is DNS cache poisoning (also known as DNS spoofing). When a name server is queried for DNS information not in its cache, it queries other servers. Because DNS information isn't authenticated, attackers can send false data to a name server; therefore, the DNS cache is said to have been "poisoned." Attackers often use cache poisoning to steer unsuspecting victims to a server of their choice instead of the Web site where victims intended to go.

A DNS name server for an organization contains database entries about every host on the network. Another problem caused by lack of authentication is DNS information leakage, which might occur if attackers accessed this database and used it to map target systems in the network. This information can be partially secured in DNS by blocking zone transfers, which replicate a name server's DNS information to other servers. Attackers could still retrieve the information by using DNS tools to query systems in an organization's IP namespace automatically one by one until they have captured a complete listing of DNS information. However, this method is slower and more painstaking.

Internet Host Security

Ironically, one of the bastions of Internet interconnectivity, the millions of host computers worldwide, is also the weakest point of the Internet infrastructure. Attackers hijack many unprotected computers around the world and use them as zombie computers to deliver spam e-mail, DoS attacks, and malicious code. Attackers often assemble these zombies into **botnets** (networks of zombie computers) to magnify the scope and intensity of their attacks.

IronPort, an antispam company, has estimated that more than 80% of the world's spam e-mail is delivered by hijacked zombie computers (*http://ironport.com/company/ironport_pr_2006-06-28.html*).

For the Internet (and its Web component) to function, many computers must be connected globally into one network. Each computer differs in the way it has been prepared to handle dangers on the Internet. The risks a careless user takes, for example, in the United States or China or South Africa can have dire consequences for careful users whose host computers are connected to the same network (the Internet). As discussed in Chapter 3, the dangers of virus, Trojan, or DDoS attacks on your system might exist simply because you're connected to the Internet. Therefore, good computing practices to minimize risks, such as antivirus software, firewalls, and system patches, are essential to survive attacks from the Internet.

NOTE Following a strict regimen of system patching isn't hard. Most major software suppliers, such as Microsoft, Red Hat, IBM, and Oracle, have automated processes for getting the most recent patches and updates for their software.

EXAMINING WEB ATTACK TECHNIQUES

To exploit the Internet's weaknesses, attackers use a variety of innovative techniques. In Chapter 3, you learned about some methods attackers use to compromise computer systems. Network reconnaissance activities—footprinting, scanning, enumeration, and social engineering—are early steps attackers use to learn more about target Web servers or host browsers and how to attack them. In the following sections, you examine attack techniques by seeing how they are constructed and then learning how to best defend against them. First, you examine attacks against Web servers, and then you learn about attacks on the client side of the Internet: Web browsers and e-mail applications.

Attack Techniques Against Web Servers

The World Wide Web operates on the principles of a client/server network, and its basic building blocks are Web servers and client computers. Because millions of these network components are distributed around the world and their hardware and software configurations are so similar in nature, they are the Internet components that attackers target most often. It's simply a question of numbers. Thousands of attackers probing a few common hardware/software server configurations (such as Windows running Internet Information Services or Linux running Apache Web Server) are more likely to discover security holes than a few attackers probing scores of different configurations.

Sensitive transactions, such as banking and e-commerce, are commonplace now on the Internet, so attackers often select Web servers handling these transaction as targets for activities such as identity theft of a business's customers. The following sections explain ways a Web server can be compromised.

Buffer Overflow Attacks

A buffer overflow attack exploits software vulnerabilities over which users and even network security personnel have little, if any, control. These common attacks often come with no warning and are almost impossible to detect and, therefore, fix. They have been around since the mid-1980s, when attackers discovered how to manipulate computer memory remotely by using worms and Trojans.

Generally, commercial software (such as OSs, Web servers, and databases) is more vulnerable to buffer attacks than customized software that companies create for internal use. The source code is wrapped in a "black box" to protect it from tampering, but many attackers have the skill to access this code. Word of pinhole vulnerabilities in black boxes travels fast through the hacker community, and decompile tools for commercial software are readily available. After attackers have access to an application's code structure, they can look for weaknesses and errors in the source code—the root of buffer overflow attacks.

Keep in mind that buffer overflows themselves aren't a cause for concern. These errors are common in computer operations. You've seen system errors similar to the one in Figure 6-4; they indicate that the buffer might have been corrupted during normal operations. The security problem starts when attackers discover poorly written code that causes buffer overflows and inject malicious code into this breach.

Figure 6-4   A common system memory error message

A buffer is a section of memory (RAM) shared by application processes that depend on one another but operate at different speeds or with different priorities. Its purpose is to coordinate data intended for use by separate activities. A critical buffer component for this coordination is the call or function stack (usually referred to as just "the stack"), and buffer overflow attacks are usually aimed at this component, in which case they're sometimes called stack smashing attacks.

The stack stores information about an application's currently running processes as well as return addresses (where processes go when they finish running), local variables, and parameters. For example, if Process1 calls Process2 several times, Process1 pushes the instruction for the return addresses of Process2's calls onto the stack. When Process2 finishes running, it pulls its return address from the stack, and program control is transferred back to Process1's return address.

Stacks are allocated a fixed size in memory when they're created. Local variables for each running process occupy (are "buffered in") some of that fixed memory space. If pushing instructions onto the stack consumes all the space allocated for the stack, a buffer overflow occurs. The problem is that the program code doesn't adequately police how local variables are loaded and used in the buffer. For a buffer to be effective, its size and the algorithms for moving data in and out need to be protected, so good buffer design in programming is crucial in preventing attacks.

More specifically, buffer overflow attacks exploit a lack of "bounds checking" on the size of data stored in a buffer array. By writing data larger than the size allocated to an array, the attacker causes the buffer to overflow. Take a look at the following program code:

NOTE The code examples are shown in the C language because many C programs have buffer overflow vulnerabilities caused by a lack of bounds checking in some library functions, such as strcopy and gets.

```
void buffSmash(void)
{
char *strOne = "abcdefghijklmnopqrstuvwxyz0123456789";
char buffOne[15];
strcpy(buffOne, strOne);
return;
}
```

The buffOne variable has been allocated 15 bytes in memory to store data assigned to it. The strOne string is larger than 15 bytes, but the code attempts to stuff it into buffOne's memory space. The result is a buffer overflow: buffOne spills over into memory space allocated for another purpose. This error is only an annoyance until attackers discover it, and then it becomes a security problem.

With this attack, attackers might be looking for an error message such as the one shown previously in Figure 6-4, which reveals a critical instruction pointer (0x06c4eaa8). Attackers attempt to overwrite this pointer with a return instruction injected through the buffer that redirects the process to run malicious code—with the ultimate goal of seizing control of the program and server.

Defending against a buffer attack is usually reactive rather than proactive because you can't foresee vulnerabilities in commercial software. The best defense is to install patches and updates as soon as they're available. Most buffer attack damage is inflicted on unpatched systems. On the proactive side, installing intrusion detection software can be beneficial, such as Sourcefire Snort (*www.snort.org*) and McAfee Entercept (*www.mcafee.com*).

SQL Injection Attacks

Structured Query Language (SQL, pronounced "sequel") is used to communicate with most relational database management systems (RDBMSs), such as Oracle, MySQL, SQL

Server, and DB2. Because SQL is used so widely, particularly in e-commerce databases, it's a favorite target of attackers for data theft and destruction. As you've learned, buffer overflows are a result of poor coding. The same is true for SQL injection attacks: Web sites that haven't been sanitized correctly are vulnerable to attack.

The term "sanitized" is used to describe computer applications or processes that have been protected against attacks.

NOTE

A buffer overflow attack requires a lot of programming expertise, thus limiting the number of potential attackers. SQL injection, however, is plaintext scripting that's easy to learn and apply, making it a favorite language for fledgling attackers (often called script kiddies). No special tools are needed—just a computer connected to the Internet, a Web browser, and patience. The good news is that unlike buffer code written by a third-party programmer, Web pages usually consist of custom-written code. Therefore, coding vulnerabilities can be fixed, if they're detected in time.

SQL injection doesn't attack a Web server directly. It attacks the database used to support Web sites housed on the Web server, and more sophisticated attacks can be extended to attack the database server and its partner Web server. The next sections examine two SQL injection attack methods and their effects on database and Web servers.

SQL Injection: Web Form Attacks

Web forms used to gather information, such as login pages or order forms, are potential entry points for attackers probing for Web site vulnerabilities. These forms are usually connected to a Web server's database, and a verification process checks information entered in the form and rejects incorrect entries. If the form's entry text boxes aren't verified correctly, however, attackers can use them to send malicious code to the database, the database server, and perhaps even the partner Web server.

If attackers are targeting a specific Web site, any form on the site (login, information, e-mail, and so on) is the starting point to look for vulnerabilities. More likely, however, attackers have to search for vulnerable candidates, which requires patience. A common method of finding candidates is using a Google search for login pages.

To find login pages, go to *www.google.com* and try these search terms: login.htm, login.html, login.asp, login.aspx, login.php, and login.jsp. These keywords return thousands of possibilities. You could also substitute index and logon for login.

TIP

The attacker might work down the Google results one by one or pick certain types, such as bank or e-commerce sites, and then start probing. The simplest method is entering a single quote (') in the first text box on a form and submitting it. An unsanitized form allows sending an unpaired single quote in the SQL command to the database, which generates an error message. The database expects to receive a SQL command something like this:

```
SELECT somefields FROM sometable WHERE field1 = 'username' and
field2='password'
```

At this point, an attacker has no idea what the table or field names are but is just hoping to generate an error to find information. Here's an example of the SQL the attacker sends to the database:

```
SELECT somefields FROM sometable WHERE field1 = ''' and field2=''
```

Notice the three single quotes following the equal sign after feild1. They represent an unpaired quote, which generates an error message similar to Figure 6-5.

Figure 6-5   A database-generated error message

With this input, the attacker might be able to learn the following:

- The Web page is not well protected from intrusion.
- The database uses SQL Server, and the Web server uses Internet Information Services.
- A careless administrator hasn't changed the default database username (sa).
- Pages are constructed with Active Server Pages (ASP), which could be a clue about the coding languages used on this Web site.

Another approach, or one to supplement the previous probe, is to inject SQL code that always evaluates to true (such as x=x). Attackers probe for familiar SQL patterns used to perform certain Web functions, such as verifying usernames and passwords or checking for valid e-mail addresses. Here's an example of an attacker's entry in a text box requesting an e-mail address:

```
SELECT somefields FROM sometable WHERE field = 'xyz@home.com' OR
'x=x'
```

It doesn't matter what e-mail address or text is entered between the first and second single quotes (in this case, xyz@home.com). The attacker is speculating about the SELECT statement's structure and has added another SQL command, OR 'x=x'. The statement x=x always evaluates to true, so this SQL statement asks for fields that *either* contain the bogus e-mail address *or* in which x=x (which is always true). If either condition is met, a return should be made.

This query might generate different responses, such as delivering all rows of a table or displaying a message stating that a correct password has been delivered to a specified e-mail address. With either response, the attacker has gained more information for creating a database footprint—a map of tables and fields in the database—that can be used to launch more serious exploits.

This method requires patience, but attackers with a destructive intent could learn enough to cause serious damage. For example, if attackers know the type and name of the database and table names, they might be able to enter a SQL command to shut down the database or drop a table, as shown in this example:

```
SELECT knownfield FROM knowntable WHERE knownfield='' or 1=1;
DROP TABLE knowntable; -- ' AND otherfield=''
```

NOTE

The semicolons denote the start of a new SQL command, and the double dash (--) indicates that what follows is a comment, not code.

With this access, attackers could add users to tables or print lists of information, such as credit card numbers. The most serious result is attackers gaining administrative access to a database and running stored procedures used to issue server commands, which could give them access to the entire Web site operation.

SQL Injection: Query String Attacks

The second SQL injection attack method involves the query string used to send information to a database. When a user clicks a link on a Web page, information is sent to the Web server. For instance, on a retail site, a user might click a product picture to see more information, which is stored on a database supporting the Web server. The product's ID code (and perhaps other information) is attached to the Web page address and sent to the Web server for action. This information being sent is clearly visible in the browser address bar and can be the source of an attack on the Web site's database. In the following activity, you see how this attack works.

Activity 6-2: Examining Query String Attacks

Time Required: 20 minutes

Objective: Examine the SQL injection attack method used with query strings.

Description: In this activity, you visit a Web site that uses query strings to retrieve and display information to users. You then examine how an attacker could exploit the query string to retrieve additional information.

1. Start your Web browser, and go to **www.asp101.com/tips/**.

This Web site is carefully protected from hacker intrusion. It's used only to demonstrate information that might appear in a browser address bar.

NOTE

2. Click the first tip in the list of Quick Tips, and then examine the code in the browser address bar. Write the code on the following line:

_____

This query string code directs the Web server to display the index.asp Web page and pass it the ID of 1 (index.asp?Id=1) to deliver information from a table row with a unique ID of 1.

NOTE

3. Delete the last character in the address bar (1, in this case), and type **2**. Then click **Go** or press **Enter** to rerun the address. A new tip appears on the index.asp Web page.

4. At the end of the string in the address bar, delete the 2 and replace it with a **'** (single quote). Then click **Go** or press **Enter** to rerun the address. Observe what happens. Write the message the Web page returns:

_____

_____

5. A well-structured error-handling response is returned. Notice that the message reveals no information about the Web site's operation; if the error weren't handled correctly, information the attacker could use might have been revealed. This site is well protected, however.

6. Find another Web site that uses Web pages with a .php extension and repeat Steps 3 to 5.

6

TIP

To find these pages, do a Google search on php?id=. That's what attackers do!

7. Exit your browser, and leave your system running for the next activity.

The preceding activity demonstrates using a query string to extract information from a database. Attackers use this method to probe Web databases for vulnerabilities; it's the same technique used in Web form attacks, just a different injection point. To generate more information from an error message, attackers might try to add extra code to the end of the query string, as shown:

```
index.asp?id=1 AND password=1
```

As with the Web form attack, the goal of any query string probe is to gain additional information about a database structure for further attacks.

SQL Injection Defense

The good news is that SQL injection attacks are isolated to custom applications, so administrators can prevent them, unlike buffer overflows, which require third-party vendors to make code adjustments. The first course of action is to prevent malicious code from being entered in Web pages that allow user input. A common mistake is for site administrators to stop there and take no further protective measures. Attackers can exploit SQL in many other ways, however, so you should take the following steps to close all potential holes:

- Tighten database authentication and limit table access. Always require password access to the database, and never leave default usernames set up during installation in place. Most attackers are familiar with the default administrative username sa, so make sure that username in particular is changed.

- Use stored procedures to eliminate passing any SQL commands to the database.

- Validate (in several places, if necessary) all user entries to make sure they're formed properly. There should be two layers of validation: form-level validation at the browser before the Web page is submitted and server-level validation when the information reaches the server for processing.

- Place the Web server and database server in a network DMZ.

- Use nonstandard naming conventions in database construction. To thwart attackers, database names, table names, and field names should be difficult to guess.

- Inevitably, database errors do occur, so configure a custom error message to display that doesn't reveal information attackers could exploit. The standard 404 error message often reveals server information attackers can use.

With these simple precautions, a Web server and its database server can be made immune to SQL injection attacks.

Attack Techniques Against Web Users

In the previous section, you learned about attack techniques directed against computer or network systems. Now you examine attacks directed at Web users through commonly used applications, such as Web browsers and e-mail programs. These attacks fall into the category of social engineering because they prey on emotions such as curiosity, anxiety, fear, and greed. Unlike some attacks against systems, almost all attacks against Web users can be prevented.

Every user takes on a measure of security risk when interacting on the Web. Attacks on Web users center on a variety of objectives. From identity theft to simple malicious behavior, informed Web users should understand these attack methods and know how to prevent them on their computers. In the following sections, you explore some of these risks and measures to eliminate or at least minimize the risk.

Phishing Attacks

Phishing, an attack through a Web browser, displays false information masquerading as legitimate information. It's a type of deception designed to steal personal information such as credit card data, account numbers, usernames, and passwords.

Phishing attacks can take many forms and range from simple to quite sophisticated. A simple form that has persisted for many years is the Nigerian money scam. The perpetrator sends out millions of e-mails to a random selection of addressees, asking for help in transferring a large sum of money from Nigeria to the United States. To be rewarded with a 10% fee, all the e-mail recipient must do is provide personal banking information to assist in making the transfer. This phishing scam persists because it works. It has even grown in popularity to include letters from China, North Korea, and Russia. The letters are almost comical in their wording, and it's hard to imagine that anyone would take them seriously. People are still taken in by this scam, however.

Another form involves Web page deception. An attacker sends out millions of e-mails that appear to come from trusted sources, such as banks, insurance companies, or payment sites (PayPal or eBay, for example). The phony e-mails, at first glance, look legitimate with corporate graphics that mimic those of a real organization. Figure 6-6 shows a typical corporate phishing e-mail.

Following are some characteristic traits of corporate phishing e-mails:

- The e-mail is unsolicited and unexpected.
- The logo and other graphics are copies of corporate imagery and seem to be legitimate.
- The message uses a generic greeting, such as "Dear valued customer" or "Corporate bank user," instead of the recipient's real name.
- The message conveys a sense of urgency, such as "Please respond immediately," "Your account has been locked," "Your credit card has expired," or "There is a security problem." These phrases are intended to make readers hurry and perhaps overlook illegitimate aspects of the e-mail.

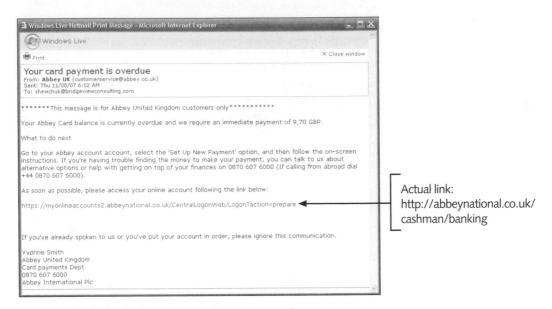

Figure 6-6 A typical corporate phishing e-mail

- Personal account information is requested, usually by asking that the information be confirmed.

- The e-mail contains a link that seems to be a secure HTTPS link. When you navigate to a Web page with this link, a lock symbol depicting an SSL-encrypted site appears at the lower right. If you hover the mouse pointer over the link, however, the real Web page address appears at the lower left. Other links in the e-mail, such as "Security Policy" or "For further information," point to the same illegitimate link.

- Usually the link to which you're being redirected is no longer active after several hours. Phishing attackers play a game of hit-and-run with the authorities who are trying to catch them, so they don't stay stationary for long.

In the early days of phishing, e-mail messages were crude and filled with grammar and spelling mistakes, and the graphics were poor copies. Attackers have become more sophisticated, however, and now these e-mails are often well crafted and difficult to discern from the real thing.

The phishing attackers' objective is to entice e-mail recipients to click the bogus link, visit the fake Web site, and enter personal information that could be used to steal personal assets or identities. These attacks are prevalent because they're easy and inexpensive to create and carry out. All an attacker needs is a Web site address, which can be purchased for under $10 (or even stolen by hacking into a legitimate Web site) and an e-mail list. E-mail lists are collected in a number of ways, such as surfing through newsgroups or blogs or purchasing lists from spammers or other phishers.

A couple of phishing variations have surfaced. In **pharming**, traffic to a legitimate Web site is redirected to the attacker's Web server. To do this, the attacker modifies the user's host file (a local file on the hard drive that assigns an IP address to a domain name) or uses DNS manipulation, such as cache poisoning. Pharming is more insidious than phishing because it doesn't require users to click a URL to go to the attacker's server.

For an in-depth look at pharming, read the article at *www.symantec.com/ avcenter/reference/Driveby_Pharming.pdf*.

TIP

Another phishing variation, **spear phishing**, focuses on specific targets, usually financial institutions or government agencies. The attacker identifies users or groups in an organization by using common avenues: e-mail, telephone, MySpace, and corporate Web pages. He might even gather names and job titles from assigned parking spaces. The attacker then mounts a campaign to exploit employees' vulnerabilities with the goal of using their access rights to penetrate the corporate infrastructure. Even the best corporate security measures are vulnerable to this attack because it's an inside job, launched within the corporate security perimeter by using employees' authentication credentials. Spear phishing is becoming more common because people are increasingly careless about revealing personal information on the Web through chat sites, blogs, and retail shopping.

Preventing most phishing attacks is a matter of educating Web users. Train employees to follow these simple guidelines for preventing phishing attacks:

- Check the browser address bar and footer. If a Web site doesn't have an HTTPS address or a lock icon, it's not a secure site, and no personal information should be entered. (A note of caution: The lock icon can be faked, so users shouldn't rely on seeing it to consider the site secure.)

- If you get an e-mail from a company you're familiar with, call the company to confirm that the request is legitimate. Companies usually have an 800 number for this purpose.

- Forward any obvious phishing e-mails to the company being faked. PayPal and eBay, for example, have forwarding addresses set up for this purpose.

- Delete any unsolicited e-mails about foreign banking (unless you have a Swiss bank account).

As a network security administrator, you must remind users of these simple preventive measures frequently. Send out regular e-mail reminders so that prevention again phishing attacks becomes second nature.

For a look at actual phishing e-mails, do a Google search using the company name and the word phishing. Two examples are at *https://www.citicards.com/cards/ wv/detail.do?screenID=607* and *www.cibc.com/ca/legal/fraud-examples.html*.

TIP

Phishing is sometimes referred to as Web page spoofing. The term spoofing, however, is usually reserved for IP spoofing.

File Attachment Attacks

E-mail attachments are a common vehicle for sending malicious code into a network. These attacks first occurred in 2002 when JPEG attachments were discovered to have virus code embedded in the file header code. Until then, data files had been fairly immune to infection.

The attack requires two virus parts. The first part spreads in the form of a traditional Win32 executable virus, arriving via e-mail or portable media. This virus makes changes to the Registry so that JPEG files are run through an extractor before they're displayed. The virus strikes if the user attempts to view a JPEG image and the extractor finds the second virus part in the graphics file header. Having both parts on the same computer is rare, however, because standard virus protection typically detects the presence of a virus arriving via e-mail or portable media. However, users should be cautious about viewing image file attachments from unknown sources.

A more recent file attachment attack involved PDF attachments; Symantec has tagged it as Trojan.Pideief.A. This attack arrives via spam e-mail with a PDF attachment, usually named Bill.pdf or Invoice.pdf to make it seem important. Adobe allows authors of PDF files to embed scripted programs and executable code in a file. If virus code is embedded in a PDF, the e-mail might be able to bypass filters in e-mail programs that normally screen out virus scripts. A flaw in certain Adobe Acrobat products (not Adobe Reader) allows malicious code in the PDF file to run, which disables Windows Firewall and then downloads a Trojan program via FTP.

The immediate solution for preventing this attack is to patch Adobe products according to their posted advisories. A patch is available for download from *www.adobe.com/support/ security/bulletins/apsb07-18.html*. A network administrator could also block delivery of e-mails with PDF attachments or advise users not to open PDFs from unknown sources, and access to known network and IP addresses usually involved in this attack could be blocked.

ActiveX Control Attacks

An ActiveX control is a Windows object coded in languages such as C++, Visual Basic, and Java. Its purpose is to deliver dynamic, interactive content to Web pages. A control object is compiled and stored in a CAB file, which is stored on a Web server and accessed by referencing the object's assigned CLASSID, as shown in the following code from the Developer Connection Quick-Time site (*http://developer.apple.com/quicktime/compatibility.html*):

```
<OBJECT CLASSID="clsid:02BF25D5-8C17-4B23-BC80-D3488ABDDC6B"
WIDTH="160"
```

```
HEIGHT="144"
CODEBASE="http://www.apple.com/qtactivex/qtplugin.cab">
<PARAM name="SRC" VALUE="sample.mov">
<PARAM name="AUTOPLAY" VALUE="true">
<PARAM name="CONTROLLER" VALUE="false">
<EMBED SRC="sample.mov" WIDTH="160" HEIGHT="144" AUTOPLAY="true"
CONTROLLER="false"
PLUGINSPAGE="http://www.apple.com/quicktime/download/">
</EMBED>
</OBJECT>
```

6

When used for legitimate purposes, an ActiveX control can be a beneficial addition to a Web site; however, attackers have discovered that an ActiveX control can be programmed to run malicious code on a user's Web browser. ActiveX controls don't require user action to be activated. They run automatically when the browser loads the Web page containing them. ActiveX controls have almost full access to the Windows OS and can perform many functions, including running code on an unprotected computer, which could involve accessing and downloading files, planting Trojan programs and worms, or destroying system programs.

The defense against malicious ActiveX controls is to make sure all ActiveX controls are scrutinized by using security settings on Web browsers. Browsers can be set to block the functioning of ActiveX controls on Web pages, for example. You can also adjust browser settings to permit certain types of ActiveX controls to run and block others. In the following activity, you check Microsoft Internet Explorer security settings to determine how ActiveX controls are handled.

Activity 6-3: Examining Internet Explorer Security Settings

Time Required: 15 minutes

Objective: Observe changes to ActiveX control settings at different security levels.

Description: In this activity, you examine Internet Explorer's settings for handling ActiveX controls. You examine the default settings first, and then make changes to determine how they affect browser security.

You need Windows XP Professional with SP2 and Internet Explorer 6.0 installed.

1. Start Internet Explorer, and click **Tools**, **Internet Options** from the menu. In the Internet Options dialog box, click the **Security** tab. How many Internet zone icons are displayed at the top?

_____

_____

2. Verify that the **Internet** icon is selected. In the Security level for this zone section, click the **Default level** button to open the Security Settings dialog box. What's the default security level? What is the note at this level about the treatment of ActiveX controls?

_____

_____

3. Click the **Custom level** button. In the Reset custom settings section, what reset levels are available?

_____

4. Scroll to the ActiveX controls and plugins section. For the first ActiveX control setting, click the **Disable** option button. For all remaining ActiveX control settings, click the **Enable** option button.

5. Click **OK** to close the Security Settings dialog box. When you see a warning message about changing security settings for this zone, click **Yes**.

6. In the Internet Options dialog box, drag the security level slider to the bottom of the scale. You should see a message box advising you that the recommended security level is Medium. Click **OK**, and the slider moves back to the Medium setting automatically.

7. Drag the slider to the topmost position, and then click the **Custom level** button. Observe the settings you changed for ActiveX controls in Step 4. What has happened to these settings?

_____

8. Click **OK** and **OK** again to close the Security Settings and Internet Options dialog boxes. Exit Internet Explorer, and leave your system running for the next activity.

Java Applet Attacks

A Java applet is a small program sometimes used as embedded code in Web pages. Java applets were considered immune to hacking because they were encased in a "sandbox" that couldn't interact with a host computer outside the confines of a browser; they could communicate only back to their codebase. However, on several occasions involving Internet Explorer and Netscape, Java applets have been used to exploit the OS and access system files. In the Internet Explorer attacks, malicious code embedded in a Java applet was used to exploit a proxy server network connection. The user's session was then redirected to a location of the attacker's choice without the user being aware of it, so the attacker was able to capture the user's information.

In the Netscape attacks, vulnerabilities in Netscape Communicator and Navigator made it possible for Java applet code to gain unauthorized local and remote file access. A malicious Java applet could read files from the local file system by opening a connection to a URL and gaining complete file access. The applet could then send files back to the server from which it originated.

With this method, the connection is reversed, and the Web browser user is sending information to the applet originator. This communication reversal negates the protection of the user's firewall, which watches for incoming vulnerabilities, not outgoing ones.

Although the combination of circumstances in these attacks is rare, it does emphasize the need to make sure your system is patched with the most recent updates and hot fixes. Furthermore, only signed applets should be permitted to run on Web browsers. In the Java applet exploits discussed previously, software patches from vendors fixed the problem.

TIP

For more information on Java applets and their use in Web pages, visit *www. cafeaulait.org/course/week5/index.html.*

6

HARDENING WEB AND INTERNET RESOURCES

Establishing and maintaining a hardened network with secure hosts requires continuous vigilance and updating components regularly. New versions of software, hardware, and network media are released frequently, but the threats against networks and systems change just as often. A network security administrator alone can't hope to keep up with the daily deluge of security concerns. By enlisting the help of security experts and adopting a preventive stance toward network security, the task is far less daunting.

Seeking the assistance of security experts need not be an expensive venture. Most help you need is free. Your first stop should be the supplier of your firewall and antivirus software. All reputable vendors maintain informative Web sites with excellent guidelines on how best to use their products. They also offer automatic, timely downloads of the latest virus signature databases so that your systems are protected as soon as protection is available. With your network systems protected, you can then push updates to all connected host computers automatically. Two of the best in the antivirus business are Sophos at *www.sophos.com* and Trend Micro at *http://us.trendmicro.com/us/home.* Both sites offer a wealth of information on the latest threats and protective measures.

Additionally, security organizations offer timely threat analysis to make your job easier. The largest of these organizations is the SANS Institute, with a worldwide membership of about 165,000 security professionals. In the following activity, you visit the SANS Web site and learn more about the information it offers.

ACTIVITY

Activity 6-4: Exploring the SANS Web Site

Time Required: 30 minutes

Objective: Learn about the Internet security information available on the SANS Web site.

Description: In this activity, you visit the SANS Web site to find information on current Internet threats and security resources.

1. Start your Web browser and go to **www.sans.org**.

2. On the SANS home page, scroll down to the Free Resources section, and click the **Top 20 Vulnerabilities** link. Under the heading for 2007 vulnerabilities, click the link for the executive summary, and read the first paragraph. What were the two major attacker targets during 2007?

   _____

3. Read the attack scenarios described in the executive summary, and then scroll down to read the vulnerabilities for Microsoft Office products. Approximately how much did vulnerabilities for these products increase from 2006 to 2007?

   _____

4. Scroll back to the top of the page. Place your mouse pointer over the **storm center** menu item, and click the **reports** entry in the drop-down list. On the Reports page, click the **Trends** link at the left, and examine the graph on the Trends report page. Which port is currently showing the highest increase in attack activity?

   _____

5. Click the browser's **Back** button to return to the Reports page, and then click the **Top Ports** link at the left. On the Port Reports page, change the year portion of the date to **2006**, enter **80** in the Port text box, and click the **Update** button. How many attack reports are listed in the results for port 80?

   _____

6. At the top of the page are color indicators for Internet threat levels. Note the colors for each level, and write down the current Internet threat level:

   _____

7. Click the **sans.org** link at the upper left to return to the SANS home page. Place your mouse pointer over the **resources** menu item, and then click the **s.c.o.r.e.** entry. What does s.c.o.r.e. stand for? Examine this page for useful security techniques and information. The links to the right lead you to more detailed information (guides, checklists, tools, and so forth) for establishing and maintaining Internet security.

   _____

8. When you're finished, exit your Web browser, and leave your system running for the projects at the end of the chapter.

Hardening DNS Servers

When attackers probe networks to look for vulnerabilities, they are footprinting the network, as you learned in Chapter 3. They pay special attention to servers hosting Internet services, such as DNS or Web servers, because these servers store valuable personal and corporate information. In this section and the following ones, you learn techniques for hardening these servers against attacks.

A primary DNS server is authoritative for specific domains and has DNS zone files (instructions for resolving domain names into IP addresses) that change as needed. A secondary DNS server receives a read-only copy of the zone file to improve the query performance of DNS services. An internal DNS zone file contains entries of all internal hosts on a network, and an external zone file contains only host entries that are visible to the public. A **zone transfer** occurs when a zone file is sent from the primary DNS server to secondary DNS servers for updating. A zone is just an abbreviated way of referring to the domain name for which a DNS server is configured. If the domain name is myschool.edu, for example, its parts are the name (myschool) and the generic top-level domain (edu). A subdomain might be staff.myschool.edu, for example. Figure 6-7 shows an example of a small zone file.

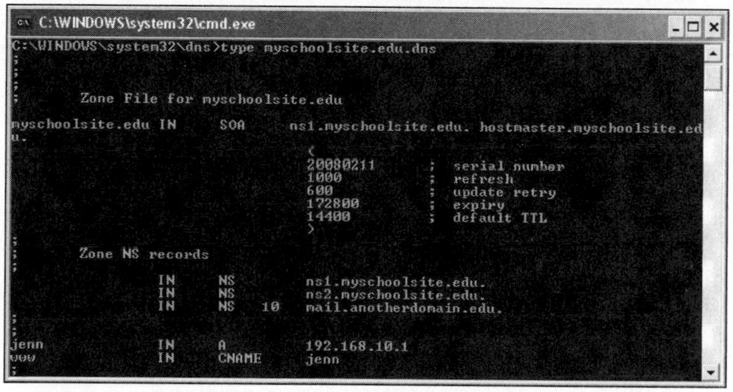

Figure 6-7   A zone file for myschoolsite.edu

If zone transfers aren't secured, attackers might be able to intercept them and retrieve a complete listing of network resources and possible targets for attack. One of the most serious configuration mistakes a network administrator can make is to allow untrusted Internet users (any host outside the network) to perform zone transfers. Transfers should be allowed only between primary and secondary DNS servers. If the DNS server doesn't use a segregation method to separate external DNS information from private internal information, internal IP address and hostname information could be exposed to attackers, who would then have an electronic road map of the organization. The following example shows probing code that an attacker might try as a starting point:

```
C:\Nslookup
```

This code might yield the following information:

```
Server: somedomain.com
Address: 10.10.10.10
```

With this information, the attacker could attempt to change the server to the network's primary DNS server and list and pull records from it.

Securing zone transfers is usually straightforward; you simply configure all DNS servers to restrict zone transfers to specific authorized servers. Using selective transfers minimizes the risk of unauthorized users getting a copy of a zone file.

If your organization has a DNS server that's authoritative for your domain on the Internet, make sure DNS servers are in a DMZ and a split DNS architecture is used. A **split DNS architecture** physically separates public DNS servers (for authoritative DNS services to the Internet) from the organization's internal DNS servers. Additionally, internal DNS servers use a non-Internet domain name, such as .corp or .local; the authoritative DNS servers conform to Internet domain requirements. A split DNS architecture, like the example in Figure 6-8, prevents internal zone information from being stored on an Internet-accessible server and prevents internal DNS entries from being sent over Internet DNS.

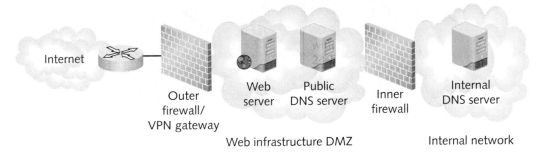

Figure 6-8   A split DNS architecture

Another layer of DNS security is at the network perimeter, where you should configure firewalls and routers with rules or filters to prevent zone transfers to the Internet. Zone transfers typically occur over TCP port 53.

In Windows Server 2003 DNS, take the following steps to restrict zone transfers:

1. Open the DNS management console.
2. Right-click the DNS zone and click Properties.
3. Click the Zone Transfers tab, and then click to select the Allow Zone Transfers check box.
4. Select Only to the following servers, and then enter IP addresses of the secondary DNS servers. (You could also click Only to the servers listed on the Named Servers tab.)
5. Click OK to close the Properties dialog box.

You can also use the dnscmd command to add secondary servers to the list by using the zone's DNS name and the servers' IP addresses. Here's an example of the code you might add:

```
dnscmd ZoneName /SecureList ServerIPaddress
```

DNS Registry entries should also be secured with permissions on the Registry key. DNS entries are located at HKEY_LOCAL_MACHINE\System\CurrentControlSet\Services\DNS. In Windows Server 2003, permissions on this key are enabled.

If an address is requested from a DNS server that doesn't have it, that server attempts to get the address from another DNS server and then add the address to its cache for possible future use. Attackers try to pollute this cache with an IP address that could redirect clients to an attacker's server or use the planted IP address to initiate a DoS attack. The cache should be protected from pollution. To check this setting in Windows Server 2003, open the DSN server's Properties dialog box and select the Advanced tab. The Secure cache from pollution option should be enabled by default.

Hardening Web Servers

Generally, regardless of platform, a Web server is secured by hardening the underlying OS, installing patches, disabling unused services, and restricting the number of user accounts and their access permissions. In addition, you can use platform-specific software tools.

Configuring Security Settings in Internet Information Services

Internet Information Services (IIS) is the Web server in Windows 2000, Windows XP Professional, Windows Server 2003, and Windows Vista. The current versions are 7.0 for Windows Vista and 6.0 for Windows Server 2003. Both have many security improvements over version 5.x, including an integrated lockdown tool for securing the Web server. For users of IIS 5.x, Microsoft has released a lockdown tool that functions much like the integrated tool in newer IIS versions. This tool is intended for servers that continue to use IIS 5.x, but it's also recommended for networks upgrading from IIS 5.x to IIS 6.0 or 7.0 in case any configurations from old IIS 5.x installations are still in use and need to be locked down. The IIS 5.x lockdown tool performs the following actions on the Web server:

- Disables unneeded Web services to reduce the number of available attack targets.

- Protects files that are vulnerable to a malicious script by mapping unused or forbidden file extensions to the 404 DLL to return a "HTTP 404 – file not found" message when these file extensions are requested from the Web server. The 404 DLL that the lockdown tool installs protects files with these extensions from being accessed.

- Removes sample and unneeded files from virtual directories. Sample files can be exploited for vulnerabilities or used as a place to store malicious code.

- Prevents anonymous access to system utilities and Web content directories by requiring a logon username and password.

- Disables Web Distributed Authoring and Versioning (WebDAV), which is vulnerable to a specially crafted HTTP request that causes the server to fail or allows attackers to run malicious code.

- Installs a URLScan Internet Server Application Programming Interface (ISAPI) filter. This filter reviews incoming URL requests for any suspicious content or characters, such as unusually long URLs or URLs with unusual characters. These URL request strings could contain malicious code intended to attack the server.

NOTE   You can download the IIS lockdown tool from *www.microsoft.com/technet/ security/tools/locktool.mspx*. Hands-On Project 6-1 takes you through the process of installing this tool on a Windows XP SP2 system.

Although the lockdown tool for IIS 5.x and the default security settings in IIS 6.0 and 7.0 result in a more secure Web server, they don't guarantee a hardened system with the fewest possible vulnerabilities. You should also follow these precautions:

- The underlying Windows OS must be hardened and maintained by installing the latest service packs, patches, and hot fixes and removing or disabling unnecessary services.

- A domain controller shouldn't also function as an IIS Web server. Domain controllers store Active Directory information and control network access and authentication. Making a server that handles such critical services available on the Internet isn't a good security practice. Domain controllers should be kept in the protected internal network and separated from the Internet with firewalls.

- Place the Web server in a secure room. An organization can't achieve information security without physical security. With all the passwords and firewalls used on a network, a Web server can still be compromised if it's kept in an unsecured area. Restrict access to Web servers with physical security measures, such as surveillance cameras, locks, and other access control systems (smart cards, for example).

- Don't connect the IIS Web server to the Internet before it's fully hardened. When a server is connected to the public Internet, it usually doesn't take long for an attacker's scan to occur.

- Remove NTFS write and execute permissions when possible to minimize the risk of unauthorized users changing files or running programs. To change NTFS permissions in Windows XP, open Windows Explorer, right-click the system root drive (usually C), and click Properties. In the Properties dialog box, click the Security tab, and then click the Advanced button. In the Advanced Security dialog box, you can view all authenticated users and change their file access permissions.

- Grant permissions to modify and view IIS logs to system and local administrators only. This step makes it harder for attackers to modify log files to hide their activities. As an added precaution, store logs on another server, not the IIS Web server.

- Allow only the administrator to log on locally to the Web server. Secure services outside the OS, such as SQL Server, to prevent them from being exploited as user accounts.

- If you're serving Web pages to the Internet, place the Web server in a firewall-protected DMZ.

As with all Microsoft products, service packs, patches, and hot fixes for IIS are released periodically. Installing them as soon as possible is important, especially when they address security issues. Subscription to the automatic Microsoft Security Notification Service is recommended for update news on IIS as well as all Microsoft products. The following activity shows you how to configure automatic OS notifications and updates for Windows XP Professional.

ACTIVITY

Activity 6-5: Configuring Automatic OS Updates

Time Required: 20 minutes

Objective: Learn how to configure automatic updates for your Windows XP SP2 system.

Description: In this activity, you set up an automatic updating service for a Windows XP SP2 system with IIS 5.1 installed.

1. Start your Web browser and click **Tools**, **Windows Update** from the menu to go to the Windows Update site. Click **Microsoft Update** at the top of the page.

2. On the welcome page, click the **Start Now** button to begin the subscription process.

3. Review the license, and then click **Continue** to download update software to your computer. Click the **OS Automatic Updates** link to open the Automatic Updates dialog box, where you define an update schedule (see Figure 6-9). Select your settings, and then click **OK**.

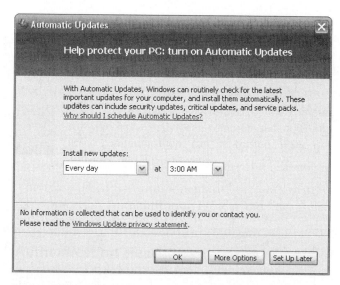

Figure 6-9   Scheduling automatic updates

4. Click the **Check for Updates** button. You're prompted to select an Express or a Custom update method. Notice on the right that your computer is set to receive automatic security and critical updates at the times you scheduled in Step 3. Click the **Custom** button to begin a scan of your Windows OS and Microsoft applications. During the update process, no information is sent to or collected by Microsoft; however, you might be asked to download and install the Windows Genuine Advantage Validation Tool, which verifies that your OS is a valid licensed copy before allowing downloads.

5. When the scan is finished, a results window similar to Figure 6-10 is displayed. The results are categorized by priority, and high-priority updates should always be installed. Click the **Review and install updates** arrow button. You have the option of examining each result and determining whether to install the update. After you have decided, click the **Install Updates** button on the left. (A download size and estimated installation time are shown next to the button.)

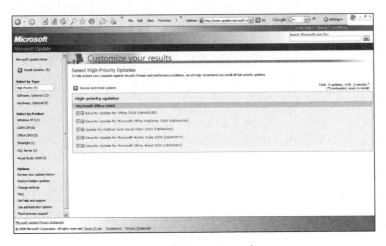

Figure 6-10   Windows update scan results

6. When the installation is finished, click the **Restart** button for the update installation to take effect. Your Windows system now has the latest security patches from Microsoft and will be updated automatically on the schedule you specified.

7. Close any open windows, and leave your system running for the projects at the end of the chapter.

If Windows Server 2003 is the OS for your IIS Web server, a lot of the security guesswork has been removed from installation and maintenance. Windows Server 2003 has many default security policies that govern every aspect of servers that can be installed on the OS, such as Web servers, DNS servers, file servers, and so on. These security policies form the basis for Web server security. (Chapter 8 discusses Windows Server 2003 security policies in more detail.)

Configuring Security Settings in Apache Web Server

Apache Web Server, the most widely used Web server application, is installed mainly on UNIX/Linux systems, although a Windows version is available. Apache's vulnerabilities aren't publicized as much as those for Windows Web servers; however, they do exist. Some misguided Apache administrators believe that Apache is secure out of the box and don't pay much attention to hardening, but this belief can be a fatal mistake. Even the Apache.org Web site was hacked in 2000! Therefore, like any Web server, Apache requires hardening to ensure security for Web sites and users. The following are security settings for Apache that the Center for Internet Security (CIS) recommends:

 For more information on these settings, visit *www.cisecurity.org*.

- Harden the underlying OS as you would any OS, by removing unused applications and sample code and updating OS patches and hot fixes. (Hardening Linux is discussed in more detail in Chapter 7.) A good resource for checking recent patches is *www.apache.org/dist/httpd/patches/*.

- Install the latest Apache binary distribution code from the OS vendor. This method is usually easier than compiling your own binary code for installation because the vendor has already done most of the configuration work for you. Apache binary distributions are available at *www.apache.org/dist/binaries*.

- Disable unnecessary Apache modules and services, disable processing of server-side includes (SSIs), and delete unneeded or default Apache files and sample code. These measures reduce the number of Web processes that are available to attackers.

- Create Web groups so that these users can be granted limited administrative rights without having root access. (Chapter 7 explains creating group and user accounts and granting permissions in Linux.)

- Create user and group accounts with limited privileges for running Apache Web Server, and never run Apache as the root account. If the Web service runs with root permissions, any compromise results in attackers having root access to the Web server.

- Subscribe to OS vendor and Apache security advisories to stay informed on security issues.

- Minimize indicators of Web server information. For example, in IIS, the Server-Tokens variable controls whether the Web server's HTTP response header field includes information about the Web server's OS and installed modules. Attackers might be able to use this information for malicious purposes, so edit the httpd.conf file to change ServerTokens to Prod or ProdOnly and ServerSignature to "off" to prevent this information from being revealed.

- Modify Web pages displaying error information with a custom message. As you learned previously, attackers can use errors messages to gather information about server setup.

- Install the ModSecurity module to have URLs in Web traffic inspected for anomalies. For example, an attacker might send this URL request to a Web server to delete the accounts database table: *http://www.myweb.com/login.asp?username=admin';DROP %20TABLE%20accounts--*. The ModSecurity module adds a filter to prevent carrying out this type of request.

NOTE

In Hands-On Project 6-2, you install the ModSecurity module and learn how to modify an error message.

- To secure access, use Digest authentication instead of Basic authentication for accepting usernames and passwords. (If you need a review of these authentication methods, conduct an Internet search for articles.)

- When setting access control lists (ACLs), determine whether allow or deny rules are evaluated first. An ACL's effect could change if the correct order of evaluation isn't used. Refer to Chapter 4 in *Guide to Tactical Perimeter Defense: Becoming a Security Network Specialist* (Course Technology, 2008, ISBN 1428356304) for more information on ACLs.

- Use Secure Sockets Layer (SSL) to encrypt the communication from user to Web server. To do this, you must download and install the mod_ssl module from *www.modssl.org/source/*. Then install an SSL certificate purchased from a recognized certification authority (CA), such as VeriSign or Geotrust. The CA includes directions on how to install the certificate. For example, VeriSign provides instructions at *www.verisign.com/support/ssl-certificates-support/install-ssl-certificate.html*.

- Limit the Web server to accepting and processing only certain HTTP request methods, such as GET, POST, HEAD, and PUT.

- Disable HTTP traces to prevent attackers from investigating HTTP request paths for potential targets. An HTTP trace asks the Web server to echo back an HTTP request's contents and is often used for debugging. Attackers could use this information to access sensitive data, such as authentication data or cookies from an established connection. For more information, see *https://www.kb.cert.org/vuls/id/867593*.

- Enable logging on the Web server so that you can spot potential problems and suspicious activity. If the server is compromised, logs also give you a record for forensics analysis, if needed. To prevent attackers from accessing and altering logs, store them on a separate network server, not the Web server.

CHAPTER SUMMARY

- The Internet is an interconnected web of networks and computers that work together to provide worldwide communication. In this tiered system, the Internet backbone is connected via network access points (NAPs) to regional ISPs, which service point of presence (POP) ISPs that connect to business, education, or home networks.

- Domain Name System (DNS) is a hierarchical system that provides name resolution services for translating hostnames to IP addresses. The foundation of the DNS hierarchy is 13 root servers located around the world. Root servers communicate with servers lower in the hierarchy that are responsible for top-level domains, and these servers delegate responsibility for domain name–to–IP address resolution to name servers farther down the hierarchy.

- Internet weak points are caused by problems in IP address authentication, routing protocol security, DNS security, and Internet host security.

- TCP/IP doesn't authenticate IP addresses, so attackers can change the source IP address in headers of malicious packets to match a trusted host's IP address (called IP spoofing). In addition, routing information isn't authenticated, so it's vulnerable to compromise.

- DNS was originally designed as a public database for name resolution services, so checking the authenticity and integrity of information stored in name servers wasn't considered necessary. This lack of security has resulted in attacks involving DNS cache poisoning and DNS information leakage.

- The millions of host computers around the world are the weakest point of the Internet infrastructure. Attackers hijack unprotected computers and use them as zombies for delivering spam e-mail, DoS attacks, and malicious code. These zombies are often assembled into botnets (networks of zombie computers) to magnify the scope and intensity of attacks.

- Web servers are the Internet components that attackers target most often. Attackers take advantage of shortcomings in configuring or programming these servers, such as poor programming practices or neglecting to patch system vulnerabilities.

- A buffer overflow attack exploits coding flaws in common commercial software, such as OSs. Attackers try to use this flaw to generate system memory errors in a running process and then inject malicious code through the memory buffer.

- A SQL injection attack uses plaintext scripting in an effort to generate information attackers can use to destroy data, disrupt Web site operations, and launch further attacks. Because this attack targets custom-written code, vulnerabilities can be fixed, if they're detected in time.

- There are two types of SQL injection attack methods. In Web form attacks, malicious SQL code is passed to servers through login pages or entry text boxes on Web page forms. In query string attacks, malicious SQL code is added to query strings (URLs) in a Web browser's address bar.

6

❏ Web user attacks make use of social engineering techniques to target users and take advantage of vulnerabilities in Web browsers by using e-mail, ActiveX controls, Java applets, and file attachments.

❏ Phishing, an attack through a Web browser, uses e-mail to send users false information masquerading as legitimate information in an attempt to steal personal information such as credit card data, account numbers, usernames, and passwords. Two variations of phishing are pharming and spear phishing.

❏ ActiveX controls don't require user action to be activated, run automatically when the browser loads the Web page containing them, and have almost full access to the Windows OS. Therefore, attackers can program ActiveX controls to run malicious code on users' Web browsers, plant Trojan programs and worms, or destroy system programs.

❏ Attackers have been able to use embedded code in Java applets to exploit the OS and access system files. These attacks involve redirecting user sessions in an effort to capture users' information.

❏ To harden DNS servers, make sure you allow zone transfers only between primary and secondary DNS servers. In addition, place DNS servers in a DMZ and use a split DNS architecture to physically separate public DNS servers from internal DNS servers. At the network perimeter, configure firewalls and routers to prevent zone transfers to the Internet so that DNS information isn't revealed to attackers.

❏ IIS 6.0 and 7.0 include an integrated lockdown tool, but for version 5.x, Microsoft has a separate lockdown tool that can be installed to secure Web servers. You should also take additional preventive steps, such as hardening the underlying OS, placing the server in a secure room, and positioning the server in a firewall-protected DMZ.

❏ The CIS recommendations are helpful guidelines for configuring server processes to harden Apache Web servers. You can also install the ModSecurity module for firewall and intrusion detection capabilities.

KEY TERMS

anycast addressing — A network addressing scheme that make its possible to decentralize DNS services among a group of servers, even servers in different locations.

botnets — A network of zombie computers that attackers assemble to magnify the effect of an attack.

Domain Name System (DNS) — A hierarchical name resolution service for translating hostnames to IP addresses; used mainly on the Internet.

network access points (NAPs) — Highly secure public facilities where commercial Internet backbones and ISPs exchange routing and traffic data.

pharming — A variation of phishing that intercepts traffic to a legitimate Web site and redirects it to a phony replica of the legitimate site.

phishing — Using social engineering techniques via e-mail to trick users into entering personal information into the attacker's Web site (designed to look like a legitimate business site).

point of presence (POP) ISPs — ISP facilities that provide connectivity to the Internet for business, education, and home users.

spear phishing — A variation of phishing that's directed at specific users (employees of an organization, for example) instead of using spam e-mail.

split DNS architecture — A network architecture that divides DNS services between two servers: a public DNS server on the organization's DMZ for Internet services and an internal DNS server on the internal network for service to internal hosts.

zone transfer — The communication to secondary DNS servers of the zone file, which contains DNS information for the domain the primary DNS server manages.

6

REVIEW QUESTIONS

1. The Internet backbone is connected to regional ISPs via which of the following?
   a. POP ISPs
   b. network service points
   c. network access points
   d. carrier network points

2. How many root servers are in the DNS infrastructure?
   a. 10
   b. 11
   c. 13
   d. 14

3. Attackers can exploit routing information updates to do which of the following? (Choose all that apply.)
   a. Launch DoS attacks.
   b. Poison DNS caches.
   c. Use IP spoofing to intercept packets.
   d. Launch man-in-the-middle attacks.

4. Attackers often use DNS cache poisoning to do which of the following?
   a. Query systems on the network one by one.
   b. Steer unsuspecting users to a server of their choice instead of the Web site where users intended to go.
   c. Flood the network with packets and cause it to crash.
   d. Install a virus on the network.

5. Which of the following is caused by a flaw in how a running process allocates memory to a variable?

   a. unsecured cryptographic storage

   b. buffer overflow

   c. broken authentication

   d. SQL injection

6. Which of the following is a common type of SQL injection attack? (Choose all that apply.)

   a. Web form attack

   b. browser executable attack

   c. system tray attack

   d. query string attack

7. In a SQL injection attack, which character is an attacker most likely to use?

   a. asterisk

   b. single quote

   c. exclamation mark

   d. double quote

8. Which of the following attack methods are used against Web users? (Choose all that apply.)

   a. social engineering

   b. phishing

   c. SQL injection

   d. pharming

9. What is a requirement for a successful file attachment attack?

   a. The user must open the file attachment.

   b. The user must reply to the e-mail containing the attachment.

   c. The user must delete the file attachment immediately.

   d. The attachment must be an image file.

10. Which of the following factors makes it possible for attackers to program ActiveX controls to run malicious code on a user's Web browser? (Choose all that apply.)

   a. ActiveX controls run in a sandbox that allows interaction with the OS.

   b. ActiveX controls don't require user action to be activated.

   c. ActiveX controls run automatically when the browser loads the Web page containing them.

   d. ActiveX controls have almost full access to the Windows OS.

11. Which of the following has an integrated lockdown tool for Web servers?
    a. Apache 6.0
    b. IIS 6.0
    c. IIS 5.0
    d. Apache 4.0

12. Which of the following is not a task the lockdown tool in Question 11 performs?
    a. enabling unneeded services based on administrator responses during installation
    b. mapping certain scripts to the 404 DLL for security
    c. removing sample and unneeded files from virtual directories
    d. locking down anonymous access to system utilities and Web content directories
    e. disabling WebDAV

13. A Web server can be hardened just by configuring the Web application correctly. True or False?

14. For optimum efficiency, configure a domain controller to also function as an IIS Web server. True or False?

15. In securing an Apache Web server, which of the following tasks isn't necessary?
    a. installing the latest Apache patches
    b. disabling processing of server-side includes (SSIs)
    c. deleting unneeded or default Apache files and sample code
    d. creating a privileged user ID for the Apache Web User account with root access

16. In a DNS zone transfer, what is actually transferred?
    a. network domain names and IP addresses
    b. usernames and passwords
    c. server MAC addresses
    d. UDP/ICMP messages

17. To keep log files organized, store them on the server you're monitoring. True or False?

6

HANDS-ON PROJECTS

Hands-On Project 6-1: Installing and Configuring the IIS Lockdown Tool on a Windows XP Web Server

Time Required: 30 minutes

Objective: Install and configure the IIS lockdown tool on a Windows XP Web server.

Description: In this project, you install and configure the Microsoft IIS lockdown tool designed to enhance the security of IIS 5.x. You need Windows XP Professional SP2 with IIS 5.x installed. IIS must be installed as a separate component with the installation CD.

1. Start your Web browser, and go to **www.microsoft.com/technet/security/tools/locktool.mspx**. Click the **iislockd.exe** link to download a copy of the lockdown tool.

2. On the IIS Lockdown Tool 2.1 Web page, click the **Download** button. When the File Download – Security Warning dialog box opens, click the **Run** button. (*Note:* If you see an Internet Explorer security warning, click **Run**.)

3. In the welcome window of the installation wizard, click **Next**. Accept the license agreement, and then click **Next**. In the Select Server Template window, click the **Dynamic Web server (ASP enabled)** option, and then click to select the **View template settings** check box. What other type of Web server is available?

   _____

4. Click **Next**. In the Internet Services window, verify that the **Web service (HTTP)** check box is the only one selected, and then click **Next**. In the Script Maps window, verify that the **Active Server Pages (.asp)** check box is cleared. All other scripts should be disabled. Click **Next**.

5. In the Additional Security window, accept the default settings. Which two actions are blocked for anonymous users? Click **Next**.

   _____

6. In the URLScan window, accept the default setting, and then click **Next** to install this filter.

7. The Applying Security Settings window shows the progress of installing the settings you selected. When it's finished, click **Next** to have these security settings applied and IIS security reconfigured. When reconfiguration has finished, click **Next** and then **Finish** to exit the wizard.

8. In Windows Explorer, navigate to **C:\Windows\System32\Inetsrv**, and double-click the **inetmgr.exe** file to open the Internet Information Services console. In the left pane, click to expand your local computer and then **Web Sites** and **FTP Sites**. Notice that the Default Web Site is enabled, but the Default FTP Site and Default SMTP Virtual Server have been stopped because you specified enabling only HTTP services in Step 4 (see Figure 6-11).

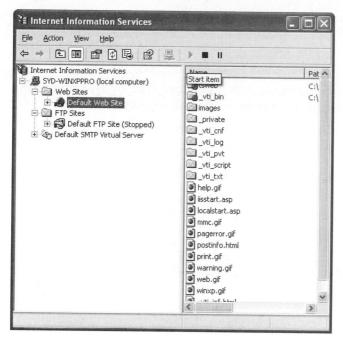

Figure 6-11 Viewing the results of installing the IIS lockdown tool

9. Close the Internet Information Services console and Windows Explorer, and leave your system running.

Hands-On Project 6-2: Installing ModSecurity on a SUSE Linux Apache Web Server

Time Required: 45 minutes

Objective: Install ModSecurity for Apache Web Server.

Description: In this project, you install the ModSecurity module for firewall and intrusion detection services. You need SUSE Linux with Apache 2.0 installed to perform these steps.

Linux is discussed in detail in Chapter 7, so if you're not familiar with using Linux commands, you might want to wait until you've read that chapter to do this project.

1. Start your Web browser, go to **www.modsecurity.org**, and download the ModSecurity for Apache module to your **/usr/src** directory. Download the MD5 checksum value for the application, too.

2. Open a terminal window, and use the **md5sum** command to generate an MD5 hash of the downloaded application. If it matches the MD5 checksum value you downloaded, continue. If not, delete the file and download the module again.

3. ModSecurity has software dependencies that must be installed before using the module. Use SUSE YaST to install these packages, if necessary: **libxml2-devel**, **apache2-devel**, and **pcre-devel**.

4. With the dependencies installed, you can start installing ModSecurity. Change the directory to **/usr/src**, and uncompress the source code by typing **tar zvxf modsecurity-apache_2.x.x.tar.gz** and pressing **Enter**.

5. The installation should have created a new directory in your current working directory, similar to modsecurity-apache_2.x.x/apache2. This directory contains the source code and makefile you must modify for SUSE Linux use. Start a text editor (such as Notepad), and open the makefile.

6. Change the top_dir variable to **/usr/share/apache2**, the APXS variable to **apxs2**, and the APACHECTL variable to **apache2ctl**. Save your changes, close the file, and leave the text editor open.

7. Return to the terminal window, and make sure you're in the directory for the source file. Type **make** and press **Enter**. Then type **make install** and press **Enter** to compile the source code and store it in the correct location.

8. Next, type **make clean** and press **Enter** to delete any files that are no longer needed. To verify the installation, make sure the mod_security2.so file is in the /usr/lib/apache2 directory.

9. Next, you need to configure Apache to load the module. In your text editor, open the **httpd.conf** file in the /etc/apache2 directory. In the [Global Environment] section, add the following lines to the end of the file:

```
# Load libxml2
LoadFile /usr/lib/libxml2.so
```

10. Save your changes, and close the file. Next, open the **/etc/sysconfig/apache2** file from the same directory. Change the APACHE_MODULES variable as shown by inserting the values shown in bold:

```
APACHE_MODULES="unique_id security2 actions alias auth_basic
authn_file..."
```

11. Save your changes, and close the file. In the terminal window, test your configuration by typing **service apache2 configtest** and pressing **Enter**.

12. Next, in the text editor, open the **mod_security.conf** file from the /etc/apache2 directory. Change the SecDebugLog variable to **/var/log/apache2/modsec_debug.log** and the SecAuditLog variable to **/var/log/apache2/modsec_audit.log**.

13. At the end of the file, add the following variable and value:

```
# Set Server Signature
SecServerSignature "Microsoft IIS"
```

NOTE This entry changes the error message so that an attacker would be fooled into thinking it's a Microsoft IIS Web server instead of Apache.

6

14. Save your changes, and close the file. Next, you need to configure the mod_security. conf file for the correct permissions (644, which is root user and root group ownership). In the terminal window, change to the **/etc/apache2** directory, if necessary. Type **chmod 644 mod_security.conf** and press **Enter**, and then type **chown root:root mod_security.conf** and press **Enter** again.

15. To check that permissions have been modified correctly, type **ls –l mod_security.conf** and press **Enter** to view the contents of this file. Scroll through the contents. You should see the following line displayed (with a different date):

```
-rw-r—r—1 root root    771 Aug 22 18:23 mod_security.conf
```

16. Next, you edit the httpd.conf file to include the mod_security.conf file. In the text editor, open the **httpd.conf** file from the /etc/apache2 directory, and add the following lines under the Load libxml2 lines you added in Step 9:

```
# Mod_security policy file
Include /etc/apache2/mod_security.conf
```

17. Save your changes, and exit the text editor. In the terminal window, test the configuration again by typing **service apache2 configtest** and pressing **Enter**.

18. Start the Apache service by typing **service apache2 start** and pressing **Enter**.

19. Next, check whether the modified error message you created is displayed. Use Telnet to connect to your Web server and issue a GET query, as shown in the following bold entries (substituting the IP address of your Web server):

```
telnet 127.0.0.1
Trying 127.0.0.1...
Connected to 127.0.0.1.
Escape character is '^]'.
GET / HTTP/1.0
HTTP/1.1 200 OK
Date: Mon, 3 Mar 2008 18:56:23 GMT
Server: Microsoft IIS
```

20. Exit the terminal window and Linux, and leave your system running for the next project.

TIP To learn more about modifying ModSecurity's policy file, visit *www.modsecurity. org/documentation/index.html*.

CASE PROJECTS

Case Project 6-1: Securing Green Globe's Web Server

Green Globe's Web infrastructure DMZ is shown in Figure 6-12. The Web administrator was fired, and you have been hired to install an Apache Web server. Currently, the server has SUSE Linux installed, and the OS has been hardened. Create a security plan to protect this Web server and Green Globe's Internet transactions from attacks.

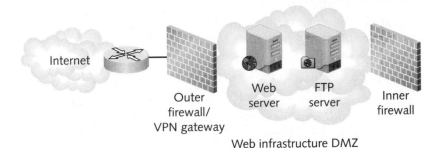

Figure 6-12   Green Globe's Web infrastructure DMZ

To assist in developing your plan, visit the SANS Web site. (Review Activity 6-4 for help in finding items on this site.) Explore the links on the s.c.o.r.e page to find resources you can use. In particular, you might find the System Security Plan, a step-by-step development guide that Michael Kirby created, helpful.

7

HARDENING LINUX SYSTEMS

After reading this chapter and completing the exercises, you will be able to:

♦ Explain how to navigate the Linux file system

♦ Describe methods of secure system management

♦ Describe ways to manage security for user accounts, directories, and files

♦ Install and secure network services, such as Kerberos, Network File System, Network Information System, and Samba

♦ Describe methods of managing security for services, processes, and system integrity

L inux is a popular operating system that is widely used to provide network server services. In fact, if you use Google to search for information on the Internet, you have connected to a Linux Web server. Besides server systems, Linux is used on desktop computers for business and personal use. It is not as common on desktop computers as Windows or Macintosh systems, but its use is growing.

This chapter examines how to harden a Linux system. Like any computer OS, Linux is vulnerable to attackers if you neglect to take steps to protect it. Attackers can find their way into a Linux system through a network, over the Internet, or while sitting at an unprotected Linux computer. By learning how to harden a Linux system, you can thwart attackers.

In this chapter, you begin by reviewing the Linux file system and how to navigate through it. Next, you learn how to secure user accounts, directories, and files—all of which are at the heart of a Linux system. You move on to securing a Linux system by using management techniques that block attackers, such as removing unneeded software and using secure access methods.

Connecting a Linux computer to a network or the Internet involves special concerns about hardening. To address these concerns, you learn how to use secure network authentication of users and how to secure network services. Finally, you learn about tools for keeping Linux secure, including firewall software, shutting down unused services and ports, and applying time-tested security tools.

UNDERSTANDING THE LINUX FILE SYSTEM AND NAVIGATION

The file system is the foundation of any OS. It contains system files, software, documents, and data—all elements that attackers can mine or malware can damage. In the sections that follow, you review file system basics and see how to navigate through the Linux file system.

Reviewing File System Basics

The information in an OS is managed, stored, and retrieved through a file system, which performs the following general tasks:

- Partitions and formats disks to store and retrieve information
- Organizes files in directories
- Establishes filenaming conventions
- Provides utilities to maintain and manage the file system and storage media
- Provides file and data integrity
- Enables error recovery or prevention
- Secures information in directories and files

In a file system, there must be a way to write digital information to disk, track and update it, and call it back when a user or program wants it. To do all this, the OS typically groups disk sectors logically, creates a record of this structure, and builds a directory to track the type of data stored in each file.

A directory is an organizational structure containing files and sometimes subdirectories in an inverse tree hierarchy. It connects names to files stored on disk, which makes it easy for users and programs to find data when needed. In addition to names and disk locations, directories and files store the following information:

- Date and time the directory or file was created, last modified, or last accessed
- Size
- Attributes such as security information or backed-up status
- Whether the information is compressed or encrypted (recorded by some file systems)

When setting up and organizing a file system, you should consider how to secure and access files. Create directories that enable you to group files containing similar information. Also, to avoid confusion, design the file and directory structure carefully from the start, particularly on servers that many users access. Plan a directory structure that complements the one the OS has already set up. The default OS structure, along with the structure you add, might consist of directories for the following:

- Operating system files (typically set up by the OS at installation)
- Software applications (often set up by the OS, software applications you install, and decisions you make about how to install these applications)

- Work files, such as word processing, graphics, spreadsheet, and database files (set up by you and by applications)

- Public files that you share over the network (set up by you)

- Utilities files (set up by the OS, utilities applications, and your decisions about how to install specific utilities)

- Temporary files (set up by the OS, applications that use temporary files, and your decisions about where to store temporary files)

Structure of Linux File Systems

Linux is versatile because it supports many different file systems. Some file systems are native to Linux and others provide compatibility with different OSs, such as Windows.

The native Linux file system is **extended file system (ext)**, which is installed by default. The first version of ext contained some flaws, supported files to only 2 GB, and didn't offer journaling. With the addition of **journaling** in later file systems, a log (journal) of the file system's activities is maintained. So if a system crashes unexpectedly, you can reconstruct files or roll back recent changes to minimize damage to file or data integrity. If the OS crashes because of an attack or isn't shut down properly (such as during a power failure), it reads the journal file when it's restarted. Information in the journal file enables files to be brought back to their previous or stable state before the crash. This feature is particularly important for files that were being updated before the crash and didn't have time to finish writing updates to disk.

Newer Linux distributions use the second (ext2), third (ext3), or fourth (ext4) versions of the extended file system. Ext2, a more reliable file system than ext, handles large disk storage; ext3 has the enhancements of ext2 with the addition of journaling. Released in 2006, ext4 allows a single disk volume to hold up to 1 exabyte (more than 1.1 quintillion bytes) of data and enables the use of extents. An extent is a logical block of data on a logical drive used to reduce file fragmentation; a block of contiguous disk storage can be reserved for a file. For example, a file of names and addresses grows continuously as you add people. Each time you add people to the file, the new data is stored next to the old in the extent of contiguous disk space reserved for that file. This feature is an improvement over other file systems, in which new data can be stored in different random locations on the disk. Over time, data in a file (without the use of an extent) could be spread all over the disk, resulting in more time to locate data and more disk wear.

NOTE   Ext3 and ext4 are compatible unless extents are used in ext4. Ext3 is also compatible with ext2. Therefore, many disk utilities, including security tools, that work with ext2 are likely to work with ext3 and ext4 (without the use of extents).

Besides ext, Linux supports a variety of other file systems that can be used for specific purposes. For example, Linux supports the NTFS file system native to Windows Server OSs and used in Windows XP and Vista, which makes transporting files from a Linux system to a Windows Server system easier, for example. Another example is support for the traditional UNIX file system (ufs), which makes porting files between Linux and UNIX easier. Linux also supports ReiserFS. This file system is similar to ext3 and ext4, has journaling capabilities, and is up to 15 times faster than ext3 and ext4. It's intended to encourage programmers to create efficient code by using smaller files.

Disk partitions containing directories and files in the ext file system are built on the concept of information nodes, called **inodes**. In Linux, a directory is actually a specialized file capable of storing other directories and data files. Each directory or file has an inode and is identified by an inode number. Inode 0 contains the root of the directory structure and is the jumping-off point for all other inodes. In Linux, the root directory, denoted with a forward slash (/), is the start of the directory hierarchy, and all other directories and files are under it.

An inode contains the following information about a directory or file:

- Name
- General information—user and group ownership, access mode (read, write, and execute permissions, discussed later in this chapter), size and type of file, and date the file was created, last modified, and last read
- A pointer indicating how to locate the directory or file on a disk partition

The pointer information is based on logical blocks. Each disk is divided into logical blocks ranging from 512 to 8192 bytes or more, depending on the Linux distribution. (Blocks can also be divided into subblocks or fractions.) The inode contains a pointer (number) that tells the OS how to locate the first in a set of logical blocks containing the directory or file contents (or it specifies the number of blocks or links to the first block the directory or file uses). In short, the inode tells the OS where to find a complete file on the hard disk.

Everything in the ext file system is tied to inodes. Space is allocated one block, or fraction of a block, at a time. Directories (specialized files) are marked with a directory flag in their inodes. The file system is identified by the **superblock**, which contains information about the layout of blocks on a specific partition. This information is the key to finding anything on the file system, and it should never change. If the superblock is lost because of disk damage or damage caused by attackers or malware, the file system can't be accessed. For this reason, many copies of the superblock are written to the file system when the file system is created by partitioning and formatting. If the superblock is destroyed, you can copy one of the superblock copies over the original, damaged superblock to restore access to the file system.

You can use the following at the Linux command line to view the primary and backup superblock locations on a Linux system (see Figure 7-1):

```
dumpe2fs /dev/hda1|grep -i  superblock
```

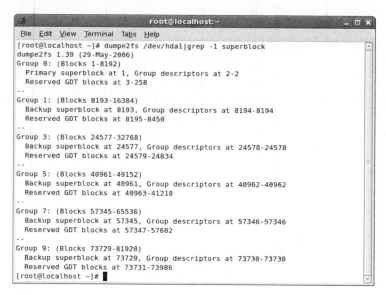

Figure 7-1   Viewing superblock locations

NOTE   Using commands is discussed in the next section. When you use the dumpe2fs command, you specify the name of the disk (hda1, in this case). To view the disks mounted on your Linux system, you use the mount command. Also, to run dumpe2fs, you need to be logged in to an account with authorization to fully manage a Linux system (covered later in "Using Commands for Directory and File Navigation").

If you need to repair a partition on which the superblock is damaged, use this command:

```
e2fsck -f -b 8193 /dev/hda1
```

Using the Linux Command Line

Linux offers a full-featured graphical desktop similar to Windows desktops, including menu bars, windows, icons, and drag-and-drop capabilities. It also offers a rich command-line environment that gives you extensive control over Linux features. The command-line environment is particularly valuable to know when you're configuring security to harden a Linux system. Also, even though there are more than 100 distributions of Linux, they have the same commands in common—so learning Linux commands means you can work on nearly any Linux system. For this reason, this chapter emphasizes using the Linux command line for configuring security.

Through the Linux command line, you can navigate the Linux file system in the following ways:

- Locate directories and files.
- Create, save, delete, and edit directories and files.

- Secure files.
- Run program (executable) files.

Linux systems that aren't configured to use a GUI, such as some server systems, boot into the command-line environment. Other Linux systems that have a GUI desktop include a terminal window for entering commands (refer back to Figure 7-1 for an example). With a GUI desktop, you can often open a terminal window from the Terminal or Terminal Window icon in the panel (taskbar in Windows) at the bottom or top of the desktop. If there's no icon for the terminal window, look for a Terminal selection in one of the menus, such as the Applications, Accessories, or System Tools menu.

This is the general syntax for a Linux command:

```
command_name [-option] [argument]
```

Command_name is the main command to enter and is always in lowercase. Using an option after the command enables you to run the command in a certain way or with a specific style. Some commands require specifying an option, and some do not. An option is usually preceded by a hyphen (-). An argument is typically optional, depending on the command, and is usually a directory name or filename.

NOTE

Traditionally in Linux syntax documentation, showing an option that's not enclosed in brackets means the command won't work without using an option. Brackets signify that the option is truly optional.

Now that you have reviewed the basics of commands, you're ready to learn some commands to perform a few basic security tasks and navigate the Linux file system.

Using the Man Command to Find Documentation

One of the most useful commands is the man command. It displays an online manual, called the man pages, that has complete information about Linux commands, including each command's options and arguments. Although some commands contain more information than others, most man pages list the following items:

- *Name*—The name of the command and a short statement describing its purpose
- *Synopsis*—A syntax diagram showing how the command is used
- *Description*—A more detailed description that includes a list of options and their descriptions
- *Author*—Name or the person who developed the command or program (if available)
- *Reporting Bugs*—Information on how to report bugs or problems
- *History*—Information included sometimes to show where the command originated

- *Other Versions*—Information included if other versions of the command are available
- *See Also*—Other commands or man pages that provide related information

The man command usually accepts only one argument—the name of the command. As an example, to see information about the who command (introduced in the next section), enter the following at the command line:

```
man who
```

Figure 7-2 shows the output of this command.

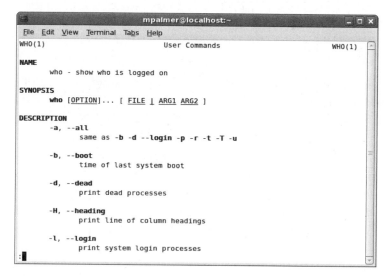

Figure 7-2   Accessing the man documentation for the who command

Use the spacebar to advance through the man documentation. To close the online manual, type q.

A Brief Introduction of Commands for Basic Security Tasks

Security administrators often use the who command to get information about who's logged in to a system. In a multiuser server system, knowing who is logged in is important so that administrators can verify authorized users and levels of use periodically. Knowing who is logged in is also valuable for ordinary users, who can use that information to judge how busy the system is at a given time or who might want to contact another user.

These are frequently used options for the who command:

- –H—Show column headings.
- –u—Show idle time for each user.
- –q—List logged-in users and display a total.

- ■ –b—Show the time the system was last booted.
- ■ am i—Display information about your own session.
- ■ whoami—See what account you're using.

NOTE Notice that the am i option is two words, and the whoami option is one word. Also, options can be combined by using only one hyphen in front, such as -uH.

For example, enter the following command to view the users logged in to a server, assess their amount of activity, and keep an eye on what they are doing:

```
who -uH
```

The advantage of using the who command often is that you can get an idea of the normal user load, plus who is typically logged in and for how long. An unexpected user or an account logged in for an atypical amount of time could be a red flag.

Another useful command for security purposes is top, used to audit system performance, such as watching CPU use as it relates to activities users or computer processes perform. If a system is slowing down because a process is in the control of malware, the system administrator can use top to identify the process and even stop (kill) it.

Later in this chapter, you learn how to automate the top command to run at regular intervals and record the results in a file you can view at your convenience. Figure 7-3 shows the use of the top command. Notice that the root account is using 98.4% of the CPU to run the yum-updatesd process (process ID 2107), which is used to download OS updates from the Internet. Also notice that this process is using 9.9% of memory.

```
root@localhost:~
File  Edit  View  Terminal  Tabs  Help
top - 19:40:37 up  5:01,  2 users,  load average: 0.41, 0.10, 0.03
Tasks: 102 total,   2 running, 100 sleeping,   0 stopped,   0 zombie
Cpu(s): 82.4%us, 17.3%sy,  0.0%ni,  0.0%id,  0.0%wa,  0.3%hi,  0.0%si,  0.0%st
Mem:    514684k total,   506468k used,     8216k free,    66936k buffers
Swap:  1048568k total,        0k used,  1048568k free,   291576k cached

  PID USER      PR  NI  VIRT  RES  SHR S %CPU %MEM    TIME+  COMMAND
 2107 root      25   0 64220  49m 4992 R 98.4  9.9 27:47.17 yum-updatesd
 2351 root      16   0  103m  16m 6000 S  1.0  3.2  0:05.39 Xorg
 2521 root      15   0 16440 7484 5912 S  0.3  1.5  0:01.19 metacity
 6726 root      15   0  2168 1008  792 R  0.3  0.2  0:00.21 top
    1 root      15   0  2036  640  548 S  0.0  0.1  0:01.05 init
    2 root      RT   0     0    0    0 S  0.0  0.0  0:00.00 migration/0
    3 root      34  19     0    0    0 S  0.0  0.0  0:00.00 ksoftirqd/0
    4 root      RT   0     0    0    0 S  0.0  0.0  0:00.00 watchdog/0
    5 root      10  -5     0    0    0 S  0.0  0.0  0:00.00 events/0
    6 root      10  -5     0    0    0 S  0.0  0.0  0:00.00 khelper
    7 root      10  -5     0    0    0 S  0.0  0.0  0:00.00 kthread
   10 root      10  -5     0    0    0 S  0.0  0.0  0:00.00 kblockd/0
   11 root      20  -5     0    0    0 S  0.0  0.0  0:00.00 kacpid
   72 root      20  -5     0    0    0 S  0.0  0.0  0:00.00 cqueue/0
   75 root      10  -5     0    0    0 S  0.0  0.0  0:00.00 khubd
   77 root      10  -5     0    0    0 S  0.0  0.0  0:00.00 kseriod
  136 root      25   0     0    0    0 S  0.0  0.0  0:00.00 pdflush
```

Figure 7-3   Using the top command

After using top regularly to monitor a system, you can begin detecting problem areas and narrow them down to specific users and processes. This command is also useful for finding ways to make a system run more efficiently and spotting problems caused by malware or attackers.

Using Commands for Directory and File Navigation

As you reviewed earlier, the root directory (denoted with a /) is the start of the directory hierarchy in Linux. Under the root directory, Linux stores several main directories that house subdirectories and files roughly grouped by function. The following is a list—not exhaustive—of typical directories under the root directory:

- */bin*—Contains executable files of the programs needed to start the system and perform other essential system tasks
- */boot*—Stores the files needed by the bootstrap loader, which is the utility that starts the OS; /boot also contains the kernel OS images
- */dev*—Holds the files needed to access system devices, such as drives, printers, modems, and memory (files that enable access to devices are called device special files)
- */etc*—Contains configuration files used when the system boots, such as the fstab file to map system devices and the passwd file containing user information
- */home*—Holds working directories for user accounts (called "home directories"); an account named sbrown, for example, has a home directory at /home/sbrown
- */lib*—Holds files containing security information, kernel modules, and shared library images that programs use for sharing code sections
- */mnt*—More common to legacy systems; contains temporary mount points for removable storage devices, such as USB/flash storage and CD/DVD devices

Mount points tell Linux where removable storage, such as a CD/DVD drive, is located for access.

- */media*—Used by newer distributions; stores temporary mount points for removable storage
- */root*—The home directory for the root account
- */sbin*—Contains files used to help start or repair the system
- */tmp*—Contains files used temporarily by programs
- */usr*—Stores software available to users

7

When you log in, you begin in your home directory, which is a subdirectory of the /home directory. To change to a different directory, use the cd command along with the path to the new directory. If you want to return to your home directory, type cd (with no path specified) and press Enter.

Linux Paths

In Linux, you can refer to a path as an absolute path or a relative path. An absolute path begins at the root level and lists all subdirectories to the destination file. For example, Sara has a subdirectory named lists under her home directory of /home/sara. She has a directory called todo in her lists subdirectory, so the absolute path to this directory is /home/sara/lists/todo. This pathname shows each directory in the path to the todo directory. Using the absolute path, Sara enters the following command to navigate to the todo directory:

```
cd /home/sara/lists/todo
```

A relative path takes less typing because it assumes your home directory as the starting point. Using the relative path from her home directory, Sara could simply enter the following:

```
cd /lists/todo
```

In another form of the relative path, Sara could use the tilde (~)character, which is shorthand for her home directory. To go to the todo file, she enters the following:

```
cd ~/lists/todo
```

The advantage of using the tilde is that it works from any directory on the system, not just from the home directory. For example, if Sara is working from a directory called /public and she enters cd ~/lists/todo, the command takes her to the /home/sara/lists/todo directory because the tilde represents /home/sara.

 You can go back to your home directory while in any directory by entering cd ~. Also, if you aren't sure which directory you are currently in, enter the pwd command to find out.

Two other directory-change commands that come in handy are a single period and two periods. A single period refers to the current directory, and two periods refer to the directory just above the current directory. For example, if Sara is in her home directory, she could enter this command to go to the todo directory (/home/sara/lists/todo):

```
cd ./lists/todo
```

Also, after she is in the /todo directory, she can enter cd .. twice to go back to her home directory.

Using the Ls Command

To see the contents of a directory, use the ls (list) command, which displays files and subdirectories. When you use the ls command with no options or arguments, it displays the names of regular files and directories in your current working directory. You can provide an argument to the ls command to see the listing for a specific file or directory. For instance, you have a file called myfile in the /etc directory. You could enter ls myfile to just list myfile in the /etc directory, or enter ls /etc to see a list of all subdirectories and files in the /etc directory.

One of the most useful options for the ls command is -l for a "long directory listing," which provides more in-depth information about files and subdirectories. Figure 7-4 shows a long listing for the /etc directory. Notice that the following command is used:

```
ls -l /etc | more
```

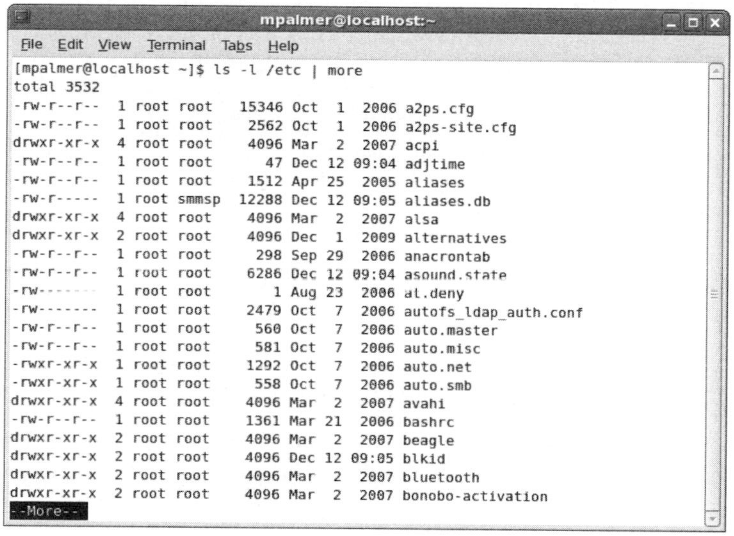

```
                    mpalmer@localhost:~
File  Edit  View  Terminal  Tabs  Help
[mpalmer@localhost ~]$ ls -l /etc | more
total 3532
-rw-r--r--  1 root root    15346 Oct  1  2006 a2ps.cfg
-rw-r--r--  1 root root     2562 Oct  1  2006 a2ps-site.cfg
drwxr-xr-x  4 root root     4096 Mar  2  2007 acpi
-rw-r--r--  1 root root       47 Dec 12 09:04 adjtime
-rw-r--r--  1 root root     1512 Apr 25  2005 aliases
-rw-r-----  1 root smmsp   12288 Dec 12 09:05 aliases.db
drwxr-xr-x  4 root root     4096 Mar  2  2007 alsa
drwxr-xr-x  2 root root     4096 Dec  1  2009 alternatives
-rw-r--r--  1 root root      298 Sep 29  2006 anacrontab
-rw-r--r--  1 root root     6286 Dec 12 09:04 asound.state
-rw-------  1 root root        1 Aug 23  2006 at.deny
-rw-------  1 root root     2479 Oct  7  2006 autofs_ldap_auth.conf
-rw-r--r--  1 root root      560 Oct  7  2006 auto.master
-rw-r--r--  1 root root      581 Oct  7  2006 auto.misc
-rwxr-xr-x  1 root root     1292 Oct  7  2006 auto.net
-rwxr-xr-x  1 root root      558 Oct  7  2006 auto.smb
drwxr-xr-x  4 root root     4096 Mar  2  2007 avahi
-rw-r--r--  1 root root     1361 Mar 21  2006 bashrc
drwxr-xr-x  2 root root     4096 Mar  2  2007 beagle
drwxr-xr-x  2 root root     4096 Dec 12 09:05 blkid
drwxr-xr-x  2 root root     4096 Mar  2  2007 bluetooth
drwxr-xr-x  2 root root     4096 Mar  2  2007 bonobo-activation
--More--
```

Figure 7-4   Viewing a long listing of the /etc directory's contents

The /etc directory holds many screens full of files and subdirectories. The | character used with "more" pipes the output of the ls command as input to the more command so that the display shows one screen and then stops. Each time you press the spacebar, you advance to the next screen of the listing.

In Figure 7-4, the long listing shows the following columns of information about subdirectories and files:

- *File type and access permissions*—The first column of information is the following set of characters: -rw-r--r--. The first character, which is a hyphen (-), indicates a file. A d indicates a directory. An I/O device file might display a, b, or c. The remainder of the characters indicate the file's access permissions, which you review later in "Configuring File and Directory Permissions."

- *Number of links*—The second column is the number of files that are hard-linked to this file. For a directory, this column shows the number of subdirectories it contains.

- *Owner*—The third column is the owner of the file. The root user owns all the files and directories shown in Figure 7-4.

- *Group*—The fourth column is the group that owns the file or subdirectory. The root group owns all but one of the files and subdirectories in Figure 7-4.

- *Size*—The fifth column shows the size of the file or subdirectory in bytes, which is 15346 for the first file listed in Figure 7-4.

- *Date and time*—The sixth, seventh, and eighth columns show the date a file or subdirectory was created; if information has been changed for a file or subdirectory, they show the date and time of the last modification.

- *Name*—The ninth column shows the file or subdirectory name.

Several other useful options for the ls command are:

- -S to sort by size of the file or directory

- -s to show the size of each file in blocks

- -X to sort by extension

- -r to sort in reverse order

- -t to sort by the time the file or directory was last modified

- -a to show hidden files (some files, such as files containing code to set the user's work environment when the user logs in, are hidden to help keep them from being deleted inadvertently)

- -i to view the inode value associated with a directory or file

NOTE

Linux supports the use of wildcards, such as the asterisk or question mark. For example, to view all files with the .pl extension in your current working directory, enter ls *.pl.

ACTIVITY

Activity 7-1: Navigating the Linux File System

Time Required: 15 minutes

Objective: Use the pwd, cd, and ls commands for navigation.

Description: Navigating the Linux file system is vital for identifying the locations of directories and files you need to secure. In this activity, you use the pwd, cd, and ls commands to navigate in a Linux system. Ensure that you have access to a regular Linux user account; you don't need access to the root account.

1. Log in to your Linux account and access the command line or a terminal window.

You might need to consult your instructor for details about an account and how to access Linux.

2. Type **pwd** and press **Enter** to determine your current working directory. Write down the absolute directory path and note whether you are in a home directory:

   _____

   _____

3. Type **cd .** and press **Enter**. (There's one space between cd and the period.) Use the **pwd** command to verify that you are still in the same directory as in Step 2.

4. What command can you use to go to the directory just above your current working directory?

   _____

5. Type **cd /dev** and press **Enter** to change to the /dev directory. Next, type **ls –l | more** and press **Enter** to view the contents of the /dev directory. (Notice that you use a lowercase L, not the numeral 1.) Press the spacebar to advance through each screen of information. Because this command can produce a lot of files to look through, you can press q at any time to exit and go back to the command prompt.

6. Type **cd /** and press **Enter** to go to the root directory. Now type **ls –l** and press **Enter** to view the directories under the root (/) directory. Record the main directories on your system under the root directory:

   _____

   _____

   _____

7. Type **cd ~** and press **Enter** to go back to your home directory. Verify that you're in your home directory by using the **pwd** command.

8. Log out of your account. (Consult your instructor, if necessary, about how to log out for your particular Linux system.)

After you locate a file by using the ls command, you might need to view its contents. For example, you want to see what parameters are set in a configuration file that affects system security. Two commands work well for viewing the contents of a file: more and less.

Besides being used to view a directory's contents, as in Activity 7-1, the more command is also commonly used to view file contents. You can view the file contents one screen at a time and scroll down as needed by pressing the spacebar. For example, to view the contents

7

of the /etc/xinetd.d/telnet file (discussed next in "Using Secure Shell Instead of Telnet"), enter the following:

```
more /etc/xinetd.d/krb5-telnet
```

The less command is more versatile than the more command because it displays file contents one screen at a time and lets you scroll up or down. To scroll one line at a time, use the up and down arrow keys. To scroll down a screen, press the spacebar or Page Down key. To scroll up a screen, press Page Up. To use less to view the /etc/xinetd.d/krb5-telnet file, enter the following (see Figure 7-5):

```
less /etc/xinetd.d/krb5-telnet
```

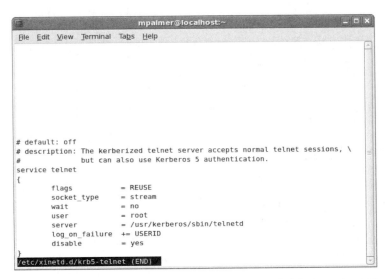

Figure 7-5   Using less to view the /etc/xinetd.d/krb5-telnet file's contents

EXAMINING SECURE SYSTEM MANAGEMENT

Linux system administrators can take many steps to harden a system. One of the most basic steps is to have remote users, including the administrator, use secure software when they log in. This practice applies to all users who access a Linux computer through a network or over the Internet. Other steps involve configuring computers to use built-in security options.

The steps for securing user access and system management include the following (and are discussed in the sections that follow):

- Using Secure Shell
- Ensuring root security
- Removing unnecessary packages
- Maintaining system patching

- Configuring system accounting
- Configuring auditing and logging
- Configuring automated system monitoring

Using Secure Shell Instead of Telnet

Two common programs are used to access a Linux computer remotely: Telnet and Secure Shell (SSH). **Telnet**, a terminal emulation program, runs on the remote computer. For example, in most versions of Windows, including XP and Vista, you can run Telnet from a command prompt window. Some older Linux systems also have Telnet. To use Telnet, the remote computer must be running the Telnet client service, and the Linux host computer must be running the Telnet server service. Also, when you configure firewalls on the client and host computers, they must be configured to allow Telnet communications.

To access the host computer, Telnet uses an IP address or a computer and domain name. For example, on a Windows client computer, you open a command prompt window and enter one of the following:

```
telnet 191.85.10.2
```

or

```
telnet science.campus.edu
```

The problem with Telnet is that it isn't secure, so one important step to hardening your Linux system is to ensure that the Telnet server service is not running. Also, block Telnet at your firewall. (You learn to configure a firewall later in "Closing Network Ports by Configuring a Firewall.") Make sure you take these steps because attackers and malware can use Telnet to enter your system to cause harm.

On many Linux host servers, you can disable Telnet by editing the /etc/xinetd.d/telnet or /etc/xinetd.d/krb5-telnet file and making sure the disable parameter is set to yes (disable = yes)—refer back to Figure 7-5. On other systems, edit the /etc/inetd.conf file by adding a pound sign (#) at the beginning of the telnet line to convert the command to a comment. The next time you boot the server, Telnet is disabled. To make sure it's disabled, try to use Telnet. You should get a message such as the following: Connection refused.

Secure Shell (SSH) was initially developed for UNIX and Linux to provide authentication security for remote access communication over networks. Historically, authentication for remote connections, such as through Telnet, has largely consisted of providing an unencrypted account and password, making both extremely vulnerable. SSH applies techniques such as encryption and tunneling to secure the authentication of a communication session. Unlike Telnet, SSH encrypts communications as they go across a network or the Internet.

In most Linux distributions, the ssh command can be used instead of telnet at the client computer to establish a secure connection to a remote host computer running Linux that's compatible with OpenSSH. OpenSSH is a version of SSH that includes protocols and software intended for free distribution and can be used with many Linux distributions.

You can learn more about OpenSSH and download a free copy by going to *www.openssh.org*. In addition, commercial and noncommercial versions of SSH are available at *www.ssh.com*, which is the Web site of SSH Communications Security founded by the originator of SSH, Tatu Ylönen in Finland.

To use ssh, enter ssh –l along with the names of the user account and host computer. Two other options are entering ssh with *user@hostname* or ssh with the IP address. For example, to access a computer with the IP address 191.85.10.2, enter the following:

```
ssh 191.85.10.2
```

Next, the SSH connection asks for your username and then your password.

Alternatively, to log in to a computer named research with the account mkehettry, enter the following:

```
ssh research -l mkehettry
```

In this example, the -l option specifies the user account mkehettry.

Ensuring Root Security

The root or superuser account enables its user to do almost anything on a Linux computer and to go anywhere in the file system because it's the account used to administer Linux. The root account owns system files and is used for installing software and hardware, modifying system files, and configuring hardware devices. For this reason, use care with the root account. The following list gives you some guidelines for protecting the root account:

- Make sure the root account has a hard-to-guess password. For example, the password should be more than eight characters, should not include common words or personal information, and should consist of a mixture of uppercase and lowercase letters, numbers, and symbols.

- Change the root password often, at least every two weeks.

- When working from a remote client computer, log in to root only with SSH.

- Spend as little time as possible logged in to the root account, reserving this account only for specific tasks. When these tasks are completed, log out of root and log in to your personal account to do other work.

- Make sure the /etc/securetty file contains only the names of sources authorized to access the root account.

- Be careful when you work in root so that you don't make mistakes with unintended consequences, such as inadvertently deleting a system or configuration file when you meant to just view its contents.

- When you need to perform tasks from the root account, use the sudo command (explained in the following paragraphs) from your own account instead of logging in to root.

NOTE Some tasks are still better performed from root, such as installing new software or doing system configuration. In many organizations, the system administrator does these tasks at night and disables users from logging in, which protects the system.

- Use the su (superuser) command to run commands from your own or another person's account, when this method is appropriate for the actions you want to accomplish in root.

You can run the sudo command while you are logged in to your own account. To use it, enter sudo plus the command you want to run. For example, to run the top command as root, enter the following:

```
sudo top
```

Enter the password for root, and the top command runs from the root account. One advantage of running top from sudo is that you have the latitude to stop any running process, such as a process an intruder is using that you want to stop instantly. In another example, you might want to use the less command to view the contents of a file that only root has permission to display, or you might need to create a new user account quickly or shut down the system instantly from your account.

By default, when you run sudo the first time and enter the root password, the password is remembered for 5 minutes. If you run another command from sudo within 5 minutes, you don't have to reenter the password.

The configuration file /etc/sudoers, which enforces sudo security, contains a list of users and the commands they are authorized to use. Use the special visudo edit command to edit the /etc/sudoers file.

NOTE The visudo command is the only edit command that should be used to modify the /etc/sudoers file because it creates a safe environment in which to edit. After you have made changes to the file, you can use q to quit and save your changes or x to exit without saving your changes. To learn more about visudo, use the man visudo command or visit *http://linux.about.com/library/cmd/blcmdl8_visudo.htm*.

Another use of sudo is to give specific users limited privileges. For example, an IT employee needs to mount CDs or DVDs per users' requests. In many Linux distributions, only root has privileges to mount a CD or DVD. To ensure that your system is hardened, you can't give the IT employee full privileges to use the root account. As a solution, you can edit the /etc/sudoers file to allow him to mount a CD or DVD by using the sudo command. In this case, his root privileges are strictly limited to mounting the CD or DVD.

An important feature to remember is that all commands issued via sudo are recorded in a log file, /var/log/messages, that the administrator should view periodically. Further, if your Linux system is used for accounting, payroll, or other financial transactions, your company's financial auditors are likely to be interested in finding out how sudo is used and in seeing the log file.

You can also use the su command to log in to root while still in your account or while you are working from someone else's account. To log in as root by using su, enter this command:

```
su root
```

The system asks for the root password. After you provide the password, you're logged in temporarily, so you can use many root privileges. However, the access granted to su can vary by Linux distribution. In some distributions, for example, using su doesn't allow you to create a directory or file. When you're finished, make sure you type exit and press Enter to log out of the root account.

Integrity Checking and Removing Unnecessary Packages

Software used in Linux generally comes in a "package" or installation file. The advantage of this approach is that all pieces of the software are in one place. On most systems, a software package is unpacked and installed by a program designed for this purpose. The most commonly used one is Red Hat Package Manager (RPM). The commercial Red Hat Enterprise Linux and its free cousin, Fedora, are among the most popular Linux distributions. Because RPM simplifies package installation and removal, many Linux distributions use it (or a customized version of it). If your system doesn't have RPM, contact the source of the Linux distribution to see whether a compatible version is available.

NOTE

You can download an open-source version of RPM from *www.rpm.org*. Other open-source package manager options are available, such as GNOME RPM (visit *www.gnome.org*) or Kpackage (see *www.kde.org*). This chapter discusses the Red Hat version of RPM because it's so commonly used. When you use a package manager, be sure it's compatible with your Linux distribution and the software packages you use. Also, if you have Debian Linux or a distribution based on it, use the Debian package manager, dpkg, and note that packages for Debian have the .deb extension.

RPM can be used in two modes: graphical and command line. The graphical mode is easiest to use because it offers point-and-click features. However, the command-line mode is consistent across Linux distributions. For this reason, the command-line mode, typically referred to as rpm (because commands are lowercase), is discussed in this chapter.

A software package intended for use with RPM has the .rpm extension. The name of the package is often rather long to indicate its purpose and version level. For example, backuponcd-0.9.1-6mdk.rpm is the name of a package for CD backup shell scripts.

Integrity Checking

When you download a package to your system, make sure you check its integrity before opening it to verify that the package hasn't been altered. Many packages have a digital signature with encrypted keys that's used for this purpose. Recent versions of rpm do a limited integrity check automatically when you install a package. However, this check doesn't always verify all the headers and signatures in a package. For a more thorough integrity check before you install the package, use one of these options:

```
rpm -K packagename
```

or

```
rpm -checksig packagename
```

Use these options without the -i, --install, -U, or --upgrade options for installing or upgrading a package.

Removing Unnecessary Packages

A good way to reduce a Linux system's attack surface is to remove software packages that aren't in use. This step is a good practice for several reasons. The most important is that the software might contain security flaws. For example, it might leave a network port open on your system that creates an opening for attackers. Even if a patch for a security flaw is available, you might not have it installed if you're no longer using that software. Unnecessary software could also start processes or open services that increase the attack surface on your system. Removing unnecessary software can also increase system performance and free disk resources. Even software that's not in use could still load processes or services that take up CPU or memory resources.

To view the software packages installed on your system, enter the following command (see Figure 7-6):

```
rpm -qa | more
```

If you're unsure what a software package does, use the -qi option to view information about it (see Figure 7-7):

```
rpm -qi packagename
```

When you're ready to uninstall a package, use the -e or --erase options as follows:

```
rpm -e packagename
```

or

```
rpm --erase packagename
```

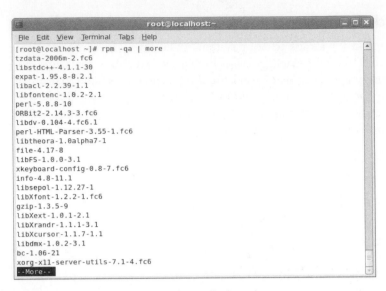

Figure 7-6   Viewing a list of installed packages

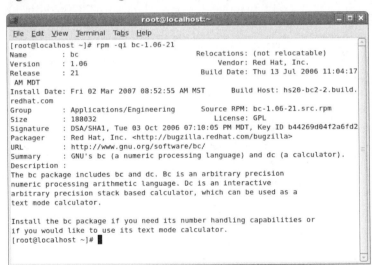

Figure 7-7   Displaying more detailed information about a package

Activity 7-2: Inventorying the Packages on a Linux System

Time Required: 15 minutes

Objective: Determine the packages that are installed on a Linux computer.

Description: You can make a Linux computer run more efficiently and reduce its vulnerability to attacks by removing unused software packages. In this activity, you inventory the packages installed on a Linux computer so that you can decide which ones to remove.

1. Log in to the root account (or use **sudo** from your own account, if you have the right privileges).

2. Access the command line or open a terminal window.

3. If you're in the root account, type **rpm –qa | more** and press **Enter**. If you're in your own account, type **sudo rpm –qa | more** and press **Enter**.

4. Record the first four packages listed in the first screen of information:

   _____

   _____

5. Review the remaining names of installed packages in the first screen.

6. Press the spacebar as needed and review the packages on the next 10 screens. You can press **q** to exit the listing.

7. After you have reviewed the packages, type **rpm –qa | more** (from root) or **sudo rpm –qa | more** (from your own account) and press **Enter** again. Determine the number of packages installed on your system and record that number on the following line. You'll notice many packages installed by default that aren't in use.

   _____

8. Type **exit** and press **Enter** to return to your user account. Leave the terminal window open for the next activity.

Maintaining System Patching

One of the best ways to harden a system is to stay current on patches and updates, which are often designed to plug security holes that have shown up after a system or software release. Generally, two kinds of updates or patches are available: those for the Linux OS and those for software packages (although sometimes the two overlap). To download and install updates and patches, you need to be logged in to the root account.

Most Linux distributions have automated tools for updating a system, and many have an icon in the panel you can use for downloading updates and patches, such as the Security Updates icon in Red Hat Enterprise Linux and Fedora. In some Red Hat and other distributions, you can also run the Update Agent program from the desktop or command line. For example, on the desktop in recent Red Hat Enterprise Linux and Fedora versions, click the Applications menu, click System Tools, and select Software Updater. From the command line in some distributions, enter up2date or up2date *packagename* (for a specific software package).

As another example, SUSE Linux has an Online Update option in its Yet another Setup Tool (YaST) system management tool. To open YaST (you need root privileges), click the Computer menu on the desktop, select More Applications, and then find and open YaST.

Configuring System Accounting

Recent Linux distributions have a system accounting capability built in to the main OS software (the kernel). If your distribution is built on version 2 or later of the kernel, it most likely has system accounting. You can determine your kernel's version by using the uname -r command.

 At this writing, the most recent Linux kernel version is 2.6.23.9. To learn more about the Linux kernel, visit *www.kernel.org*.

When you enable system accounting, Linux tracks information about commands that have been entered on the system. This information is stored in the /var/log/pacct file. If you suspect an intrusion in your system, you can examine the pacct log to find out more. You can also use this log to monitor what software users run routinely. With this information about commonly run programs, you can optimize your system for these programs.

Before you enable system accounting, be aware that the pacct file can grow fast and eventually take up lots of disk space. One way to manage it is to use the cp command to copy the current pacct file to an archived file (pacct1, in this example):

```
cp pacct pacct1
```

Then delete and re-create the pacct file from scratch. Later, delete the old pacct1 file or archive it to CD/DVD or tape, and replace it with a more recent one. In this way, you keep only current data without using up too much disk space.

The first step in configuring system accounting is to modify the init process script, which is the /etc/inittab file (also called the init file). A **script** is a file of Linux commands used to carry out a certain task. The /etc/inittab file is a script that runs when you boot the system.

You can create or modify a script or other file by using the vi editor, which is a simple screen editor installed by default in most Linux distributions. For example, log in to root (don't use sudo for this task) and enter this command:

```
vi /etc/inittab
```

You begin in command mode, which doesn't allow you to enter text. Use the down arrow to scroll to where you want to insert the modifications. Next, press the letter i to go into insert mode. After entering text, review it carefully for typing mistakes, and correct any you find. Press Esc to enter command mode again. At the : prompt at the bottom of the screen, type x or wq and press Enter to exit and save your work.

TIP

If you're new to using the vi editor, review the documentation first by typing man vi. Also, if you're uncertain about your vi editor skills, or as a good precaution, make a copy of the /etc/inittab file before you edit it by typing cp /etc/inittab /etc/inittab.bak and pressing Enter.

7

When you modify the init script, you add a command that starts system accounting and directs the information to the pacct log. The following are sample code lines you could enter:

```
#Start system accounting
/sbin/accton /var/log/pacct
echo "System accounting started"
```

As you have probably guessed, the line /sbin/accton /var/log/pacct is used to start system accounting. (Note the space after "accton.")

Before you reboot or before you start system accounting, you need to create the pacct file with this command:

```
touch /var/log/pacct
```

The touch command is used to create a file when one with that name doesn't exist. If one already exists, touch changes only the timestamp and doesn't overwrite the file. Plan to modify the init script and create the pacct file from the root account to ensure that root owns the file and has the necessary access to manage its contents. However, keep in mind that changes you make to the init script don't go into effect until you reboot the system.

Finally, after the pacct file starts tracking information, you can use the sa command to view a summary of information accumulated in this log.

ACTIVITY

Activity 7-3: Viewing the Init File's Contents

Time Required: 10 minutes

Objective: Determine whether system accounting starts automatically.

Description: The init file is important to your system because it sets up the system environment, runs programs and scripts, and performs other initialization functions. In this activity, you view its contents to find out whether it's set up to start system accounting.

1. If you aren't already logged in, log in to your regular account, and access the command line or open a terminal window.

2. Type **less /etc/inittab** and press **Enter** (see Figure 7-8).

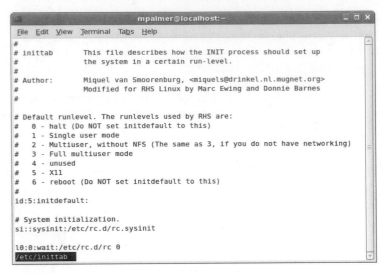

Figure 7-8   Viewing the contents of the init file

3. Use the spacebar to display additional pages.

4. Did you see any entries to start system accounting? If so, record the specific lines of code used to start it:

_____

_____

_____

5. When you come to the last page, type **q** to exit. Leave the terminal window open for the next activity.

Configuring Auditing and Logging

Distributions with the Linux kernel 2.6.x and later come with an auditing package that can be installed to set up "watches" on specific files. For example, your organization's financial auditors might recommend that you set a watch on accounts receivable and payable files or on the payroll file. You might also decide to set up a watch on system files used to control user accounts so that you can monitor when these files are written to, such as for changing passwords.

The first step is to install the audit package with the rpm, up2date, or yum commands (depending on what your system supports). The yum command is available in popular Linux distributions, such as Red Hat and Fedora, and is a good command for installing packages because it can simplify installation steps, such as setting up dependencies (additional files the audit system uses). For example, to install auditing with yum, enter the following:

```
yum install audit
```

The program that handles auditing is called auditd. You can start this program from the command line or from the init file by using the following:

```
/etc/init.d/auditd start
```

After you install auditd, you can set up watches on specific files, such as the /etc/passwd and /etc/shadow files that manage user accounts (explained in more detail later in this chapter). To set up a watch on the /etc/passwd file, enter the following:

```
auditctl -w /etc/passwd -p wr -k password-file
```

In this example, the -w option sets up a watch on the /etc/passwd file. The -p sets the filter for which permissions to watch, which can be w for write, r for read, and x for execute. In this example, w and r permissions are specified, but not x permissions. Therefore, audit information is recorded each time someone writes to or reads the password file. Finally, the -k option sets a filter key called password-file that's used to find information in the audit logs related specifically to the password file.

Two important commands for viewing the information auditd collects are ausearch and aureport. The ausearch command pulls out specific information from the audit logs, such as who has accessed the passwd file. The aureport command generates summary data of the audit log contents. For example, if you want to see who has made changes to the /etc/passwd file, enter the following:

```
ausearch -f /etc/passwd | less
```

In this example, the -f option is used to specify the file, and the results are piped into the less command (| less) because there are multiple pages of data to view.

When you use the aureport command, you can view a wide variety of summarized data, including the following:

- System configuration changes
- Account and group changes
- Successful logins and failed logins
- Number of successful and failed authentications
- Number of users
- Number of executables (programs)

Using Antivirus Solutions

You have already learned about the value of antivirus software in this book. This section is just a reminder to obtain an antivirus software package and automatic update service for your system. Many commercial and open-source antivirus programs are available for Linux, such as Panda Antivirus for Linux, MacAfee LinuxShield, F-PROT Antivirus for Linux, BitDefender, and OpenAntivirus.org. You can search the Internet for options to evaluate.

MANAGING USER AND FILE SYSTEM SECURITY

The goal of network security is to secure resources against intrusions yet enable authorized users to access the resources they need. The tools administrators use for this purpose are user accounts, groups, directories, and files. In the sections that follow, you learn how to work with these tools to improve security.

Configuring User Accounts and Groups

Access to a Linux computer is enabled through user accounts, groups, and access permissions (discussed later in "Configuring File and Directory Permissions"). Each user account in Linux is associated with a **user identification number (UID)**. Also, users who have common access needs can be assigned to a group via a **group identification number (GID)**, and then the permissions to access resources are assigned to the group instead of to each user. When a user logs in to access resources, a password file is checked to permit login authorization. This file, named passwd, is in the /etc directory and contains the following information for each user:

- The username
- An encrypted password or a reference to the **shadow file** (a file associated with the passwd file that's restricted to the root user, which makes it difficult for intruders to determine passwords)
- The UID, which can be a number as large as 60,000
- A GID associated with the username
- Information about the user, such as a description or a job title
- The location of the user's home directory
- A command that runs as the user logs in, such as which shell to use

 Usually, you give users a unique UID; however, if there's more than one Linux server on a network, you might create accounts on each server with the same account name and UID to simplify access and account administration.

In many Linux distributions, any account with a UID of 0 has access to anything in the system automatically. Occasionally, you should audit the /etc/passwd file to make sure only the root account has this UID. To view the /etc/passwd file's contents from the root account, enter less /etc/passwd.

The shadow file (/etc/shadow) is normally available only to the system administrator (root account). It contains password restriction information that includes the following:

- Minimum and maximum number of days between password changes
- When the password was last changed

- Warning information about when a password will expire
- Amount of time the account can be inactive before access is prohibited

Information about groups is stored in the /etc/group file, which typically contains an entry for each group consisting of the group's name, an encrypted group password, the GID, and a list of group members. In most Linux distributions, every account is assigned to at least one group and can be assigned to more than one group simultaneously. In some Linux distributions, when an account is created, by default a group with the same name is created, and that account becomes a member of the group.

You can create user accounts and groups by editing the passwd, shadow, and group files, but a safer method is using Linux commands created for this purpose. If you edit the files, you run the risk of a typing error that can cause unanticipated problems. Also, making sure each group has a unique GID is important because groups using the same GID can pose a serious security risk. An obvious risk is that permissions given to one group might not be appropriate for the other group to have.

You use the useradd command to create a new user. The options you can use with it include the following:

- -c—Gives an account description
- -d—Specifies the user's home directory location
- -e—Specifies an account expiration date
- -f—Specifies the number of days the account can be inactive before access is prohibited
- -g—Specifies initial group membership
- -G—Specifies additional groups to which the account belongs
- -m—Establishes the home directory if it hasn't been set up previously
- -M—Means do not create a home directory
- -n—Means don't set up a group with the same name as the account (the default is creating a group with the same name as the account name)
- -p—Specifies the account password
- -s—Designates the default shell associated with the account
- -u—Specifies the UID

To see how some of these options are used, take a look at this example:

```
useradd -c "Lisa Ramirez, Accounting Department, ext 221" -p
green$thumb -u 700 lramirez
```

This command creates an account called lramirez with a comment containing the account holder's full name and department, a password set to green$thumb, and a UID of 700. (In Hands-On Project 7-1, you set up a user account.)

You can automate account creation by writing a script containing prompts for the information.

In many Linux distributions, a UID under 500 is typically used for system accounts, and user accounts have a UID of 500 or higher. In this example, several parameters aren't included in the command but are set by default: to create a group called lramirez, to create the home directory (/home/lramirez, with lramirez as owner), and to set the shell as bash (Bourne Again Shell). If you don't want a group created automatically at the time you create a user account, use the –n option to assign the account to a general group called users (with GID 100) instead. Not all Linux distributions set up a default group with the same name as the user account, however.

In many Linux versions, if no password is specified when the account is created, the account is disabled by default. This feature adds a measure of security because it closes possible doorways into the system.

To modify a user account's parameters, you use the usermod command. For instance, to change the password for the lramirez account, you enter this command:

```
usermod -p applebuTTer# lramirez
```

To delete an account, use the userdel command, which enables you to specify the username and delete the home directory and its contents, if needed. In some distributions, such as Red Hat Enterprise Linux and Fedora, you use the -r option, as shown, to delete an account, the home directory, and all files in the home directory:

```
userdel -r lramirez
```

When employees leave an organization, it's a good practice to ensure that all important business files they own are archived or transferred to other accounts before they leave. Then as soon as they leave, disable their accounts or change the passwords. In a few days, after you are certain the accounts don't own files important to the business, delete them.

Information about groups is typically stored in the /etc/group file (see Figure 7-9), and group security information is in the /etc/gshadow file. To create groups, you use the groupadd command, usually with the –g option to establish the GID and a string to specify the group name. For example, to create the auditors group with a GID of 2000, you enter groupadd –g 2000 auditors. After a group is created, you can modify it with the groupmod command or delete it with the groupdel command. (In Hands-On Project 7-2, you create a group.)

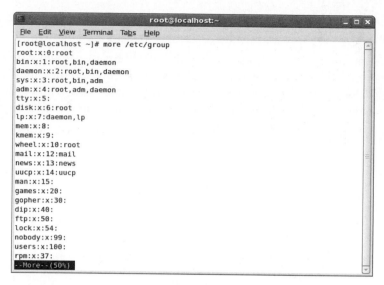

Figure 7-9 Viewing the contents of the /etc/group file

Monitoring User Account Activity

Good network management includes being aware of users on a system and how they are using it. You already learned to use the who command for this purpose. Two other commands—last and ac—are useful for monitoring user activity so that you can gain a sense of what's normal and what could signal a problem. Monitoring user activity not only helps maintain good security, but also ensures that legitimate users can use the system without interference from intruders or malware.

The last command lists users who have logged in recently. It retrieves this information from the /var/log/wtmp and /var/log/btmp files. When you use last, you can view the account name, dates of login, login duration, terminal or type of login, and other information. At the end of the display is the date when the information started being recorded. If you suspect there has been an intruder since a certain date, you can use last to review who has been logging in.

The ac command displays a summary of connection times for users, so you get an idea of who uses the system most and least. If you use the ac command by itself, you see only the total time of all user connections. For connection totals by user, add the -p option.

Managing Password Security and Password Restrictions

When you create accounts for new users, make sure they understand the policies for changing passwords. Even with a policy in place, encourage them to change their passwords regularly, such as every month. In addition, make sure users are familiar with the passwd command for changing their passwords. When using this command, you must type the new password twice to verify it. Also, in most Linux distributions, you have to provide the old password before changing the new one.

An account owner can use passwd without entering the account name. When system administrators use the command to change another user's password, however, they must enter the account name, such as passwd lramirez. The system administrator also can use the passwd command to set account restrictions for a specific user account by using the following options:

- -l—Locks the password, which means the user can't access that account; only root can access it

- -u—Unlocks an account after the -l option is used

- -f—Requires that the user change the password at the next login

- -n *days*—Configures the minimum number of days a password can be used; before that time, the password can't be changed

- -x *days*—Specifies the maximum number of days a password can be used before it expires and the user has to change it

- -w *days*—Is often used with the -x option to give users warnings at login of a password's expiration; for example, -w 5 starts the login warning five days in advance

NOTE

One advantage of learning to write scripts in Linux is that you can use one command to run a script that applies the same password restrictions to all or specific accounts.

If your organization uses password expiration, you can use the chage command to fine-tune this restriction. Useful options for this command include the following:

- -m *days*—Sets the minimum number of days the current password must stay in effect before it can be changed

- -M *days*—Sets the maximum number of days before the password expires

- -I *days* (uppercase I)—Locks the account if it isn't used in the specified number of days

- -E *date*—Sets a specific date on which the account is locked

- -l *accountname* (lowercase l)—Displays the password expiration information for a specific account

Using the Shadow File

As you learned earlier, the shadow file (/etc/shadow) is used to protect user account passwords. If the shadow file is not enabled, passwords are written to the /etc/passwd file and are fairly easy to view because they aren't hidden or encrypted. When the shadow file is enabled, the password field for each account in /etc/passwd contains a pointer to the shadow file. Passwords in the shadow file are encrypted, so even if intruders can view the file, they can't read the passwords. Also, by default only the root account has permissions for the shadow file.

Most modern Linux distributions are set up so that the shadow file is enabled automatically when the OS is installed. If you have an older Linux distribution, enable the shadow file before you begin creating user accounts by entering the following from the root account:

```
/usr/bin/pwconv
```

In many modern Linux distributions, you can also enable the shadow file with the Authentication Configuration utility, which uses the authconfig command. To enable the shadow file with this utility, enter one of the following commands:

```
authconfig --enableshadow
```

or

```
authconfig --useshadow
```

As an alternative, many Linux distributions offer a GUI system tool to enable the shadow file. Consult the documentation for your distribution or search through the menu to find it.

Configuring File and Directory Permissions

In Linux, the security of files and directories is managed through **permissions**, which specify access rights and privileges. Permissions are part of **access control lists (ACLs)** that are associated with the information about each file and directory. In Linux, three main permissions are used to protect files and directories:

- read (r)
- write (w)
- execute (x)

Use the Linux chmod command to set directory and file permissions. In its simplest form, the chmod command takes as arguments a symbolic string (characters that are abbreviations for permissions) followed by file or directory names. The symbolic string specifies permissions that should be granted or denied to categories of users.

Here's an example: ugo+rwx. The characters ugo stand for user (same as owner), group, and other. The next character, the + sign, means permissions are being granted. The characters rwx indicate the permissions being granted: read, write, and execute, in this example. Therefore, ugo+rwx means that read, write, and execute permissions are being granted to the owner, group, and other. The following example shows how the symbolic string is used in a command to modify myfile's access permissions:

```
chmod ugo+rwx myfile
```

The following command grants read permission to the customers file for the group:

```
chmod g+r customers
```

Programmers often use the "other" designation for programs they write so that users can run those programs. In this situation, the programmer is the owner, and users who run the program are the "other."

NOTE

You can also deny permissions by using the – sign with a symbolic string. The following command denies the group and other write and execute permissions for the account_info file:

```
chmod go-wx account_info
```

The octal permission format is another way to assign permissions; this format uses a number that indicates the type of permission and owner, group, and other. For example, execute permission is assigned 1, write is 2, and read is 4. These permission numbers are added for a value between 0 and 7. For instance, read and write permission is a 6 (4 + 2) and read and execute is a 5 (4 + 1), as shown in the following list:

- 0—No permissions
- 1—Execute (same as x)
- 2—Write (same as w)
- 3—Write and execute (same as wx)
- 4—Read (same as r)
- 5—Read and execute (same as rx)
- 6—Read and write (same as rw)
- 7—Read, write, and execute (same as rwx)

One of these numbers is associated with each of three numeric positions after the chmod command. The first position indicates the owner, the second position indicates the group, and the final position indicates other. For example, the chmod 755 myfile command assigns these permissions for myfile: read, write, and execute permissions (7) to owner; read and execute permissions (the first 5) to group; and read and execute permissions (the second 5) to other. Here are some other examples of assigning permissions to myfile:

- chmod 711 myfile—Assigns read, write, and execute to owner; execute to group; and execute to other
- chmod 642 myfile—Assigns read and write to owner; read to group; and write to other
- chmod 777 myfile—Assigns read, write, and execute to owner, group, and other
- chmod 504 myfile—Assigns read and execute to owner; no permissions to group; and read permission to other

Three advanced permissions deserve mention. Typically, system administrators use them for special purposes: **sticky bit**, **set user id (SUID) bit**, and **set group id (SGID) bit**.

In older Linux distributions, the sticky bit is used to cause an executable program to stay resident in memory after it's exited. This action ensures that the program is ready immediately to use the next time around or stays ready for multiple users on a server. In current OSs, the sticky bit is used instead to allow a file to run, but only the file's owner or root have permission to delete or rename it. The symbol for the sticky bit is t. Therefore, when you view permissions for a file by using a long listing (ls -l), you see a t instead of the usual x for execute permission, as in this example: –rwxr-xr-t.

The SUID bit is generally used on programs and files used by programs. SUID gives the current user (user ID) temporary permissions to run program-related files as though he or she is the owner. For example, programs on a multiuser system or server are usually installed by root. However, ordinary users might need to run and possibly modify files to use those programs as though they are the root account. Setting the SUID bit gives them the access they need to use the programs—temporarily treating these users as root (the owner). Even though someone is using the program with the SUID bit permission, root still retains actual ownership. The symbol for the SUID bit is s, which is used instead of x (execute) when you view permissions, as in this example: –rwsr-xr-x.

The SGID bit works similarly to SUID, but it applies to groups. For example, your company might have a group of people who use accounting files. The system administrator can create a group called accounting and use the SGID bit to give each member of the group temporary access as an owner while she or he is using the accounting files. The symbol for SGID is also an s, so when both SUID and SGID are set, the file permissions might look like this: –rwsr-sr-x. Notice that the x permission is replaced with s for the owner and group.

Determining Permissions on a File or Directory

When you use ls -l to get a long listing of a directory, you can also view permissions for files and subdirectories in that directory (refer back to Figure 7-4). For example, you might see the following: –rwxr-xr-x. Recall that the first position indicates a file (–) or a directory (d). The next three positions are the owner's permissions (rwx, in this example). Positions 5 to 7 (which are r-x) indicate the group's permissions. This specification applies to all users (other than the owner) who are members of the owner's group. Positions 8 to 10 (r-x) indicate permissions for other. In the example –rwxr-xr-x, here's what each character indicates:

- First hyphen—Specifies a file
- r—File's owner has read permission
- w—File's owner has write permission
- x—File's owner has execute permission
- r—Group has read permission

- Second hyphen—Group does not have write permission
- x—Group has execute permission
- r—Others have read permission
- Third hyphen—Others do not have write permission
- x—Others have execute permission

Activity 7-4: Determining Permissions

Time Required: 15 minutes

Objective: Determine the permissions associated with key directories in Linux.

Description: You should know the permissions associated with important files and directories in Linux so that you're aware of potential vulnerabilities. In this activity, you determine the permissions associated with some of the main directories under the root directory.

1. Access the command line from your own account.

2. Type **cd /** and press **Enter**.

3. Type **ls –l** and press **Enter**.

4. What are the file permissions for the /bin directory?

   _____

5. What permissions are associated with the /home directory?

   _____

6. What permissions are on the /root directory?

   _____

7. Do the permissions set on your system match the security you need?

   _____

   _____

   _____

8. Type **exit** and press **Enter** to close the terminal window.

Configuring File and Directory Ownership

File and directory ownership is important because the owner has complete control, such as the ability to set or change permissions. When a file or directory is created, the default owner is the account that created it. Sometimes changing ownership is necessary because control of the file or directory could change hands when someone leaves the company or the responsibility for it is passed from root to a specific user.

The owner uses the chown command to transfer ownership. For example, to change ownership of the vendors file to the user account rzubrow, you enter the following:

```
chown rzubrow vendors
```

You might also want to change ownership of a directory and all the files and subdirectories it contains. To do this for a directory called data so that rzubrow is the new owner, use the –R option as shown:

```
chown -R rzubrow data
```

EXAMINING NETWORK CONFIGURATION SECURITY

Linux systems are often connected to a network or the Internet for sharing information. However, these connections can also make computers vulnerable to attacks unless steps are taken to protect them. In the sections that follow, you review popular methods of sharing information in Linux and learn how to protect systems by using these methods: Network File System, Network Information System, and Samba. Before you focus on these methods, however, read the next section on the value of enabling Kerberos for network authentication to help protect the integrity of communication.

Enabling Kerberos Authentication

Linux supports Kerberos, as do Windows systems. When you share resources on a network, such as accessing shared files on a Linux or Windows computer, using Kerberos for connection authentication can increase security. Further, most Windows systems use Kerberos, and communication with these systems, such as through Samba, is safer when Kerberos is enabled.

 Chapter 8 covers Kerberos in more detail. You can also refer to *Guide to Tactical Perimeter Defense: Becoming a Security Network Specialist* (Course Technology, 2008, ISBN 1428356304) for more information.

On modern Linux systems, use the Authentication Configuration tool to enable Kerberos. It's available from the command line and often as a GUI tool. As a GUI tool, it's usually in the System or Administration menu in the popular GNOME GUI desktop. For example, to start it in Red Hat Enterprise Linux or Fedora, click the System menu, point to Administration, and click Authentication. In the dialog box that opens, click the Authentication tab, and select the option to enable Kerberos. To enable Kerberos authentication as the default from the command line, use the authconfig command with the following option:

```
authconfig --enablekrb5
```

Using Network File System

Linux enables resource sharing by using **Network File System (NFS)**. With NFS, a Linux computer can mount a partition on another Linux computer and then access file systems on the mounted partition as though they are on the local Linux computer. When a client mounts NFS volume on a host server, both the client and host use **Remote Procedure Calls (RPC)**, which enables services and software on one computer to use services and software on a different computer. Further, for NFS to work, RPC services should be enabled on the server.

Configuring NFS on the Server Side

To configure NFS on the computer offering the partition to share, you create a file called /etc/exports. If the file doesn't already exist on your computer, you can create and edit it with the vi editor. If it already exists, use the vi editor to open and edit it. Either way, you enter the following:

```
vi /etc/exports
```

Here are some sample lines for the /etc/exports file:

```
# This file provides an access control list for NFS file systems
to export to clients
/home/lramirez/data            brown.ourcomp.com(rw,sync)
/home/anderson/lists             *(secure,sync)
```

As mentioned previously, the pound sign (#) indicates a comment. Typically, you add a comment to document the purpose of the file. In the next line, the contents of the /home/lramirez/data directory are made available exclusively to the computer brown.ourcomp.com, giving that computer read and write (rw) access to the directory's contents. The sync option is used so that write operations are written to disk synchronously to ensure data integrity and avoid data loss. Note that specifying ro instead of rw gives the client read-only access. In the third line, the /home/anderson/list directory is made available to anyone via a secure reserved communication port.

NOTE
There are more options for specifying export file systems in the /etc/exports file; these examples are meant only as an introduction. You can use the man NFS command to find more documentation.

After your /etc/exports file is set up, you can have it go into effect without restarting by using the following command:

```
exportfs -a -v
```

The security that controls which clients can access NFS on a server is handled through entries in two files. The /etc/hosts.allow file contains the clients allowed to use NFS, and the /etc/hosts.deny file contains computers that aren't allowed to use NFS. Besides configuring the /etc/hosts.allow and /etc/hosts.deny files, the resources mounted through NFS are also protected by permissions on directories and files.

In the /etc/hosts.deny file, for the best security, specify that all clients (hosts) are denied except those listed in the /etc/hosts.allow file. To do this, put the following line in the /etc/hosts.deny file:

```
portmap: ALL
```

In the /etc/hosts.allow file, you enter the portmapper service plus the IP addresses of those computers allowed to access the shared resources. For example, the following line allows access only to the host with the IP address 192.168.0.30:

```
portmap: 192.168.0.30
```

In another example, you could allow all users on the local network and the user with remote network IP address 22.44.0.15 by using the following line:

```
portmap: 192.168.0.0/255.255.255.0, 22.44.0.15
```

Configuring NFS on the Client Side

On the client side, users can mount an NFS shared partition automatically when their computers start by creating an entry in the /etc/fstab file. For example, to mount the /pub partition, which is made available from a server to all users on a network, each user might have the following /etc/fstab entry:

```
server.mynet.com/pub          /home/public     nfs      timeo=30
```

This line means mount the server's /pub directory on the client computer as /home/public and wait 30 seconds for a response from the server before terminating the mount request.

The client computer can also mount an NFS partition manually by using the mount command. Using the previous example, this is the command:

```
mount -t nfs -o timeo=30  server.mynet.com/pub /home/public
```

Using Network Information System

Network Information System (NIS) provides a naming system for shared resources on a Linux network. One computer acts as the NIS server. Through the NIS server, a user can access shared resources, such as a shared partition offered through NFS, by using a single user designation and password. NIS is intended for users on a local network.

Configuring the NIS Server

NIS is set up in several stages. First, you specify a domain name for the NIS server in the /etc/sysconfig/network file by using the NS_DOMAIN parameter, such as NIS_DOMAIN=mycompany.nis.

Second, configure the /var/yp/Makefile file. Some of the available options include the following:

- Set the NOPUSH option first to indicate whether there are slave NIS servers (backup servers, in case the master or main NIS server goes down).

- Set the minimum user and group IDs to 500.

- Enable the shadow and group files.

- Specify the directories in which to find passwd and other files NIS uses.

- Specify the configuration files that NIS manages, such as the passwd and shadow files.

- Specify the files to be shared through NIS.

Next, start the NIS server service by using this command:

```
service ypserv start
```

NOTE   The "yp" in these commands stands for yellow pages because NIS was originally called Yellow Pages when Sun Microsystems created it.

After the NIS service is started, create the NIS database by entering the following:

```
ypinit -m
```

Finally, edit the /var/yp/securenets file to list the clients of the NIS server. This step is important because it sets up basic security for the NIS environment. If you decide to list hosts separately, you can do this by specifying each IP address, such as:

```
host        192.168.0.22
```

If all users on the network are to have access to the NIS server, you can simply enter the following line in the /var/yp/securenets file:

```
255.255.255.0    192.168.0.0
```

Configuring the NIS Client

For NIS clients, the client software is already installed in many Linux distributions. However, each client needs to use the Authentication Configuration tool to specify the NIS domain name and NIS server name. For most users, the easiest method is using the Authentication Configuration GUI tool. (Consult the documentation for your Linux distribution to learn how to open the tool.) As you learned earlier, in Red Hat Enterprise Linux, click the System menu, point to Administration, and click Authentication. To enable NIS, click the User Information tab and select the option to enable NIS. Next, click the button to configure NIS and provide the names of the NIS domain and server.

The next step for clients is to edit the /etc/yp.conf file to contain the NIS server's IP address, as in this example:

```
ypserver 192.168.0.2
```

After the /etc/yp.conf file is edited, users can start the NIS client server by entering this command:

```
service ypbind start
```

Using Samba

Linux computers can access shared Windows files (and Windows computers can access Linux shared files) through the use of Samba. **Samba** is a utility that uses the Server Message Block (SMB) protocol, which is also used in Windows for sharing folders and printers. With Samba, a Linux computer appears to other Windows computers as just another Windows server. Samba provides Windows-compatible services for the following:

- File services
- Print services
- Authentication services (such as through Kerberos)

Samba configuration information is stored in the smb.conf file. Programmers of older Windows systems might notice that this file uses parameters and a structure reminiscent of Windows initialization (.ini) files. Depending on your Linux distribution, smb.conf is in the /etc, /etc/ samb, or /usr/local/samba/lib directories. This chapter simply introduces you to configuring the smb.conf file; discussing the many options for configuring it is beyond the scope of this book. Figure 7-10 shows the beginning instructions and configuration lines in a generic smb.conf file.

The beginning of the default smb.conf file offers instructions for learning more about setting up the file. The file is divided into sections with information on many configuration parameters, including the following:

- Specification of the Windows workgroup
- Server string (description) information
- Security parameters
- Share parameters
- Printer list and printer options
- Samba passwording options
- Connection interfaces
- Paths to shared folders

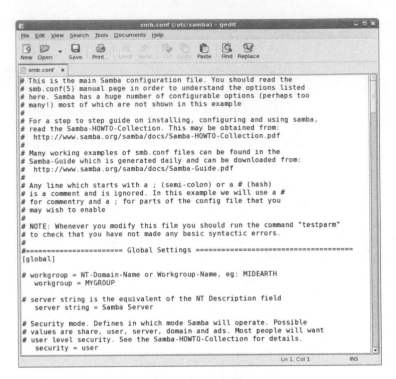

Figure 7-10 Viewing the smb.conf file

You can use a screen editor, such as vi, to modify the smb.conf file. A Web-based configuration tool called SWAT is also available.

Besides providing basic information, such as the Windows workgroup name and share parameters, setting security parameters is important to protect the Linux and Windows servers from intruders.

A minimal smb.conf file might look similar to the following:

```
[global]
workgroup = myworkgroup
netbios name = Computer1
[homes]
guest ok = no
read only = no
[share1]
path = /pub
[share2]
path = /spreadsheets
comment = Shared spread sheets
```

In this simple example, the [global] section provides the name of the Windows workgroup and the Linux computer's name as seen by other Windows computers. The [homes] section has two entries that carry out security measures. The first entry, guest ok = no, means that only accounts on the server hosting Samba can connect; users on other servers on the network or through the Internet can't connect. The read only = no parameter gives read and write permissions to shared directories and files. If this parameter is set to yes, users have read-only permission and no write permission. Finally, the [share1] section offers a share from the /pub directory, and the [share2] section offers access to the /spreadsheets directory.

Besides the security parameters shown in this smb.conf example, you can include several others. For example, one of the most secure setups is to specify which IP addresses can access the Samba server and block all others. Consider the following lines:

```
hosts allow = 192.168.1.1/41 192.168.2.10/22 127.0.0.1
hosts deny = 0.0.0.0/0
```

The hosts allow parameter gives access to users with private network addresses 192.168.1.1 through 192.168.1.41 and 192.168.2.10 through 192.168.22. It also enables the loopback address 127.0.0.1 for test purposes. The host deny parameter 0.0.0.0 blocks all other addresses that aren't specified.

Another security measure is to limit the types of interfaces that can access the Samba server. This setting can be important because if no interfaces are listed in the smb.conf file, Samba assumes that all types of interfaces are welcome, including interfaces from the Internet or over a remote network connection, such as through a DSL or wireless connection. If, for example, you have an Ethernet network using hard-wired and local wireless connections, you can lock down who accesses a Samba server by using the following lines in the smb.conf file:

```
interfaces = eth* lo
bind interfaces only = yes
```

These lines tell the server to only accept local Ethernet (eth*) connections and a connection through the loopback interface (lo). All others get a message such as "Connection Refused."

Yet another way to improve security is to specify which users and groups can access the Samba server, as with the following lines:

```
valid users = lramirez, sbach, rzubrow, @research
```

This parameter allows only the usernames lramirez, sbach, and rzubrow and the Linux security group @research to access the server.

After you have set up the smb.conf file, you can test it before you start Samba by using the following command (with the directory location /etc/samba as an example):

```
testparm /etc/samba/smb.conf
```

Finally, encrypting passwords used on accounts for accessing Samba is a good idea. You can specify encrypted passwords by including the following lines in the smb.conf file:

```
encrypt passwords = yes
smb passwd file = /etc/samba/smbpasswd
```

The second line specifies the location of the smbpasswd file, which holds usernames and passwords. The password file must be created at the same time as the smb.conf file by running the mksmbpasswd.sh script. Usernames and passwords are obtained from the Linux passwd file. You can add new users and passwords to the Samba password file by using the smbpasswd command.

 Make sure the passwd file's permissions are set so that only root has access, such as by entering chmod 600 /etc/samba/smbpasswd. (chmod 600 is equivalent to chmod u+rw.)

NOTE

The testparm utility examines the smb.conf file and reports any parameters that are entered incorrectly. After the smb.conf file is set up, you can start Samba by using the following command:

```
service smb start
```

SECURING LINUX

In addition to the techniques you have learned so far, there are many tools you can use to harden a Linux system. In this section, you learn about tools to close network ports, remove unused services, monitor and stop processes, track attackers, check the integrity of systems, and examine and set security settings on a system.

Closing Network Ports by Configuring a Firewall

Most Linux distributions come with a firewall that can be configured easily by using the GUI desktop. You can usually find the firewall GUI tool in a system tools or system administration menu from one of the panel's menus. In SUSE Linux, for example, you can configure the firewall by opening YaST with root privileges. In recent versions of Red Hat Enterprise Linux and Fedora, click the System menu, point to Administration, and click Security Level and Firewall. (The menu sequence might change, depending on the desktop version.)

Through the firewall configuration software, you can block specific services, such as the following, by closing their TCP/IP ports (see Figure 7-11):

- FTP
- SMTP (Internet mail)

- NFS
- SSH
- Samba
- HTTPS

Blocking ports is one of the best ways to foil attackers and malware because open ports can be an open door into your network.

Figure 7-11   Configuring firewall settings

Before you connect any Linux desktop or server to a network, using a firewall to block network services/ports that aren't used or aren't permitted in your organization is a good security practice. In many Linux distributions, you can configure the firewall when you install Linux. If this option is available, plan to enable and configure the firewall during installation so that the system is protected before it's connected to a network.

Removing Unused Services

Services can be a source of risk if attackers and malicious software can use them to access a system. As you learned with software packages, a good practice for hardening a Linux system is to remove services that aren't used to reduce the attack surface.

You can use the chkconfig command with the --list option to view the services that start automatically when a Linux system boots, as shown in Figure 7-12. This command shows each service and its runlevel. The on or off information shows whether a service is started or stopped at a specific runlevel. Use the following command to view services one screen at a time:

```
chkconfig --list | more
```

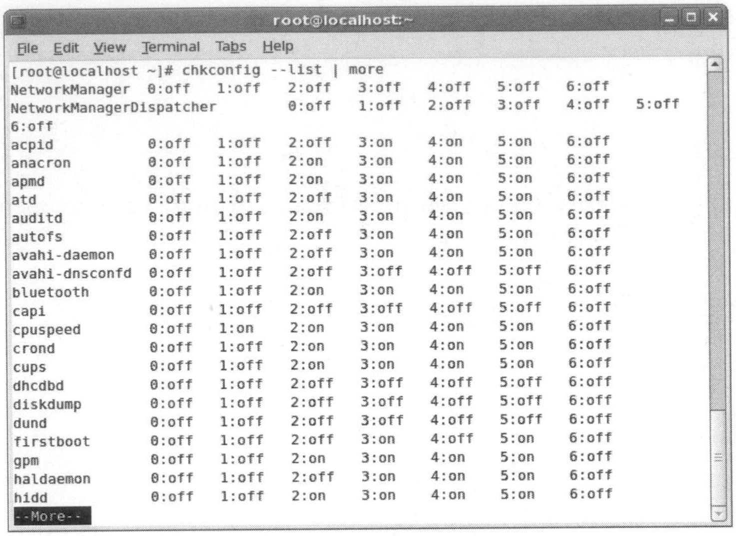

Figure 7-12 Using chkconfig to view services

In Linux, a **runlevel** is the level in which a computer boots or a service runs. As shown in Table 7-1, there are seven runlevels, ranging from 0 to 6; however, most services use only levels 1 through 5. The startup scripts containing the services to start for each runlevel are usually in /etc/rc.d but might be in other locations, depending on the distribution.

Table 7-1 Linux runlevels

Runlevel	Description
0	Halts or shuts down the system
1	Operates in single-user mode, which does not configure network interface services, does not start daemons, and allows only root to log in
2	Operates in multiuser mode, in which network interface services and daemons are not started
3	Operates in multiuser mode, in which the system starts all normal services but does not start the GUI desktop (X Window and desktop services)
4	Unused in Linux (reserved for future purposes)
5	Operates in multiuser mode and starts X Window and desktop services
6	Reboots the OS

Editing multiple runlevel scripts to remove services can be complex. Fortunately, many Linux distributions offer command-line and GUI tools for managing services. A common command-line tool is the System V Configuration tool, ntsysv, which enables you to start or stop services at bootup based on the runlevel. For example, to manage services at runlevel 1, you enter the following:

```
ntsysv 1
```

If you enter only ntsysv without specifying a runlevel, it uses the runlevel you are currently in, such as runlevel 5 for systems using a GUI desktop. However, to manage all services, you must run the tool for each runlevel used by Linux (1 to 5). The tool displays a text-based screen listing the installed services (see Figure 7-13). Use the up and down arrow keys to view the services. A hyphen inside the square brackets in front of the service means the service starts on bootup. Press the spacebar to remove a service flagged with the hyphen. (The spacebar toggles between on and off.) Also, you can use the Tab key to go from the services list to the Ok or Cancel buttons. When you're finished configuring services, tab to the Ok button and press Enter.

Figure 7-13   Using ntsysv to configure services to start or stop

A few Linux distributions, such as Ubuntu and Debian, use a command-line tool called sysvconfig, which is similar to ntsysv.

NOTE

Stopping Rogue Processes

When a program runs, it starts one or more processes. Sometimes a process hangs, or if it has bugs, it might take over system resources so that other processes run too slowly or grind to a halt. Also, an attacker or malware can introduce a rogue process.

Currently running processes are identified by a **process id (PID)**. (See the first column in Figure 7-3, for example.) The first step in identifying the resources a process uses is to run the top command you learned earlier in this chapter. You can also use the ps command to view the processes running on a system, but this command doesn't provide the resource use information that top does.

When you identify a process in top that needs to be stopped, you can press k (for kill), enter the PID, and then press Enter. If you aren't using top, you can use the kill command to stop a process. For example, to stop a process called badprocess with the PID 243, enter either of the following:

```
kill 243
```

or

```
kill %badprocess
```

Monitoring and managing processes is an effective way to optimize your system and stop an attacker or malware early before the damage is too serious. Try Hands-On Project 7-3 to use top to manage processes.

Other Linux Security Tools

A host of open-source and third-party Linux security tools are available. The following sections briefly cover three of them: TCP Wrappers, Integrity Checkers, and Bastille.

TCP Wrappers

TCP Wrappers offers a way to track attackers on a system and includes the following features:

- Uses standard Linux system logs to track connections to services
- Enhances authentication so that both a user account plus the password to log in come from the same authorized location
- Offers a way to trap attackers who are using network services
- Adds more extensive authentication for services such as ftp, exec, rsh, rlogin, telnet, finger, and others
- Uses the /etc/hosts.allow and /etc/hosts.deny files for enforcing security

You can download TCP Wrappers from *ftp://ftp.porcupine.org/pub/security*.

Integrity Checkers

Integrity checkers are used to track changes in a system, such as changes to files. They aren't quite the same as the integrity checking done with packages to verify file integrity before installing a package, although sometimes the integrity-checking methods are similar. In this case, an integrity checker is software that tracks changes to files already on a computer. It provides an audit trail for financial auditors, ensures that files and systems aren't damaged or corrupted, and determines whether damage has been done by attackers or malware.

Tripwire, a popular integrity checker, uses cryptographic hashes or signatures to monitor whether files have been changed. When you first run Tripwire, it calculates hashes of files you've selected to monitor. Then each time it runs, the hashes are recalculated to determine whether they have changed. Tripwire can be configured to track both authorized and unauthorized changes so that integrity problems are spotted right away. You can purchase a commercial version of Tripwire at *www.tripwire.com*. Free open-source versions are also available.

Advanced Intrusion Detection Environment (AIDE), another integrity checker, checks the attributes of files for changes, such as permissions, links, group associations, and inode numbers. It also creates an encrypted checksum for specified files to determine whether changes have occurred to the file contents. You can download AIDE from *sourceforge.net/projects/aide*, which is an open-source development Web site.

Bastille

Bastille can be used to help security administrators harden security. When run in interactive mode, Bastille examines security on a system so that it can be hardened interactively through a range of choices. Interactive mode is also a good tool for beginners to learn about Linux security. When Bastille runs in automated mode, it uses preconfigured security profiles the administrator selects to harden security. Through Bastille, you can configure system security settings, configure security programs and processes that run in the background for security, and add a firewall to a system. You can download Bastille from *www.bastille-linux.org* or *http://sourceforge.net/projects/bastille-linux*.

Chapter Summary

- There are many steps in hardening a Linux system. One of the best places to begin is to understand the Linux file system structure and how to navigate through it.

- The Linux command line offers a rich environment for using and managing security features and tools. The who and top commands are basic yet vital commands to use for protecting a system.

- Secure Shell offers a way to secure remote network and Internet connections to a Linux computer.

- The root account is used to administer a Linux computer. Take steps to protect this account fully, such as configuring a secure password that's changed regularly and using this account only when necessary.

- Many Linux systems have software packages that can be removed to harden the system. Other ways to harden a system include enabling system accounting, auditing, and logging and using an antivirus program that's kept updated. In addition, make sure patches are up to date.

❏ User accounts and passwords provide a basic defense for authorizing access to a Linux system.

❏ Directory and file permissions and ownership should always be configured to protect files on a system.

❏ Kerberos offers a way to encrypt communication on a network between clients and servers. Plan to use Kerberos for stronger authentication.

❏ When you use network services such as Network File System, Network Information System, and Samba, learn how to configure their built-in security features before they are made available to users.

❏ Use firewall software to close network ports that aren't in use, such as ports for FTP, SMTP, NFS, and other services that might not be used.

❏ Use tools such as ntsysv to stop unused services that increase a system's attack surface and use top to monitor and stop rogue processes.

❏ Consider using open-source and commercial security software, including TCP Wrappers, integrity checkers, and Bastille.

KEY TERMS

access control list (ACL) — Information stored in the OS that specifies the access rights users and groups have to resources, such as files and directories.

extended file system (ext) — The native file system in Linux, which comes in the following versions: ext, ext2, ext3, and ext4.

group identification number (GID) — A unique number assigned to a Linux group that distinguishes it from all other groups on a Linux computer.

inodes — A system for storing essential information about directories and files in the ext file system.

journaling — The process of keeping chronological records of data or transactions so that if a system crashes without warning or is brought down by an attack, the data or transactions can be reconstructed or rolled back to avoid data loss or information that isn't synchronized correctly.

Network File System (NFS) — A Linux service that enables file transfer and other shared services on Linux computers.

Network Information System (NIS) — A Linux service that provides a naming system for shared resources on a Linux network; makes resources easier to locate and identify.

permission — An element in a file or directory's access control list that specifies who can access a file or directory and in what way. Linux has three essential ACL permissions: read, write, and execute.

process id (PID) — An identification number that the OS assigns to a process for managing and tracking it.

Remote Procedure Calls (RPC) — A service that enables services and software on one computer to use services and software on a different computer over a network.

runlevel — The level in which a computer boots or a service runs.

Samba — A Linux service that enables Linux, UNIX, and Mac OS X systems to access shared Windows resources and vice versa.

script — A file of Linux commands for performing a certain task.

Secure Shell (SSH) — A form of authentication originally developed for Linux and UNIX to secure remote connections between a client computer and a host computer over a network or the Internet.

set group ID (SGID) bit — An advanced permission that enables a program owner to retain full ownership but gives group members temporary ownership while running the program.

set user ID (SUID) bit — An advanced permission that enables a program owner to retain full ownership but gives ordinary users temporary ownership while running the program.

shadow file — A file in Linux containing critical information about user accounts, including the encrypted password for each account; access to the shadow file is limited to the root user.

sticky bit —An advanced permission that causes a program to stay resident in memory (in older Linux distributions) or ensures that only root or the owner can delete or rename files (in newer distributions).

superblock — A special data block on a Linux partition containing information about the layout of blocks. This information is the key to finding directories and files in the file system.

Telnet — An Internet terminal emulation program that can be a security risk when used over a remote connection to a computer running Linux.

user identification number (UID) — A number assigned to a Linux user account as a way to distinguish it from all others on the same computer.

REVIEW QUESTIONS

1. Which of the following is a file permission in Linux? (Choose all that apply.)

   a. write

   b. block

   c. execute

   d. protect

2. What happens if the superblock is corrupted in Linux?

   a. Linux switches to the NTFS file system automatically.

   b. The Linux file system can't be accessed.

   c. Account access security is compromised because the use of passwords is eliminated.

   d. The disk containing the file system is unmounted automatically.

3. Which of the following commands can you use to kill a process? (Choose all that apply.)

   a. who

   b. scan

   c. top

   d. kill

4. Which of the following can be found in the /etc/shadow file?

   a. a copy of all recent changes made to data files

   b. a copy of the system kernel, which can be restored from this file

   c. password restriction information

   d. network connection timeout parameters

5. In what file are Samba security restrictions specified?

   a. smb.conf

   b. sec.conf

   c. smbd.ini

   d. sam.ini

6. You are attempting to change permissions on a file, but the system will not allow you to change them. Which of the following might be the problem?

   a. Only the root account can change permissions on any file.

   b. Your account does not have ownership of the file.

   c. The file is in the /pub directory, which means the permissions are permanently set.

   d. The file is disabled, so it can't be accessed.

7. Which of the following commands do you use to view the services started on a Linux system automatically?

   a. bootser

   b. services -l

   c. started -c

   d. chkconfig --list

8. All processes have a _____ .

   a. start code

   b. PID

   c. start/stop flag

   d. permission flag

9. AIDE and Tripwire are examples of _____ .
   a. integrity checkers
   b. network services for users
   c. spyware used to obtain user account names and passwords
   d. inode intimidators

10. Which of the following files contains security information important to NFS? (Choose all that apply.)
   a. /etc/hosts.allow
   b. /usr/net.access
   c. /usr/net.block
   d. /etc/hosts.deny

11. What does the chmod 777 budget command do?
   a. It copies the budget file to the directory currently in use.
   b. It scans the budget file to test the checksum, starting bit, and ending bit.
   c. It assigns the budget file to the user with GUID 777.
   d. It enables all users to run the budget file as well as read its contents and write to the file.

12. The passwd command is used to _____ . (Choose all that apply.)
   a. enable the security administrator to check for passwords that are not "strong"
   b. enable a user to change her or his password
   c. enable the system administrator to set account restrictions
   d. encrypt all passwords

13. After you install the auditd program, you must set up which of the following?
   a. signatures
   b. watches on specific files
   c. penalties
   d. yum monitors

14. Which command can you use to run a command sequence that requires root privileges?
   a. rootrun
   b. superu
   c. rqn
   d. sudo

15. You have been working to set permissions on files in several directories, and now you want to return to your home directory quickly. Which of the following commands should you use?

   a. !home

   b. ls -h

   c. cd ~

   d. cd ...

16. You're having trouble accessing your CD/DVD drive because of malware on your system, and you need to troubleshoot it. In which directory should you look to examine files that control use of the drive? (Choose all that apply.)

   a. /dev

   b. /mnt or /media

   c. /usr or /user

   d. /drivers

17. While logged in with the root account, you have been creating security files for new integrity-checking software you've just installed. The problem is that the files go into three different directories. Which of the following commands can you use to make sure you're in the right directory before you create a security file?

   a. whereami

   b. pwd

   c. who --dir

   d. ?dir

18. Which file can you modify to ensure that system accounting starts when the Linux system is booted?

   a. /var/account

   b. /root/systable

   c. /dev/sysscript

   d. /etc/inittab

19. When you install NIS, you need to configure which of the following? (Choose all that apply.)

   a. the NIS server

   b. the NIS security file /etc/nis/passwd.nis

   c. the NIS gatemaster

   d. the NIS client

20. You're considering removing a software package but want to be sure you know what it does before you remove it. Which of the following commands do you use to determine what the package does?

   a. rpm –qi

   b. su –i

   c. packlst

   d. ps –l

HANDS-ON PROJECTS

HANDS-ON PROJECTS

7

Hands-On Project 7-1: Creating an Account

Time Required: 15 minutes

Objective: Create a secure account in Linux.

Description: Creating accounts in Linux is the front line for authorizing access. You can create accounts by using a GUI tool, but you have more control and versatility when you use the command line. In this project, you create an account and then view the passwd file to verify that it's created as you intended.

1. Log in to root. (Or check with your instructor about using the sudo command from your account. If you use the sudo command, add it in front of the commands in the following steps. Also, you need a password to use sudo.) Access the command line or open a terminal window.

2. When you set up the account, use your own name or initials plus the word "test." For example, type **useradd –c "Mac Arthur, practice account" –p practice –n MArthurtest** and press **Enter**.

When you don't specify the UID, Linux uses the next available number higher than 500.

NOTE

3. What is the purpose of typing **–n** in Step 2?

   _____

   _____

4. Type **more /etc/passwd** and press **Enter** to view the contents of the passwd file. Do you see the account you created? (You might need to press the spacebar one or more times to go to the end of the file—and you can press **q** to exit the file contents listing.)

5. Test your new account by logging in to it.

6. If your instructor wants you to delete the account after you finish, type **userdel –r** plus the name of the account and press **Enter**.

7. Leave the terminal window or command line open for the next project (or log out, if you can't proceed to the next project during this lab session).

Hands-On Project 7-2: Creating a Security Group

Time Required: 15 minutes

Objective: Create a new group in Linux.

Description: Creating groups can save you headaches when managing resource access security in Linux. In this project, you create a group, change the group's name, and then delete the group.

1. If you aren't already logged in, log in to root (or use sudo and add it in front of the commands you use). Make sure you're at the command line.

2. At the command prompt, type **groupadd –g GID** (provided by your instructor) *groupname* (your first and last initials plus test), such as **groupadd –g 800 jptest**, and press **Enter**. Note that if the GID is already in use, the system reports this information and doesn't create the group. If you omit the **–g** option, the system uses the next available GID.

In some Linux versions, you see a return code of zero that indicates you added the group successfully. If a return code other than zero is displayed, make sure you typed the command correctly, used a unique GID and group name, and have proper access to create groups. If you're still getting the wrong return code, ask your instructor for help.

3. Change the group name by adding your first and middle initial after test, using the command **groupmod –n** *newname oldname*, such as **groupmod –n jjtest jptest**, and press **Enter**. (Again, in some versions of Linux, you see a zero return code to indicate that you have changed the group name successfully.)

4. Type **more /etc/group** and press **Enter** to view the groups and verify that you changed the group name successfully. (You might need to press the spacebar several times to get to the end of the file and press **q** to exit the listing.)

5. Delete the group by entering **groupdel** *group name*, such as **groupdel jjtest**, and pressing **Enter**.

6. Type **more /etc/group** and press **Enter** to verify that the group you created is truly deleted.

7. If you have a terminal window open, type **exit** and press **Enter** to close it, or log out if you don't have time to perform Hands-On Project 7-3 right after this project.

Hands-On Project 7-3: Managing Processes

Time Required: 15 minutes

Objective: Manage and kill processes in Linux.

Description: Managing processes is critical for ensuring that a system is running efficiently and is hardened against attackers and malware. In this project, you use the top command to view and kill processes.

1. If you aren't already logged in, log in to root (or use sudo and add it in front of the commands you run) and be sure you're at the command line.

2. Display the CPU and process activity by typing **top** and pressing **Enter**.

3. Notice the far-left column of information labeled PID. This column lists the process ID of each process shown. The processes are listed by the amount of CPU time they use. Record the PID of the top command:

_____

4. Press **k** to initiate the kill command. The top utility asks you to enter the PID to kill. Enter the PID of the top command and press **Enter** to kill the process. (You might have to press **Enter** a second time to return to a command prompt.) Type **clear** and press **Enter** to clear the lines from the screen. (You might have to type **clear** more than once.) The top utility is no longer running.

5. What other commands can you use to view running processes and kill a process?

_____

CASE PROJECTS

Case Project 7-1: Applying Security Policies to a Linux Server

Green Globe is installing a new Linux server and is concerned about securing the server to follow its new security policies, such as the password security policies you created for the case project in Chapter 3. Explain how you would address the security policies in the following ways:

- What tools enable you to address the security policy for the password security of accounts, and how would you use these tools to carry out the policy?

- Green Globe plans to use NFS and Samba to enable both Linux and Windows client computers to share Linux files. How would you control access to the NFS and Samba server to match the security policies?

- What tools can you use to secure important system directories to follow the security policies?

- How would you train users to secure files in their home directories?

- What software would you train users in for accessing the Linux server, and why would you choose this software?

8

WINDOWS SERVER 2003 SECURITY FUNDAMENTALS

After reading this chapter and completing the exercises, you will be able to:

♦ Describe the Windows Server 2003 infrastructure

♦ Explain Windows Server 2003 authentication methods

♦ Describe auditing and logging in Windows Server 2003

This chapter introduces you to the fundamentals of Windows Server 2003 security. Like Windows 2000 Server, Windows Server 2003 uses Active Directory, Microsoft's directory service that catalogs network resources and gives administrators a centralized management interface for working with resources, managing access, and monitoring security, among other tasks. Another tool for network management is Group Policy, used to manage configuration settings for objects.

Next, you examine authentication methods used in a Windows Server 2003 environment, including Internet Authentication Service for remote authentication. Finally, you learn how auditing and logging are crucial activities for monitoring and tracking security-related events and see how Windows logs can be used to identify security problems.

EXAMINING THE WINDOWS SERVER 2003 INFRASTRUCTURE

Windows Server 2003 has many security enhancements over Windows 2000 Server; however, network administrators must remember that the default security settings are merely a starting point and aren't intended to be completely secure right out of the box. Even though Windows Server 2003 is far more secure than previous versions, it still must be fine-tuned. A correctly designed, implemented, and managed Windows Server 2003 network can be robust and secure, but the key words are *correctly designed, implemented, and managed*. Most security breaches are a result of poor planning, flawed configurations, and management errors. In addition, remember that there are no absolutes in security. What works for one organization might not work for another.

A Windows Server 2003 network is managed, secured, and monitored by using Microsoft's powerful directory service, Active Directory. **Active Directory** is a distributed hierarchical database service that stores objects, manages resources, and makes those resources available for use. This chapter and Chapter 9 give you a solid foundation for designing a secure Active Directory deployment on your Windows Server 2003 network.

Examining Active Directory

The X.500 specification from the International Organization for Standardization (ISO) sits at the OSI model's Application layer as a set of protocols. Its goal was to provide standards and interfaces for an interoperable, global, distributed directory service. Its many components function together as a single entity. One component is the Directory Information Base (DIB), which provides information about objects stored in the database. Objects in the DIB are set up in a tree structure, or Directory Information Tree (DIT).

By now, you're familiar with the upside-down tree structure—the hierarchy—used throughout the digital world. The root of the tree is at the top, serving as a common frame of reference for locating resources, and the branches of the tree project downward. X.500 follows this tree structure, too. Objects in the X.500 tree represent containers for information about people, places, or things, and the main container objects are country, location, and organizational unit (OU). Objects are also grouped into classes, such as groups of countries, companies, geographical locations, and so on.

Although X.500 was ahead of its time in many ways, it had some serious limitations. It was developed to facilitate open communication, but developers weren't as concerned with interoperability standards or global information sharing as with market competition. Another problem was the surging popularity of the Internet; as a result, TCP/IP became the dominant protocol suite. X.500 was the basis for new technologies, however, and serves as the grandfather of modern directory services.

Another X.500 specification, Directory Access Protocol (DAP), provided a way for services to access information stored in a database. DAP was too complex, however, and proved too cumbersome to use. A simplified version was developed to enable clients to access and manipulate database information. After several further revisions, the IETF adopted Light-weight Directory Access Protocol (LDAP) as a directory service standard, and it's the access interface for Active Directory clients. Notably, LDAP sits on top of the TCP/IP protocol stack, so TCP takes care of transport details, and any client supporting TCP/IP can access directory information with LDAP. Like X.500, LDAP uses the upside-down tree structure.

Active Directory and DNS

Active Directory uses the same type of Domain Name System (DNS) as on the Internet, so administrators can organize networks with the same hierarchy of top-level domains, organizational domains, and computers. Active Directory requires DNS to function correctly. There are three main components of DNS:

- *Namespace*—The DNS hierarchical domain structure
- *DNS zones*—One or more DNS domains grouped for administrative purposes
- *Name server*—A DNS server containing records for a DNS zone

A namespace is the logical area on a network that contains directory services and named objects and can perform name resolution. The Active Directory namespace is coordinated with the DNS namespace and can be on a single server or distributed among several servers. Active Directory uses two namespaces: disjointed and contiguous. In a contiguous namespace, every subdomain name contains the root domain's name, as *marketing.course.com* contains the root domain name *course.com*. In a disjointed namespace, subdomains don't contain the root domain's name.

The object-naming scheme uses distinguished names and relative distinguished names. A **distinguished name (DN)** represents the entire path to an object in the directory, from the object all the way up to the root domain. DN is synonymous with fully qualified domain name (FQDN). A **relative distinguished name (RDN)** is an attribute representing the object's name without its directory path. This name isn't always unique because another object with the same name can exist elsewhere in the directory structure (meaning it has a different distinguished name). An RDN is denoted in LDAP Interchange Format (LDIF) as the object's canonical name (CN, sometimes called "common name").

Name resolution is enabled by tables of information, called **resource records**, such as records linking computer names to IP addresses. Each table is associated with a partition on a DNS server called a **zone**. The zone that maps hostnames to IP addresses is called the forward lookup zone. It contains a host address (A) resource record that DNS can locate and is the zone most often used to locate resources. A reverse lookup zone maps IP addresses to hostnames.

Each DNS zone has a primary DNS server (authoritative server) that's the "top-level" administrative server for the zone. Zones can also have secondary DNS servers that serve as a backup for the primary DNS server. Secondary DNS servers can also be used for load-sharing DNS requests on a network but aren't used for administering DNS services.

8

Table 8-1 summarizes some types of DNS resource records that are important to name resolution in an Active Directory network.

Table 8-1   DNS resource records

Resource record	Description
Host address (A)	Links a hostname to an IPv4 IP address; in IPv6, it's an AAAA resource record
Canonical name (CNAME)	Links a common name or alias to its distinguished name (FQDN) so that a network's actual computer-naming scheme is difficult to determine
Mail exchanger (MX)	Provides the IP addresses of SMTP servers that can accept e-mail for users in a domain
Name server (NS)	Provides links to secondary DNS servers for an authoritative server and links to off-site primary servers that aren't authoritative for the domain
Pointer record (PTR)	Associates an IP address with a hostname
Service (SRV) locator	Associates a TCP/IP service with a server, domain, and protocol
Start of authority (SOA)	The first record in a zone; also indicates whether the server is authoritative for the current zone
Windows Internet Naming Service (WINS)	Forwards lookup requests for NetBIOS names to a WINS server when DNS can't locate the hostname
Windows Internet Naming Service Reverse (WINS-R)	Forwards a reverse lookup (IP address to NetBIOS name) request to a WINS server
Load sharing	Distributes DNS lookup requests among DNS servers

NOTE   Although this chapter's projects can be completed with only Windows Server 2003, having one or more client computers running Windows 2000 Professional or Windows XP Professional is helpful. It's best to begin these projects with a clean installation of Windows Server 2003 (Standard or Enterprise Edition) to prevent any problems with previous configurations. Make sure you've installed Service Pack 2 (SP2), and keep your Windows Server 2003 installation CD handy.

Activity 8-1: Installing and Configuring DNS

ACTIVITY

Time Required: 15 minutes

Objective: Install and configure the DNS service on your Windows Server 2003 SP2 computer.

Description: In Windows Server 2003, the DNS service isn't installed by default; you must add it. Although DNS can be installed and configured automatically when Active Directory is installed, if an existing DNS server is detected, Active Directory uses that information. After DNS is installed, it's configured and managed from the Administrative Tools menu or the DNS Microsoft Management Console (MMC). No zone or name resolution information exists on the DNS server until it's configured. In this project, you install and configure DNS. Consult with your instructor about what zone name to use in Step 9.

Many administrative tasks can be performed in the MMC, which can be customized. You customize the MMC in Activity 8-3 later in this chapter.

NOTE

1. Log on to your server as an administrator, and open Control Panel.

2. Click **Add or Remove Programs**. In the Add or Remove Programs window, click the **Add/Remove Windows Components** button to start the Windows Components Wizard.

3. Double-click **Networking Services**. In the Networking Services dialog box, click to select the **Domain Name System (DNS)** check box. (If any other check boxes are already selected, leave them selected.) Click **OK**, and then click **Next**.

If you see a message that the server has a dynamically assigned IP address, click OK. The Connection Properties dialog box opens, where you can reconfigure Internet Protocol (TCP/IP) to have a static address. The DNS server should have a static (fixed) address, so consult with your instructor about assigning one and which IP address to use. If you don't have an IP address to use at this time, click Cancel to close the dialog box. Keep in mind, however, that in most situations, a server should have a static IP address. You might see the warning box about a dynamically assigned IP address again. If so, click OK.

NOTE

4. Click **Finish**, and then close the Add or Remove Programs window. The DNS service is installed.

5. Click **Start**, point to **All Programs**, and point to **Administrative Tools**. Click **DNS** to configure the DNS server.

6. Click the server name, and then click **Action**, **Configure a DNS Server** from the menu.

7. In the Configure a DNS Server Wizard window, click the **DNS Checklists** button to open an MMC help file with checklists and information to guide you through planning and configuring your DNS server.

8. Click **Deploying DNS** in the left pane, and in the right pane, read the information for planning your DNS deployment.

9. You need to determine your namespace scheme, DNS zones, and interface configurations and consider interoperability issues, among other planning tasks. Consult your instructor, and enter your domain/zone name:

_____

8

10. Close the MMC window, and return to the Configure a DNS Server Wizard. Click **Next** to continue.

11. Make sure the **Create a forward lookup zone (recommended for small networks)** option button is selected, and then click **Next**.

12. In the Primary Server Location dialog box, make sure the **This server maintains the zone** option button is selected, and then click **Next**.

13. Enter your zone name, and then click **Next**. You're creating a new zone, so accept the default value in the Zone File window, and then click **Next**.

14. Make sure **Do not allow dynamic updates** is selected, and then click **Next**.

15. Click **No, it should not forward queries**, and then click **Next**. Click **Finish**.

16. Your DNS server is now installed, and you can examine or refine your configurations in the DNS management window (see Figure 8-1). Notice the differences in this window after configuring a DNS server.

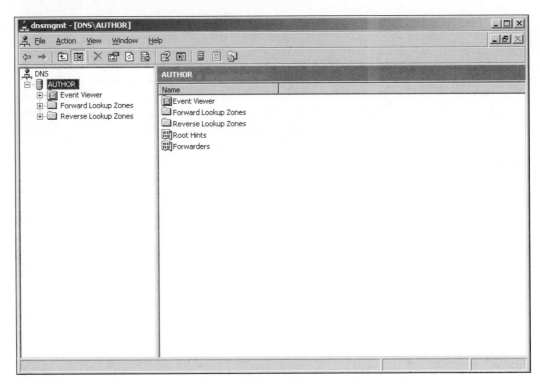

Figure 8-1   The DNS management window after configuring a DNS server

17. Close all open windows, and leave your system running for the next activity.

Active Directory's Database Structure

Active Directory is made up of containers and has a schema defining how data is stored, organized, retrieved, manipulated, and reviewed. Containers store attributes of the information in Active Directory, which is organized as collections of records. Active Directory is more than a database, however; it's also a database management system (DBMS) with a user interface and a mechanism for managing stored data.

Although Active Directory shares the upside-down tree structure of X.500, it uses LDAP as its access protocol and relies on DNS for locater services. The most basic components of the Active Directory database are objects, which represent users, computers, printers, files, and so on. Most are **container objects** that can hold other containers or objects, such as a user or computer object. **Leaf objects** (also called node objects) nest inside container objects and can't contain other objects. Containers can nest until a leaf object is added. You can think of Active Directory as one big container holding all containers for all objects in your network, nested in a hierarchical fashion. The container structure is important to the way you apply policies and security settings.

Every object has its own set of attributes, such as a printer's name, a user's department, or a file's access permissions, and a globally unique identifier (GUID), a unique number associated with the object name. Object classes organize objects into groups according to their nature or purpose, such as user account, computer, and network classes.

The **schema** (also called the Directory Information Tree) defines every type of object stored in Active Directory and the type of information that can be stored in Active Directory, including object classes and attributes. Some attributes in the schema are mandatory, and others are optional. For example, password and domain are required attributes for a user account, but telephone number and account description are optional attributes. Some common object classes are computer, group, printQueue, securityPrincipal, server, user, and volume.

Security Accounts Manager (SAM) is a local database file that stores user and group information on standalone servers, provides security interfaces, and ties in LDAP for access in Active Directory. When a Windows Server 2003 computer is configured as a domain controller, information in the SAM database is transferred to the Active Directory database. An administrator account and password are still stored in SAM, however, and this account is used to boot the server into Recovery Console and Directory Services Restore modes.

Active Directory's Physical Structure

The physical structure of Active Directory is made up of the components representing what you can use to optimize network traffic. **Sites** are groups of computers in reliable, well-connected IP subnets. "Well-connected" means a sustained bandwidth of at least 10 Mbps. Sites are designated to enable efficient Active Directory operations on a network and have the following characteristics:

- Consist of one or more IP subnets
- Used for efficient Active Directory replication (copying updated information) between domain controllers

- Enable a client to access the closest domain controller for faster logon
- Composed of two types of objects: servers and configuration objects
- Typically reflect the same boundaries as the network the sites represent

Site links are objects representing connectivity between sites and are composed of four parameters:

- *Replication schedule*—Indicates when the link is available for replication traffic
- *Replication interval*—Polls a domain controller on the opposite end of a site link for changes
- *Transport*—Connection used for replication traffic
- *Cost*—A measure of a link's reliability, used to determine which path is used for replication traffic

Sites and site links can be used to schedule replication at off-peak times. All domain controllers in the same physical site are assumed to share the same network connection, and connections between sites that aren't 100% reliable must have replication managed with replication schedules and frequency intervals. For example, if your domain has domain controllers in different time zones, you don't want them to replicate major changes in Active Directory during peak load times.

Domain controllers (DCs) are Windows Server 2003 computers that contain a copy of the Active Directory database and schema for the domain. A DC can be located near users to speed up logon and authentication processes. This placement is better in terms of bandwidth use and speed than having users log on to a DC across the country, where traffic could be routed through dozens of hops in each direction. Even with high-speed, high-capacity connections, designing physical and logical resource access to minimize network congestion is still a good idea.

Windows Server 2003 member servers are members of the domain and generally provide services for the domain, such as file and print sharing and remote access. Member servers don't participate in Active Directory replication, perform authentication, or store domain security policy information.

Standalone servers are Windows Server 2003 servers that are independent of the domain. They are usually connected to a workgroup and can share resources with other computers on their networks but can't take advantage of Active Directory's capabilities.

NOTE

Role servers are member servers that perform specific services, such as DNS, DHCP, or WINS, and are installed when the server OS is installed. A server in a domain environment can function as a member server or a DC. Sometimes you need to promote a member server to a DC or demote a DC to a member server, which changes that server's role in the domain.

The **global catalog** is a Windows Server 2003 database that stores information about every object in a forest (described in the next section), essentially serving as an index. The first DC installed in a forest becomes the global catalog server by default and stores a full replica of every object in its own domain and partial replicas of objects in the forest's other domains. Partial replicas contain the information most often used to search for an object. These are the main purposes of a global catalog server:

- Authenticate users

- Provide lookup for and access to all resources in the domain

- Perform replication of key Active Directory elements

- Maintain a copy of objects' most used attributes for quick access

TIP

You can configure other DCs to be global catalog servers, which is a good way to provide redundancy, manage traffic, and improve performance.

Active Directory's Logical Structure

The main component of Active Directory's logical structure is a **domain**. Microsoft views a domain as a partition in an Active Directory forest, and it's usually thought of as the network's administrative and security boundary. Therefore, domain policies and settings affect only objects in that domain, not objects in other domains. (Domain-level policies are discussed in "Group Policy" later in this chapter.)

A domain also serves as a replication boundary. Inside this boundary, all DCs replicate information automatically to all other DCs in their domain. In other words, all domain controllers are equal, and each has a complete copy of directory information about the domain.

Any changes to an object on one DC are replicated to all other DCs automatically. Administrators can modify intrasite (DCs in one site) replication to happen at specified intervals instead of when the change takes place. Intersite (DCs in different sites) replication can also be configured to take place at specific times, which helps minimize replication traffic at undesirable times, such as when users are logging on.

The root domain is the first domain object you configure after installing Active Directory and is the first container object created. It represents your local network in its entirety and contains objects representing all network resources, including subdomains. For example, if your root domain is *course.com*, you can create additional domains beneath it, such as *marketing.course.com*.

If the root domain is also your Internet domain, you should register it with an Internet domain administration authority. If you have a registered domain already, your root domain is the object you create in Active Directory to represent it.

An **organizational unit (OU)** is another logical Active Directory component used to organize objects in the domain. Because OUs can be used to group classes of objects, they are key components for security and administrative purposes. For example, you can create an OU to group all users in the Finance Department so that you can apply security settings to them.

Trees and forests are also logical components of Active Directory used to further organize objects. **Trees** include everything from the bottom of the object path to the root domain and encompass domains with a common relationship, such as sharing a contiguous namespace and global catalog. Member domains in a tree use the same schema and global catalog. **Forests** are collections of trees, as you have probably guessed. They are useful when you want to combine trees that don't have a contiguous namespace but share a global catalog and schema. Forests are the highest level container in Active Directory's design. Figure 8-2 shows the hierarchical structure of Active Directory. The most important difference between Active Directory's logical structure and physical structure is that the logical structure is used to organize resources, and the physical structure is used to control network traffic.

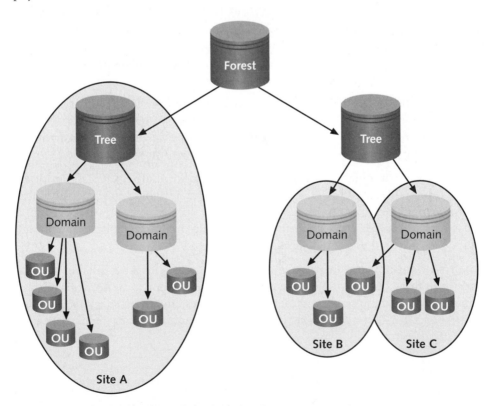

Figure 8-2   Active Directory's logical structure

Trust Relationships

A trust is simply an arrangement between two or more parties that enables secure resource sharing between domains. The default trust relationships in Active Directory are Kerberos **transitive trusts**, meaning they flow to all other domains in the tree. Security between clients and servers is based on Kerberos and uses a combined protocol and encryption approach. If a new domain joins the tree, it has a two-way (trusting and trusted) relationship with all other domains in the tree automatically, so every domain has access to every resource in the tree. A two-way trust flows in both directions, meaning each party is both trusting and trusted. Two-way trusts exist between child and parent domains, for example.

Nontransitive trusts are bound by the two domains in a trust relationship. They don't flow to other domains in the forest and are one-way by default. **One-way trusts** can be created in both directions of the trust relationship or can flow in one direction. They are useful when you want to allow access to resources on one domain without allowing access to the trusted domain.

Active Directory creates tree-root, parent, and child trusts automatically, and you can create shortcut, external, realm, and forest trusts manually. Table 8-2 summarizes the trust types in Active Directory.

Table 8-2   Trust types

Type	Direction	Nature of the trust
Tree-root	Two-way	Transitive
Parent	Two-way	Transitive
Child	Two-way	Transitive
Shortcut	One-way or two-way	Transitive
External	One-way or two-way	Nontransitive
Realm	One-way or two-way	Transitive and nontransitive
Forest	One-way or two-way	Transitive

Planning an Active Directory Deployment

As with any deployment, lack of planning can result in wasted resources, poor performance, or a failure to meet business needs. Most important from a security perspective, poor planning results in vulnerabilities. The main consideration when planning any major deployment is to keep it as simple as possible. Adding complexity to your design makes it harder to manage and more prone to errors. Another important consideration is to plan for future changes and growth. Keeping your design flexible enough to accommodate changes in the business environment makes administration easier. These are the major areas you must plan before deploying Active Directory:

- Domains
- Site topology

- Forests

- Trusts

- Organizational units

For your domain plan, first decide how many domains you need. Domains provide administrative boundaries, enabling you to apply settings according to the resources that clients in the domain require. You could set up an Accounting Department domain, for instance, so that employees in this department have full access to financial databases, but other departments have limited access to them.

After determining your domain plan, you can turn your attention to the site topology plan, which delineates the physical layout of your Active Directory environment and network connections and includes information such as the placement of network services and domain controllers. In addition, by examining network traffic, you can manage bandwidth better and determine the most efficient placement of domain controllers.

The first rule is to position domain controllers as close to users as possible to ensure availability of Active Directory. It makes no sense to have users logging on to a DC in another site, which creates unnecessary traffic and slows performance. The second rule is to have at least two DCs capable of hosting Active Directory, even in a small office. If you have only one DC and it crashes, your domain is unavailable until you can replace the hardware, reinstall and configure the server, and restore your domain from backups. Even so, all work since your last backup is lost. A large enterprise network should have several DCs to help with load balancing and provide redundancy.

 RAID is another way to maintain Active Directory availability in a small office.

TIP

Another main factor in site topology is replication within (intrasite) and between (intersite) sites. Because sites represent physically distinct locations, replication occurs across site links, which are usually slow and might be leased lines. Understanding how intrasite and intersite replication happen is important to knowing how to manage bandwidth; you don't want heavy replication traffic during peak load times. Replication also passes through routers and can increase the load on your Internet gateway, which reduces performance and could result in a bottleneck. As a domain hierarchy grows, the resources consumed grow with it. Table 8-3 summarizes how intersite and intrasite replication work.

Table 8-3 Intersite versus intrasite replication

Intersite replication	Intrasite replication
Uses Remote Procedure Calls (RPC)	Uses SMTP or TCP/IP transport protocol
No compression	Compression

Table 8-3 Intersite versus intrasite replication (continued)

Intersite replication	Intrasite replication
Replication partners notify each other when a change has occurred	No notification between replication partners
Bridgehead servers maintain replication connections between sites	DCs in the same site are connected

Next, you need to develop a forest plan. This structure dictates the methods you use to administer the network and how users interact with the directory. From a top-down view, applying forestwide policies and keeping more specific policies to a minimum is easier, faster, and less error prone. For most situations, a single forest is enough. The trusts are created for you, all users can see the entire directory, and settings need to be applied only once. If you need to manage different departments in an organization, creating multiple forests might be justified, but you must create trust relationships between them so that users can access resources in forests other than their own. With your forest plan, you should also include change control management procedures that specify who can make changes, what types of changes can be made, and what circumstances prompt changes.

A trust plan helps you determine trust relationships between forests, trees, and domains. A forest trust plan outlines the trust relationship between forest roots. A trust established between two forest roots causes Active Directory to create transitive trusts automatically between all domains in the forests. Creating a forest trust requires all DCs to run Windows Server 2003 because previous versions don't support forest trusts at the Windows Server 2003 functional level.

The OU plan specifies how containers in a domain are laid out and how objects nest in the hierarchy and are grouped. You can design OUs to reflect the physical structure of business groups, such as Marketing, Finance, and Sales OUs for users in those departments, or you can create OUs with management in mind, such as creating an OU for backup administrators.

ACTIVITY

Activity 8-2: Installing Active Directory

Time Required: 15 minutes

Objective: Install the Active Directory service on your Windows Server 2003 SP2 computer.

Description: As a network grows, managing network resources can become overwhelming. Active Directory simplifies network management by providing a centralized interface for configuring, managing, and monitoring resources. In this activity, you install Active Directory, and then lay the foundation for your new root domain. Make sure the Windows Server 2003 computer is connected to the network before you start.

1. If necessary, log on to your server as an administrator.

2. Click **Start**, **Run**, type **dcpromo**, and then click **OK** to start the Active Directory Installation Wizard.

3. Click **Next** twice. Make sure **Domain controller for a new domain** is selected, and then click **Next**.

4. Make sure **Domain in a new forest** is selected, and then click **Next**.

5. In the New Domain Name window, enter the DNS domain name you used in Activity 8-1, and then click **Next**.

6. Make sure your assigned domain name is displayed in the NetBIOS Domain Name window, and then click **Next**.

7. Click **Next** twice, accepting the default values.

8. In the DNS Diagnostics window, wait for the diagnostics to finish, and then click **Next**.

9. Click **Next** in the Permissions window. In the Directory Services Restore Mode Administrator Password window, enter a password and confirm it, and then click **Next**.

10. Click **Next** in the Summary window, after ensuring that the installation parameters are configured correctly. If necessary, insert your Windows Server 2003 installation CD when prompted, and then click **OK**.

11. Click **Finish**, and then click **Restart Now**.

12. After your system restarts, log on as an administrator. Active Directory is ready to be configured in the Manage Your Server window, shown in Figure 8-3. Notice that in the example in Figure 8-3, the server has been assigned the roles of Application Server, Domain Controller (Active Directory), and DNS Server. The Application Server and DNS Server roles were assigned before installing Active Directory. Also, if the Manage Your Server window isn't displayed automatically when you restart, you can open it by clicking **Start**, pointing to **All Programs**, pointing to **Administrative Tools**, and clicking **Manage Your Server**.

13. Close the Manage Your Server window, and leave your system running for the next activity.

TIP

After Active Directory is installed, new tools are available to manage and configure Active Directory elements, such as Active Directory Domains and Trusts, Active Directory Sites and Services, Active Directory Users and Computers, Domain Controller Security Policy, and Domain Security Policy. To access these tools, click Start, point to All Programs, point to Administrative Tools, and click the tool you want.

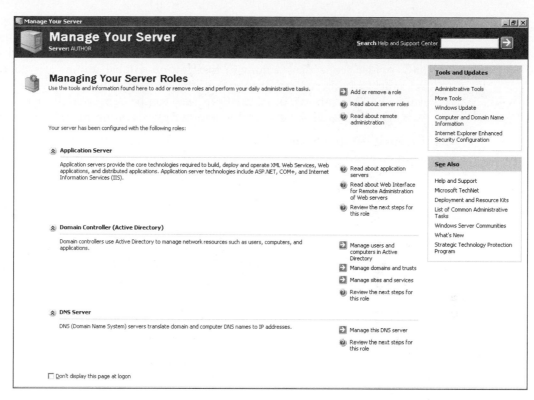

Figure 8-3   The Manage Your Server window

Managing Groups

You can create security groups and distribution groups for management purposes. These groups are used to eliminate the repetitive steps of applying and changing settings for groups of users with similar characteristics, such as users who access the same files and folders. Security groups are used to manage resource access in domains or across an entire forest. Distribution groups, such as e-mail or telephone lists, are used to send information to groups of people easily. Using groups can save a lot of time and help ensure consistency because you can manage all group members as one entity. Note that user accounts can be members of several groups.

Four types of security or distribution groups can be created in Active Directory, and each has a different scope of influence, meaning it applies to different levels of the domain hierarchy:

- *Local*—A **local group** is used on standalone servers that aren't part of a domain and don't use Active Directory; the scope is limited to the local server.

- *Domain local*—A **domain local group** is used to manage resources in a single domain and provide resource access in a domain to global and universal groups. This group type can contain user accounts, global groups, and universal groups.

- *Global*—A **global group** is used to manage group accounts in the same domain so that those members can access resources in their own domain and other domains. Because members can access resources in other domains, this group type has a wider scope than a domain local group. Global groups can contain user accounts and other global groups from the domain in which they're created and can be nested, as shown in Figure 8-4. They can be converted to universal groups as long as they aren't nested within another global group or universal group.

- *Universal*—A **universal group** is used to enable members to access all resources in a forest. These groups are forestwide in scope and can contain user accounts, global groups, and other universal groups from any domain in the forest.

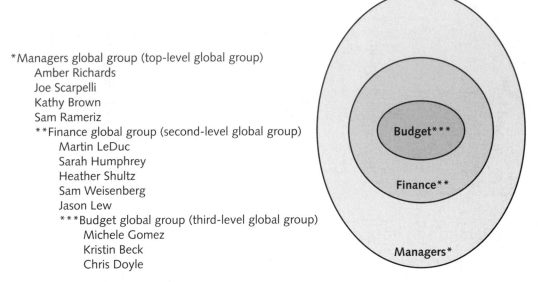

```
*Managers global group (top-level global group)
    Amber Richards
    Joe Scarpelli
    Kathy Brown
    Sam Rameriz
    **Finance global group (second-level global group)
        Martin LeDuc
        Sarah Humphrey
        Heather Shultz
        Sam Weisenberg
        Jason Lew
        ***Budget global group (third-level global group)
            Michele Gomez
            Kristin Beck
            Chris Doyle
```

Figure 8-4   Nested global groups

NOTE   Local groups are created in the Local Users and Groups MMC. Other groups in an Active Directory environment are created and managed in the Active Directory Users and Computers MMC snap-in.

You can convert domain local groups to universal groups as long as they don't contain other domain local groups and the domain is running in Windows Server 2003 mode (meaning you have only Windows Server 2003 servers). Windows 2000 mixed mode means the domain has Windows NT, Windows 2000 Server, and Windows Server 2003 servers. Windows 2000 native mode means no servers are running an OS before Windows 2000 Server, so you can have Windows 2000 Server and Windows Server 2003 servers. These modes are also referred to as domain functional levels in Active Directory. To take full advantage of Windows Server 2003 capabilities, your domain must be running at the Windows Server 2003 functional level.

TIP To check or change the level, open Administrative Tools, and click Active Directory Domains and Trusts. Right-click the domain you want to work with, and click Raise Domain Functional Level. The dialog box shows the current level, and you can raise or lower it. After you raise the level, it can't be lowered, so be sure you don't need to support older servers that require the lower domain functional level.

Here are some guidelines for using groups:

- Use global groups to store user accounts as members.
- Give global groups access to resources by adding them as members of domain local groups in the domain where the resources are located or adding them as members of universal groups.
- Keep nesting of global groups to a minimum to avoid confusion and complexity.
- Use domain local groups to allow access to resources in a particular domain.
- Add domain local groups to access control lists (ACLs) for specific resources in a domain, such as shared printers or files.
- Avoid placing user accounts in domain local groups as much as possible. Add the accounts to global groups, and add those groups to domain local or universal groups for access, depending on the scope of access needed.
- Use universal groups for extensive access. For example, add a universal group to the ACL for resources in any domain, forest, or tree.

CAUTION Starting with limited access to resources and increasing access as needed is better than granting unlimited access to everything. You can expand rights more easily (and with less complaining from users) than removing rights.

Group Policy

Group Policy is an administrative tool that uses Active Directory to manage users and computers by applying group policy settings to them. These settings are stored in **Group Policy Objects (GPOs)** that can be linked to an Active Directory domain, site, or OU. An OU is the smallest Active Directory container you can link a GPO to.

When the first domain is created, a default domain policy is created that applies to that domain and any child domains created under it. This policy can be modified for child domains, however. Default containers created when Active Directory is installed, such as the Builtin, Users, and Computers containers, are actually folders. They are non-OU folder containers and, therefore, can't have GPOs linked to them.

NOTE

Two default GPOs are created when Active Directory is installed. The Default Domain Policy applies to the domain container. The Default Domain Controllers Policy applies to the domain controller's OU.

There are also local and nonlocal GPOs. A local GPO applies to the local computer. This GPO doesn't support many of the functions of Active Directory GPOs, and in an Active Directory hierarchy, it's overwritten by nonlocal GPOs, which apply to sites, domains, and OUs. If you have multiple GPOs, they are applied in the following order of increasing precedence:

- Local

- Site

- Default domain

- OU

When a computer starts, computer GPOs are applied incrementally, starting with the local policy and proceeding through the OU policies. An easy way to remember this order is with the acronym LSDOU. When a user logs on to the computer, the process starts again for user GPOs.

Group policies can apply to user or computer accounts or both, but computer policies override user policies. To be applied to a user or computer, a GPO must be linked to the object's container and have read and apply group policy permissions set. For example, to prevent a GPO from being applied to an administrator, you can remove the administrator's read access to the GPO. Authenticated users have read and apply group policy permissions by default. A GPO can be linked to any number of containers, and deleting the link to one container doesn't affect other containers. Linking several policies to one container is also possible. In this situation, the GPO at the top of the hierarchy is applied last and, therefore, takes precedence.

Administrators can use two other settings to fine-tune how policies are applied: Block Policy Inheritance and No Override. Block Policy Inheritance is used when you don't want a container to inherit certain settings. For example, you might not want a restrictive software policy preventing users from installing applications and patches applied to IT support staff. To do this, you set Block Policy Inheritance on the OU containing IT support staff. No Override prevents blocking policies for a container. You might use it, for example, when you don't want a user to prevent a policy from being applied to a container. No Override always takes precedence over Block Policy Inheritance.

TIP

No Override is changed to Enforce on computers where the Group Policy MMC is installed.

There are many uses for group policies, but they are mainly used to control the user environment and, of course, for security. Table 8-4 describes the key extensions in the Group Policy tool.

Table 8-4 Key extensions in the Group Policy tool

Extension	Purpose
Administrative Templates	Configure Registry settings that control desktop appearance
Security Settings	Set local computer, domain, and network security options for computers and users
Software Installation	Manage software installation centrally by assigning or publishing software to users or assigning software to computers
Scripts	Automate computer startup and shutdown and user logon and logoff with standard DOS batch files or VBScript, Perl, and JavaScript files
Remote Installation Services	Control remote OS installation on client computers
Internet Explorer Maintenance	Maintain Internet Explorer and control users' access to Internet Explorer options
Folder Redirection	Redirect special Windows folders, such as My Documents, Application Data, Start Menu, and Desktop Settings, from their default locations to a network location

You might be confused about how different groups fit into Active Directory's physical and logical framework. Security groups are a type of container object created and managed in Active Directory. GPOs are a type of container that holds policy settings. You create containers, create security groups inside them, add computer and user objects as group members, and then apply GPOs to the containers. The goal is to manage the largest possible *container* groupings to reduce administrative overhead and possible errors and maximize efficient resource use.

 Remember that all child objects inherit their parent objects' policies by default. Keep this inheritance in mind when planning your Active Directory logical structure and designing group memberships.

Using Group Policy Objects

For administrators to assign a group policy to an Active Directory object, they must have read and write permissions for the Sysvol (system volume) folder and modify permission for the object. (The Sysvol folder is created automatically when you install a DC or promote a server to a DC.)

GPOs are the foundation of security in Windows networks. They're used to supply logon and logoff scripts, maintain Internet Explorer, and manage software, among other tasks. To create, edit, and manage GPOs, you must install the Group Policy Object Editor MMC snap-in, which you do in Activity 8-3.

Activity 8-3: Adding the Group Policy Object Editor Snap-in

Time Required: 15 minutes

Objective: Add an MMC snap-in to create and manage GPOs.

Description: This activity walks you through adding an MMC snap-in to your Windows Server 2003 domain controller for creating and managing group policies. To complete this activity, you need administrative access to a Windows Server 2003 domain controller and must have completed Activities 8-1 and 8-2.

1. If necessary, log on to your domain controller as an administrator.

2. Click **Start**, **Run**, type **mmc**, and then click **OK**.

3. Click **File**, **Add/Remove Snap-in** from the MMC menu to open the Add/ Remove Snap-in dialog box. Click **Add** to open the Add Standalone Snap-in dialog box.

4. In the Available standalone snap-ins list box, click **Active Directory Users and Computers**, and then click **Add**. Scroll down and click **Group Policy Object Editor**, and then click **Add**.

5. In the Select Group Policy Object dialog box, verify that **Local Computer** is selected under Group Policy Object. Click **Finish** to add the local computer GPO, and then click **Close** in the Add Standalone Snap-in dialog box.

6. In the Add/Remove Snap-in dialog box, click the **Extensions** tab. In the Snap-ins that can be extended list box, click **Active Directory Users and Computers**, if necessary. Verify that the **Add all extensions** check box is selected. Repeat this procedure for the Group Policy Object Editor snap-in, and then click **OK**.

7. To save the changes, click **File**, **Save As** from the MMC menu. Type **GroupPolicy** in the File name text box, and then click **Save**. Maximize the Console Root window inside the GroupPolicy window, if you haven't already. Your console should look similar to Figure 8-5. (In the left pane, you can double-click Active Directory Users and Computers (*computer name*) and Local Computer Policy to view the elements listed under them, as shown in Figure 8-5.)

8. Leave your GroupPolicy console open and your system running for the next activity.

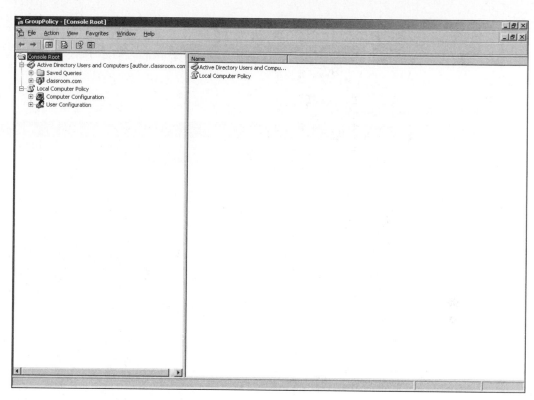

Figure 8-5   The GroupPolicy MMC

Creating a GPO

You can create two main types of GPOs that apply to security in particular: software policies and security policies. Software policies manage applications, the Windows Server 2003 environment, and related user settings. For example, you can create a policy that prevents users from changing their desktop backgrounds. To configure a software policy for an object, right-click it in the Active Directory Users and Computers snap-in and click Properties. Click the Group Policy tab, and enter the settings you want.

Security policies govern logons and logoffs, communication, file services, and more. You can use them on every port or service that poses a risk to the network. To modify a domain's properties, right-click the domain, such as classroom.com in Figure 8-5, and click Properties. Select the Group Policy tab, select a GPO, and click Edit to open the Group Policy Object Editor for that GPO. Table 8-5 summarizes the categories of security policies you can configure in the Group Policy Object Editor.

8

Group policies can be set for a site, a domain, or an OU, but not for a non-OU folder container. The default non-OU folder containers in Windows Server 2003 include Builtin, Computers, ForeignSecurityPrincipals, and Users.

Table 8-5   Security policies

Group policy category	Purpose
Account Policies	Passwords, account lockout, authentication, and Kerberos
Local Policies	Auditing, user rights definitions, security options
Event Log	Settings for recording event logs, such as log file size and how long to retain a log
Restricted Groups	Manage group membership for security-sensitive groups, such as the built-in Administrator or Guest group
System Services	Security and default startup parameters (Automatic, Disabled, or Manual) for services running on the computer
Registry	Security for Registry keys
File System	File system security
Wireless Network Policies	Wireless network security, such as controlling unauthorized access, protecting data transmissions, and establishing certificate or password authentication
Public Key Policies	Encrypted data recovery agents, trusted certification authorities, and other settings related to PKI
Software Restriction Policies	Restrictions on running software, such as setting disallowed or unrestricted software access, restrictions by file types, and others
IP Security Policies	IPSec parameters

A key concept in using group policies is change management, which is enforced on users. The goal of GPOs is to ensure that users can't change their settings in a harmful way. For example, applying a redirect on users' My Documents folders from their local hard drives to a network drive on a server prevents them from storing files on their own workstations. This setting is important for a number of reasons. First, files stored on a local hard drive are rarely (if ever) backed up; files on the server are backed up regularly. Second, files stored on a network server can be checked for malware with up-to-date software. Even using antivirus software on every workstation doesn't guarantee that virus definition files are current, and managing one server is easier than managing thousands of workstations. Third, keeping files on a centrally located, managed server ensures that users always have access to the same files, no matter where they log on. All these goals can be achieved by using GPOs to enforce settings without user intervention.

NOTE Windows Server 2003 GPOs have no effect on clients older than Windows 2000. If you do need to support downlevel clients, you must use older security technologies, such as Windows NT 4.0 System Policy Editor. The best option is to upgrade clients and servers as soon as possible to at least Windows 2000.

ACTIVITY

Activity 8-4: Creating and Applying a GPO

Time Required: 15 minutes

Objective: Create a GPO on a Windows Server 2003 domain controller.

Description: To manage a Windows Server 2003 Active Directory network, you must be able to create custom GPOs to apply security and other settings to users, computers, groups, and network resources. In this activity, you create a simple GPO. You need administrative access to a Windows Server 2003 domain controller and must have completed Activities 8-1, 8-2, and 8-3.

1. If necessary, log on to your domain controller as an administrator, and open the GroupPolicy.msc console you created in Activity 8-3. (Click **Start**, point to **All Programs**, point to **Administrative Tools**, and click **GroupPolicy.msc**.) Maximize the Console Root window.

2. If necessary, double-click **Active Directory Users and Computers** (*computer name*) in the left pane. Right-click the domain you want to modify and click **Properties**. Click the **Group Policy** tab. Your dialog box should look similar to Figure 8-6.

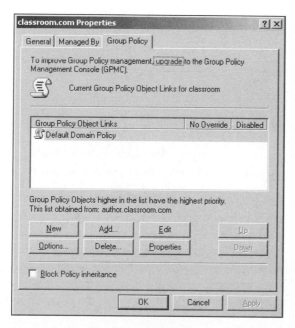

Figure 8-6   The Properties dialog box for the domain

3. Click the **New** button, type the policy name **GPO1**, and press **Enter**. If necessary, click **GPO1** to select it, and then click the **Edit** button to open the Group Policy Object Editor.

4. In the left pane under Computer Configuration, double-click to expand **Windows Settings** and then **Security Settings**. Under Security Settings, double-click to expand **Account Policies**, and then click **Password Policy** (see Figure 8-7).

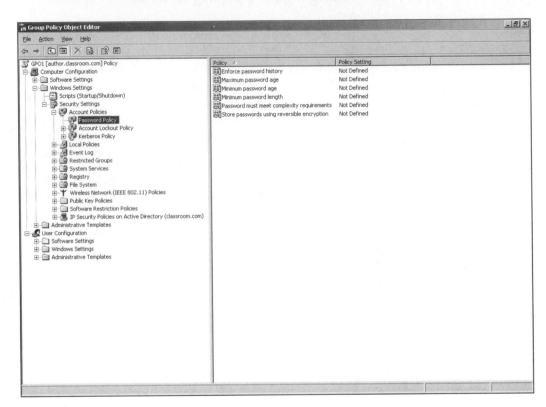

Figure 8-7   Selecting a GPO to edit

5. Double-click each password policy in the right pane, and click the **Define this policy setting** check box to configure a password policy according to standard best practices.

6. Close all open dialog boxes, and leave your system running for the next activity. When prompted to save your GroupPolicy.msc console settings, click **Yes**.

Another tool for managing group policies in Windows Server 2003 is the Group Policy Management Console (GPMC). To learn more about this tool and download it, visit Microsoft's Web site.

UNDERSTANDING WINDOWS SERVER 2003 AUTHENTICATION

The authentication process is a key component of network and server security because it ensures that users trying to access the network or domain are who they claim to be. In general, authentication depends on exchanging information that tells one entity that another entity is recognized as an authorized user. That information can be a password; a long encrypted block of code called a key; a checksum (a formula for verifying digital information); a physical object, such as a smart card; or biometric data from fingerprints, retina scans, or voiceprints.

In general, there are three types of authentication—user, client, and session authentication. They are set up in various combinations, methods, and protocols, explained in the following sections. In Windows Server 2003 Active Directory environments, Kerberos-based authentication is the default. Kerberos uses a combined authentication approach, authenticating a user via the client computer configured to use Kerberos with a ticket that's valid for a given session. Internet Authentication Service, RADIUS and TACACS+, Extensible Authentication Protocol, and NT LAN Manager version 2 (NTLMv2) are also used.

User Authentication

User authentication identifies a person who's authorized to access network resources. A user who submits the correct credentials can log on to the network from any location or any computer, which offers a measure of flexibility. You don't need to require users to log on every time they access the network; instead, you can configure the authentication to be automatic and based on the exchange of keys.

In addition, you can specify time-based restrictions that control when a user is allowed to access the network, such as only on weekdays during daytime hours. Setting time-based restrictions adds another level of security for your network if you don't have IT staff available around the clock to handle intrusion attempts. By blocking authorized access during overnight hours, you make it more difficult for attackers to launch exploits in the middle of the night.

If you prevent users from accessing the network on evenings or weekends, you might run into complaints from employees who need to work after hours. Make sure employees don't need to work during off-hours before you set time-based restrictions.

Client Authentication

Client authentication grants access to network resources based on a source IP address, computer MAC address, or computer name rather than user information. As with user authentication, the identification process can be automatic or manual. Manual authentication, which requires users to enter a username and password to access resources, takes more effort but increases security because you restrict access based on the source computer and username/password in one process. Even if an intruder steals a user's username and password, using client authentication means the computer could be accessed only with the required IP address—or by spoofing the IP address, which the intruder would also have to obtain.

Session Authentication

Session authentication authorizes a user or computer on a per-connection basis by using software installed on the client computer that exchanges information with the authentication server. The connection between the client computer and server is authorized instead of the person or a machine name or address. Session authentication gives users more flexibility than user or client authentication; it enables any user and any computer (configured with the client software) to access any network resources they have permission to use.

Session authentication takes place in the background; however, the user making the connection does need to enter a password. You can configure it so that a user is asked to enter a password every time a file or other resource is requested, once per session, or after a specified number of minutes of inactivity. The third option prevents unauthorized users from working at a machine connected to a protected resource that the original user has abandoned.

How do you decide which type of authentication is right for your needs? Table 8-6 compares the advantages and disadvantages of these three approaches.

Table 8-6   User, client, and session authentication

Method	Advantages	Disadvantages
User authentication	Gives users flexibility because they can access the network from any location	If username/password information is stolen, unauthorized users can gain access
Client authentication	Provides better security than user authentication; can be configured to work with all applications and services	Users must work at computers configured for client authentication
Session authentication	Gives users the most flexibility; can provide password-based security for resources after a period of inactivity or per session	The authentication software must be installed on each client computer

Authentication Methods

Windows authentication can be fine-tuned for maximum security or support for legacy clients, but rarely for both. Many networks still contain older Windows client OSs that must be supported. Windows Server 2003 supports all Windows authentication methods for backward compatibility, but administrators should know the limitations of these authentication methods so that they can use them effectively.

LAN Manager and NT LAN Manager, two early Microsoft authentication methods, aren't secure and should not be used if a stronger method is possible. For this reason, they aren't covered in this chapter.

NTLMv2 Authentication

The second version of NT LAN Manager was released as part of Windows NT 4.0 SP4 and is called NTLMv2 authentication. This version has several improvements over previous authentication protocols, such as mutual authentication between server and client, longer keys to create stronger passwords, and passwords up to 128 characters.

NTLMv2 is mainly used to support legacy clients and servers, UNIX clients that need to communicate with NT servers, or UNIX clients using the Server Message Block (SMB) daemon to authenticate. Because NTLMv2 uses fewer resources than more advanced authentication methods, it can also be used when you want to conserve resources. NTLMv2 does not support single sign-on or transitive trusts and can't be configured as much as Kerberos can. Upgrading clients to support stronger forms of authentication, such as Kerberos, is strongly recommended.

NTLMv2 is included with Windows 2000 and later, but support for Windows 98 can be added by installing Active Directory Client Extensions. You can download the necessary software from Microsoft's Web site. However, keep in mind that Microsoft closed extended support for Windows 98 and Windows 98 Second Edition (SE) on July 11, 2006. This means no new security updates for these legacy systems are available.

Kerberos in Windows Server 2003

MIT developed Kerberos version 5 as a secure authentication protocol. Microsoft adopted this protocol and modified it to use as the default authentication protocol for Windows Server 2000/2003. Kerberos, which is superior to NTLMv2, authenticates users' identity with a simple method called "authentication by assertion." The computer that connects to a server and requests services asserts that it's acting on behalf of an approved user of those services. Although this method sounds simple, the process by which computers communicate the assertion and response is not. Figure 8-8 shows how Kerberos works.

The following list outlines what happens at each step in Figure 8-8:

1. A client requests a file or other service.

2. The server prompts the client for a username and password (user account credentials).

3. The client submits the credentials, and the request is sent to an authentication server (AS) that's part of the Kerberos system. The Kerberos AS is known as the

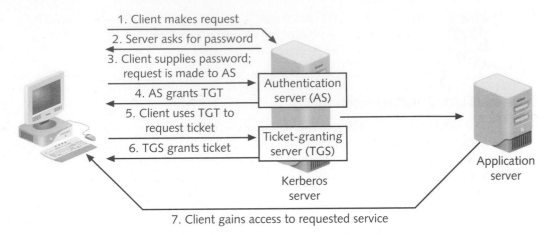

1. Client makes request

2. Server asks for password

3. Client supplies password; request is made to AS

4. AS grants TGT

5. Client uses TGT to request ticket

6. TGS grants ticket

Authentication server (AS)

Ticket-granting server (TGS)

Kerberos server

Application server

7. Client gains access to requested service

Figure 8-8   Kerberos authentication

Key Distribution Center (KDC). A domain controller can also serve as the AS in Windows 2000 or XP.

4. The AS creates an encrypted code called a session key, based on the client's password plus a random number associated with the service being requested. This session key is called a ticket-granting ticket (TGT).

5. The AS grants the TGT.

6. The client presents the TGT to the ticket-granting server (TGS). The TGS is also part of the Kerberos system but may or may not be the same server as the AS.

7. The TGS grants the session ticket and forwards the session ticket to the server holding the requested file or service on behalf of the requesting client.

8. The client gains access to the requested service or file.

A major advantage of Kerberos is that passwords aren't stored on the system, so they can't be intercepted. A ticket is specific to a user and typically expires after a set period (usually eight hours). Kerberos does allow postdated tickets and renewable tickets, but users can't modify tickets; they must request these flags when requesting their tickets.

In addition, Kerberos has a lower network overhead than a Public Key Infrastructure (PKI) system, so you don't need to install a central server and perform as many management tasks as you might with PKI. Most of the Kerberos authentication process is handled on the client side, and each domain controller shares the load by operating as a KDC.

There is a major concern with Kerberos, however. The KDC is a single point of failure for Kerberos, so if it goes down (and no backup servers can take over this role), no one can be authenticated. Administrators using a single KDC should take measures to ensure that authentication services can continue to function in the event of failure. Other major security flaws in Kerberos have emerged, making it possible for attackers to run arbitrary code on

KDCs, launch man-in-the-middle or DoS attacks, or cause the domain controller to shut down. Patches to address these flaws are available, however.

NOTE Kerberos is defined in RFC 4120 (which made RFC 1510 obsolete) and several related RFCs. Make sure you're looking at the current document, however, because standards change or become obsolete. For additional information on Kerberos, read related RFCs and visit MIT's Web site at *www.mit.edu*.

Single Sign-On

The Windows Server 2003 implementation of Kerberos solves the problem of cross-domain authentication, which can be a factor in large networks with multiple trees. For resources in domains other than their own (even though they're in the same forest), users had to supply username/passwords that authorized them to access those resources. Remembering different username/passwords for each domain was difficult, and having several username/passwords meant more opportunities for users to cause a security breach inadvertently.

Windows servers use an authentication strategy known as **single sign-on (SSO)**, an automatic process that works by using Kerberos. SSO enables users to log on once and have access to all resources they have permission to use, regardless of which domain they're in, for the duration of the session without needing to log on again. Resources in other domains are made available by trusts between Kerberos realms. Every domain in a Windows 2003 network is also a Kerberos realm, and every Active Directory domain controller is a KDC. Support for Kerberos-based SSO is one of the major reasons that trusts in a Windows Server 2003 environment are transitive.

Remote User Authentication

With laptops and handheld devices, employees can stay connected to the office while working at home or during business trips. Each time an employee connects to the corporate network remotely, however, a potential security breach is possible. An intruder or unauthorized user who gains access to the remote user's system could access files on the corporate network. Special authentication systems have been designed to address remote access needs. These are the two best-known systems:

- Terminal Access Controller Access Control System (TACACS+), commonly called "Tac-plus," is a set of proprietary authentication protocols that Cisco Systems developed. TACACS+ uses TCP as its transport protocol and separates the authentication and authorization processes. It also uses the MD5 algorithm to produce an encrypted digest of transmitted data.

- Remote Authentication Dial-In User Service (RADIUS) is generally considered less secure than TACACS+, even though it's supported more widely. RADIUS transmits authentication packets unencrypted across the network, which means they are vulnerable to attacks from packet sniffers. It combines authentication and authorization in a user profile.

TACACS+ is not backward compatible with Standard TACACS or Extended TACACS (XTACACS). For more information on TACACS, TACACS+, or XTACACS, search at *www.cisco.com*.

In TACACS+ or RADIUS, authentication is carried out by a server. A TACACS+ or RADIUS server is set up with the usual dial-up server used to receive connection requests from remote users, and the dial-up server can configure requests to the TACACS+ or RADIUS server for authentication. A TACACS+ or RADIUS authentication server needs its own IP address and uses special ports for communication, which means the network administrator must configure authentication for filtering, proxying, and NAT, as discussed in the following list:

- *Filtering characteristics*—TACACS+ uses TCP port 49; RADIUS uses UDP ports 1812 or 1645 for authentication and UDP ports 1813 or 1646 for accounting. (For more information on RADIUS client/server accounting, see RFC 2866.) You need to set up packet-filtering rules that enable clients to exchange authorization packets with the TACACS+ or RADIUS server.

- *Proxy characteristics*—A RADIUS server can function as a proxy server, but it doesn't work with generic proxy systems set up for Web access or other services. TACACS+, however, does work with generic proxy systems.

- *NAT characteristics*—RADIUS isn't compatible with NAT without additional configuration, but TACACS+ does work well with NAT systems. Static NAT works best because some TACACS+ systems use source IP addresses to create encryption keys.

RADIUS and TACAS+ systems are becoming less critical because remote employees and business partners often have direct connections to the Internet and can establish connections through VPNs. However, these systems still play a role in many corporate networks' security schemes.

A Windows Server 2003 computer can act as a RADIUS server or client. A RADIUS client (usually acting as a dial-up or VPN server) accepts authentication requests from users or computers and forwards them to a RADIUS server. A RADIUS server accepts authentication information from RADIUS clients and authorizes or denies requests based on authentication information in the Active Directory or local user database. Figure 8-9 shows the process of RADIUS authentication.

Windows Server 2003 Routing and Remote Access Services (RRAS) can be configured as a RADIUS client when used for remote access. For a Windows Server 2003 system to act as a RADIUS server, Internet Authentication Service (IAS, discussed in the following section) must be installed.

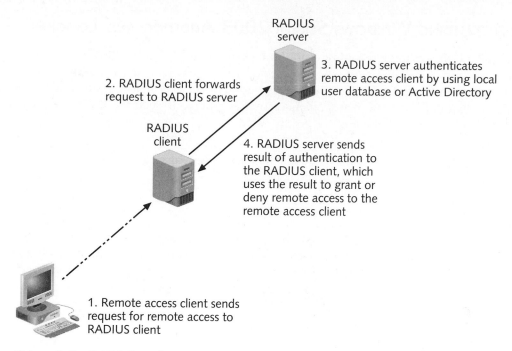

Figure 8-9   RADIUS authentication

Internet Authentication Service

Internet Authentication Service (IAS) is a standard component of Windows Server 2003 that allows a Windows Server 2003 system to act as a RADIUS server or RADIUS proxy (an intermediary between RADIUS clients and RADIUS servers) to provide remote authentication services. If IAS isn't going to use the Active Directory database to authenticate RADIUS clients, you configure it by using the IAS snap-in. You enter information about the identity of RADIUS clients and a shared secret (password) for authenticating requests between the RADIUS server and client. IAS servers don't respond to requests from RADIUS clients unless they are listed in the IAS configuration.

> **NOTE**   RADIUS proxies are new in Windows Server 2003. In previous versions of IAS, Windows servers could act only as RADIUS servers.

If IAS is configured to use Active Directory for authorization, it must be registered in Active Directory before it can read users' remote access properties. Integrating IAS with Active Directory makes it more convenient for remote users, who can use their regular Active Directory authentication credentials for the domain.

UNDERSTANDING WINDOWS SERVER 2003 AUDITING AND LOGGING

Auditing creates a record of events (a log) that enables you to check for suspicious activity, such as attempted access to a restricted file or changes in user permissions. The most common events to audit are users logging on or off, object access (including files), and user and group account management activities, but your security policy is most useful in determining what to log.

NOTE   Log file auditing is also useful for tracking performance and diagnosing problems, but the focus of this book is on security auditing.

New administrators often make the mistake of auditing too much and then can't possibly check all the log files. Too much auditing can be worse than no auditing because security events can get lost in the huge volume of information and go unnoticed, creating a false sense of security. Administrators must make time each day to examine every security event; however, if log entries are so numerous that checking them all is impossible, you should consider logging less data or investing in a third-party utility that helps evaluate your log files for suspicious entries.

Determining What to Audit

Before setting up auditing, you must decide on the categories of events to audit, the size of log files and how they are handled, and whether to audit object or directory service access. The Windows Server 2003 audit policy for domain controllers has auditing disabled by default; however, auditing account management is enabled by default. Table 8-7 explains the nine event categories you can choose to audit. Keep in mind that auditing can consume a lot of resources (computer and personnel), so keep auditing to the minimum needed to provide an adequate audit trail.

Table 8-7   Event categories

Event category	Purpose
Account logon events	Generated when a domain user account is authenticated on a domain controller.
Account management events	Generated by account management, such as creating a user or group, renaming a user or group, disabling an account, or changing a password.
Directory service access events	Generated by a user accessing an Active Directory object. Applies only to Active Directory objects, not file system or Registry objects.

Table 8-7　Event categories (continued)

Event category	Purpose
Logon events	Generated by a user logging on or off a computer. Logon events aren't the same as account logon events; they are generated by logging on to a computer at the console, not logging on to the domain.
Object access events	Generated by a user accessing an object, such as a file or printer, that has its own system ACL.
Policy change events	Generated by a change to user rights assignments, trust policies, or audit policies.
Privilege use events	Generated by each instance of a user exercising a user right.
Process tracking events	Generated by any event related to processes, such as program activation, process exit, and so on (events typically displayed in Task Manager). Mainly used to troubleshoot OS errors because of the high number of events it produces.
System events	Generated by a user starting or shutting down a computer or any event that affects system security or the Security log.

The default settings for these audit categories are to audit only success events or no auditing at all. Depending on the amount of security needed and the server's role, you might need to audit failure events, too. For example, auditing account logon events for failure means you can detect whether someone is attempting to access the system by guessing at an administrator's password. Similarly, you should audit object access failures to know whether someone is attempting to access files or folders they don't have permissions for. A log entry contains several pieces of information, such as the event's success or failure, time the event occurred, username of the account that caused the event, and actions the user performed.

In addition to monitoring security, logs can be used to track performance and plan resource allocation and access strategies. For example, if a group of users frequently accesses a resource stored on a server in another site, placing a replica of that resource on a local server can speed up access and lower bandwidth demands. Sometimes even managers don't know exactly what resources are needed, and tracking resource use helps improve operational efficiency.

Managing Event Logs

Event Viewer is used to view System, Security, and Application event logs on a local or remote system. DCs have three additional logs: File Replication Service, Directory Service, and DNS Server.

The System log contains events such as software driver problems, hardware errors, disk errors, memory errors, and others. The Security log tracks logon access, file and folder access, group policy changes, and more. It's used for file auditing, for example, so that you can track activity related to critical files, such as financial records. The Application log tracks software use and problems, when software programmers have designed their software to interface with this log. If, for example, an attacker or malware has interfered with software to cause it to abort, the Application log might contain clues about how to fix it or prevent future intrusions.

The File Replication Service log shows changes to file replication services, including when these services are started or stopped. For example, if an attacker has stopped replication services, the log shows this event has occurred. The Directory Service log shows events such as modifications to the Active Directory database, when the database has been replicated to DCs, and startup and shutdown events.

The DNS Server log records when DNS data has been modified, reports DNS server problems, and records DNS server startup and shutdown. Monitoring the DNS Server log is often a prime defense against attackers. An attacker might try to modify the DNS server contents, such as via DNS cache poisoning (which replaces legitimate IP addresses with false addresses). This means the attacker can redirect users to a hijacking program that downloads malware or spyware to users' computers. In another form of DNS cache poisoning, the attacker modifies a DNS server's contents so that all messages are directed through his Web server and then bounced to the real destination. Besides monitoring the DNS Server log, your best defense is to make sure current DNS server updates are installed.

Figure 8-10 shows details about an object access event from a DC's Security log. Event types are categorized as Informational, Error, Warning, Success Audit, and Failure Audit. Each event shares some common fields with all other events: Type, Date, Time, Source, Category, Event, User, and Computer. (The fields are mostly self-explanatory, but the Event field is the ID number the system gives to the event. Event IDs are covered in the next section.)

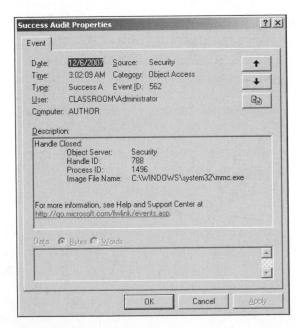

Figure 8-10   Details about an object access event

Some events are routine and easy to recognize, but others aren't. It's important to learn to differentiate the routine from the unusual. Obviously, error and warning events take priority, but informational events must also be checked regularly to keep tabs on server health. Event Viewer makes it easier to filter log file searches and archive log files. If you're looking for a specific problem or event, you can filter a log's contents by any or a combination of the common fields. For example, if you want to view failed logon attempts by a specific computer, you can create a filter to do so.

TIP

Plan to use Event Viewer often so that you become familiar with the information that's logged. When you know what's normal for your system, you can spot what's not normal quickly.

You also use Event Viewer to set the maximum size of log files and determine how files are handled when the maximum is reached. You can overwrite older events when file size reaches the maximum, overwrite files older than a specific number of days (up to 365), or stop logging until an administrator clears the event log. As you can imagine, the last option is a security risk and should be avoided. The option to overwrite files older than a specific number of days can also result in events not being logged if the log file is full and there are no events older than the specified number of days.

You must ensure that log files haven't been tampered with, maintain a reasonable retention policy, and ensure consistent, regular review of log data. Storing a backup copy of log files on a separate computer is a good idea, especially for sensitive data. If the server storing log files is compromised, an attacker could erase or modify log files, and there would be no evidence. Worse, you might not realize the server has been compromised. Often, log file review is the only way you can discover a breach. Including log files in backups is a sensible precaution for the same reason.

Using a database with third-party log file analysis tools can help you keep up with log file reviews, and an integrated database that stores server, remote access, firewall, and intrusion detection logs can help you correlate events. Every device records different information, so collecting all the data in one place gives you a clearer picture of an event.

Security-Related Event IDs

Learning some common security-related event IDs can help you spot events that require immediate attention. Table 8-8 lists some common event IDs created from daily network activity, such as users logging on or computers shutting down.

Table 8-8   Common server event IDs

Event ID number	Description
513	Computer shutdown
528	Successful user logon
529	Logon failure caused by unknown username or incorrect password

Table 8-8 Common server event IDs (continued)

Event ID number	Description
530	Logon failure caused by logon time restriction
531	Logon failure caused by a disabled account attempting to log on
532	Logon failure caused by an expired account attempting to log on
533	Logon failure caused by a user restricted from logging on at this computer attempting to log on
535	Logon failure caused by an expired user password
539	Logon failure caused by a user account being locked out
540	Successful network logon
624	New user account created
642	Change in user account management—reset password, enable account, and so on

Many of these events show up hundreds of times during the course of an average day. Remember that the OS also has several built-in accounts, which are logged each time the account accesses the system.

Policies must be audited to make sure organizations have a well-defined security policy and users are in compliance with it. The organization's security policy defines standards for connecting to the company network from any host. Enforcing these policies can be difficult, however. Policies should be defined for different levels of restriction; you might want to define tighter controls for business partners than you do for company employees, for example. Access controls for administrators might be less restrictive, but they should be required to have stronger passwords and change them more often.

Remember to strike the best balance between productivity and security. It's easy to err on the side of caution and lock a system down too tightly, which hinders productivity and frustrates users. It's equally easy to err on the side of productivity and leave systems open to attack. Try to provide the best security possible, within your security policy's guidelines, yet give your users enough freedom to be productive.

CHAPTER SUMMARY

□ Windows Server 2003 has a number of security enhancements over Windows 2000 Server, but default installations must still be tailored to meet organizations' needs.

□ Active Directory is a distributed hierarchical database service that stores objects, manages resources, and makes resources available for use. Almost everything in Active Directory is considered an object, and each object has associated attributes. Active Directory depends on DNS to function correctly.

□ Active Directory's logical structure is composed of domains, organizational units (OUs), trees, and forests. Active Directory's physical structure is composed of what can be used to optimize traffic, such as sites. Sites are groups of well-connected computers in a domain and can be used to adjust Active Directory replication.

- Trust relationships in Active Directory are arrangements between entities that enable secure resource sharing. Trusts can be nontransitive or transitive (the default relationship in Active Directory).

- Group Policy is an administrative tool that uses Active Directory to manage users and computers. Group policies are stored in Group Policy Objects (GPOs), which can be linked to an Active Directory domain, site, or OU.

- The two main types of GPOs are software policies and security policies. GPOs are applied in the following order: local computer, site, domain, OU. To be applied to a user or computer, a GPO must be linked to the container where the object resides.

- The Block Policy Inheritance setting prevents a container from inheriting settings, and the No Override setting prevents a policy from being blocked.

- Authentication is a key component of network and server security. The main Windows Server 2003 authentication methods are NTLMv2 and Kerberos. Single sign-on is enabled by Kerberos authentication (the default method in Windows Server 2003).

- Internet Authentication Service is a standard component of Windows Server 2003 that allows the server to act as a RADIUS server or RADIUS proxy to provide remote authentication services.

- Auditing, a critical part of security, enables you to check for suspicious activity. New administrators make the mistake of auditing too much, which makes log files overwhelming. The key is to produce an adequate record of events without generating a huge log file you can't review efficiently.

- Event Viewer is used to examine event logs on a local or remote system and can be customized to manage log file size, location, and other specifications.

KEY TERMS

Active Directory — A distributed hierarchical database and directory service that stores objects, manages resources, and makes those resources available for use.

container objects — Objects in a directory service that can hold objects and other container objects.

distinguished name (DN) — A naming scheme that represents the entire directory path to an object; also known as the fully qualified domain name (FQDN).

domain — Active Directory's main logical organizing component that serves as a security and replication boundary.

domain local group — A type of Active Directory group used to manage resources in a single domain and provide resource access in a domain to global and universal groups.

forests — Logical Active Directory components that represent collections of trees. *See also* trees.

global catalog — A Windows Server 2003 database that stores information about every object in a forest. Global catalog servers provide authentication, manage access to domain objects, and perform replication of key Active Directory elements.

global group — A type of Active Directory group used to manage group accounts from the same domain so that those domain users can access resources in their own domain and other domains.

Group Policy Objects (GPOs) — Containers that store group policy settings and can be linked to an Active Directory domain, site, or OU.

Internet Authentication Service (IAS) — A standard component of Windows Server 2003 that allows a server to act as a RADIUS server or RADIUS proxy to provide remote authentication services.

leaf objects — Objects in a directory that nest inside containers and can't contain other objects.

local group — A type of Active Directory group used on standalone servers that aren't part of a domain; the scope is limited to the local server.

nontransitive trusts — Trust relationships bounded by the two domains in the trust relationship. Nontransitive trusts don't flow to other domains in the forest and are one-way by default.

one-way trusts — Trust relationships that allow the trusted entity to access resources of the trusting entity; they apply in only one direction.

organizational units (OUs) — Logical components of Active Directory used to organize objects in a domain; can be used to group classes of objects.

relative distinguished name (RDN) — A naming scheme that refers to an object's name without including its directory path; also known as the canonical name (CN).

resource records — Tables of information used for name resolution that contain computer names, IP addresses, and similar locating information for a zone.

schema — The method of defining each object in Active Directory, including an object class and its attributes.

Security Accounts Manager (SAM) — A local database file that stores user and group information for standalone servers.

single sign-on (SSO) — An authentication strategy that enables users to log on once and have access to all resources they have permission to use for the duration of the session without needing to log on again.

sites — Groups of reliable, well-connected computers in the same IP subnet.

transitive trusts — In this arrangement, trusts are inherited by all domains in the tree or by all subcontainers of the parent container where the trust relationship is established.

trees — Logical Active Directory components representing everything from the bottom of the object path to the root domain. Trees contain multiple domains that share contiguous namespaces, schemas, and global catalogs or other commonalities.

universal group — A type of Active Directory group used to enable access to all resources in a forest.

zone — A namespace partition on a DNS server.

REVIEW QUESTIONS

1. Which of the following statements about Active Directory is true? (Choose all that apply.)

    a. It's a relational database.

    b. It's a distributed database.

    c. It's hierarchical.

    d. It allows decentralized management of network resources.

2. A domain is considered a _____ and _____ boundary.

    a. physical, logical

    b. security, logical

    c. security, replication

    d. replication, physical

3. Which of the following terms describes a group of computers in a reliable, well-connected IP subnet?

    a. organizational unit

    b. tree

    c. domain

    d. site

4. Group policies are applied in a specific order, represented by which of the following acronyms?

    a. LDSOU

    b. LSDOU

    c. DLOUS

    d. LSOUD

5. To prevent users from blocking policies being applied to their containers, you could set which of the following options?

    a. No Override

    b. Block Policy Application

    c. No Policy Inheritance

    d. Block Policy Inheritance

6. Administrators must have which of the following object permissions to assign a group policy to an Active Directory object?

    a. read

    b. write

    c. delete

    d. modify

8

7. To assign a group policy to an Active Directory object, an administrator must have _____ permission to the Sysvol folder. (Choose all that apply.)

    a. modify

    b. delete

    c. read

    d. write

8. Which of the following is the default authentication method in Windows Server 2003 Active Directory environments?

    a. LM authentication

    b. NTLM authentication

    c. Kerberos authentication

    d. NTLMv2 authentication

9. Every server in a network using Kerberos for authentication operates as a Key Distribution Center. True or False?

10. In which of the following authentication methods do users log on to the domain once and access all resources for which they have permissions?

    a. one-time authentication

    b. single key authentication

    c. smart cards

    d. single sign-on

11. If local, domain, and OU policies are set on a computer logging on to a domain, which one takes precedence?

    a. none

    b. local

    c. OU

    d. domain

12. Authenticated users have which of the following group policy permissions by default?

    a. read and write

    b. read and modify

    c. read and apply

    d. read and change

13. Which of the following is a main container object in X.500? (Choose all that apply.)

    a. OU

    b. domain

    c. country

    d. site

14. What is the DNS zone that maps IP addresses to hostnames?
    a. forward lookup zone
    b. reverse lookup zone
    c. address resolution zone
    d. resource record

15. What is the unique number associated with an object name in Active Directory?
    a. object class
    b. object attribute
    c. GUID
    d. GID

16. Which of the following defines every type of object stored in Active Directory?
    a. global catalog
    b. default domain policy
    c. schema
    d. GUID

17. Which of the following trusts is one-way by default and bound by the two domains in the trust relationship?
    a. nontransitive trust
    b. one-way trust
    c. transitive trust
    d. realm trust

18. What is the smallest Active Directory container you can link a GPO to?
    a. OU
    b. forest
    c. domain
    d. site

19. How do you prevent a container from inheriting policies?
    a. Use No Override.
    b. Use Block Policy Inheritance.
    c. Create and apply a separate GPO for that container.
    d. Place the container in a different OU.

8

20. In which event log would you find a record of someone trying unsuccessfully to log on to the Administrator account in Windows Server 2003?

  a. DNS Server log

  b. Directory Service log

  c. Security log

  d. Application log

HANDS-ON PROJECTS

HANDS-ON PROJECTS

Hands-On Project 8-1: Configuring IAS

Time Required: 15 minutes

Objective: Configure your Active Directory DC as an IAS server.

Description: Managing remote users can be challenging and can frustrate users who need to remember different sets of logon credentials. By using IAS, you can integrate remote access authentication with users' authentication credentials stored in the Active Directory database. You need administrative access to a Windows Server 2003 DC and must have completed all in-chapter activities.

1. If necessary, log on to your domain controller as an administrator.

2. Open Control Panel, and click **Add or Remove Programs**. Click the **Add/Remove Windows Components** button to start the Windows Components Wizard.

3. Scroll down in the Components list box, and double-click **Networking Services**. Click to select the **Internet Authentication Service** check box, and then click **OK**. Click **Next** to install IAS.

4. Click **Finish**, and then close the Add or Remove Programs window.

5. Click **Start**, point to **All Programs**, point to **Administrative Tools**, and click **Internet Authentication Service**. The IAS management console is shown in Figure 8-11.

6. Because your server is an Active Directory domain controller, the option to register the IAS server in Active Directory is available. Right-click **Internet Authentication Service (Local)** in the left pane and click **Register Server in Active Directory**.

7. When prompted to allow the computer to read users' dial-in properties, click **OK**. Click **OK** again in the Server registered dialog box.

8. In the left pane, right-click **Remote Access Policies** and click **New Remote Access Policy**.

9. Click **Next** in the New Remote Access Policy Wizard. Enter **VPN access policy 1** as the policy name, and then click **Next**.

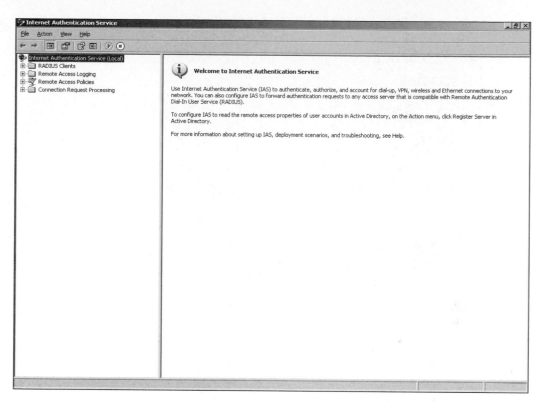

Figure 8-11   The Internet Authentication Service management console

10. In the Access Method window, verify that the **VPN** option button is selected, and then click **Next**.

11. In the User or Group Access window, click the **User** option button, and then click **Next**.

12. For the authentication method, accept the default (MS-CHAPv2), and then click **Next**.

13. In the Policy Encryption Level window, click to clear the **Basic encryption (IPSec 56-bit DES or MPPE 40-bit)** check box, and then click **Next**. Click **Finish** to complete the wizard. When Remote Access Policies is selected, you should see VPN access policy 1 listed first (see Figure 8-12).

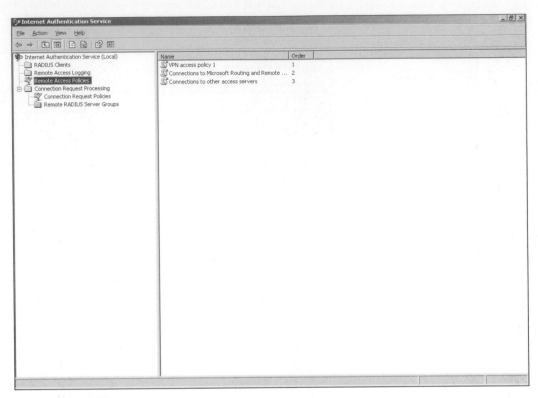

Figure 8-12   Viewing the VPN access policy 1 you added

14. To configure a new RADIUS client, right-click **RADIUS Clients** in the left pane and click **New RADIUS Client** to open the New RADIUS Client dialog box.

15. Enter the client's name and IP address. (You can use your own computer name and IP address.) Click **Verify**. Click **Resolve** to resolve the IP address you entered. Click **OK**, and then click **Next**.

16. Click **RADIUS Standard** in the Client-Vendor list box (if it's not already selected), enter and confirm a password in the Shared secret text box, and then click **Finish** to create the client.

17. Make sure **RADIUS Clients** is selected in the left pane. You should see the RADIUS client you configured in the right pane (see Figure 8-13).

18. Close all open windows, and leave your system running for the next activity.

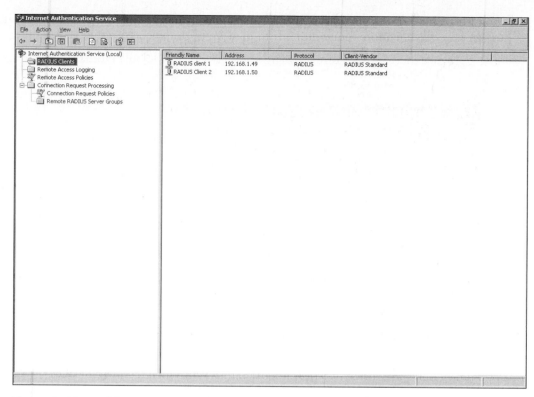

Figure 8-13   Adding a RADIUS client

Hands-On Project 8-2: Configuring Auditing in Windows Server 2003

Time Required: 5 minutes

Objective: Configure auditing on a Windows Server 2003 DC.

Description: Before you can audit object access, you must enable auditing for that audit category and then configure each object for auditing. In this project, you configure the Default Domain Controllers Policy GPO to audit object access events. This setting logs attempts to access objects that have a security ACL and provides additional monitoring for objects with special security requirements. For example, a folder containing sensitive information might have security settings that restrict access to certain groups or users. Failed attempts might indicate an attacker trying to gain access. Successful attempts might reveal an unauthorized user accessing the object, which could indicate a privilege escalation issue. For this project, you need administrative access to a Windows Server 2003 DC and must have completed all in-chapter activities.

1. Click **Start**, point to **All Programs**, point to **Administrative Tools**, and click **Active Directory Users and Computers**. Expand your domain in the left pane.

Right-click **Domain Controllers** and click **Properties** to open the Domain Controllers Properties dialog box.

2. Click the **Group Policy** tab. You should see the Default Domain Controllers Policy (see Figure 8-14).

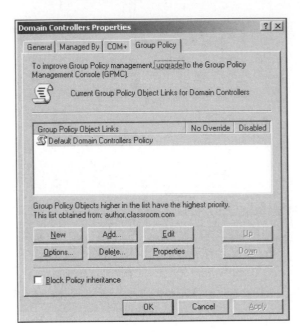

Figure 8-14   Viewing GPO links

3. Click to select **Default Domain Controllers Policy**, and then click the **Edit** button.

4. Under Computer Configuration in the left pane, expand **Windows Settings** and then **Security Settings**. Expand **Local Policies**, and then click to select **Audit Policy** (see Figure 8-15).

5. In the right pane, right-click **Audit object access** and click **Properties**. Click to select the **Define these policy settings** check box (if it's not already selected), and then click the **Success** and **Failure** check boxes. Click **OK**. Notice that Success, Failure is now listed in the Policy Setting column in the right pane.

6. Close all open windows, and leave your system running for the next activity.

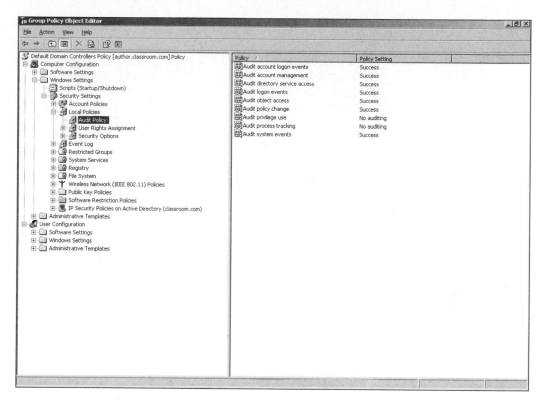

Figure 8-15 Configuring the Default Domain Controllers Policy

HANDS-ON PROJECTS

Hands-On Project 8-3: Examining Event Logs

Time Required: 10 minutes

Objective: Examine a Windows Server 2003 DC's event logs.

Description: As an administrator, you need to know how to sort through event logs to identify potential problems. You need administrative access to a Windows Server 2003 DC for this project.

1. If necessary, log on to your domain controller as administrator.

2. Click **Start**, point to **All Programs**, point to **Administrative Tools**, and click **Event Viewer**.

3. Maximize the window. Click **Security** in the left pane, and review the Security log (see Figure 8-16). Click the column headings to sort the log differently. You can double-click an event to open its Properties dialog box.

4. Right-click **Security** and click **Properties**. In the Security Properties dialog box, click the **Filter** tab. Enter **Administrator** in the User text box to filter out activities by all users other than the Administrator account, and then click **OK**. Notice that only Administrator is listed under the User column in the right pane.

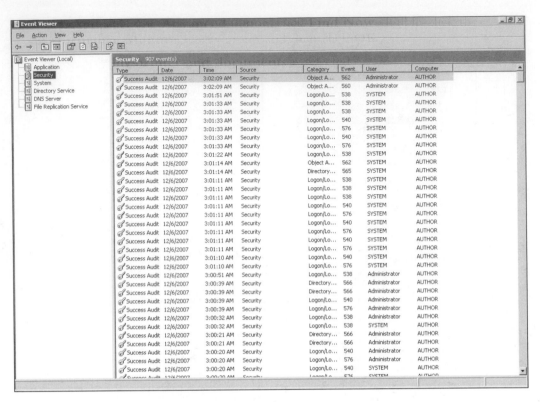

Figure 8-16 Viewing events in the Security log

5. In the left pane, right-click **Application** and click **Properties** to open the Application Properties dialog box. On the General tab, note the log file's current size, and write it down along with the maximum log file size:

_____

6. Reduce the maximum log file size to half the value you recorded in Step 5. What effect will this setting have on the logs that are recorded, and what are the security implications? What could you do to reduce the log file size yet still provide an audit trail of the most important events?

_____

_____

_____

7. If time permits, explore the remaining logs (System, Directory Service, DNS Server, and File Replication Service), and then close all open windows.

CASE PROJECTS

CASE PROJECTS

Case Project 8-1: Planning an Active Directory Deployment for Green Globe

Design an Active Directory deployment for Green Globe. Be sure to plan the site topology, domain and OU structure, and trust relationships. In addition, account for remote access and temporary memberships, such as for partners or students. Include a plan for group membership and any nested groups you plan to use for security management. Submit written documentation and a diagram showing the design's logical and physical layout.

8

CONFIGURING WINDOWS SERVER 2003 SECURITY

> ### After reading this chapter and completing the exercises, you will be able to:
> - Describe how to configure Windows Server 2003 resource security
> - Explain how to use Windows Server 2003 security configuration tools
> - Describe how to configure Windows Server 2003 network security for remote access and virtual private network services

In Chapter 8, you gained a solid footing in the basics of securing Windows Server 2003. This chapter takes the next step by showing you ways to apply what you have learned with configuration techniques and tools. By combining your knowledge from Chapter 8 with the tools in this chapter, you can protect a Windows Server 2003 network effectively and thoroughly.

The chapter begins by covering file systems, basic security attributes, and the Encrypting File System. You go on to learn about configuring permissions and auditing for folders, files, printers, and the Registry. Next, you learn how to apply account security by using group policies, the Security Configuration and Analysis snap-in, and the Security Configuration Wizard. Finally, you learn how to create remote access policies and configure Network Address Translation to secure Windows Server 2003 network services.

CONFIGURING WINDOWS SERVER 2003 RESOURCE SECURITY

In Windows Server 2003, many components can be configured for security. Some relate to the file system, and others are connected with printing, the Registry, and computer services. In the sections that follow, you learn how to configure the following important components:

- Folder and file attributes, including the Encrypt attribute
- Folder and file permissions
- Folder and file auditing
- Network printer security
- Registry security
- Services and processes

Before focusing on folder and file attributes and permissions, you review the FAT and NTFS file systems used in Windows Server 2003.

A Quick Review of FAT and NTFS

All editions of Windows Server 2003 support File Allocation Table (FAT) versions 16 and 32 and New Technology File System (NTFS). FAT is an older file system that was designed for computers with small disk systems, such as early computers with 20 to 500 MB of disk storage. Because NTFS is a more robust file system and has more security features, converting any FAT16 or FAT32 volumes to NTFS is a good idea. For example, use the following command to convert volume E from FAT (fs) to NTFS:

```
convert e: /fs:ntfs
```

NOTE Always perform a backup before converting a FAT volume to NTFS. Further, keep in mind that using the convert command is a one-time conversion because no Microsoft utility for converting back to FAT16 or FAT32 from NTFS is available.

NTFS 5 is the Windows Server 2003 file system, designed for the needs of a network server environment. It offers the following important features:

- Local security through file and folder permissions
- Compression of files to save disk space
- Disk quotas to manage available disk space
- Encryption to secure files and folders
- Indexing for faster file and folder searches
- POSIX.1 support for compatibility with other file systems

Table 9-1 compares FAT and NTFS features.

Table 9-1 FAT16, FAT32, and NTFS compared

Feature	FAT16	FAT32	NTFS
Total volume size	4 GB	2 GB to 2 TB	2 TB
Maximum file size	2 GB	4 GB	Theoretical limit of 16 exabytes
Filename length	11 characters	256 characters	256 characters
Security	Limited security based on attributes and shares	Limited security based on attributes and shares	C2-compatible extensive security and auditing options
File compression	Supported with extra utilities	Supported with extra utilities	Supported as part of NTFS
File activity tracking	None	None	Tracking via a log
POSIX support	None	Limited	POSIX.1 support
Hot fix	Limited	Limited	Supports hot fixes
Large database support	Limited	Yes	Yes
Multiple disk drives in one volume	No	No	Yes

NOTE

A hot fix repairs data automatically in hard disk areas that have become damaged or corrupted, without the need to shut down the computer or OS. When possible, the OS moves the data to a reserved good area without users noticing. The disk's damaged areas are then marked so that they aren't used again.

Folder and File Attributes in FAT and NTFS

When reviewing file security, the use of attributes is easy to leave out, but attributes represent a basic form of security in FAT16, FAT32, and NTFS. Both FAT and NTFS use file and folder attributes as a carryover from DOS, but attributes also provide a partial migration path for converting files and directories from a Novell NetWare file server. DOS and NetWare systems use file attributes as a form of security and file management. Attributes are stored as header information with each folder and file, along with other characteristics, including volume label, designation as a subfolder, and date and time of creation.

Attributes Used in FAT

The folder and file attributes available in a FAT-formatted Windows Server 2003 disk are Read-only, Hidden, and Archive. When you open a file or folder's Properties dialog box, you see these attributes on the General tab. If you enable the Read-only attribute for a folder, the folder is read-only, but not the files in the folder. This means the folder can't be deleted or renamed from the command line or by a user who's not in the Administrators group. If an administrator attempts to delete or rename the folder, a warning message states that the folder is read-only and asks whether to proceed. Some Windows Server 2003 administrators leave the Read-only check box blank and set the equivalent protection in permissions because files in the folder can inherit a folder's read-only permissions.

Folders can be marked as Hidden to prevent users from viewing their contents. For example, the server administrator at a college places new statistical software on a network but keeps the folder hidden while a few users test it. After testing is completed, the Hidden attribute is removed.

CAUTION In Windows 2000 and XP, the Hidden attribute can be defeated by selecting the option to view hidden files and folders (from the View or Tools menus in Windows Explorer or My Computer). Hidden files can also be displayed in Windows Vista by opening Folder Options from Control Panel and selecting the View tab.

The Archive attribute indicates that the folder or file needs to be backed up because it's new or changed. Some network administrators ignore the Archive attribute for folders but rely on it for files. Files, but not folders, are flagged to archive automatically when they are changed. This attribute is important to remember because you can configure server backup systems to detect files with this attribute set.

Attributes Used in NTFS

An NTFS volume also has Read-only, Hidden, and Archive attributes plus the Index, Compress, and Encrypt attributes. As with FAT attributes, you find the Read-only and Hidden attributes on the General tab in a folder or file's Properties dialog box. To access the other attributes, called extended attributes, click the General tab's Advanced button to open the Advanced Attributes dialog box shown in Figure 9-1. When you make a change to one of the attributes here, you have the option to apply that change to only the folder and files it contains or to the folder, its files, and all subfolders and files.

NTFS Index Attribute

You use the NTFS Index attribute to index folder and file contents so that you can search for text, creation date, and other properties quickly. For this feature to work, however, the Indexing Service must already be installed as a Windows Server 2003 component. Also, the service should be set to start automatically after it's installed. You learn about configuring services in "Managing Services and Processes" later in this chapter.

NTFS Compress Attribute

A folder and its contents can be stored on disk in compressed format. This option enables you to reduce disk space used for files, which is particularly useful when disk space is limited or you have directories that are accessed infrequently, such as those used to store accounting data from previous fiscal years. Compression saves space, but it takes longer to access information because each file must be uncompressed before it's read.

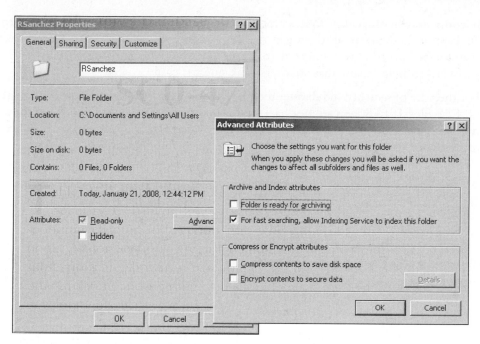

Figure 9-1   Attributes and extended attributes in NTFS

If you want to use the Encrypt attribute to increase security, do not compress files because compressed files can't be encrypted.

CAUTION

Encrypt Attribute and the Encrypting File System

With the NTFS Encrypt attribute set, only the user who encrypts the folder or file can read it. As an administrator, you might use this option to protect certain files, such as new software you aren't ready to release for general use. In organizations with sensitive file contents, such as banks or scientific research facilities, encryption can be an essential measure for ensuring security of these files.

In Windows Server 2003, you can't encrypt system files because users generally need access to these files to do their work. If you attempt to encrypt a system file, you see an "Access denied" message.

TIP

An encrypted folder or file uses **Encrypting File System (EFS)**, which sets up a unique private encryption key associated with the user account that encrypted the folder or file. The file is protected from network intruders and in situations when a server or hard drive is stolen. EFS uses both symmetric and asymmetric encryption techniques. The symmetric portion uses a single key to encrypt the file or folder. In the asymmetric portion, two encryption keys are used to protect the key for encrypting the file or folder. Because the asymmetric portion is connected to a user account, the account should have a strong password to help ensure that attackers can't guess it easily.

For the sake of security and disaster recovery, backing up EFS keys is as important as backing up EFS files. If EFS keys are not backed up, you have no access to EFS files when they are restored after a recovery. To ensure that the keys are backed up, make sure you back up the full OS, not just the EFS files.

TIP

To make finding EFS files in the Windows interface easier, you can use the Folder Options dialog box to display encrypted or compressed files in a certain color, as explained in Activity 9-1.

When you move an encrypted file to another folder on the same computer, that file remains encrypted, even if you rename it. There's no prompt to retain the Encrypt attribute when you move the file. The same holds true for copying the file to a different Windows 2003 server. If the folder or file is moved to a Windows 2000 Server, XP, or Vista computer, however, there should be a prompt to determine whether the Encrypt attribute is retained.

A folder or file's owner can decrypt it by using Windows Explorer or My Computer to remove the Encrypt attribute and then apply the change. You can also encrypt or decrypt folders and files by using the cipher command in a command prompt window. (Type cipher /? to view the command's options.)

After a folder or file is encrypted, users besides the owner can be added to enable them to view and use the encrypted information. Also, when you first encrypt a folder, you have the option to encrypt its files and subfolders, as shown in Figure 9-2.

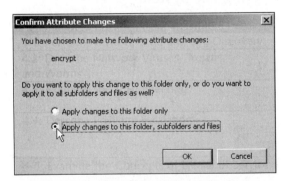

Figure 9-2   Encrypting files and subfolders in a folder

As you use EFS, consider these security guidelines for a server:

- EFS is effective, but the most effective step is to make sure a server is physically protected so that unauthorized people can't remove its hard drives.
- Encrypt all sensitive files.

- Create new sensitive files in folders that are already encrypted so that the files are encrypted automatically.

- Delete all nonencrypted versions of files that have been encrypted.

- Consider encrypting even frequently used folders, such as My Documents, for user accounts.

- Make sure laptop computers use EFS on the server so that sensitive files aren't kept on laptops that go offsite.

- If sensitive files must be used offsite, enable the use of offline files. (These files are loaded on a computer and can be used when the computer isn't connected to the network. When the computer reconnects to the network, offline files can be synchronized with the server.) At the same time, enable the Encrypt Offline Files setting in the Folder Options dialog box to secure data (see Figure 9-3). You can also enforce this practice by making it a group policy through Active Directory.

- Use group policy measures, as discussed in Chapter 8, to ensure that specific folders on servers and their workstation clients use EFS.

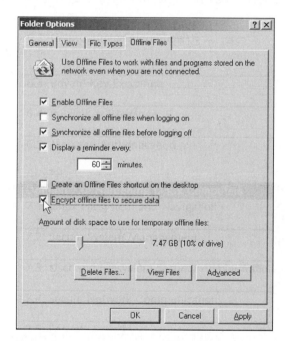

Figure 9-3 Encrypting offline files

> **NOTE**
>
> For the best results with the activities and projects in this chapter, start with a clean installation of Windows Server 2003 Standard or Enterprise Edition and make sure Service Pack 2 (SP2) is installed. Also, you need to log on using an account with Administrator privileges.

ACTIVITY

Activity 9-1: Using the Encrypting File System

Time Required: 15 minutes

Objective: Encrypt the files in a folder.

Description: One way to provide security against theft of laptops and computer drives is to use the Encrypting File System to protect files. In this activity, you practice encrypting a folder's contents.

1. Use My Computer or Windows Explorer to create a new folder in the root of the C drive. Give the folder a name that's a combination of your first initial and last name, such as RSanchez. Find a file to copy into the folder, such as a text file already in the root of drive C, or use Notepad to create a new file and place it in this folder.

2. Right-click your new folder and click **Properties**. If necessary, click the **General** tab. What attributes are already enabled? Record your observations:

   _____

3. Click the **Advanced** button. Record which attributes are already enabled in the Advanced Attributes dialog box:

   _____

4. Click to select the **Encrypt contents to secure data** check box, click **OK**, and then click **Apply**.

5. Verify that **Apply changes to this folder, subfolders and files** is selected (refer back to Figure 9-2), and then click **OK** twice.

6. How would you verify that the file you copied into the folder is encrypted? How would you decrypt the entire folder contents?

   _____

   _____

7. Close the folder's Properties dialog box.

8. The name of the folder you encrypted should be displayed in a color, such as green, in My Computer or Windows Explorer to show that it's encrypted. If not, click **Tools**, **Folder Options** from the menu. Click the **View** tab, and then scroll down and click the **Show encrypted or compressed NTFS files in color** check box (see Figure 9-4). Click **OK**.

9. Close My Computer or Windows Explorer, and leave your system running for the next activity.

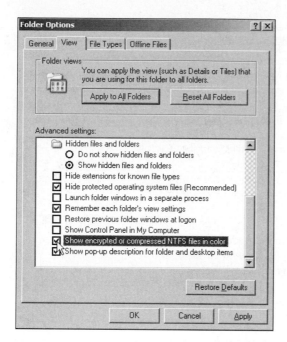

Figure 9-4 Enabling color for encrypted file and folder names

Setting File and Folder Permissions

In Windows Server 2003, permissions control access to an object, such as a folder or file. For example, when you configure a folder or file so that a group has access only to read its contents, you're configuring permissions. At the same time, you're configuring the folder or file's access control list (ACL) of security descriptors. To configure permissions for a folder or file, you can use the Add and Remove buttons on the Security tab of a folder or file's Properties dialog box to change which groups and users have permissions, as shown in Figure 9-5. Also, to modify permissions for groups and users, simply change the selections in the Allow and Deny columns. Table 9-2 lists the folder and file permissions supported by NTFS.

Table 9-2 NTFS folder and file permissions

Permission	Description	Applies to
Full Control	Can read, add, delete, run, and modify files; change permissions and attributes; and take ownership	Folders and files
Modify	Can read, add, delete, run, and modify files; cannot delete subfolders and their file contents, change permissions, or take ownership	Folders and files

Table 9-2 NTFS folder and file permissions (continued)

Permission	Description	Applies to
Read & Execute	Implies the capabilities of both List Folder Contents and Read (navigate folders, view file contents, view attributes and permissions, and run files)	Folders and files
List Folder Contents	Can navigate files in the folder or switch to a subfolder, view folder attributes and permissions, and run files; cannot view file contents	Folders only
Read	Can view file contents, folder attributes, and permissions; cannot navigate folders or run files	Folders and files
Write	Can create files, write data to files, append data to files, create folders, delete files (but not subfolders and their files), and modify folder and file attributes	Folders and files

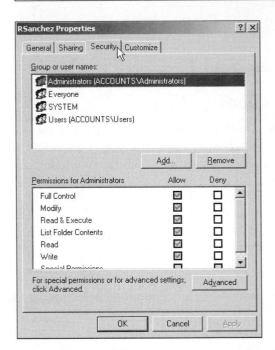

Figure 9-5 Modifying permissions on the Security tab

On the Security tab shown in Figure 9-5, if no Allow or Deny check boxes are selected, the group or user has no access to the folder or file. Also, when a new folder or file is created, typically it inherits permissions from the parent folder or the root. Inheritance is important to remember when you create a folder or file so that you consider default permissions. Always check permissions when you create a folder or file so that you know what they are.

Further, you usually have to take special steps to remove inherited permissions, or the system will prevent you from altering them. Finally, the Deny option overrides any other access. For example, if an account belongs to two groups—one with Allow selected for the permission and one with Deny selected—the Deny setting prevails.

Activity 9-2: Setting Folder Permissions

Time Required: 15 minutes

Objective: Configure permissions on a folder to enable users to access and change its contents.

Description: Many organizations have a Server Operators group for users who perform day-to-day management of servers. In this activity, you need to create a Utilities folder for the Server Operators group so that its group members can place new utilities in the folder, list the folder's contents, and run utilities in that folder.

1. Use My Computer to create a folder called Utilities plus your initials, such as **UtilitiesAL**. Right-click the new folder and click **Properties**.

2. Click the **Security** tab. What users and groups already have permissions to access the folder? Click each group and user to determine what permissions they have and record your results. Notice that some check boxes are selected but dimmed (meaning they can't be clicked) because these settings are inherited.

   _____

   _____

3. Click the **Add** button.

4. Click the **Advanced** button. In the Select Users, Computers, or Groups dialog box, click **Find Now**. Double-click **Server Operators** in the list at the bottom, and then click **OK**.

5. Click to select the **Server Operators** group. What permissions does it have by default?

   _____

   _____

6. Click the **Allow** check box for the Modify permission.

7. Click **OK** in the folder's Properties dialog box. Leave the My Computer window open for the next activity.

As you noticed in Activity 9-2, some Allow check boxes for permissions are selected but dimmed to indicate inherited permissions, which flow from a parent object to all child objects (such as files and subfolders in a parent folder). If you want to change a permission that has a selected but dimmed Allow or Deny check box, you must remove the inherited permissions first, as you learn in Activity 9-3.

ACTIVITY

Activity 9-3: Clearing Inherited Permissions

Time Required: 10 minutes

Objective: Clear inherited permissions from a folder.

Description: A folder inherits permissions from its parent folders in the NTFS hierarchy. Files also inherit permissions from the folders they are in. Reviewing inherited permissions to determine whether they need to be cleared is a good security precaution. Keep in mind that if you do not clear inherited permissions, you can't modify them in NTFS.

1. Using My Computer, find the Utilities folder you created in Activity 9-2. Right-click the folder and click **Properties**.

2. Click the **Security** tab, and then click **Advanced** to open the Advanced Security Settings dialog box.

3. Click the **Permissions** tab, if necessary, and then click to clear the **Allow inheritable permissions from the parent to propagate to this object and all child objects. Include these with entries explicitly defined here.** check box.

4. In the Security message box that opens (see Figure 9-6), notice that you can select one of three options: copying the previously inherited permissions (if you have removed them already), removing the inherited permissions, and canceling this operation. Click **Remove**.

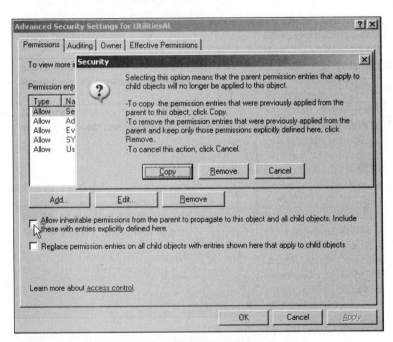

Figure 9-6   Clearing inheritable permissions

5. Click **OK**.

6. Compare the groups that now remain with those you recorded in Step 2 of Activity 9-2 and record which ones are no longer on the list:

_____

_____

7. Click **OK** in the folder's Properties dialog box. Close all open windows and leave your system running for the next activity.

Sometimes the standard set of permissions doesn't quite fit the security you want on a folder, but in Windows Server 2003, you can use special permissions to customize security settings for a user or group. Figure 9-7 shows the special permissions you can set up, which are explained in more detail in Table 9-3. Also, try Hands-On Project 9-1 at the end of this chapter to configure special permissions.

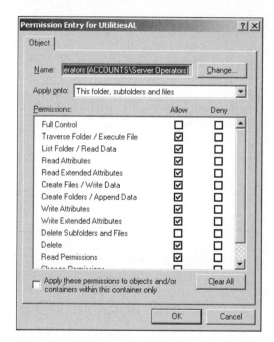

Figure 9-7   Special permissions

Table 9-3 NTFS folder and file special permissions

Permission	Description	Applies to
Full Control	Can read, add, delete, run, and modify files; change permissions and attributes; and take ownership	Folders and files
Traverse Folder/Execute File	Can list the contents of a folder and run program files in that folder; keep in mind that all users are granted this permission automatically via the Everyone and Users groups, unless you remove or deny it	Folders and files
List Folder/Read Data	Can list the contents of folders and subfolders and read the contents of files	Folders and files
Read Attributes	Can view folder and file attributes (Read-only and Hidden)	Folders and files
Read Extended Attributes	Can view extended attributes (Index, Compress, Encrypt)	Folders and files
Create Files/Write Data	Can add new files to a folder and modify, append to, and write over file contents	Folders and files
Create Folders/Append Data	Can add new folders and add new data at the end of files (but otherwise not delete, write over, or modify data)	Folders and files
Write Attributes	Can add or remove the Read-only and Hidden attributes	Folders and files
Write Extended Attributes	Can add or remove the Archive, Index, Compress, and Encrypt attributes	Folders and files
Delete Subfolders and Files	Can delete subfolders and files (the following Delete permission is not required)	Folders and files
Delete	Can delete the specific subfolder or file to which this permission is attached	Folders and files
Read Permissions	Can view the permissions (ACL information) associated with a folder or file (but doesn't imply you can change them)	Folders and files
Change Permissions	Can change the permissions associated with a folder or file	Folders and files
Take Ownership	Can take ownership of the folder or file (Read Permissions and Change Permissions accompany this permission automatically)	Folders and files

Microsoft provides the following guidelines for setting permissions:

- Protect the Windows folder, which contains OS files on Windows servers, and its subfolders from general users by allowing limited access, such as Read & Execute and List Folder Contents, or by granting the Traverse Folder/Execute File special permission to general users but giving the Administrators group Full Control access.

- Protect server utility folders, such as for backup software and network management, by giving access permissions to only these groups: Administrators, Server Operators, and Backup Operators.

- Protect software application folders with Read & Execute and Write permissions so that users can run applications and write temporary files.

- Create publicly used folders to have Modify access, so users have broad access except to take ownership, set permissions, and delete subfolders and files.

- Give users Full Control access to their own home folders.

- Remove general access groups, such as Everyone and Users, from confidential folders—for example, those used for personal mail, sensitive files, or software development projects.

To follow sound security practices, always begin with strong security when you configure permissions and adjust settings later as needed. This approach is easier than angering users by having to take away permissions.

Security Through Folder and File Auditing

You can track access to folders and files by setting up auditing to track read or write activity on a folder or file. Some organizations use auditing on folders and files containing financially sensitive information, and others monitor access to research or marketing project information. In Windows Server 2003 NTFS folders and files, you can audit a combination of any of the activities listed as special permissions in Table 9-3. As you learned in Chapter 8, you can track successful and failed access attempts. Before you can audit a specific event, you need to do the following:

- Enable auditing as a group policy, as you learned in Activity 8-2 in Chapter 8.

- Select the option to audit specific objects or events, which you learn next.

For example, your organization's financial auditors want an audit trail for all files in the Accounting folder that records each time a user with access changes the contents of a file in the folder. The financial auditors might also want to verify that only the Accounting and Administrator groups have permission to write to files in this folder. To set up this type of auditing, configure the folder to audit each successful write event, such as Create Files/ Write Data and Create Folders/Append Data. For extra information, you might track permission, attribute, and ownership changes by monitoring successful attempts at Write Attributes, Write Extended Attributes, Change Permissions, and Take Ownership events. Audited events are recorded in the Event Viewer's Security log.

The general steps for auditing a folder are as follows:

1. In My Computer, right-click the folder you want to audit and click Properties.

2. Click the Security tab, and then click the Advanced button.

3. In the Advanced Security Settings dialog box, click the Auditing tab.

4. Click Add, click Advanced in the Select Users, Computers, or Groups dialog box, click Find Now, double-click the name of the group you want to audit, and click OK.

5. Click the Successful check boxes for Create Files/Write Data, Create Folders/Append Data, Delete Subfolders and Files, and Delete. These settings enable you to monitor who's creating new information in the folder and who might be deleting information after creating it. Click OK.

6. Click OK, and then click OK again.

To configure auditing for an object, including a folder, you must set up an auditing policy. If you don't, you might see an error message when you configure auditing in the object's Properties dialog box. For a standalone server, you configure an audit policy for the local computer; for domain controllers in an Active Directory domain, you configure the domain security policy. To set the audit policy, you need Administrator privileges.

Configuring Shared Folders and Shared Folder Permissions

Along with establishing folder permissions and auditing, a folder can be set up as a shared folder for users to access over the network. To share a server folder, open the folder's Properties dialog box and click the Sharing tab (see Figure 9-8). The Sharing tab has two main options: to share or not share the folder. To share a folder so that network users can access or map it, click the Share this folder option button. Selecting the Maximum allowed option means that the number of users who can access the folder simultaneously is the same as the number of Windows Server 2003 client licenses you have. Use the other option, Allow this number of users, to specify a limit to the number of simultaneous users. This option is one way to make sure licensing restrictions for software are followed, for example.

To set permissions for the share, click the Permissions button. Share permissions for an object can differ from basic access permissions set through the Security tab, and the permissions are cumulative, which means the basic access permissions and share permissions are added together. For example, if user LAnderson has write permission for a folder and the share permission for this user is read, LAnderson has both read and write permissions. The exception is when a permission is denied. Three share permissions are associated with a folder for specified users and groups:

- *Full Control*—Provides full access to the folder, including the ability to take control or change permissions

- *Change*—Enables users to read, add, modify, run, and delete files

- *Read*—Permits groups or users to read and run files

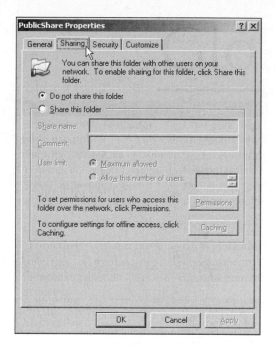

Figure 9-8   Configuring sharing in a folder's Properties dialog box

When you share a folder, there's an option to hide it so that it doesn't appear on a browser list, as in My Network Places in Windows 2000 or Windows XP or Network Neighborhood in Windows 98 or Windows NT. To hide a share, place the $ sign just after its name. For instance, if the Share name text box contains the name Budget, you can hide the share by entering Budget$.

Configuring Printer Security

Printing is configured by using the Add Printer Wizard to set up a printer, and printers are often set up for sharing so that several users can access them. As a review, these are the general steps for using the Add Printer Wizard to set up and share a printer:

1. Click Start, point to Control Panel, point to Printers and Faxes, and click Add Printer.

2. Follow the directions for setting up the printer.

3. When you come to the Printer Sharing dialog box during setup, select to share the printer and enter a share name, such as the name of the printer or the room in which it's located.

4. Complete the setup steps and print a test page when you're finished.

Also, you can configure a printer that's already set up so that it can be shared over a network by following these general steps:

1. Open Control Panel, and point to Printers and Faxes.
2. Right-click the printer to configure and click Properties.
3. Click the Sharing tab.
4. Click to select the option to share the printer, and give the printer a name.
5. Click OK to close the Properties dialog box.

Following good security practices means you should configure permissions for all printers set up for sharing over a network. On the Security tab of the printer's Properties dialog box, you can modify the following default group permissions for the printer, for example:

- *Administrators, Server Operators, Print Operators*—Print, Manage Printers, and Manage Documents
- *Everyone*—Print
- *Creator Owner*—Manage Documents

You can also add and remove groups who have access to the printer. Table 9-4 lists the printer share permissions that can be set.

Table 9-4 Printer share permissions

Share permission	Access capability
Print	Users can connect to the shared printer, send print jobs, and manage their own print requests (such as pause, restart, resume, or cancel a print job).
Manage Documents	Users can connect to the shared printer, send print jobs, and manage any print job sent (including jobs sent by other users).
Manage Printers	Users have complete access to a printer share, including changing permissions, turning off sharing, configuring printer properties, and deleting the share.
Special Permissions	Similar to configuring special permissions for a folder, special permissions can be set up for a printer on the Advanced tab.

Clicking the Advanced button on the Security tab opens the Advanced Security Settings dialog box, where you can do the following:

- Configure special printer permissions for groups and users
- Add or remove a group or user
- Enable printer auditing
- Take ownership of a printer
- Display the effective permissions for a user or group

Similar to folders and files, special permissions enable you to fine-tune shared printer permissions, such as specifying that a group with Manage Printers permission can perform all functions except taking ownership.

To audit access to a shared printer for any user account or group, click the Auditing tab in the printer's Advanced Security Settings dialog box. For printer auditing to work, you must make sure object auditing is enabled, as you learned in Chapter 8. Object auditing for shared printing includes tracking successful and failed attempts to do the following:

- Print documents.
- Manage printers.
- Manage documents.
- Read printer share permissions.
- Change printer share permissions.
- Take ownership of the printer.

 In Hands-On Project 9-2, you learn more about configuring printer security.

NOTE

Configuring Registry Security

The Registry is at the core of Windows Server 2003 because it contains a multitude of critical settings, such as the following types:

- Software configuration settings
- Desktop settings
- Hardware settings
- User profile information
- Group policy settings
- Software licensing information
- Control Panel configurations
- System initialization information
- System services information

With the critical information stored on it, the Registry is a prime target for attackers and malware and needs to be protected carefully. Even inexperienced users can pose a serious risk if they have access to make Registry changes. One false move in the Registry can mean that a system doesn't boot or exhibits problems that can be difficult to trace.

Before discussing how to protect the Registry, it is important to review the essentials of its structure. The Registry is a hierarchical database made up of keys, subkeys, and entries. A **Registry key** is a folder in the left pane of the Registry Editor that can contain subkeys and entries. It is a category or division of information in the Registry. A **Registry subkey** can contain entries or other subkeys. You might think of a Registry key as a master folder in a directory hierarchy and a subkey as a subfolder. A **Registry entry** is the lowest level in the Registry and consists of three parts: a name, the data type, and the parameter setting. For example, in the entry ErrorControl:REG_DWORD:0, ErrorControl is the name, REG_DWORD is the data type, and 0 is the parameter setting. In this entry, the option to track errors is turned off if the setting is 0, and error tracking is turned on if the setting is 1. There are three data types (formats) for Registry entries: DWORD is hexadecimal, string is text data, and binary is two hexadecimal values.

Five root keys, also called subtrees, are at the top of the Registry hierarchy, which is indicated by the HKEY at the beginning of their names (see Figure 9-9). These keys store the following information:

- *HKEY_LOCAL_MACHINE*—Information on the server's hardware components, such as loaded drivers and their version levels, IRQ (interrupt request) lines used, setup configurations, BIOS version, and more.

- *HKEY_CURRENT_USER*—Information about the desktop setup for the account logged on to the server console, including background, taskbar, icons, fonts, and other information.

- *HKEY_USERS*—Profile information for each logged-on user, which might include a customized environment.

- *HKEY_CLASSES_ROOT*—Data to associate file extensions with programs; used as the default settings for all logged-on users.

- *HKEY_CURRENT_CONFIG*—Information about the current hardware profile, such as the monitor type, keyboard, and mouse. On most servers, only one default hardware profile is set up.

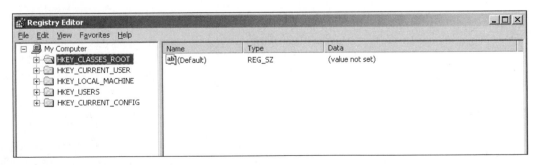

Figure 9-9   Root keys in the Registry Editor

Each root key represents an object that can have one of the three permissions listed in Table 9-5 assigned to it. You can also configure auditing on these root keys for additional protection.

Table 9-5 Registry permissions

Permission	Access capability
Full Control	Users can query entry values, set entry values, create subkeys, list and view subkeys and entries, delete Registry subkeys and entry values, control who can read the Registry, take ownership, and create links.
Read	Users can query entry values and list and view subkeys and entries.
Special Permissions	Similar to configuring special permissions for other objects, but it gives users special permissions that apply to Registry activities, such as creating subkeys and entering values.

To configure permissions and auditing, you use the Registry Editor. As is true for auditing other objects, when you audit Registry accesses and modifications, the information is stored in the Security log. Try Hands-On Project 9-3 to practice using Registry permissions and auditing.

Managing Services and Processes

Servers are always running a number of services, which vary depending on the number and types of installed components. A few examples of services include the following:

- *Alerter*—Sends notification of problems on the server
- *Eventlog*—Enables server events to be logged for later review or diagnosis, in case problems occur
- *IPSEC*—Enables IPSec security
- *Plug and Play*—Enables automatic detection of new hardware devices or devices that have changed

Allowing unneeded services to run reduces server efficiency and, as you've learned in previous chapters, leaves potential targets open to attackers. For the health of your server, disable services that aren't needed, and disable and remove services from sources you can't identify, especially if you suspect they are running malware. (Try disabling the service first to determine its effect and then remove it, if necessary.)

You should also plan to monitor services running on the server periodically by using the Computer Management tool (see Figure 9-10). You can open this tool from the Administrative Tools menu, or right-click My Computer and click Manage.

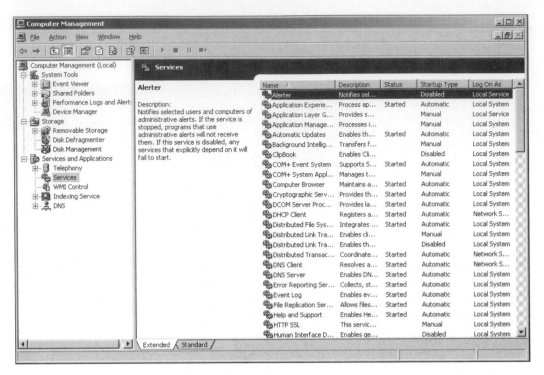

Figure 9-10   Monitoring services in the Computer Management tool

Services are displayed in the right pane, which contains the following columns:

- *Name*—Lists services alphabetically.

- *Description*—Contains a short description of each service; you can click a service name to read its description more easily in the blank area to the left of the columns.

- *Status*—Indicates the service's current status: Started means the service is running, Paused means it's started but not available to users, and a blank means the service is halted or hasn't been started.

- *Startup Type*—Shows how a service is started when the computer boots. Most services start automatically when the server is booted, but some are started manually only when they're needed. Services that aren't set to start automatically or manually are disabled.

- *Log On As*—Specifies the account the service is running under. Most services log on to a Local System account.

To disable a service that's already started, follow these general steps:

1. Double-click the service in the right pane of the Computer Management window to open the Properties dialog box.

2. Click the Dependencies tab to determine whether any other services depend on this service. (If they do, stop and disable those services.)

3. Click the General tab. In the Startup type drop-down list, click Disabled.

4. Stop the service by clicking the Stop button, and then click OK.

TIP

At times, you need to use or troubleshoot a service without making it available to users. Pausing a service takes it offline to be used only by the Administrators or Server Operators groups. To restart a paused service, right-click it and click Restart.

Another place to manage services is in the Msconfig utility. This utility doesn't show all the services listed in Computer Management, but it's worth knowing as an alternative way to view services and make your computer start faster. You can start Msconfig from the Start menu, and then click the Services tab. You can also view the Startup tab to see which programs start when you boot Windows Server 2003. If your server is slow to boot, consider removing nonessential startup programs that you can always start manually later, if needed.

Besides monitoring and disabling services, monitoring running processes is a good practice. You might need to stop a process if it represents a security threat to the server or is taking up excessive server resources. Processes that are taking too many resources can also be dropped in CPU priority. Task Manager is a useful utility for monitoring processes. These are the general steps for using it:

1. Right-click the taskbar and click Task Manager. (You can also press Ctrl+Alt+Delete and click Task Manager.)

2. Click the Processes tab, if necessary, and scroll to view all running processes. The CPU column shows how a process is affecting CPU resources and the User Name column shows who is running the process.

3. To stop a process, select it and click the End Process button. Click Yes after you see the warning about stopping a process.

4. If you want to give a resource-intensive process less CPU priority, right-click the process, point to Set Priority, and click BelowNormal or Low (depending on the importance of the process), as shown in Figure 9-11.

CAUTION

Don't set the priority to Realtime because this setting might hog CPU time.

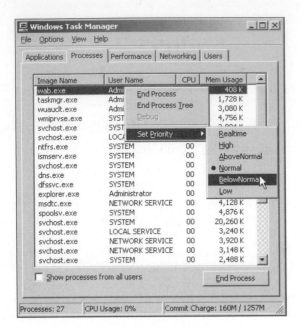

Figure 9-11   Resetting a process's priority

USING WINDOWS SERVER 2003 SECURITY CONFIGURATION TOOLS

Windows Server 2003 offers several tools for securing access to accounts and OS features. For example, you can use group policies to set up account access restrictions. You can also use the Security Configuration and Analysis MMC snap-in to create and apply security templates on a broad scale, and the Security Configuration Wizard helps you examine current settings interactively for security holes and configure essential security parameters. In this section, you learn how to use all these tools.

Configuring Account Security

An unsecured account can leave an opening for attackers to access a server. Windows Server 2003 addresses this issue with account policies, which focus on three levels of security (discussed in more detail in the following sections): passwords, account lockout, and Kerberos. In Hands-On Project 9-4, you get a chance to practice configuring these policies.

Password Security Policies

Every administrator knows that users can be careless with their passwords, even though the password is a basic line of defense. Besides teaching users not to give out passwords and to use strong passwords, another option is to configure password restrictions in Windows Server 2003. For example, with an account policy, you can require users to change passwords at regular intervals, such as every 30 days. If a user's password is compromised because of carelessness, at least you know it will be changed.

Some organizations require that all passwords be a minimum length, such as seven or eight characters. The longer a password is, the harder it is to guess. Another option is to have the OS "remember" passwords that have been used previously. For example, the system might be set to recall the most recent five passwords, which forces users to change to a different password instead of reusing the same one. An account lockout option can also be configured.

In Windows Server 2003, the password security options that can be enforced with account policies are the following:

- *Enforce password history*—Requires users to choose new passwords when they make a password change because the system can remember previously used passwords

- *Maximum password age*—Sets the maximum time allowed until a password expires

- *Minimum password age*—Specifies that a password must be used for a minimum amount of time before it can be changed

- *Minimum password length*—Requires that passwords be at least a certain number of characters

- *Passwords must meet complexity requirements*—Creates a filter of customized requirements that each account password must follow

- *Store password using reversible encryption*—Enables passwords to be stored in reversible encrypted format

Securing Administrator Accounts

Server administrators and other users with administrative functions, such as those in the Server Operators group, need to take extra precautions with their passwords. Obviously, a compromised Administrator account password can be a security nightmare. Here are some measures for protecting these accounts:

- Similar to the root account in Linux, the Windows Server 2003 Administrator account needs a hard-to-guess password. This password should be longer than eight characters, should not include common words, should not contain personal information, and should contain a mixture of uppercase and lowercase letters, numbers, and symbols.

- The password should be changed every month or sooner. Some organizations keep the Administrator password in a sealed envelope. Each time the envelope is opened and administrative tasks performed while using the password have been completed, the password is changed and placed in a new sealed envelope.

- Spend as little time as possible logged on to the Administrator account, and don't use it for ordinary activities, such as reading e-mail or writing a memo. When the task is completed, log off the Administrator account and log back on to your personal account. The less you use the Administrator account, the less likely it will attract the attention of attackers.

- Change the name of the Administrator account so that it's difficult for an attacker to determine which account has Administrator privileges. When you change this account's name, create a different account called Administrator with limited permissions; this account then acts as a decoy.

- On large networks using Active Directory, divide administrative functions between a domain administrator and an enterprise administrator. Use the No Override option in group policies to prevent the domain administrator from overriding an enterprise-level group policy that the enterprise administrator has set.

- Configure account lockout settings to help thwart password-guessing programs.

- Audit the Administrator account and check the Security log regularly.

Account Lockout Policy

In Windows Server 2003, you can lock out an account after a number of unsuccessful logon attempts. Even the true account owner can't access the account when it's locked out. The lockout can be set to release after a specified period of time or by intervention from the server administrator.

Some organizations have lockout go into effect after 5 to 10 unsuccessful logon attempts. More security-conscious organizations select three unsuccessful logon attempts. Further, the administrator can set lockout to release after a designated time, such as 30 minutes. The 30 minutes creates enough delay to discourage intruders, yet gives some leeway to a user who might have forgotten a recently changed password. The following are the available settings in the account lockout policy:

- *Account lockout duration*—Specify in minutes how long the system keeps an account locked out after reaching the specified number of unsuccessful logon attempts.

- *Account lockout threshold*—Set a limit to the number of unsuccessful logon attempts.

- *Reset account lockout count after*—Specify the number of minutes between two consecutive unsuccessful logon attempts to make sure the account isn't locked out too soon.

Kerberos Security

As you learned in Chapter 8, in Kerberos security, tickets are exchanged between the client requesting logon access and the authentication server granting access (also known as a Key Distribution Center [KDC]).

NOTE When Active Directory is installed, account policies enable Kerberos, which is the default authentication method. If Active Directory is not installed, Kerberos isn't included in account policies because the default authentication method is Windows NT LAN Manager version 2 (NTLMv2), which is not as strong as Kerberos.

The following options are available for configuring Kerberos:

- *Enforce user logon restrictions*—Enables Kerberos security, which is the default

- *Maximum lifetime for a service ticket*—Determines the maximum time in minutes that a service ticket can be used to access a service continuously in one service session

- *Maximum lifetime for a user ticket*—Determines the maximum time in hours that a ticket can be used in one continuous session for access to a computer or domain

- *Maximum lifetime for user ticket renewal*—Determines the maximum number of days the same Kerberos ticket can be renewed each time a user logs on

- *Maximum tolerance for computer clock synchronization*—Determines how long in minutes a client waits until synchronizing its clock with that of the server or Active Directory database it's accessing

Configuring Account Audit Policies

One way to track what happens through user accounts is to configure account audit policies. For example, you might want to track security changes to accounts or failed logon attempts. Some organizations monitor failed logon attempts for the Administrator account as one way to check whether intruders are attempting to access the server. This information can be important even if the Administrator account is set up as a decoy.

Further, accounts that access an organization's financial information are often audited routinely to protect their users as well as the information they access. Organizations can audit events such as the following:

- Account logon (and logoff) events

- Account management

- Directory service access

- Logon (and logoff) events at the local computer

- Object access

- Policy change

- Privilege use

- Process tracking

- System events

As with other types of object access auditing, each activity is audited in terms of success or failure of the event. For example, if account logon attempts are audited, a record is made each time someone logs on to an account successfully or unsuccessfully.

Auditing successful logons can create a mountain of data in the Security log, so make sure you maintain or back up this log regularly (see Chapter 8). Another approach is to use this auditing strategy only when needed, such as for month-end and year-end accounting periods or when you're specifically tracking account intrusions.

Using the Security Configuration and Analysis Tool

Even though you have been careful about setting up security and security policies, you might still have omissions or gaps you need to address. Also, as time passes, security requirements on a server or in a domain change. Windows Server 2003 offers the Security Configuration and Analysis MMC snap-in to help you monitor and analyze security. This tool works by creating a database for configuring a server and performing security checks. For example, if you're setting up the first domain controller hosting Active Directory, you can use this tool to configure the server for the Default Domain Policy. Later, you can use the tool to analyze the policy and determine whether you need to make modifications on the basis of increased server use. You can use the tool to import an existing or new security template you have created. The database can be built from an existing group policy or a security template, or you can construct one the first time you run the tool. After a database is in place for the domain or an OU, you should analyze it periodically to see whether it meets your server's changing security needs.

Configuring Security Templates

Windows Server 2003 includes a Security Templates MMC snap-in for creating security templates you can store in Active Directory and use with the Security Configuration and Analysis tool. This snap-in enables you to set up security templates for the following:

- Account policies
- Local policies
- Event log tracking policies
- Group restrictions
- Service access security
- Registry security
- File system security

This tool is particularly useful when you're managing many group policies or have several OUs to maintain that share a group policy. For example, you have 20 OUs set up in a domain. You want to use one group policy for eight of these OUs, a different one for seven of the OUs, and still another one for five of the OUs. In this situation, you could create three security templates to make managing group policies for these OUs easier and more efficient.

To create a new security template, use these general steps:

1. Make sure no default security template matches what you want to do. If there *is* a match, use the default security template.

2. Make sure the Security Templates and Security Configuration and Analysis snap-ins are installed in the MMC.

3. In the left pane, click the main folder under Security Templates (such as Windows\security\templates). Click Action, New Template from the menu. Enter a name for the new template, and then click OK. Double-click the new template in the left pane to open its Properties dialog box, and then configure the settings you want.

4. To import your template to an existing group policy, right-click the Security Configuration and Analysis snap-in in the left pane and click Open Database. Select a database to open and click Open. Right-click Security Configuration and Analysis in the left pane and click Import Template. In the Import Template dialog box, click the template file you created in Step 3 and click Open. Right-click Security Configuration and Analysis in the left pane again and click Configure Computer Now. Click OK.

Several default security templates come with Windows Server 2003, which you can import to an existing group policy instead of creating a new security template:

- *compatws*—Provides compatible workstation or server security settings for computers running Windows Server 2003, Windows 2000 Server, and Windows NT

- *DC security*—Default security for domain controllers

- *hisecdc*—Sets maximum (high security) protection for domain controllers running Windows Server 2003

- *hisecws*—Sets maximum (high security) protection for member servers (non-domain controllers) running Windows Server 2003

- *notssid*—Sets user security in terminal server applications

- *rootsec*—Consists of the default security settings used by the root domain in a tree

- *securedc*—Provides the recommended security for domain controllers, excluding file, folder, and Registry key security

- *securews*—Provides the recommended security for client workstations, excluding file, folder, and Registry key security

- *setup security*—Provides "out-of-the-box" security, which leaves most security settings not defined (so this template isn't recommended)

Configuring Security with the Security Configuration and Analysis Snap-in

As you see in the following activity, you can use the Security Configuration and Analysis tool to set up a preconfigured security template or one you have created with the Security Templates snap-in. You can also use this tool to create and analyze a security database.

Activity 9-4: Using the Security Configuration and Analysis Snap-in

Time Required: 20 minutes

Objective: Learn how to use the Security Configuration and Analysis snap-in.

Description: The Security Configuration and Analysis snap-in can be an invaluable way to configure security more thoroughly and analyze security on a server periodically. In this activity, you create a sample security database and then analyze it.

1. Click **Start**, **Run**, type **mmc**, and click **OK**.

2. Maximize the console window, if necessary, and click **File**, **Add/Remove Snap-in** from the menu.

3. Click the **Add** button, and then double-click **Security Configuration and Analysis**.

4. Click **Close**, and then click **OK**.

5. For this activity, create a practice database by right-clicking **Security Configuration and Analysis** in the left pane and clicking **Open Database**.

6. In the File name text box, enter a database name consisting of **Domain** plus your initials, and then click **Open**.

7. In the Import Template drop-down list, click **setup security.inf**, and then click **Open**. Wait a few moments for the system to generate the database. Notice in the right pane that you can now use this tool to configure your server (group policies) or analyze security settings.

8. To practice analyzing settings on a database, right-click **Security Configuration and Analysis** in the left pane and click **Analyze Computer Now**.

9. Make sure the error log file location is correct, and then click **OK**. The Analyzing System Security dialog box shows what's being checked.

10. Right-click **Security Configuration and Analysis** in the left pane and click **View Log File**.

11. The results written to the log are displayed in the right pane, as shown in Figure 9-12. Scroll through the log file to examine its contents. (Because you generated a sample database for demonstration purposes, your results don't necessarily reflect actual errors on your system.)

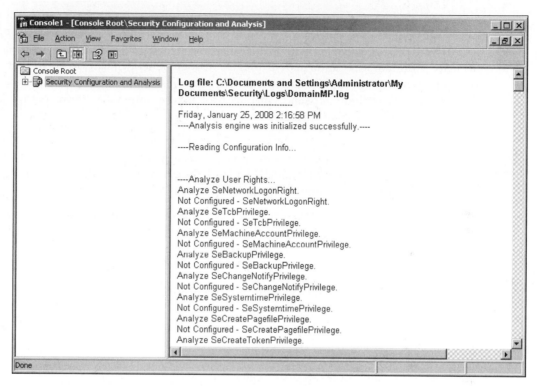

Figure 9-12 Viewing the analysis log file

12. Close the console window and click **No** if prompted to save your settings. Leave your system running for the next activity.

Using the Security Configuration Wizard

SP1 for Windows Server 2003 introduced the Security Configuration Wizard (SCW), which steps you through analyzing and configuring security settings on a server, and this wizard is also included with SP2. SCW helps you create a strong security policy to harden a server and reduce its attack surface.

Microsoft refers to these hardening tasks as security policies, but they aren't the same as GPOs you configure in the Group Policy Object Editor.

The SCW doesn't perform exactly the same security functions as the Security Configuration and Analysis tool, but there's some overlap. For example, both are used to configure security policies, enhance network security, and create a database for managing security. The Security Configuration and Analysis tool is broader in scope than SCW, in that you can configure templates to apply security at different levels, such as at the OU and domain levels. The Security Configuration and Analysis tool is also somewhat more complex to use because it's not in a wizard format.

SCW examines the roles a server plays and then tries to adjust security to match these roles. For example, it can disable unnecessary services and software, close network ports that aren't in use, and examine shared files and folders to help manage network access through Server Message Block (SMB) communications.

SCW is not installed by default. You must install it as a Windows Component from Control Panel's Add or Remove Programs (but SP1 or SP2 must have been installed earlier). After installation, SCW consists of a GUI wizard, a command-line tool, and a Security Configuration Database (SCD), which is a group of XML files that establish a security policy.

After SCW is installed, start the wizard from the Administrative Tools menu. You can use it to perform these main tasks:

- Create a new security policy.
- Edit an existing security policy.
- Apply an existing security policy.
- Roll back the last applied security policy.

The default action is to create a new security policy. When you select this option, SCW creates the SCD (see Figure 9-13). Next, the wizard identifies server roles, such as DNS, domain controller, file server, and others. You can disable or add roles. Next, you select client features to use, such as DNS client. You can also disable or add services. SCW also shows ports that are open and in use, so you can block ports that shouldn't be available. Next, SCW establishes what types of clients access the server, such as Windows NT, Windows XP, and so forth, so that it can configure the right network security. Finally, it steps you through creating a basic system audit policy.

The SCW command-line tool, Scwcmd, can be used to analyze and configure security on the local server or remote servers, which means you can configure security on several servers from one location. The advantage of Scwcmd is that it makes server administration easier and enables multiple servers to have consistent security settings. Another important advantage is that it has the transform option for converting the SCD's XML settings into GPOs that can be applied to domains or OUs in Active Directory. Therefore, you can customize

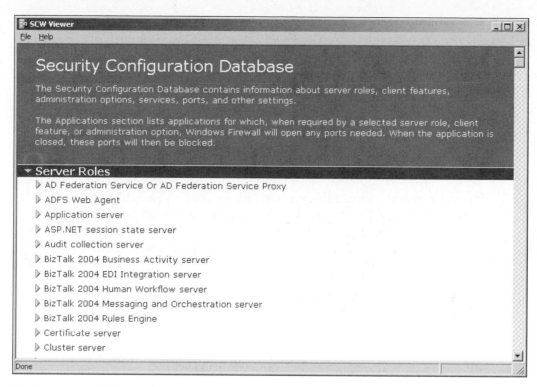

Figure 9-13 Creating the SCD

security for specific OUs. For example, if your company divides departments into specialized OUs, you can use Scwcmd to create different security settings for each OU, convert the settings to GPOs, and apply them.

When the SCW command-line tool is used to analyze security, you can view the results in an HTML display. You can also roll back SCW security policies to a previously configured group of security settings. You might need to roll back settings, for example, if you find some services or software can't function because of the security you have applied.

You should always try an SCW security configuration on a test server before you move it into production. Table 9-6 lists the options you can use with Scwcmd.

Table 9-6 Scwcmd options

Option	Description
analzye	Analyzes current security settings in the SCD
configure	Configures security settings and writes them to the SCD
register	Registers new SCD extensions
rollback	Rolls back security settings to previously configured settings
transform	Converts XML security settings in the SCD into a GPO
view	Displays current security settings in the SCD

CAUTION

If you use the transform option to convert security settings to a GPO, you can't use the rollback option to undo GPO settings. Also, some services, including firewall and IPSec services, might not respond correctly when you perform a rollback. Finally, don't apply SCD settings for a 32-bit computer to a 64-bit computer and vice versa.

CONFIGURING WINDOWS SERVER 2003 NETWORK SECURITY

Windows Server 2003 has network services that enable users to access the network and server resources remotely. These services include Remote Access Services and Virtual Private Network. Virtual Private Network services are particularly popular in organizations that need to provide secure remote access. You can configure protection for these network services by creating a remote access policy and profile and using Network Address Translation. In the following sections, you learn about configuring security for these network services.

Securing Routing and Remote Access Service and VPNs

Remote access to Windows Server 2003 is accomplished with **Routing and Remote Access Services (RRAS)**. RRAS actually contains two important methods for remote access: Remote Access Services (RAS) and Virtual Private Network services.

In addition to normal server functions, RAS servers can handle hundreds of simultaneous connections through dial-up, high-speed broadband, the Internet, and intranets for servicing remote access needs. RAS offers remote connectivity for MS-DOS and all versions of Windows clients.

Besides supporting different types of modems and communication equipment, Windows Server 2003 RAS is compatible with the following network transport and remote access protocols:

- TCP/IP
- Microsoft NWLink IPX/SPX/NetBIOS Compatible Transport Protocol
- NetBEUI
- Serial Line Internet Protocol (SLIP) and Compressed Serial Line Internet Protocol (CSLIP)
- Point-to-Point Protocol (PPP)
- Point-to-Point Tunneling Protocol (PPTP)
- Layer Two Tunneling Protocol (L2TP)

Another method of providing remote access to users is a virtual private network (VPN). A Windows Server 2003 server can be configured as a VPN server for access through the Internet, routers, and telecommunications lines, such as DSL, ISDN, SONET, and frame relay.

NOTE

VPNs are covered in extensive detail in *Guide to Tactical Perimeter Defense: Becoming a Security Network Specialist* (Course Technology, 2008, ISBN 1428356304).

To create RAS or VPN servers, open the Routing and Remote Access console from the Administrative Tools menu. As you go through the installation steps, you can install RAS or VPN, which are related remote access services. There's also the option to manage multiple RAS or VPN servers through a RADIUS server, as discussed in Chapter 8.

After the RAS or VPN server is installed, configuring a remote access policy is important for security. Windows Server 2003 uses a remote access policy plus the dial-in properties of user accounts for granting users the right to access the RAS or VPN server. Using a remote access policy reduces administrative overhead and offers more flexibility and control for authorizing connection attempts.

Granting remote access permission can still be configured in a user account's Properties dialog box with the Active Directory Users and Computers tool. The best practice, however, is to configure a remote access policy and then set remote access properties (through a profile) for accounts.

Elements of a Remote Access Policy

Before giving users remote access, you should evaluate the following components of your remote access policy:

- *Conditions*—This set of attributes (such as day and time restrictions or the group the connecting user belongs to) is compared with the connection attempt's attributes.

- *Permissions*—The combination of remote access permissions configured for the user account and the remote access policy. For example, if the user has been denied access in the user account properties, the connection attempt is rejected.

- *Profile*—Consists of settings such as multilink properties, authentication methods, and encryption settings.

When a user attempts a remote connection, the connection is first evaluated against the remote access policy's conditions, then the permissions, and finally the profile. The following steps outline what occurs when a user attempts to connect to the RAS or VPN server via a remote access policy:

1. First, the remote access policy is evaluated. If there's no policy, the connection attempt is rejected. The connection attempt must match the conditions of the policy or the connection attempt is rejected. If there are multiple policies, they

are evaluated in the order they appear under Remote Access Policies in the Routing and Remote Access console.

2. If the conditions of one of the policies match the connection attempt, the permissions are then evaluated.

3. If the user has been denied access, the connection attempt is rejected. If the user has been granted access, the settings configured for the user account and those in the profile are evaluated. If the settings match those of the connection attempt, remote access is granted. If the connection attempt doesn't match the settings, the connection is rejected.

4. If remote access permission is configured to be controlled through a remote access policy, the policy's permissions are evaluated and the user is granted or denied access. If the policy is set to grant remote access permission, the dial-in settings configured for the user account (if access is via dial-up) and the profile's settings are evaluated. Remote access is granted if the connection attempt matches the settings.

Creating and Configuring a Remote Access Policy and Profile

After RAS or VPN access is enabled, you use the Routing and Remote Access tool (accessed via Administrative Tools or as an MMC snap-in) to create a remote access policy and profile. Right-click Remote Access Policies (under the RAS or VPN server) in the left pane and click New Remote Access Policy to start the New Remote Access Policy Wizard.

You can configure several types of authentication for RAS or VPN servers, described in Table 9-7. You can use one or a combination of these authentication protocols, and if you use a combination, the RAS or VPN server negotiates with the client until it finds an authentication method that works.

Table 9-7   Authentication types

Authentication protocol	Description
Challenge Handshake Authentication Protocol (CHAP)	CHAP requires encrypted authentication between the server and the client but uses a generic form of password encryption, which enables computers running UNIX/Linux and other non-Microsoft OSs to connect to the RAS/VPN server.
Extensible Authentication Protocol (EAP)	EAP is used for clients accessing RAS through special devices, such as smart cards, token cards, and others that use certificate authentication. If you select this option, Certificate Services should be installed so that you can configure services or a particular device or certificate type. Certificate Services is installed as a Windows component by using Add or Remove Programs.

Table 9-7 Authentication types (continued)

Authentication protocol	Description
MS-CHAP v1 (also called CHAP with Microsoft extensions)	MS-CHAP v1 and MS-CHAP v2 are the defaults when you install RAS/VPN servers, which means clients must use MS-CHAP with PPP. MS-CHAP is a variation of CHAP that uses a challenge-and-response form of authentication along with encryption. Almost all Windows versions support MS-CHAP v1.
MS-CHAP v2 (also called CHAP with Microsoft extensions version 2)	Developed especially for VPNs, MS-CHAP v2 provides better authentication than MS-CHAP v1 because it requires the server and client to authenticate mutually. It also provides more sophisticated encryption by using different encryption keys for receiving and sending. Windows 2000, XP, Vista, and Server 2003 clients support MS-CHAP v2, and most Windows 9x clients can be updated to support it. VPNs attempt to use MS-CHAP v2 with a client, and then use MS-CHAP v1 if the client doesn't support version 2.
Password Authentication Protocol (PAP)	PAP can perform authentication but doesn't require it, which means that OSs without password encryption capabilities, such as MS-DOS, can connect to RAS/VPN servers.
Unauthenticated	This option isn't recommended because it means that no authentication takes place.

When you configure a remote access profile, the Edit Dial-in Profile dialog box has six tabs with configuration settings for RAS or VPN dial-in access. As a first step, always configure the options on the Authentication and Encryption tabs. Use other tabs to customize the profile for your situation, such as the Multilink tab if you're using multilink to aggregate ISDN lines. Table 9-8 describes the options in each tab.

NOTE RAS/VPN servers use Multilink Point-to-Point Protocol (MPPP) to aggregate multiple data streams into one logical network connection, which increases available bandwidth for users.

Table 9-8 Tabs in the Edit Dial-in Profile dialog box

Tab	Available settings
Dial-in Constraints	Configure idle and session timeouts, day and time restrictions, whether access is restricted to a single number, and whether access is restricted based on media.
IP	Configure how the client dialing in receives an IP address. IP filters can also be created to determine the protocols that clients can use.

Table 9-8   Tabs in the Edit Dial-in Profile dialog box (continued)

Tab	Available settings
Multilink	Configure whether a client can use multilink, the number of connections it can use, and at what point a link is dropped; you can also enable Bandwidth Allocation Protocol (BAP) for managing the network link.
Authentication	Configure the available authentication protocols.
Encryption	Configure the encryption level.
Advanced	Set RADIUS attributes that can further restrict access.

When you configure a remote access policy, you can select the data encryption options, described in Table 9-9, that specify which encryption protocol is used. The available encryption protocols are IP Security, Microsoft Point-to-Point Encryption, and Data Encryption Standard. You've already learned about IPSec and DES (or the 3DES enhancement) in Chapter 6. **Microsoft Point-to-Point Encryption (MPPE)** is a starting-to-ending-point encryption technique that uses special encryption keys varying from 40 to 128 bits. As with authentication protocols, you can use one or a combination of the RAS encryption options in Table 9-9 to match what the client is using.

Table 9-9   RAS encryption options

Encryption option	Description
Basic encryption (MPPE 40 bit)	Enables clients using 40-bit encryption key MPPE (available in Windows OSs), or clients can use 56-bit IPSec or DES encryption.
No encryption	Enables clients to connect without using data encryption.
Strong encryption (MPPE 56-bit)	Enables clients using 56-bit encryption key MPPE, 56-bit IPSec encryption, or DES.
Strongest (MPPE 128 bit)	Enables clients using 56-bit IPSec, 3DES, or MPPE 128-bit encryption.

After a remote access policy is created, it's listed under Remote Access Policies in the Routing and Remote Access console. Policies are evaluated in the order in which they appear. To change the evaluation order, right-click a policy and use the Move Up or Move Down options.

Configuring NAT

Network Address Translation (NAT) serves two important functions:

- It enables an organization to assign its own IP addresses automatically on an internal network without having to set up many globally unique addresses for use over external networks.

- It protects computers on an internal network by hiding their IP addresses; computers on external networks, including the Internet, can't view internal computers' IP addresses.

For a review of NAT, refer to *Guide to Tactical Perimeter Defense: Becoming a Security Network Specialist* (Course Technology, 2008, ISBN 1428356304).

NOTE

NAT uses a pool of private addresses for the internal network, which is a network separated from the outside world by a router or firewall, for example. Because the outside world can't view these internal addresses, there's no need to have a large pool of IP addresses that can also be used over an external network. Only one or very few globally unique IP addresses are needed for external communication. As a result, fewer IPv4 global addresses are needed. One reason for developing IPv6 was to allow more globally unique IP addresses. The widespread use of NAT has meant that organizations can delay changing to IPv6.

In a typical installation, NAT acts like a firewall so that the outside world (external networks) sees only one address, such as 129.52.0.1. However, the internal network contains many computers with addresses such as 192.168.22.1, 192.168.22.2, 192.168.22.3, 192.168.22.4, and so on. When the computer with IP address 192.168.22.4 sends a communication to the outside world, it's translated into the address 129.52.0.1. (NAT can also use a set of addresses for translation to the outside world.)

When RAS or VPN services are enabled, you can also configure NAT for networks offering remote access through RRAS by following these steps in the Routing and Remote Access console:

1. In the left pane, expand Routing and Remote Access and the RAS/VPN server.

2. Click to expand IP Routing. Right-click General and click New Routing Protocol.

3. Double-click NAT/Basic Firewall in the list of routing protocols, and then click OK.

4. In the left pane, click NAT/Basic Firewall. Right-click the interface (such as Remote Router) and click Properties.

5. In the interface's Properties dialog box, click the NAT/Basic Firewall tab. For Internet access, for example, click Public interface connected to the Internet. Under this section, select the options Enable NAT on this Interface and Enable a basic firewall on this Interface.

6. To configure the firewall portion, click the Services and Ports tab and select the service to enable through the firewall, such as IP Security.

7. Close the Routing and Remote Access console and save the changes.

9

CHAPTER SUMMARY

❑ Many of the components you configure in Windows Server 2003 for a secure server and network environment represent objects, such as folders, files, and printers.

❑ Windows Server 2003 supports FAT16, FAT32, and NTFS file systems. NTFS has better security capabilities than FAT16 and FAT32.

❑ FAT16, FAT32, and NTFS offer folder and file attributes as a form of basic security, such as the Read-only and Hidden attributes. However, NTFS adds the Encrypting File System via the Encrypt attribute, which increases protection for sensitive data.

❑ NTFS includes folder, file, and share permissions for controlling who can access information and what they can do with the information. If the standard permissions aren't adequate for your security requirements, you can set special permissions to customize security measures.

❑ With folder and file auditing, you can track who has accessed folders and files and whether they have been modified.

❑ Permissions can be applied to printers and the Registry to control access and management.

❑ Good security practices for Windows Server 2003 include disabling unneeded services and controlling problem processes.

❑ User account security includes configuring password restrictions, account lockout settings, Kerberos authentication, and account auditing.

❑ The Security Configuration and Analysis tool and Security Configuration Wizard are tools for configuring security and security policies.

❑ Networks that use RAS or VPN network services should have a remote access policy and profile for strong security. Security for these network services also entails using NAT to conceal internal network addresses.

KEY TERMS

Encrypting File System (EFS) — A file system that enables users to encrypt the contents of a folder or a file so that it can be accessed only by using the private key code of the user who encrypted the folder or file.

Microsoft Point-to-Point Encryption (MPPE) — A starting-to-ending-point encryption technique that uses special encryption keys from 40 to 128 bits.

Registry entry — A parameter in the Registry stored as a value in hexadecimal, binary, or text format.

Registry key — A category of information in the Windows Server 2003 Registry, such as hardware or software.

Registry subkey — A key within a Registry key, similar to a subfolder under a folder.

Routing and Remote Access Services (RRAS) — A group of Windows Server 2003 services that provide routing capabilities and remote access so that off-site workstations can access a Windows Server 2003 network through telecommunication lines, the Internet, or an intranet.

REVIEW QUESTIONS

1. An NTFS file is encrypted by setting which of the following?
   a. a block
   b. an attribute
   c. a permission
   d. a protection ID

2. When you back up encrypted files, you should also back up which of the following?
   a. archive ACLs
   b. search indexes
   c. retrospective permissions
   d. encryption keys

3. What tool is used to configure an auditing policy in the Default Domain Policy?
   a. Group Policy Object Editor
   b. Domain Policy Audit tool
   c. Active Directory Users and Computers tool
   d. Active Directory Domain Manager tool

4. What happens when a user attempts to access the RAS server and there's no remote access policy?
   a. The user is given full access with no restrictions.
   b. The user has full access to the RAS server but not to other network servers.
   c. The user is allowed limited remote access through a guest account.
   d. The connection attempt is denied.

5. Which of the following is an authentication type in RRAS? (Choose all that apply.)
   a. MAP
   b. EAP
   c. CHAP
   d. PAP

6. Which of the following is a tunneling protocol typically used by a Windows Server 2003 VPN? (Choose all that apply.)

   a. NetBEUI

   b. TSLIP

   c. L2TP

   d. PPTP

7. You belong to a group called Sales that has Write permission for the Marketing folder set to Deny. However, on your user account, Write permission for the Marketing folder is set to Allow. What access do you really have to the Marketing folder?

   a. You can't create files in the folder, write to files, append data to files, delete files, or create subfolders.

   b. You have permissions to create files in the folder, write to files, append data to files, delete files, or create subfolders.

   c. You can modify the contents of files but can't create new files or subfolders.

   d. You can only create subfolders under the Marketing folder.

8. Where do you set permissions on a file?

   a. Ownership tab in the file's Properties dialog box

   b. Security tab in the file's Properties dialog box

   c. ACL Configure tool

   d. Permissions Wizard

9. Which of the following is a standard permission used with the Registry? (Choose all that apply.)

   a. Modify Value

   b. Modify Key

   c. Read

   d. Full Control

10. What tool do you use to disable an unneeded service?

    a. Computer Management tool

    b. Service Control tool

    c. My Computer

    d. Service Manager snap-in

11. Which of the following is a printer permission? (Choose all that apply.)

    a. Manage Documents

    b. Full Control

    c. Manage Printers

    d. Control Print Jobs

12. A service in paused status means which of the following?

    a. The service has overrun the CPU.

    b. The service is available only to someone with Administrator or Server Operator privileges.

    c. The service is available only to a local computer user, not a remote user.

    d. The service is working in real time.

13. The bank examiners have just done a security review and are concerned that there are no restrictions on user account passwords for the Accounting server. Which of the following is a restriction that can be configured? (Choose all that apply.)

    a. password history

    b. password length

    c. password complexity

    d. password age

14. You suspect that unauthorized users are trying to access critical accounts, such as the Administrator account and the office manager's account. How can you monitor these accounts?

    a. Use the Security Monitor Wizard.

    b. Use account auditing for successful and failed logons.

    c. Use account tracking to examine logon ports.

    d. Use IPSec access attempt statistics.

15. You need to create a special set of group policies for the Research and Testing OU in your organization. Which of the following tools can assist you with this task? (Choose all that apply.)

    a. Security Templates snap-in

    b. Domain and OU Security tool

    c. Local Domain Configuration snap-in

    d. Security Configuration and Analysis snap-in

16. Which of the following types of data encryption can be configured with Windows Server 2003 RAS and VPN services? (Choose all that apply.)

    a. Microsoft Point-to-Point Encryption (MPPE)

    b. Data Encryption Standard (DES)

    c. IP Security (IPSec)

    d. TCP Point-to-Port (TPP)

9

17. In Windows Server 2003 with Active Directory, which of the following acts as a key distribution center for Kerberos?

    a. the first computer set up with Active Directory

    b. the last computer set up with Active Directory

    c. the tree manager

    d. each domain controller

18. Which of the following events can be audited? (Choose all that apply.)

    a. directory service access

    b. policy changes

    c. system events

    d. account management

19. You upgraded a Windows 2000 Server computer to Windows Server 2003, and one of its volumes is still configured for FAT32. You want to make it an NTFS volume for security reasons. Which of the following utilities can be used to convert the file system?

    a. Server Manager

    b. Disk Defragmenter

    c. the convert command

    d. the ntfs /c command

20. After you encrypt certain files and folders, how can you tell which ones are encrypted?

    a. Their names appear in color.

    b. Their names appear in italic.

    c. They are moved to the Private Encrypt folder automatically.

    d. They are flagged as hidden.

HANDS-ON PROJECTS

HANDS-ON PROJECTS

Hands-On Project 9-1: Configuring Special Permissions

Time Required: 15 minutes

Objective: Configure special permissions for a folder to give a group extra access.

Description: Sometimes regular NTFS permissions don't enable you to create exactly the type of access you want on a folder. In this project, you set up special permissions for the Server Operators group on the Utilities folder you used in Activities 9-2 and 9-3.

1. Open My Computer, and find the Utilities folder you created in Activity 9-2. Right-click the folder and click **Properties**.

2. Click the **Security** tab, and then click the **Advanced** button.

3. Click **Server Operators** in the Permissions entries list box, and then click the **Edit** button to open the Permission Entry dialog box.

4. Notice that the Server Operators group doesn't have permission to delete subfolders and files. You want them to have this permission so that they can remove old utilities and keep the Utilities folder contents up to date. Click the **Allow** check box for the Delete Subfolders and Files permission, and then click **OK**.

5. Click **OK** in the Advanced Security Settings dialog box, and then click **OK** in the Properties dialog box.

6. Close My Computer, and leave your system running for the next project.

Hands-On Project 9-2: Configuring Printer Security

Time Required: 15 minutes

Objective: Set up security on a shared printer.

Description: It's vital to configure security on a shared printer so that you can control who has access and ensure uninterrupted productivity for the printer's users. In this project, you remove the Everyone group's access to a printer and give access to the Performance Monitor Users group, which is the group of users who have permission to use Performance Monitor so that they can analyze server and network performance. You also set up auditing of failed printing attempts for the domain local group you created. A printer should already be set up in Windows Server 2003.

1. Click **Start**, point to **Control Panel**, and point to **Printers and Faxes**. Right-click the printer to configure and click **Properties**.

2. Click the **Security** tab. What security is set up already? Record your observations:

   _____

   _____

3. Click the **Everyone** group and click **Remove**. Notice that the Name text box is then updated to reflect this change.

4. Click the **Add** button, click the **Advanced** button, and click **Find Now**. Scroll to and double-click the **Performance Monitor Users** group. (You might need to expand the Name (RDN) column heading to see the entire group name.) Click **OK**. What permissions are given to this group by default?

   _____

5. Verify that the **Allow** check box is selected for the Print permission.

6. Click the **Advanced** button, and then click the **Auditing** tab.

7. Click **Add**, click the **Advanced** button, click **Find Now**, double-click the **Performance Monitor Users** group, and then click **OK**.

8. Make sure **This printer and documents** is selected.

9. Click the **Failed** check box for the Print permission (see Figure 9-14), and then click **OK**. Notice that Failed is also selected for Read Permissions automatically. What information now appears in the Auditing entries list box?

_____

_____

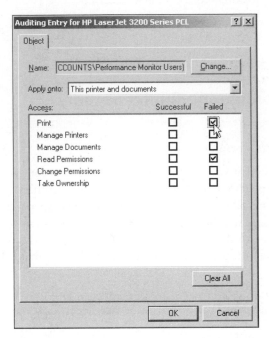

Figure 9-14   Configuring shared printer auditing

10. Click **OK**. If there's a message that auditing is not turned on as a group policy, how would you enable it?

_____

_____

11. Click **OK**.

HANDS-ON
PROJECTS

Hands-On Project 9-3: Configuring Registry Security

Time Required: 15 minutes

Objective: Verify Registry security and configure auditing.

Description: The Registry has tentacles reaching into every corner of Windows Server 2003. Make sure you configure Registry security and auditing to protect Windows Server

2003 from attackers and malware as part of a healthy computer initiative. In this project, you check existing Registry permissions and configure Registry auditing. Also, you gain practice using the Registry Editor.

1. Click **Start**, **Run**, type **regedit** in the Open text box, and click **OK** to open the Registry Editor.

2. Right-click **HKEY_LOCAL_MACHINE** and click **Permissions**.

3. Click each group or user in the Group or user names list box, and notice the permissions they are granted. Record the groups and their permissions:

_____

_____

_____

_____

4. In your organization, users in the Server Operators group typically modify some Registry values when needed for specific hardware, so you need to add this group for this limited change capability. Click **Add**, click **Advanced**, click **Find Now**, double-click **Server Operators**, and click **OK**.

5. Notice that Server Operators is given Special Permissions by default. Click **Advanced** to open the Advanced Security Settings for HKEY_LOCAL_MACHINE dialog box. Click **Server Operators**, and then click **Edit**.

6. Click to select the **Allow** check box for Query Value, Set Value, Enumerate Subkeys, and Notify, and leave Allow selected for the Read Control permission (see Figure 9-15).

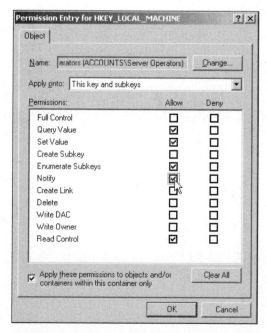

Figure 9-15 Configuring Registry special permissions

7. Click the **Apply these permissions to objects and/or containers within this container only** check box, and then click **OK**.

8. Click the **Auditing** tab.

9. Click **Add**. Click **Advanced**, click **Find Now**, double-click **Server Operators**, and click **OK**. Click the **Successful** and **Failed** check boxes for Query Value and Set Value. With these settings, you can track this group's activities by viewing the Security log.

10. Click **OK**, and then click **OK** again.

11. Click **OK** to return to the Registry Editor. Right-click the other root keys and click **Permissions** to verify their security settings.

12. Close the Registry Editor when you're done.

HANDS-ON
PROJECTS

Hands-On Project 9-4: Configuring Account Policies

Time Required: 30 minutes

Objective: Configure account policies for security.

Description: A fundamental way to protect a server is with account policies. In this project, you configure account policies for password restrictions, account lockout, Kerberos, and auditing in the Default Domain Policy.

1. Click **Start**, **Run**, type **mmc** in the Open text box, and click **OK**.

2. Click **File, Add/Remove Snap-in** from the menu.

3. Click the **Add** button, click **Group Policy Object Editor**, and then click **Add**.

4. Click the **Browse** button, and then click **Default Domain Policy**. Click **OK**, and then click **Finish**.

5. Click **Close**, and then click **OK**.

6. Maximize the console windows. In the left pane, click to expand **Default Domain Policy**, **Computer Configuration**, **Windows Settings**, and **Security Settings**, and then click **Account Policies** (see Figure 9-16).

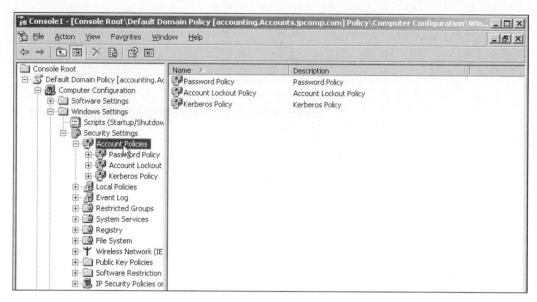

Figure 9-16 Configuring account policies

7. In the left pane, click **Password Policy**. In the right pane, notice the policies you can configure. Double-click **Enforce password history**. Verify that **Define this policy setting** is selected. Set the password history to remember the past **20** passwords (24 is the default), and then click **OK**.

8. Double-click **Maximum password age**. Verify that **Define this policy setting** is selected, and change the days text box to **30** (the default is 42 days). Click **OK**.

9. Double-click **Minimum password length**. Verify that **Define this policy setting** is selected, and change the number of characters from the default of 7 to **8** (see Figure 9-17). Click **OK**.

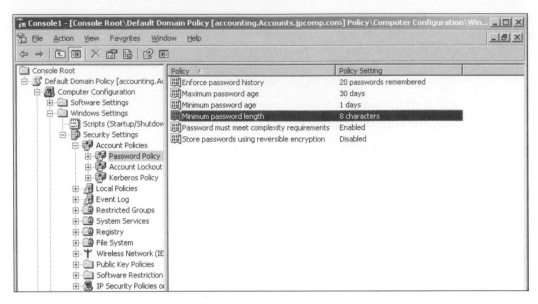

Figure 9-17   Configuring a password policy

10. In the left pane, click **Account Lockout Policy**. In the right pane, double-click **Account lockout duration** (not defined by default).

11. Verify that **Define this policy setting** is selected. Enter **40** in the minutes text box, and click **OK**.

12. Record the values in the Suggested Value Changes message box:

_____

_____

13. Click **OK** in the Suggested Value Changes message box. Notice that the suggested values are now implemented as account policies.

14. In the left pane, click **Kerberos Policy**. In the right pane, double-click **Maximum lifetime for service ticket**. Verify that **Define this policy setting** is selected. Enter **720** in the minutes text box, and then click **OK**.

15. Record the value in the Suggested Value Changes message box:

_____

16. Click **OK** in the Suggested Value Changes message box, and then notice that the suggested value is implemented.

17. In the left pane, click to expand **Local Policies**, if necessary, and then click **Audit Policy**.

18. In the right pane, double-click **Audit account logon events**. Verify that **Define these policy settings** is selected. Click to clear the **Success** check box, and then

click to select the **Failure** check box. Click **Apply** to have these settings take effect immediately, and then click **OK**.

19. Double-click **Audit object access**. Verify that **Define these policy settings** is selected as well as the **Success** and **Failure** check boxes, and then click **OK**. This setting is important because it enables you to audit object access, such as attempts to access files, the Registry, shared printers, and so forth.

20. Close the console window, and then click **Yes** to save the settings.

21. Enter **DomainSecurity.msc** as the filename, and then click **Save**.

CASE PROJECTS

CASE PROJECTS

Case Project 9-1: Configuring Security for Windows Server 2003 Servers

9

Through the work you've done in previous chapters, Green Globe already has a written security policy. Now it's time to apply these security policy measures to Green Globe's Windows Server 2003 systems.

- Explain how you would configure security on key Windows Server 2003 folders and files, including system folders, application folders, and user account folders and their contents. Make sure the security you configure matches Green Globe's written security policy.

- In light of Green Globe's security policy, how would you protect the Administrator account with tools in Windows Server 2003?

- Green Globe is designating one person in each department and another as a backup to manage network printers. What security should be given to these printer managers?

- What tools can Green Globe use to analyze its current security settings and to develop customized default domain security and security for its OUs on the basis of the company's written security policy? What are the special capabilities of the tools you recommend?

- How might setting up a VPN match the security needs specified in Green Globe's written security policy?

When you're finished, collect your case projects from all previous chapters and incorporate them into a written proposal for Green Globe to submit to your instructor. Make sure you include your research and worksheets at the end as appendixes, unless instructed otherwise, and check that your paper conforms to your school's or instructor's writing guidelines. Include a network diagram showing the physical and logical topology of your design; a list of all hardware, software, and other equipment needed with approximate costs; and any other relevant information and supporting documentation.

A

SC0-471 OBJECTIVES

Table A-1 maps the Strategic Infrastructure Security objectives in the Security Certified Professional's (SCP's) SC0-471 course to the corresponding chapter and section title where the objectives are covered in this book. Major sections are listed after the chapter number, and applicable subsections are shown in parentheses. Because the SCP exams undergo periodic updating and revising, you should check the SCP Web site for the latest developments at *www.securitycertified.net*.

Table A-1 Objectives-to-chapter mapping

Domain objective	Chapter and section(s)
Domain 1.0: Analyzing Packet Structures	
1.1: Describe the Concepts of Signature Analysis	Chapter 4: Understanding Signature Analysis Chapter 4: Understanding Packet-Capturing Techniques
1.2: Examine the Common Vulnerabilities and Exposures (CVE)	Chapter 4: Examining the Common Vulnerabilities and Exposures Standard
1.3: Examine Normal Network Traffic Signatures	Chapter 4: Detecting Network Traffic Signatures (Normal Network Traffic Signatures)
1.4: Examine Abnormal Network Traffic Signatures	Chapter 4: Detecting Network Traffic Signatures (Abnormal Network Traffic Signatures) Chapter 4: Identifying Suspicious Events
Domain 2.0: Creating Security Policies	
2.1: Examine the Concepts of Security Policies	Chapter 2: What Makes a Good Security Policy? Chapter 2: Developing a Security Policy (Seven Steps to Creating a Security Policy) Chapter 2: Handling Security Incidents (Updating the Security Policy)
2.2: Identify Security Policy Categories	Chapter 2: Developing a Security Policy (Identifying Security Policy Categories)
2.3: Define Incident Handling Procedures	Chapter 2: Handling Security Incidents
Domain 3.0: Performing Risk Analysis	
3.1: Examine the Concepts of Risk Analysis	Chapter 1: Risk Analysis Concepts
3.2: Define the Methods of Risk Analysis	Chapter 1: Risk Analysis Methods
3.3: Describe the Process of Risk Analysis	Chapter 1: Risk Analysis Process
3.4: Examine Techniques to Minimize Risk	Chapter 1: Techniques for Minimizing Risk
Domain 4.0: Ethical Hacking Techniques	
4.1: Perform Network Scanning and Discovery	Chapter 3: Network Reconnaissance
4.2: Describe Network Viruses, Trojans, and Worms	Chapter 3: Malicious Code Attacks
4.3: Examine Social Engineering	Chapter 3: Network Reconnaissance (Social-Engineering Techniques)
4.4: Describe Privilege Escalation	Chapter 3: Network Attack Techniques (Privilege Escalation and Unauthorized Access)
4-5: Examine the Concepts of Denial of Service	Chapter 3: Network Attack Techniques (Denial-of-Service Attacks)
4.6: Exploiting Password Weaknesses	Chapter 3: Network Attack Techniques (Password Exploitation)

Table A-1   Objectives-to-chapter mapping (continued)

Domain objective	Chapter and section(s)
Domain 5.0: Internet and WWW Security	
5.1: Identify and Define the Weak Points in the Structure of the Internet	Chapter 6: Examining the Structure of the Internet (Understanding Weak Points in the Internet's Structure)
5.2: Define Web Site Attack Techniques	Chapter 6: Examining Web Attack Techniques (Attack Techniques Against Web Servers)
5.3: Define Attack Techniques of Web Users	Chapter 6: Examining Web Attack Techniques (Attack Techniques Against Web Users)
5.4: Hardening Web Servers	Chapter 6: Hardening Web and Internet Resources (Hardening Web Servers)
5.5: Hardening DNS Servers	Chapter 6: Hardening Web and Internet Resources (Hardening DNS Servers)
Domain 6.0: Cryptography	
6.1: Historical Cryptography	Chapter 5: Reviewing Historical Cryptography Techniques, Examining Cryptography Standards
6.2: Cryptographic Algorithms	Chapter 5: Components of Cryptographic Protocols, Modern Cryptanalysis Techniques
6.3: Private Key Exchange	Chapter 5: Components of Cryptographic Protocols (Key Management)
6.4: Public Key Exchange	Chapter 5: Components of Cryptographic Protocols (Key Management)
6.5: Message Authentication	Chapter 5: Components of Cryptographic Protocols (Hashing Algorithms, Digital Signatures)
Domain 7.0: Hardening Linux Computers	
7.1: Linux Filesystem and Navigation	Chapter 7: Understanding the Linux File System and Navigation
7.2: Secure System Management	Chapter 7: Examining Secure System Management
7.3: User and Filesystem Security Administration	Chapter 7: Managing User and File System Security
7.4: Secure Network Communications	Chapter 7: Examining Network Configuration Security
7.5: Security Scripting	Chapter 7: Examining Secure System Management, Securing Linux
7.6: Linux Security Tools	Chapter 7: Examining Secure System Management, Examining Network Configuration Security, Securing Linux

Table A-1   Objectives-to-chapter mapping (continued)

Domain objective	Chapter and section(s)
Domain 8.0: Hardening Windows Server 2003	
8.1: Windows Server 2003 Infrastructure Security	Chapter 8: Examining the Windows Server 2003 Infrastructure (Managing Groups)
8.2: Examine Windows Server 2003 Authentication	Chapter 8: Understanding Windows Server 2003 Authentication
8.3: Implement Windows Server 2003 Security Configuration Tools	Chapter 9: Using Windows Server 2003 Security Configuration Tools
8.4: Configure Windows Server 2003 Resource Security	Chapter 9: Configuring Windows Server 2003 Resource Security
8.5: Configure Windows Server 2003 Auditing and Logging	Chapter 8: Understanding Windows Server 2003 Auditing and Logging
8.6: Configure Windows Server 2003 Network Security	Chapter 9: Configuring Windows Server 2003 Network Security

B

ADDITIONAL RESOURCES

Information security is a rapidly changing field. To keep up with the latest developments, you should visit the Web sites and other resources mentioned in this appendix regularly. Many sites offer white papers, research papers, and other background information on topics such as firewalls, packet filtering, authentication, and encryption. You can find policy hints and resources, disaster-planning guides, and tools to help you do your job. In addition, you should visit these sites to learn about the latest threats. Bugs, security holes, and patches to plug them will be available online long before you read about them in a book. You can also sign up for e-mail alerts at many of the resources listed here for news of new threats and current trends as soon as they are discovered.

Security Resources

New threats surface daily, and you need ways to keep up with them. The Web sites in Table B-1 contains resources you can use to enhance your skills and knowledge.

Table B-1   Helpful sites for IT security professionals

Web site	Description
Common Vulnerabilities and Exposures (CVE), *www.cve.mitre.org*	CVE, a dictionary of publicly known security vulnerabilities, helps vendors share information about vulnerabilities so that they can work together.
Symantec Security Response, *www.symantec.com/security_response/index.jsp*	Symantec maintains extensive information, including an outstanding virus encyclopedia and detailed assessments of other security threats.
SANS Internet Storm Center, *http://isc.sans.org/*	This site, which is affiliated with SANS, specializes in how to respond to intrusions, incidents, and security alerts. Maps and charts show security breaches reported by geographic region. The site also includes a list of current attack trends, such as frequently attacked ports and recently reported malicious software.
The Center for Internet Security, *www.cisecurity.org*	This nonprofit organization is devoted to developing security standards it calls "benchmarks." Benchmarks are available for Windows, Linux, UNIX, and other OSs. Benchmarks are also listed for network devices and applications.
System Administration, Networking and Security (SANS) Institute, *www.sans.org*	This research and education organization focuses on network security. SANS conducts seminars and workshops on security around the country.
The Cert Coordination Center, *www.cert.org*	This group, affiliated with the Carnegie-Mellon Institute, lists security alerts, incident notes, and vulnerabilities on its home page. CERT also offers tips and articles about aspects of network security and training courses and has developed many computer and network security solutions.

Table B-1 Helpful sites for IT security professionals (continued)

Web site	Description
The National Institute of Standards and Technology (NIST), *www.nist.gov* NIST Computer Security Division, Computer Security Resource Center (CSRC), *http://csrc.nist.gov*	NIST is a U.S. federal agency with the mission to develop and promote measurements, standards, and technology to enhance productivity, facilitate trade, and improve the quality of life. The Computer Security Division addresses information security topics. In addition, NIST Special Publications are available for many computer topics and can be useful as standardized guidelines.
Internet Assigned Numbers Authority (IANA), *www.iana.org*	IANA assigns and maintains number assignments for the Internet, including port numbers and protocol numbers. Also coordinates DNS and IP addressing.
Internet Engineering Task Force (IETF), *www.ietf.org/home.html*	The IETF is an international body of network designers, vendors, operators, and researchers cooperatively working toward the Internet's evolution and smooth operation. RFCs are managed primarily by the IETF.
IEEE Computer Society, *www.ieee.org/portal/site*	This organization is a major international membership association for computer professionals. Membership isn't free, but the organization offers online courses, information, and professional networking opportunities for members.
Internet Corporation for Assigned Names and Numbers (ICANN), *www.icann.org*	ICANN is responsible for global coordination of the Domain Name System and its unique identifiers. An initiative is currently underway to transition the Internet domain name and addressing system to the private sector.

INFORMATION RESOURCES

You should also join newsgroups and mailing lists for IT professionals as a way to network with your peers and learn from their experiences. Sometimes you run into a problem that you can't solve, despite poring through manuals and textbooks, searching the Internet, and running numerous tests. Table B-2 lists some resources to check.

Table B-2   Information resources

Web site	Description
SecurityFocus Mailing Lists, *www.securityfocus.com/archive*	SecurityFocus runs security-related mailing lists on topics from intrusion detection to firewalls to honeypots. One of the best features is being able to search archived messages by topic without having to subscribe. However, by joining a list, you can get news daily.
SANS Computer Security Newsletters and Digests, *www.sans.org/newsletters/*	The newsletters published by the SANS Institute include a weekly News Bites publication and a weekly Security Alert Consensus listing current security threats and countermeasures. SANS has added a monthly newsletter called OUCH!, which is a consensus security awareness report for end users.
Symantec Security Response Weblog, *www.symantec.com/enterprise/security_ response/weblog/*	Symantec maintains a forum about a wide array of security topics open to both the general public and technical experts. Symantec staff post information on the blog occasionally, although they don't usually answer questions, and information is offered on an as-is basis.
National Security Agency, *www.nsa.gov/snac/*	The NSA offers configuration guides for OSs, applications, database servers, Voice over IP (VoIP), and other products.
SANS Institute, *www.sans.org/resources/policies*	SANS offers consensus papers on security policy development, including templates and samples.
Microsoft, *www.microsoft.com/security/default.mspx*	Microsoft offers downloads, updates, and security information for its products. You can find security guides for Windows Server, Office products, client OSs, and applications such as Exchange Server. Security newsletters are available via e-mail.
Forum of Incident Response and Security Teams (FIRST), *www.first.org*	This group is a coalition of security incident response teams working in government, commercial, and academic organizations that seek to promote rapid reaction to security incidents by coordinating communication and sharing information.

Table B-2 Information resources (continued)

Web site	Description
TechRepublic, *http://techrepublic.com.com/*	TechRepublic offers white papers, blogs, Webcasts, and job postings for IT professionals. Many other downloads are available, including templates, checklists, and software tools.
Network World, *www.networkworld.com/*	Network World is a periodical covering a variety of current IT topics, including vendor news, threats, and reports on global security trends. You can access blogs, podcasts, RSS feeds, and Webcasts.
Linux Security, *www.linuxsecurity.com/*	This site offers security guidance, news, and tools for Linux OSs. You can also browse user forums and access current advisories.

Most vendors and research organizations also maintain knowledge bases and public forums where users can post problems and get answers and helpful hints from experts and other knowledgeable users. You can join vendors' IT professional forums if you meet certain criteria, such as certification from that vendor. Other resources, such as US-CERT, are available to the public.

If you need information on a specific problem, such as finding an automated tool to inventory your hardware resources or map MAC addresses of equipment, most of these sites have helpful resources. Most of the sites listed in Tables B-1 and B-2 also cover penetration-testing techniques, tools, and advice. TechRepublic, in particular, offers templates for legal liability agreements you should use before conducting any penetration testing on a system.

Finally, each chapter of this book has included tips and notes directing you to additional resources and more information. Make sure you visit these sites and consider creating a Security Resources folder in your bookmarks to organize useful sites for fast access.

SECURITY CERTIFICATION SITES

The following sites offer certifications that can be invaluable for finding employment in network security.

Global Information Assurance Certification (GIAC)

The GIAC Web site (*www.giac.org*) provides information about the SANS Institute certification exams. Programs include the CIAC Silver, Gold, and Platinum certifications (in ascending order of difficulty).

The International Information Systems Security Certification Consortium (ISC²)

ISC² (*www.isc2.org*) is an international nonprofit organization dedicated to maintaining a common body of knowledge on security. ISC² prepares and administers two well-known certifications in network security: Certified Information Systems Security Professional (CISSP) and Systems Security Certified Practitioner (SSCP).

CompTIA Certification

The Computing Technology Industry Association (*www.comptia.org/default.aspx*) is best known for the A+ certification track. The CompTIA Security+ Certification exam is also available to establish fundamental security competency in firewalls, encryption, and intrusion detection. In addition, CompTIA offers the Network+ certification, which verifies competence in fundamental networking skills, and Linux+, which tests knowledge of the Linux OS. Passing the CompTIA Security+ exam is a prerequisite for taking the SCP's Tactical Perimeter Defense and Strategic Infrastructure Security exams.

The Security Certified Program

The Security Certified Program (*www.securitycertified.net/index.htm*) is the vendor-neutral administrator of the Security Certified Network Specialist (SCNS), Security Certified Network Professional (SCNP), and Security Certified Network Architect (SCNA) exams. For the SCNS certification, candidates must pass the Tactical Perimeter Defense SC0-451 exam, which is covered in *Guide to Tactical Perimeter Defense* (Course Technology, 2008, 1428356304). For the SCNP certification, candidates must pass the Strategic Infrastructure Security SC0-471 exam, which this book covers.

PUBLIC KEY CERTIFICATE STANDARDS

Public Key Infrastructure (PKI) depends on interoperability. If one party of a transaction is using a different certificate from another party, neither can communicate. Public key cryptography standards (PKCSs), listed in Table B-4, developed over the years have improved PKI systems and made their use more widespread.

Table B-3   Published PKCSs

Standard and RFC (if applicable)	Name	Description
PKCS #1, RFC 3447	RSA Cryptography Standard	Defines the format of RSA encryption
PKCS #3	Diffie-Hellman Key Agreement Standard	Allows two parties with no previous knowledge of each other to establish a shared secret key jointly over communication channels that aren't secure
PKCS #5, RFC 2898	Password-based Cryptography Standard	Provides recommendations for using password-based cryptography; covers key derivation functions, encryption, and message authentication schemes
PKCS #7, RFC 2315	Cryptographic Message Syntax Standard	Used to sign and encrypt messages under a PKI for certificate dissemination; is the basis for S/MIME
PKCS #8	Private-Key Information Syntax Standard	Describes syntax for private key information, including a private key for some public key algorithms and a set of attributes; also describes syntax for encrypted private keys
PKCS #9	Selected Attribute Types	Defines selected attribute types for use in extended certificates, digitally signed messages, private key information, and certificate-signing requests
PKCS #10, RFC 2986	Certification Request Standard	Specifies the format of messages sent to a CA to request verification of a public key
PKCS #11	Cryptographic Token Interface (Cryptoki)	An application programming interface (API) defining a generic interface to cryptographic tokens
PKCS #12	Personal Information Exchange Syntax Standard	Defines a file format to store private and accompanying public keys protected by a password-based symmetric key
PKCS #15	Cryptographic Token Information Format Standard	Defines a Cryptoki-independent standard for cryptographic token users to identify themselves to applications

Glossary

acceptable use policy — A policy that establishes what constitutes acceptable use of company resources and offers specifics on what's considered unacceptable use.

access control list (ACL) — Information stored in the OS that specifies the access rights users and groups have to resources, such as files and directories.

Active Directory — A distributed hierarchical database and directory service that stores objects, manages resources, and makes those resources available for use.

address spoofing — A type of attack that uses a packet with the target's IP address and port. Because the source address and port are the same as the target destination, the target could crash.

Advanced Encryption Standard (AES) — The current U.S. government standard for cryptographic protocols, AES uses the Rijndael algorithm with key sizes of 128, 192, or 256 bits and a fixed block size of 128 bits.

anycast addressing — A network addressing scheme that make its possible to decentralize DNS services among a group of servers, even servers in different locations.

ASCII payload — The actual data part of the packet, given in ASCII format.

assets — The hardware, software, and informational resources you need to protect by developing and implementing a comprehensive security policy.

asymmetric algorithms — A type of mathematical formula that generates a key pair: one key to encrypt cleartext and another key to decrypt ciphertext.

auditing — The process of reviewing records of network computers' activities; these records include who is connecting to a computer, what resources are being requested, and whether access is granted or blocked.

backdoor — A set of software tools that allows an attacker to access and use a computer without the user's knowledge by hiding running processes, files, or system data. Also known as a "rootkit."

block cipher — A type of encryption algorithm that encrypts groups of cleartext characters.

botnets — A network of zombie computers that attackers assemble to magnify the effect of an attack.

buffer overflow — An attack method that takes advantage of poorly written programming code to overflow a system buffer with executable program code. If a maximum buffer size is defined, but the program is allowed to write more than the maximum to the buffer, an error condition exists that could allow a buffer overflow attack.

CAN — A prefix the CVE Web site uses to identify candidate vulnerabilities. In October 2005, this prefix was replaced with "CVE," and a vulnerability's status is now noted as Entry, Candidate, or Deprecated.

Common Gateway Interface (CGI) scripts — Scripts used to process data submitted over the Internet.

Common Vulnerabilities and Exposures (CVE) — A standard that enables security devices to share information about attack signatures and other vulnerabilities so that they can work together to provide network protection.

container objects — Objects in a directory service that can hold objects and other container objects.

control connection — An initial FTP connection between client and server.

cost-benefit analysis — A technique for comparing the costs of an investment with the benefits it proposes to return.

413

cryptanalysis — The study of breaking encryption methods. Some common attack methods against cryptographic systems include differential and integral cryptanalysis, random number generator attacks, side channel attacks, and XSL attacks.

cryptographic primitives — Modular mathematical functions that perform one task reliably. They form the basic building blocks of modern cryptography.

cryptographic protocol — A detailed description that incorporates standardized requirements and guidelines for key generation and management, authentication, encryption, hashing functions, nonrepudiation methods, and other aspects of message security.

cryptography — The process of converting plaintext into ciphertext by using an encoding function.

cyber risk insurance — A type of insurance policy that protects businesses from losses resulting from attacks, viruses, sabotage, and so on. It typically has specific coverages and exclusions like any insurance policy.

Data Encryption Standard (DES) — An older protocol composed of a 16-round Feistel network with XOR functions, permutation functions, 6x4 S-box functions, and fixed key schedules. DES generates 64 bits of ciphertext from 64 bits of plaintext by using a 56-bit key.

denial-of-service (DoS) attack — An attack that floods a host with more requests than it can handle, effectively preventing the host from responding to legitimate requests.

digital signatures — A method of verifying nonrepudiation and integrity in messages.

distinguished name (DN) — A naming scheme that represents the entire directory path to an object; also known as the fully qualified domain name (FQDN).

distributed denial-of-service (DDoS) attack — A DoS attack that uses multiple computers to attack a single target.

domain — Active Directory's main logical organizing component that serves as a security and replication boundary.

domain local group — A type of Active Directory group used to manage resources in a single domain and provide resource access in a domain to global and universal groups.

Domain Name System (DNS) — A hierarchical name resolution service for translating hostnames to IP addresses; used mainly on the Internet.

due process — A legal concept that ensures the government respects a person's rights or places limitations on legal proceedings to guarantee fundamental fairness, justice, and liberty.

dumpster diving — A form of social engineering that involves using a company's carelessly discarded trash to find information. Security policies, employee personal information, and bills are valuable sources of information in gaining access to a system.

electronic assets — The word processing, spreadsheet, Web page, and other documents on your network computers.

Encrypting File System (EFS) — A file system that enables users to encrypt the contents of a folder or a file so that it can be accessed only by using the private key code of the user who encrypted the folder or file.

encryption algorithm — A precise set of instructions that provides an encoding function for a cryptographic system or generates output for use in additional operations.

enumeration — A method for obtaining information on valid account names, network resources, shares, and applications; uses protocols such as ICMP and SNMP to scan remote hosts. Enumeration can also provide information about well-known services that identify the function of a remote host.

escalation procedure — A set of roles, responsibilities, and measures taken in response to a security incident.

exclusive OR (XOR) function — This cryptographic primitive based on binary bit logic is used as a linear mixing function, combining values for use in further computations.

exposure — Vulnerability to loss resulting from the occurrence of a threat, such as accidental or intentional disclosure or destruction or modification of information resources. Exposure increases with the presence of multiple threat factors.

extended file system (ext) — The native file system in Linux, which comes in the following versions: ext, ext2, ext3, and ext4.

extranet — A private network a company sets up as an extension of its corporate intranet for the purpose of allowing outside entities (contractors, suppliers, partners, and so on) access to only a limited portion of the network infrastructure.

fault tolerance — The capability of an object or a system to continue operations despite a failure.

Feistel network — A cryptographic primitive that forms the basis of many symmetric algorithms. Feistel networks combine multiple rounds of repeated operations, such as processing cleartext input with XOR functions. A key schedule is used to produce different keys for each round.

footprinting — A method attackers use to create a profile of a target system, including the organization's security level, DNS architecture and server names, e-mail system, IP addresses, contact information for employees, and so on.

forests — Logical Active Directory components that represent collections of trees. *See also* trees.

Fourth Amendment — The Fourth Amendment in the U.S. Bill of Rights provides constitutional protection from illegal search and seizure and guarantees the right to due process. It also implies an expected right of privacy, even though no such right is stated specifically.

global catalog — A Windows Server 2003 database that stores information about every object in a forest. Global catalog servers provide authentication, manage access to domain objects, and perform replication of key Active Directory elements.

global group — A type of Active Directory group used to manage group accounts from the same domain so that those domain users can access resources in their own domain and other domains.

group identification number (GID) — A unique number assigned to a Linux group that distinguishes it from all other groups on a Linux computer.

Group Policy Objects (GPOs) — Containers that store group policy settings and can be linked to an Active Directory domain, site, or OU.

hashing algorithms — Sets of instructions applied to variable-length input (the message) that generate a fixed-length message digest representing the input. Hashing algorithms don't provide confidentiality because they don't encrypt the message contents, but they do provide verification that a message hasn't been altered.

hashing functions — Processes a computer runs to verify message integrity by generating a hash value (also known as a message digest), which is a fixed-size string representing the original input's contents. Hashing functions are also used for error detection.

hexadecimal payload — The actual data a packet is communicating, expressed in hexadecimal format.

hop — The movement of a packet from one point on the network to another.

ID number — For packets in general, it's an identifying number used to reassemble a packet that's divided into fragments. For ICMP packets, it identifies the ICMP packet so that the originating computer can make sure the response came from its original request.

inodes — A system for storing essential information about directories and files in the ext file system.

International Data Encryption Algorithm (IDEA) — A common European symmetric algorithm that uses 64-bit blocks and eight and a half rounds of modular addition/multiplication math and XOR functions. IDEA has a 128-bit key.

Internet Authentication Service (IAS) — A standard component of Windows Server 2003 that allows a server to act as a RADIUS server or RADIUS proxy to provide remote authentication services.

Internet Protocol Security (IPSec) — A set of standard procedures that the Internet Engineering Task Force (IETF) developed for enabling secure communication on the Internet.

Internet use policy — A policy that defines how users can access and use the Internet and specifies what rules apply to e-mail and other communications, such as instant messaging.

IP spoofing — The process of inserting a false address into the IP header to make the packet more difficult to trace back to its source.

journaling — The process of keeping chronological records of data or transactions so that if a system crashes without warning or is brought down by an attack, the data or transactions can be reconstructed or rolled back to avoid data loss or information that isn't synchronized correctly.

key management — A way to prevent keys from being discovered and used to decipher encrypted messages. One method is changing keys frequently.

keystroke loggers — Devices or computer programs used to capture keystrokes on a computer.

leaf objects — Objects in a directory that nest inside containers and can't contain other objects.

local group — A type of Active Directory group used on standalone servers that aren't part of a domain; the scope is limited to the local server.

malware — Executable code designed to damage target systems. Malware can be a virus, worm, Trojan program, or macro.

maximum transmission unit (MTU) — The maximum packet size that can be transmitted over a type of network, such as an Ethernet network.

Message Authentication Code (MAC) — A hashing algorithm that uses a shared secret key to generate a MAC tag for a message.

Message Digest 5 (MD5) — A widely used hashing algorithm that produces a 128-bit hash value displayed as a 32-character hexadecimal number.

Microsoft Point-to-Point Encryption (MPPE) — A starting-to-ending-point encryption technique that uses special encryption keys from 40 to 128 bits.

monoalphabetic substitution — A one-for-one character substitution scheme; this encryption method is vulnerable to frequency analysis.

Monte Carlo simulation — An analytical method meant to simulate a real-life system by randomly generating values for variables.

multiple-packet attacks — Attacks that require a series of packets to be transmitted.

network access points (NAPs) — Highly secure public facilities where commercial Internet backbones and ISPs exchange routing and traffic data.

network assets — The routers, cables, bastion hosts, servers, and firewall hardware and software that enable employees to communicate with one another and other computers on the Internet.

network baselining — The process of determining what's normal for your network so that you can identify anomalies.

Network File System (NFS) — A Linux service that enables file transfer and other shared services on Linux computers.

Network Information System (NIS) — A Linux service that provides a naming system for shared resources on a Linux network; makes resources easier to locate and identify.

network reconnaissance — The process of gathering as much information about a potential target system as possible, using scanning methods, ping sweeps, social engineering, packet capture and analysis, and other means.

network security policy — A policy that defines and establishes responsibility for protecting the network and the information processed, stored, and transmitted on the network.

nontransitive trusts — Trust relationships bounded by the two domains in the trust relationship. Nontransitive trusts don't flow to other domains in the forest and are one-way by default.

null packets — TCP packets with no flags set.

one-way trusts — Trust relationships that allow the trusted entity to access resources of the trusting entity; they apply in only one direction.

organizational units (OUs) — Logical components of Active Directory used to organize objects in a domain; can be used to group classes of objects.

packet capture and analysis — A procedure administrators use to identify problems, analyze and monitor traffic conditions, locate security violations, and perform other network-monitoring tasks. Attackers also use it to gather information about a network.

packet sniffer — Software or hardware that monitors network traffic and captures information about TCP/IP packets it detects.

permission — An element in a file or directory's access control list that specifies who can access a file or directory and in what way. Linux has three essential ACL permissions: read, write, and execute.

permutation functions — Bit-shuffling cryptographic primitives that reorder sets of objects randomly.

pharming — A variation of phishing that intercepts traffic to a legitimate Web site and redirects it to a phony replica of the legitimate site.

phishing — Using social engineering techniques via e-mail to trick users into entering personal information into the attacker's Web site (designed to look like a legitimate business site).

ping of death — A DoS attack that sends an oversized packet to the target system, causing the target to crash, reboot, or hang. Most systems are patched to prevent this type of attack, but it was a successful method in the mid-1990s.

ping sweep — A tool that sends ICMP Echo packets to multiple targets, identified by a range of IP addresses, to build a map of a target network.

point of presence (POP) ISPs — ISP facilities that provide connectivity to the Internet for business, education, and home users.

polyalphabetic substitution — This encryption method applies multiple substitution ciphers to different parts of a message, often to each plaintext character.

port scan — An attempt to connect to a computer's ports to see whether any are active and listening.

private key exchange — In symmetric cryptography, the same key is used to encrypt and decrypt a message. Public Key Infrastructure is often used for private key exchange.

privilege escalation — A type of attack that exploits a software bug to gain access to resources that would normally have been protected.

privileged access policy — A policy detailing additional access, functions, and responsibilities of users with privileged (administrative or root) access to resources.

probability — The possibility that a threat will actually occur, influenced by geographic, physical, habitual, or other factors that increase or decrease the likelihood of occurrence.

process id (PID) — An identification number that the OS assigns to a process for managing and tracking it.

pseudorandom number generators (PRNGs) — Cryptographic primitives used to generate sequences of numbers that approximate random values.

public key cryptography standards (PKCSs) — A set of standards RSA developed to provide standardization guidelines for cryptography. Many of these 15 standards have moved into the IETF standards track.

public key exchange — In asymmetric cryptography, two keys are required: the public key and private key. The public key, used to encrypt the message, is shared freely. The private key, used to decrypt the message, is kept secret.

Registry entry — A parameter in the Registry stored as a value in hexadecimal, binary, or text format.

Registry key — A category of information in the Windows Server 2003 Registry, such as hardware or software.

Registry subkey — A key within a Registry key, similar to a subfolder under a folder.

relative distinguished name (RDN) — A naming scheme that refers to an object's name without including its directory path; also known as the canonical name (CN).

remote access and wireless connection policy — A policy that defines what security measures need to be in place on a remote desktop or wireless connection before connecting to the organization's network.

Remote Procedure Calls (RPC) — A standard set of communication rules that allows a computer to request a service from another computer on a network.

residual risk — The risk remaining after countermeasures and defenses are implemented.

resource records — Tables of information used for name resolution that contain computer names, IP addresses, and similar locating information for a zone.

Rijndael — The encryption algorithm used in AES is a symmetric block cipher composed of 10 to 14 rounds of S-box and XOR functions. It supports 128-bit, 192-bit, or 256-bit keys and block sizes. Rijndael applies 10 rounds for 128-bit keys, 12 rounds for 192-bit keys, and 14 rounds for 256-bit keys.

risk — The possibility of incurring damage or loss.

risk analysis — A process of analyzing the threats an organization faces, determining precisely what resources are at risk, and deciding the priority to give each asset.

risk management — The process of identifying, choosing, and setting up countermeasures justified by the risks you identify.

role-based authentication — A method of authentication that grants users limited access based on the role they are assigned in the company and defines what resources the role is allowed to use.

Routing and Remote Access Services (RRAS) — A group of Windows Server 2003 services that provide routing capabilities and remote access so that off-site workstations can access a Windows Server 2003 network through telecommunication lines, the Internet, or an intranet.

runlevel — The level in which a computer boots or a service runs.

safeguards — Measures you can take to reduce threats, such as installing firewalls and intrusion detection systems, locking doors, and using passwords and encryption.

Samba — A Linux service that enables Linux, UNIX, and Mac OS X systems to access shared Windows resources and vice versa.

scanner — A device that scans a network for open ports or other potential vulnerabilities.

scanning — A method attackers use to identify active hosts on a network. Also used by security personnel to identify vulnerable hosts.

schema — The method of defining each object in Active Directory, including an object class and its attributes.

script — A file of Linux commands for performing a certain task.

search warrant — A legal document issued by the court allowing a search of a specified place for specific evidence. The warrant must detail what the search is seeking and where law enforcement is permitted to look for it.

Secure Hash Algorithm (SHA) — A hashing algorithm that the NSA designed as a replacement for MD5. SHA-1 produces a 160-bit message digest.

Secure Shell (SSH) — A form of authentication originally developed for Linux and UNIX to secure remote connections between a client computer and a host computer over a network or the Internet.

Security Accounts Manager (SAM) — A local database file that stores user and group information for standalone servers.

security incident response team (SIRT) — A group of people designated to take countermeasures when an incident is reported.

security policy — A statement that spells out exactly what defenses will be configured to block unauthorized access, what constitutes acceptable use of network resources, how the organization will respond to attacks, and how employees should handle the organization's resources safely to discourage loss of data or damage to files.

security user awareness program — A training program designed to educate users about security topics, answer their questions about security, and prepare users to accept changes made for security purposes.

selective acknowledgements — Acknowledgements that selected packets in a sequence have been received instead of acknowledging every packet.

server security policy — A policy that regulates IT staff who have privileged access to company servers. This policy should cover all servers, including Web and database servers.

set group ID (SGID) bit — An advanced permission that enables a program owner to retain full ownership but gives group members temporary ownership while running the program.

set user ID (SUID) bit — An advanced permission that enables a program owner to retain full ownership but gives ordinary users temporary ownership while running the program.

shadow file — A file in Linux containing critical information about user accounts, including the encrypted password for each account; access to the shadow file is limited to the root user.

signature — A set of characteristics—such as IP numbers and options, TCP flags, and port numbers—for defining a type of network activity.

signature analysis — The practice of examining TCP/IP communications to determine whether traffic is legitimate or suspicious.

single sign-on (SSO) — An authentication strategy that enables users to log on once and have access to all resources they have permission to use for the duration of the session without needing to log on again.

single-packet attack — An attack that can be completed by sending a single network packet from client to host.

sites — Groups of reliable, well-connected computers in the same IP subnet.

social engineering — A method attackers use to gain information or access to a system by tricking users into voluntarily giving them the requested information. Social engineering can be done over the phone or in person.

spear phishing — A variation of phishing that's directed at specific users (employees of an organization, for example) instead of using spam e-mail.

split DNS architecture — A network architecture that divides DNS services between two servers: a public DNS server on the organization's DMZ for Internet services and an internal DNS server on the internal network for service to internal hosts.

spyware — Software that gathers information from users' computers about their Internet surfing habits. Spyware can also gather personal information, such as credit card numbers, e-mail account information, passwords, or logon names. Spyware is usually installed without the user's knowledge or permission.

sticky bit —An advanced permission that causes a program to stay resident in memory (in older Linux distributions) or ensures that only root or the owner can delete or rename files (in newer distributions).

stream cipher — A type of encryption algorithm that encrypts one bit at a time.

strobe scan — A type of port scan that probes ports commonly used by certain programs in an attempt to see whether the program is present and can be used.

subpoena — A legal document requiring a person to appear, provide testimony, or cooperate with law enforcement. Testimony consists of written or oral declaration of fact under penalty of law.

substitution box (S-box) function — A cryptographic primitive that transforms a number of input bits into a number of output bits and produces a fixed or dynamic lookup table.

substitution cipher — A type of encryption method in which one character in the message is replaced with another character in a one-to-one substitution scheme.

superblock — A special data block on a Linux partition containing information about the layout of blocks. This information is the key to finding directories and files in the file system.

survivability — The capability to continue functioning in the presence of attacks or disasters.

Survivable Network Analysis (SNA) — A security process that starts with the assumption that a computer system will be attacked and follows a set of steps to build a system that can survive such an attack.

symmetric algorithms — A type of mathematical formula in which the key for encrypting cleartext is the same key for decrypting ciphertext.

SYN flood — A type of DoS attack that takes advantage of the TCP three-way handshake by sending multiple packets with the SYN flag set to a target. The target responds by sending a SYN/ACK packet, which the attacking system ignores, leaving the session half-open. The target system is eventually overwhelmed with half-open sessions and can't respond to legitimate requests.

Telnet — An Internet terminal emulation program that can be a security risk when used over a remote connection to a computer running Linux.

Threat and Risk Assessment (TRA) — An approach to risk analysis that starts from the standpoint of threats and accounts for risks to an organization's assets and the consequences of those threats and risks if they occur.

threats — Events and conditions that haven't occurred but could potentially occur; the presence of these events or conditions increases risk.

time to live (TTL) — A value that tells a router how long a packet should remain on the network before it's discarded.

transitive trusts — In this arrangement, trusts are inherited by all domains in the tree or by all subcontainers of the parent container where the trust relationship is established.

Transport Layer Security (TLS) — A protocol designed to provide additional security for Internet communication. TLS uses a hashed message authentication code (HMAC) to combine the hashing algorithm with a shared secret key. TLS splits input data in half, processes each half with a different hashing algorithm, and recombines them with an XOR function.

transposition cipher — A type of encryption method that rearranges the order of characters in each word of a message.

trees — Logical Active Directory components representing everything from the bottom of the object path to the root domain. Trees contain multiple domains that share contiguous namespaces, schemas, and global catalogs or other commonalities.

Triple DES (3DES) — An enhanced variation of DES that uses three 64-bit keys to process data. *See also* Data Encryption Standard (DES).

Trojan scan — A type of port scan that looks for Trojan programs that have already circumvented security measures and are running on the scanned system. If attackers can find one already installed, they can use it instead of having to install a new one.

tunneling protocols — Network protocols that encapsulate (wrap) one protocol or session inside another.

two-factor authentication — Authentication requiring at least two forms of verification from a user to be granted access. Verification requires something the user has, knows, or is.

type of service (TOS) — The part of a packet header used to express a packet's precedence—whether it should have low delay, whether it needs high reliability, and so on.

universal group — A type of Active Directory group used to enable access to all resources in a forest.

user identification number (UID) — A number assigned to a Linux user account as a way to distinguish it from all others on the same computer.

vanilla scan — A type of port scan in which all ports from 0 to 65535 are probed one after another.

virus signature file — A file prepared by antivirus software vendors that contains patterns of known viruses. Antivirus software uses these files to identify known viruses.

vulnerabilities — Situations or conditions that increase threat, which, in turn, increases risk.

worst-case scenarios — Descriptions of the worst consequences that befall an organization if a threat occurs.

X.509 — An International Telecommunication Union standard for PKI that specifies standard formats for public key certificates, a strict hierarchical system for CAs issuing certificates, and standards for certificate revocation lists. X.509 certificates use RSA for key generation and encryption and MD5 hashes to verify the certificate's integrity.

zombie — A computer that has been compromised and can be used to attack another computer; also known as a "bot." Usually, an attacker compromises hundreds or thousands of computers to launch an attack.

zone — A namespace partition on a DNS server.

zone transfer — The communication to secondary DNS servers of the zone file, which contains DNS information for the domain the primary DNS server manages.

Index